The
Popular
Literature
of Medieval
England

•

The Popular Literature of Medieval England

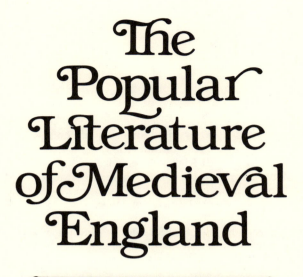

Edited by

THOMAS J. HEFFERNAN

VOLUME 28
TENNESSEE STUDIES IN LITERATURE
The University of Tennessee Press
Knoxville

Publication of this book has been aided by a grant from The
Better English Fund, established by John C. Hodges at The
University of Tennessee, Knoxville.

After its inception in 1956, the distinguished series, "Tennessee
Studies in Literature," sponsored by the Department of English
at the University of Tennessee, Knoxville, published 26 volumes.
Beginning with Volume 27, the series presents a new format.
Each book deals with a specific theme, period, or genre, for which
the editor of that volume has invited contributions from leading
scholars in the field. No longer an annual series, the volumes will
be published as they are ready. As with all University of Tennessee
Press clothbound books, the "Tennessee Studies in Literature"
volumes are printed on paper that meets the guidelines for permanence and durability of the Committee on Production Guidelines
for Book Longevity of the Council on Library Resources, and
binding materials are chosen for strength and durability.

Library of Congress Cataloging in Publication Data
Main entry under title:
The Popular literature of medieval England.

(Tennessee studies in literature; v. 28)
Includes bibliographies.
1. English literature—Middle English, 1100–
1500—History and criticism—Addresses, essays,
lectures. 2. Popular literature—England—History
and criticism—Addresses, essays, lectures. I. Heffernan, Thomas J., 1944– . II. Series.
PR275.P65P6 1985 820.9′001 84-26959
ISBN 0-87049-453-8 (alk. paper)
ISBN 0-87049-589-5 (pbk.: alk. paper)

Tennessee Studies in Literature

Inquiries concerning this series should be addressed to the Editor, *Tennessee Studies in Literature,* Department of English, The University of Tennessee, Knoxville, Tennessee 37996-0430. Those desiring to purchase additional copies of this issue or copies of back issues should address The University of Tennessee Press, 293 Communications Building, Knoxville, Tennessee 37996-0325.

In memory of my beloved son
THOMAS JOHN

Preface

We have all had the experience of attending a conference in which a paper is given, let us say, on the *Ormulum*. During the presentation and succeeding discussion period one invariably hears questions such as the following: how does the *Ormulum* fit into the established canon of Middle English literature? If it does not belong in the canon, are we still to consider it a work of literature to be studied by literary historians? Conversely, if we do agree that it is "literary," how do we discuss it and with what kind of critical language? Someone in the audience may offer the observation that it is a document of the literature of catechesis, or another (with a taste for the ironic) that the *Ormulum* is part of the literature of the non-literate; the speaker may suggest that it belongs to a large and as yet undefined corpus of medieval popular literature. Such comments, whether they offer insight into the text in question or not, are of moment for Middle English scholars, for the comments do illustrate two serious issues: there are important Middle English texts, which given our current critical bias, continue to resist explication and hence are virtually ignored, and terms such as "catechesis," "non-literate," "didactic," "courtly," and "popular" remain misunderstood and poorly defined.

Let us first look at one of these above terms. For example, what exactly do I mean when I use the epithet "popular" when considering the *Ormulum*? Can we use the expression when discussing medieval literature without regard to its modern connotations? Does the term impute something to a text on the basis of the number of the surviving manuscripts? Were those compositions which survive in the most numbers the most popular? Or were they the products of a small, zealous minority intent on spreading this particular message? Might the number of surviving manuscripts simply be the result of historical serendipity? Is the term "popular" inherently tied to a place and class of individuals, to the country rather than the court, to the many and not the few? Does it represent an intuition of the modern scholar, an intuition that while inchoate and resisting definition sees those texts as popular that somehow pertain to *das volk* and are in some manner a part of an indigenous culture? To be sure, there are other questions we might ask, but these are meant merely to underline the lack of some basic agreement.

A striking thing about this otherwise perfectly appropriate scholarly discussion is that we are not talking here of a small fraction of the corpus of Middle English. On the contrary, there is a veritable cornucopia of texts which create this cold feeling of uncertainty in Middle English scholars. And texts which—unlike the unique *Ormulum*—survive in large numbers: the "Pricke of Conscience," to cite one example from among many, is extant in more manuscripts (115 at the last count) than any other Middle English work. Yet it too inhabits this aesthetic limbo, neither accepted nor rejected from the canon but rather recognized as an important, indeed indispensable, part of English literary culture. It is recognized but ignored—in short, damned with faint praise. This situation reminds me of a childhood game in which we had to fit pegs of varied shapes into their respective holes, and how, after being given a peg of a different shape for the first time, it would resist stubbornly, despite the severity of our hammering, our best efforts to force it home. Oh, the recalcitrance of that wood! There is an analogy here between the child's pique with the game and the scholars' uncertainty with the material. Both make similar assumptions about the unfamiliar, the strange; after all it is invariably the new peg and the text that are blamed for not fitting their respective molds and not the wisdom of human judgment. The scholarly communities' interest has been directed elsewhere, to the virtuoso items of the Middle English canon.

Surely part of the reason for the discomfort we have when we consider medieval literary texts of a so-called "popular nature" is related to our sense of their difference. After all they do not conform to the aesthetic norms we have been trained in and which have been cherished, codified, and established into a canon at least since the Enlightenment. I believe we can safely avoid a discussion of what these norms are and how they work, and simply collapse the attitudes which underlie this sense of unease— without doing permanent damage to the philosophy of aesthetics—into what I would like to call the ideal of virtuosity. I am using "virtuosity" in a singularly modern sense to suggest excellence in a particular endeavor, to suggest that unique mark of accomplishment that allows us to recognize that individual's work amongst all others. But how does this ideal of virtuosity affect our appreciation of popular literature? How does it play a role in the ambivalent attitude of our fictitious scholar in his or her discussion of the *Ormulum*? Let me suggest that virtuosity in an artistic performance, whether literary or theatrical, requires an audience trained to recognize and distinguish between previously established categories of excellence. Hence there is at least a nominal symbiosis of values that must exist between reader and text; ideally, for this system to function most effectively, an interdependence should exist between the text and the listener/reader; an interdependence which is grounded in a shared ancestry, in a shared understanding and acceptance of an aesthetic norm, in an understanding of established moral and pedagogical laws, and in an inheritance of a canon of established values on what constitutes excellence in art. While none of these observations is terribly novel, it is important to refresh ourselves concerning their pertinence, and what better place than a book that has as its subject the popular literature of medieval England?

Needless to say this symbiosis between text and audience ceases to exist when the scholar moves outside these established bounds. And clearly much of medieval literature is excluded *a priori* when literary judgment—or as in the case of our fictitious *Ormulum* scholar—literary uncertainty is founded on assumptions about excellence which are themselves indebted to the ideal of virtuosity. Does such a situation exist presently? I think the evidence for it is indisputable, especially if we examine the critical literature since the last World War—a period in which "New Criticism" (now with the advent of post-modernism considered positively antediluvian) came to dominate the teaching of literature in our schools. What immediately strikes one is that the field of Middle English studies has invested its energies somewhat eccentrically. In a period that spans the three centuries between 1150 and 1450, the vast majority of research concerns the closing decades of the fourteenth century. And within this brief span, clearly the research choice of most modern Middle English scholars is some aspect of the Chaucerian canon. A conservative estimate of the secondary literature written on Chaucer during the past five years is approximately 225 items per year. Even the most cursory perusal of any of the standard bibliographies containing Middle English will reveal an enormous differential between Chaucer scholarship and all others. For example, to return to our *Ormulum* scholar, he or she can take cold comfort in the fact that there has been one item of moment published on the *Ormulum* in the last five years, whereas there have been in excess of 1,125 books, monographs, articles, and notes written on some aspect of the Chaucerian canon. Ratios not too dissimilar result if we compare the secondary literature on Chaucer with, for example, that on Capgrave, Julian of Norwich, Richard Rolle, the *Cloud of Unknowing,* Margery Kemp, the "Katherine Group," the *Cursor Mundi,* sermons and saints' legends in verse and prose, and selected romances. Indeed even *Piers Plowman* scholarship on average is about one sixth as voluminous as that on Chaucer. Enthusiasts might be tempted to exclaim that the proof is in the pudding; that the preponderance of scholarship illustrates *a posteriori* the relative merit of the subject. The logic of this argument I shall leave for others to debate, but it would appear that one effect of this sort of argument would be to reduce the rest of Middle English Literature to a codicil to the end of the fourteenth century.

Moreover, this acute focus on Chaucer has perforce been a focus on an urban courtly society, a society with a mercantile class who took delight in literature and reading and who acted, at times, as patrons of the arts. It was a society clearly more mobile and secular in outlook than that of its provincial cousins. In short it was atypical. English society of this period was chiefly agrarian, with a barter economy probably the norm in most areas, and the bulk of the populace were illiterate, non-mobile peasants dwelling in small self-sufficient vills with strong ties to their local traditions. London and the court for these people was as far away as the fabled lands the mendicants delighted them with in their sermons. Froissart gives us a homely picture of the differences between the urban courtier and the common people when he comments "Et trop fort se diffèrent en Engleterre les natures et conditions des nobles aux hommes mestis et villains, car li gentilhomme sont de noble et loiale condition, et li communs peuples est de fèle, perilleuse, orguilleuse et desloiale conditions." Leaving aside Froissart's obvious delight in class fractiousness, the society of London was clearly a culture that was a "rara avis" at the close of the fourteenth century. To be sure, the entire scholarly community is indebted to much of the secondary literature I have been discussing, as it has contributed greatly to our understanding of late medieval English literature and culture. Indeed it has also contributed, albeit indirectly, to the entire tapestry of medieval English culture and provided us with an indispensable critical legacy with which to work. But in the singularity of its focus, in its primary concern with the closing decades of the fourteenth century, in its essential concern with the virtuoso writers of this period, something has been lost. It is my hope that the essays in this book might stimulate a search for that lost world.

THOMAS J. HEFFERNAN

Contents

Preface
Thomas J. Heffernan   *page ix*

Who Were "The People"?
D.W. Robertson, Jr.   3

The Fourth Lateran Council and Manuals of Popular Theology
Leonard E. Boyle, O.P.   30

The Influence of Canonical and Episcopal Reform on Popular
Books of Instruction
Judith Shaw   44

Medieval Popular Literature: Folkloric Sources
Bruce A. Rosenberg   61

Secular Life and Popular Piety in Medieval English Drama
Stanley J. Kahrl   85

Romance
Edmund Reiss   108

The International Medieval Popular Comic Tale in England
Derek Brewer   131

Chaucer and Erasmus on the Pilgrimage to Canterbury:
An Iconographical Speculation
John V. Fleming   148

The Middle English *Planctus Mariae* and the Rhetoric of Pathos
George R. Keiser   167

Some Versions of Apocalypse: Learned and Popular Eschatology
in *Piers Plowman*
    Robert Adams   194

Chaucer and the Written Language
    John H. Fisher   237

The "Tone of Heaven": Bonaventuran Melody and the Easter
Psalm in Richard Rolle
    William F. Pollard   252

The Beguines of Belgium, the Dominican Nuns of Germany,
and Margery Kempe
    Ute Stargardt   277

Contributors   314

Index   316

The
Popular
Literature
of Medieval
England
•

Who Were "The People"?

D.W. Robertson, Jr.

The term *popular literature* is actually not very specific, and it quite naturally suggests for the period of the late Middle Ages "vernacular" literature, or where England is concerned, literature in Middle English. It may well be argued that even where Middle English works are translations or adaptations from Latin, Anglo-Norman, or French they are still "popular" by virtue of the language in which they are written. However, M.T. Clanchy has recently suggested that it was often "the most sophisticated and not the most primitive authors who experimented with vernaculars," so that "we should not be misled by the prefatory apologies in vernacular works, or by their unusual orthography, into thinking that they were composed by the less educated."[1] Today we often associate popular literature with unlettered folk, or, alternatively, with best-selling books, the most popular of which at the moment are romances written for women, cook books, diet or exercise books, or books on sexual techniques. Except for certain books falling under the general category "religious instruction," like *The Prick of Conscience,* for example, and perhaps certain songs and carols, it would be difficult to describe Middle English works generally as being popular in this sense. It is probably fair to say that there was no popular literature in the modern sense in late medieval England and except for certain religious beliefs held in common, it lacked a "mass culture." For this reason, it should be helpful to know something about the various kinds of audiences that did exist at the time.

No one who studies English dialects or local customs, social, legal, or, to use a rather inappropriate modern term, "political,"[2] can escape the conclusion that England was a highly diversified country during the late Middle Ages. Each shire had its own distinctive customs, and some shires, like Kent in the south or Cheshire in the north, had their own

3

peculiar laws and organizational structures. The same principle holds, perhaps to an even greater extent, for English towns. The national economy was basically agricultural, but agricultural procedures varied enormously with soil and climate, and with other features like proximity to the coast, proximity to waterways, the availability of pasture, or even proximity to towns that sheltered a preponderant population of trades-men, as not all towns did. Proximity to active mining areas, like the tin mines of Cornwall, might also have a marked effect on manorial practices and agricultural prosperity. Areas of "open field" agriculture, sometimes regarded as being "typical," were actually extremely diversified, for manorial customs varied from manor to manor. Manors under the lordship of large ecclesiastical or monastic organizations were generally more closely supervised than those under lay jurisdiction, even when these were controlled by "liberties," like the Duchy of Lancaster; and, finally, the relationship between lord and tenant was determined in part by whether the lord was resident, occasionally resident, or nonresident, with his jurisdiction in the hands of stewards or local bailiffs.

Much depended also on the character of the lord and his relationships with other lords in the vicinity. Land in the hands of the Crown, or in "ancient demesne," enjoyed access to royal legal jurisdiction, and lands in the hands of lords who enjoyed liberties were sometimes subject to local jurisdiction for offenses that would ordinarily be referred to royal courts. Other factors that influenced manorial communities were the proportion of free and unfree tenants, the absence of one of these classifications, the proportion between demesne and tenant lands, susceptibility to inclem-ent weather, whether flood or drought, and, finally, the little understood local variation in the effects of plague or murrain. Tenants in some areas, moreover, were more exposed than those in others to mistreatment by extortionate sheriffs, bailiffs, summoners, archdeacons, rural deans, or diocesan officials. Again, some areas suffered more than others from the activities of royal purveyors or purveyors acting for noblemen, from the itinerant jurisdiction of the marshall and his court, from the intervention of the Court of the Admiralty, or from the depredations of soldiers moving to and from the coast or awaiting departure in the neighborhood of ports,[3] or from raiders from France or Castile. We should, I think, understand that agricultural workers or "peasants" were not by any means all alike, that their immediate interests were not the same through-out the country, and that they did not constitute "the masses" of the time. Community interests were still very strong, and manorial communities tended to arrange themselves in hierarchies. The easy generalizations of

Marxist and post-Marxist rhetoric should be restrained when we think about them.

It is true that many agricultural workers underwent extreme hardship during the early years of Edward III,[4] and that the plagues, murrains, droughts, and floods of the second half of the fourteenth century (not to mention the wars) produced a great deal of suffering. On the other hand, plague left many survivors with larger holdings that could be more efficiently managed, encouraging a new prosperity resulting from greater productivity. At the same time a shortage of labor inconvenienced landlords, who were forced to pay higher wages, while artisans in towns demanded higher prices or engaged in the production of substandard goods. People and their attitudes not only varied from place to place; they also varied in time.

For these reasons the question, Who were the people? is very difficult to answer, but a few details may be helpful. The "peasantry," with whom we shall begin, included not only free and unfree tenants of manors but miscellaneous agricultural workers (including Welshmen in border areas) who could be hired legally by the year, like those, for example, compelled by the Statute of Laborers to bring their implements to town and offer their services publicly where everyone could see and hear (so that landlords could not offer wages beyond the statute).[5] Both manorial lords and tenants with larger holdings after the great plague could afford to hire workers of this sort. There were also cottagers or small artisans on many manors who worked for more prosperous tenants. A manor might contain tenants who held only a portion of a virgate,[6] a virgate, more than one virgate, or several virgates. This matter is also complicated by the fact that a nobleman (or noblewoman) or a merchant might hold tenements under the manorial lord operated by local families. In any event, by the later fourteenth century, social status on a manor generally depended on wealth rather than legal status, so that a bondman might have a higher status in the manorial community than many of his free neighbors. It is also true that a tenant might hold both free and unfree lands, since rents and services were often attached to the land rather than to the person. In the years preceding the Great Revolt of 1381 (which involved ecclesiastics and minor noblemen as well as villeins, of whom there were none in Kent), there is evidence that some villein tenants were withdrawing their services. In 1377 it was alleged in Parliament that they were the victims of "Counsellors, Maintainers, and Abettors in the Country, which hath taken Hire and Profit of the said Villaines and Landtenants, by Color of certain Exemplifications made out of the Book of Domesday of the Manors and Towns where they have been dwelling, and by virtue of the same Exemplifications, and their evil Interpretations of the same, they affirm them to be quite and utterly discharged of all Manner Servage, due as well of their Body as of their said Tenures, and will not suffer any Distress or other Justice to be made upon them; but do menace the Ministers of their Lords of Life and Member, and, which more is, gather themselves together in great Routs, and agree by such Confederacy, that everyone shall aid other and resist their Lords with strong Hand."[7] In the following year there was a complaint that many agricultural laborers had gone to "vills, boroughs, and towns" and there "become artificers, mariners, or [surprisingly] clerks," making it difficult to keep lands in cultivation.[8] This sort of exodus apparently continued throughout the remainder of the century in spite of efforts on the part of the justices of the peace to stop it, for the temptation of ready cash afforded by wages by the day was very great.[9] Villeins on manors generally held the offices of ordinary manorial servants at stipends fixed by manorial custom and were elected by the manorial court. That is, the reeve, carter, shepherd, ponder, oxherd, butcher, dairymaid, and, at times, the miller or other regular servants of the manor (whose offices varied from manor to manor) were now demanding higher stipends. The examples afforded by hired laborers, or by laborers turned "artificers, mariners, or clerks" probably stimulated them to demand what was regarded as "outrageous and excessive Hire," so that a statute seeking to control them was passed in 1388.[10]

On many manors landlords, who were also interested in ready cash, commuted the labor services of their villeins for cash in the form of higher rents, or leased their demesne lands, often the most productive on the manor, so that labor services were no longer of interest to them. At the same time efforts on the part of lords to maintain the traditional work obligations of villeinage were ultimately doomed to failure, and this fact was becoming more and more obvious.[11] A rather amusing petition in the parliament of 1393–1394 complained that some religious had avoided the statute of Mortmain by arranging to have their villeins marry women holding free lands so that such lands might be inherited by the sons of villeins and, concomitantly, fall into the seizin of religious houses.[12] One can imagine the good brothers furbishing their more prosperous villeins to make them attractive to the ladies in prospect. Considering the agricultural economy as a whole, one should not assume that later fourteenth-century peasants were generally very poor persons gaining a mere subsistence in lamentable circumstances. The "spirit of enterprise" sometimes said to be characteristic of the age[13] extended to agricultural communities, often at the expense of community spirit and mutual cooperation, a fact that troubled the moralists of the age, but, nevertheless, at least from a rigorous economic point of view, seems a promising development, although the promise was not fulfilled in the fifteenth century, when real wages declined generally.

An ordinary peasant lived in a "long house," a rectangular structure, one end of which, containing perhaps two chambers, sheltered the tenant and his family while the other was used for his beasts. A more prosperous family might have a separate building for farm animals, placed at a right angle to the dwelling so as to form a kind of courtyard, and some tenants boasted two or three residential buildings. Although in a few areas these houses may have been of stone, ordinarily they were walled with wattles and clay set within a timber framework.[14] The resultant walls were not very sturdy and, as the coroners' rolls reveal, could be broken down by a determined robber, or by persons inside seeking to escape pursuit. Surrounding the house or houses was a tract of land, usually rectangular, with a short side on the lane. This might contain four or five acres more or less, affording room for a garden of vegetables and herbs, some fruit trees, and a small pasture. In some instances several families along a lane shared a common pasture at the rear of their tenements bordered by a service lane. Poor cottagers lived in smaller houses, perhaps with the "bower and hall" divided by a hanging. The animals might be cows, pigs (especially in Cheshire), sheep, goats, and fowl, and occasionally horses or oxen. Not infrequently a peasant wife brewed ale, which she sold, but each new batch was supposed to be judged by the local ale-taster, who also kept a watchful eye for violations of the assize and on some manors saw to it that the lord received a portion of each brew. Violations of the assize of ale had to be reported to the bailiff of the hundred or to the manorial court if its lord held the "View."[15]

Before the ill effects of plague (which varied from place to place) weakened traditional manorial communities there was a considerable amount of cooperation among manorial tenants, free and unfree, practically necessitated by overpopulation. This did not entirely disappear in the later fourteenth century, although some tenants were clearly more interested in making money than they were in the welfare of their fellows. The tenants elected their own jurors or "affeerors," who imposed fines in the manorial court. They determined in cooperation with the lord and his steward the customs of the manor, reached decisions about such matters as alterations in manorial field systems, and cooperated in keeping the peace. In accordance with the frankpledge system, male tenants of twelve years or more who were neither ecclesiastics nor persons under the direct jurisdiction of noblemen were divided into groups or "tith-ings," ideally of ten (although the number varied), presided over by a chief tithingman, who was bound to report transgressions by any of his men at the View.[16] The whole tithing could be fined for a transgession by any one of them; indeed, the whole vill or township might be fined in severe cases or on occasions when the tithingmen had failed to report transgressions of which they were clearly aware. The behavior of one's neighbors was thus a matter of some interest to everyone. Anyone being attacked or molested was required to raise the "hue and cry" so that the perpetrator might be seized by his neighbors. Those who raised the hue falsely or who failed to raise it when they should have done so could be fined. Transgressors might find "pledges" among their neighbors to guarantee payments of fines or future good behavior. On some manors the tenants might be divided into rather rigorous hierarchies, depending on the kind of tenure they held and on the size of their holdings.[17] Although these hierarchies often became fictions when demesnes were leased, they were replaced by hierarchies depending on wealth.

The peasant diet has received much attention, and here one must allow for considerable local variation, although the widespread impression that peasants for the most part ate little more than gruel is probably erroneous. The gardens referred to above, not to mention the livestock, probably afforded ample supplements of vegetables, eggs, milk, cheese, and some meat, like the "seynd bacoun" of Chaucer's abstemious dairy-maid. Food offered at "boonworks" when tenants assisted at the lord's harvest varied from place to place. Thus gruel might be served on some manors, but at Stoneleigh Abbey workers received a small white wheaten loaf, four eggs, pottage, sometimes cheese, and ale.[18] At Waltham in Essex a worker was given at dinner (in the early afternoon) bread and ale, pottage, a dish of either pork or mutton, or a dish of fish and some herrings. In the evenings he had bread, ale, and herrings or milk and cheese.[19] At Stretham, a manor of the Bishop of Chichester in Sussex, a bond tenant received wheaten bread and ale for breakfast; at dinner wheaten bread, soup, beef and mutton or other meat of two kinds and cheese; and for supper a wastel (gateau), a drink, two herrings, and cheese.[20] There is no reason to think that agricultural workers generally suffered from a lack of protein, even in those areas where their bread was made of oats, in the fourteenth century. After the great plague they often demanded better food as well as higher wages. By modern standards they may have been somewhat injudicious in asking for white bread, as they sometimes did.

The most important centers of social activity for agricultural workers were the church and the manorial court. Unfortunately, we have little first-hand evidence of parish entertainments in the fourteenth century.[21] Writers on morals like Robert Mannyng may complain about dances in the churchyard, beauty contests, and "summer games," but such complaints are often traditional so that it is difficult to determine whether they reflect current activities. It would be safe to assume, however, that parish priests organized pilgrimages to nearby shrines, which, in accordance with late-medieval attitudes toward decorum on "religious" occasions, might be very pleasant without being scandalous. There were processions on Rogation Day governed by similar prepuritanical standards, and festive celebrations on major holy days, probably with an element of pageantry. Itinerant friars interlaced their sermons with songs and stories,[22] some of which modern scholars would call folk tales, and weddings offered occasions for community celebration. Less decorous forms of entertainment, organized by the men of the vill, might give rise to difficulties. Thus in 1381 a football (soccer) game produced a "fray" between men of two villages under different lordships in Durham, and the prior's tenants were heavily fined in court.[23] Dice playing had been forbidden in one of the prior's vills in the previous year.[24] A statute of 1388 stipulated that no "servant of husbandry" carry a "buckler, sword, or dagger," but have bows and arrows to use on Sundays and holy days, and that such servants leave all "playing at Tennis or Football, and other games called Coits, Dice, Casting the Stone, Kailes [skittles], and other such importune Games."[25] We may assume that such games had been popular and that archery gradually came to replace them, although statute law, in spite of being proclaimed at county courts and marketplaces, was notoriously ineffective until the fifteenth century. Other opportunities for entertainment were afforded at fairs, where professional singers, dancers, and prostitutes might well be found among the merchants in their stalls. In the late fourteenth century there were still large fairs at St. Ives and Stourbridge, as well as lesser ones elsewhere. Local marketplaces probably afforded occasion for discussion of current events and the exchange of witty tales, not to mention songs airing current grievances.

Meetings of the manorial court, theoretically "from three weeks to three weeks," but often less frequently, gave everyone an opportunity to gain new insights into the character and behavior of his neighbors as well as to observe their land transactions of various kinds and to effect his own. Trespasses and other grievances were aired, including failures to clean ditches (which might become dangerous if blocked), digging in or otherwise obstructing highways, and failure to pay debts.[26] Licenses to marry were granted, and fines were imposed on women of villein status for fornication, pregnancy out of wedlock, or adultery. Occasionally young men were warned about illicit affairs; a Durham tenant was warned, for example, in 1380 not to keep a certain Katerina within the vill nor to come with her to a suspect place on pain of a heavy fine.[27] Among the various trespasses against the lord were allowing children to raid his orchard, pasturing beasts on his land, or taking thorns,[28] an event immortalized, so to speak, in the lyric "The Man in the Moon."[29] There were frequent cases of defamation, or verbal assault. For example, on the estates of Crowland Abbey a man was fined 2s. for saying to a villein that he wished he would burn.[30] It was, in effect, illegal to call a woman a prostitute or a man a robber.[31] A woman could not lightly be called a witch,[32] although it was considered worse to call a man a thief than for him to call her a whore,[33] probably because theft might be a felony punishable by hanging if the perpetrator were found guilty before royal justices. The punder, who impounded stray beasts, must have often aroused the ire of negligent tenants, so that in a Durham vill it was a trespass to insult him.[34] The Durham court also forbade calling a tenant a "native" (villein) in 1364 on pain of 20s., and in the following year began fining tenants for calling their fellows "rustics."[35] Women were especially prone to use abusive language.[36] In the vills of Durham shrewish women seem to have become a problem after 1378.[37] At the court of Carshalton in Surrey, five women were accused in 1393 of being "communes garulatores, ad grave nocumentum patrie."[38] Occasionally a woman might become sufficiently obstreperous to beat a man.[39] Generally, manorial courts sought to keep the peace as best they could and to prevent contentiousness among neighbors. When courts were held, food was sometimes served, and the occasion was social as well as legal. The various cases and judgments undoubtedly produced much discussion, some of it amusing.

The question of peasant literacy is a difficult one. Clanchy contends that reeves, who were required to make fairly elaborate accounts annually to a steward or auditor and were admonished not to alienate anything without a writ, might have been able to read;[40] but P.D.A. Harvey has pointed out that reeves' accounts at Cuxham were compiled by clerks, probably from wooden tallies simply labeled with drawings (not unlike labels used to mark bundles of some government documents) and kept by the reeves.[41] It has also been noted that some peasants had seals and conveyed land by charter.[42] Ada E. Levett noted that villeins at St. Alban's Abbey frequently conveyed lands by charter, registered wills, some of which (unlike wills made by freeholders under the common law) conveyed lands, and that they sometimes held copies of records describing their holdings.[43] The fact that peasants of villein status often sought and obtained for a fee permission to send off their sons to acquire sufficient education to enter the clergy suggests strongly, moreover, that small schools for boys conducted by priests, chaplains, monks,[44] or canons were probably more numerous in rural areas than has been generally supposed, for the boys in question had probably shown some aptitude in elementary instruction. This may well have included, in addition to some psalms, "Cato," the *Liber parabolum* of Alanus de Insulis *(PL,* 210.581–94), the *Cartula (PL,* 184.1307–14), the *Facetus* on good manners, and Bishop Grosseteste's *Stans puer ad mensam.*[45] Some peasants, especially reeves, who traditionally acted as pledges for those elected to parliament, guaranteeing their attendance, probably attended sessions of the shire courts, and in the general round of social activities that accompanied such sessions may have been exposed to some "literary" entertainment. Meanwhile, it is undoubtedly true that peasant mothers often sang to their infants or children,[46] or told them stories, about which we know very little, although there is reason to believe that they may have included ghost stories.[47] And men in the countryside, like men anywhere else, probably relished jocular stories, or, as folklorists call them, "merry tales."

If we turn to the more prosperous towns, especially to chartered boroughs with their own governments, the "literary" situation immediately improves, and here we find a ready audience for songs, romances, plays, and for popular works of religious instruction, which were numerous and varied, ranging from simple creed or confessional formulas to much more elaborate works of doctrine or spirituality, not to mention informative or instructive works that we should be inclined to call literary.[48] The *Canterbury Tales* contains a reworked saint's legend, an elaborate moral treatise by Albertanus of Brescia, and a sermon (or treatise) on penance.[49] But Chaucer was fortunate in having a court audience that included noblemen, ecclesiastics, clerks, and officials about the royal court.[50] These are, of course, "people" too, although their tastes were not exactly "popular." Audiences in lesser towns were somewhat less sophisticated and less responsive to various kinds of literary subtlety. Perhaps a few brief remarks about boroughs and their inhabitants may be helpful.

A borough was, as H.P.R. Finberg wrote, "a place where the tenements were held in burgage tenure," or for rents without services, although the terms under which various persons held could and did vary,[52] and in some boroughs there were remnants of heriot, fealty, and alienation and entrance fees.[53] By population the largest towns were London (about three times as large as the next largest town), York, Bristol, Coventry, Plymouth, Norwich, Lincoln, and Salisbury. Coventry was a monastic town, the largest of some thirty such towns in England and a thriving commercial center. Town governments varied a great deal, for, as J.S. Furley wrote, "in the Middle Ages . . . there was no uniformity; the system of government in a town depended on its individual history."[54] Borough customs, involving such matters as inheritance, the treatment of felons, and so on, varied from place to place.[55] In some boroughs primogeniture was the rule, as under the common law (except in Kent); in others, "borough English," in accordance with which the youngest son inherited, prevailed. Wives ordinarily took over the shops and tenements of their deceased husbands, whereas under the common law they were entitled to only a third of their husbands' lands for life, except in Kent, where they received half for life, or for so long as they remained single and did not become pregnant.[56] And many borough tenants, like many villein tenants, had the right to will or devise their holdings to others, a privilege denied free tenants under the common law. Chartered boroughs or towns with their own courts and governments tended to have a great deal of civic pride and to be very jealous of their privileges.[57]

Beverley affords a good example of a large agricultural town, in this instance dependent on the raising of oxen, cows, pigs, horses, and sheep, supported in common pastures, although sheep were allowed to wander about the town. It was governed by twelve "keepers" (*juratores, custodes, gubernatores*) selected from among the more substantial citizens. They were granted the power to collect amercements of the green wax (from the exchequer) by Edward III, thus depriving the Sheriff of York of this privilege—one, incidentally, that sheriffs often abused in spite of King Edward's reforming statute of 1368 (42 Ed. III 9), which was widely disregarded, as a parliamentary complaint of 1393 *(RP, 3.222)* reveals. Such abuses are reflected in the Wakefield *Last Judgment* (line 281). The keepers of Beverley were also responsible for the assize of bread and ale, the amercements from which were delivered to the bailiff of the Archbishop of York, and they themselves heard cases of fraud. The town had a merchant guild and other craft guilds, but here the merchant guild was not the government of the town, as it was at Southampton, where the alderman of the guild was called the "mayor" in the fourteenth century. Among the ancient customs of the town was one in which if a burgess begat offspring upon a concubine, no such offspring could become a citizen of Beverley, even though the father later married the concubine.[58] Beverley Minster, noted for its magnificent Percy tomb (c. 1335–1340), celebrated the feast of "The King of Fools" until it was abolished by Bishop Thomas Arundel in 1388,[59] and the town sponsored plays.[60]

A small town might develop within the confines of an agricultural manor. Thus a settlement of cutlers, smiths, brewers, drapers, and carpenters grew up during the fourteenth century at Thaxted (Essex) near the manor house and the church. These tenants owed biennial attendance at the manorial court and elected a bailiff, but did not acquire a charter until the sixteenth century.[61] Generally, most boroughs included tenements and adjacent agricultural lands which could be held independently of the tenements themselves. Some boroughs were dominated by prominent noblemen. Thus the lord of Leicester was the Earl of Derby (or later the Duke of Lancaster), although the town itself was governed by a mayor and twenty-four "jurats," or wealthy members of the merchants' guild. In 1375 John of Gaunt leased the bailiwick to this government for £80 a year for a period of ten years, the sum being a substitute for the profits from the fair court (which sat for a week at Michaelmas), the piepowder (i.e., "dusty-foot") or merchants' court, and the portmanmoot (presided over by the mayor and the twenty-four), granting at the same time relief from toll and tallage. But the duke kept his rents of mills and ovens, rents collected by the porter of the castle, and his right to the escheat of free tenements. The lease expired in 1385 and was not renewed until 1402. The town had its own elected coroner and chamberlain. There were a number of social guilds (neither craft guilds nor parish guilds), the oldest of which was the guild of Corpus Christi. Members of such guilds attended the funerals of deceased brethren, provided chaplains, held ceremonial dinners, and supported impoverished members. They also sought to supervise the moral behavior of their members, some of whom might be women. Here as elsewhere guilds proliferated after the great plague.[62] Guilds of various kinds, like that of St. Mary at Boston, supported plays, and some parish guilds supported dancing.[63] A guild like that of the Holy Trinity at Louth might also maintain in connection with its chantry a chaplain to instruct boys in manners and "polite letters."[64]

Although Winchester was not a royal manor, the king held the soil of the city, which paid an annual rent of 100 marks to the exchequer in the fourteenth century. It boasted the first mayor in England, legendary in 1184 and actual in 1200. He had twenty-four jurats or "peers" who made up his council, and he presided over a city court that recorded property transfers, and that dealt with breach of contract or warranty, debt, and trespass. He also held a merchants' court mostly concerned with debts involving foreigners (or noncitizens from elsewhere). When the bishop held his fair at St. Giles, he received the keys to the city from the mayor for sixteen days, since all trade had to be carried out at the fair. The city's two bailiffs, selected from among four nominated by the jurats, were royal officers who acted as property custodians upon the death of a tenant, kept records of property transfers, collected rents and amercements, made presentments at royal courts, and supervised standards of workmanship. The city had a chamberlain, two coroners, whose records were checked against those of the bailiffs, and a cofferer, who kept records but not treasure. There were six wards, each with a chief tithingman (without the judicial powers of London aldermen) who supervised the bedels. Weaving was the chief trade, the products being blankets and burel cloth, so that the chief import was wool.[65]

Other towns might house prosperous merchants engaged in overseas trade. Southampton, for example, was granted freedom from the jurisdiction of the sheriff by Henry III, long before the larger and more prosperous cloth-exporting town of Bristol achieved "county status" in 1373. Southampton did not acquire freedom from tolls, passage, and pontage throughout the realm until the time of Edward III, although that freedom had been bestowed on Bristol by Henry II.[66] The city was dominated by the merchants' guild, which met at prime on the Sunday after Saint John's Day (June 24) and on the Sunday after Saint Hilary (Jan. 13). Such meetings lasted all day and might, indeed, extend for several days. The guild forbade quarrels among its members, punished swearing (without, incidentally, any taint of Lollardy), attended the sick, participated in funerals, and relieved the poor among its members. Members, either by heredity or purchase (not unlike the citizens of London in this respect, although some franchised citizens were here not members), shared purchased merchandise, and enjoyed freedom from local tolls and customs. The alderman of the guild held courts, supervised officers, kept the peace, summoned meetings, and kept records. His seneschal (steward) oversaw the maintenance of guild and town property, and he was assisted by a council of twelve and four "discreets" or echevins, who were respected older citizens. Two of the twelve were elected bailiffs; there were four jurats of the markets who maintained the quality of fish, meat, poultry, and bread; and twelve guardians kept the peace in five wards. Brokers supervised sales, and there were some sergeants and a clerk. Although local patriotism was intense, heirs of wealthy merchants often abandoned the town to become wealthy freeholders or "franklins."

Like many other towns, Southampton welcomed the Franciscans, providing stone buildings for them (contrary to the rule of the order).[67] A visiting provincial had them destroyed, but his timber and plaster houses were replaced by a stone church and other structures in the late thirteenth century. The church, like many other churches elsewhere, was used for business deals, and the Franciscans were widely respected in the town, for which they provided water systems, as they also did in Bridgenorth, Bristol, Chichester, Coventry, Lichfield, Lincoln, London, Richmond, Carmaethan, Newcastle, Oxford, Scarborough, and Exeter. Friars' churches became popular burial sites, to the disgust of writers like Jean de Meun and, later, Erasmus, and the burgesses often remembered the friars in their wills. It is quite probable, however, that the friars stimulated the growth of lay spirituality, and that their influence included the popularization of devotional literature and penitential treatises, and the conversion of popular lyrics and carols into more obviously devotional songs, however innocent of anything except a certain amount of figurative language the originals may have been. Their sermons, with the literary adornments characteristic of Franciscan preaching, evidently captured the attention and sympathy of their local benefactors and their wives, and it is likely that they sponsored pageantry of one kind or another on high feast days.

The wealth of the friars, which sometimes contrasted sharply with their professed ideals, especially where Franciscans were concerned, and their rivalry with parish priests in preaching, hearing confessions, and burying the dead, promoted controversy not only among the learned but among lesser folk as well. The friars were sometimes accused of seducing women,[68] and it is quite possible that some popular lyrics are counteraccusations in kind inspired by the friars themselves. A historian of the manor of Winton in Sussex wrote, "It is curious that in the fifty years during which clergy are mentioned (1356–1408) only one name of a rector occurs, but it can hardly have been the same person throughout."[69] The name in question was "Sir John," which was indeed a common epithet for a rector. The songs "A Betrayed Maiden's Lament," "Our Sir John," and "Jolly Jankyn," where "Jankyn" is a contemptuous diminutive of "Sir John,"[70] may have been inspired by friars, although it is true that others besides friars, like Chaucer's Parson, for example, or Bishop Brinton, complained about lecherous priests; and the peace rolls afford many specific examples. Antifraternal songs are not always obvious at first glance. Thus the equation of fox with friar was a common enough bit of iconographic humor. In the lyric "The False Fox"[71] the predator "assoils" the geese before seizing his chosen victim, thus revealing his identity.[72] At times, as in the Vernon Lyrics, praise and blame of the friars may appear in the same collection.[73] It is true also that oppressive ecclesiastics like the Summoner at the Trial of Mary in the *Ludus Coventriae*[74] are often ridiculed in popular writings.

Southern coastal towns suffered especially from the wars. In 1360 Southampton, like Winchester and Plymouth, was exempted from war taxes on account of poverty. And in 1376 the town asked the king to take it into his own hands (a considerable sacrifice) and to prepare its defenses. After the coastal raids of 1377, the great architect Henry Yevele was asked to build a new keep for the castle, the construction of which was carried out during the anxious years 1382–1388. The same kind of danger affected towns elsewhere. On 30 November 1377 a writ was addressed to Leicester, as well as to other towns, to prepare a balinger for use in defense "at the cost of only the most honorable and richest men of the towns aforesaid."[75] The wine trade, important especially to merchants who exported cloth to Gascony, was often threatened. Thus in 1377 the king commanded that the vintage fleet be accompanied by the royal fleet, and orders were issued in 1384, 1385, 1386, and 1388 for the wine fleet to proceed in convoys.[76]

In times of peace, however, life, especially for the wives of well-to-do merchants, must have been rather pleasant, anticipating the situation discovered among wives of English merchants by Van Meteren during his visit to England in the sixteenth century. There are at least hints of this sort of thing in the song "On the Follies of Fashion,"[77] in Chaucer's description of the wives of his fraternal craftsmen in the General Prologue to his *Tales,* and in the Prologue to the Wife of Bath's Tale, all, of course, disapproving. The Wife likes to dress in her best clothes and go to vigils, processions, and sermons, to go on pilgrimages, and to attend marriages. She also likes to see "pleyes of myracles," which must have appealed to persons of all degrees. Finally, like Van Meteren's wives, she liked to spend a great deal of time with her "gossips," although in Chaucer's time she might well have qualified as a "scold" because of the calumny she heaped on her old husbands. Guilds and fraternities held processions on the days of their patron saints, or on Corpus Christi, and members of town governments and guildsmen paraded through the streets with carols and minstrelsy on festive occasions dressed in colorful costumes. In London, Saint John's Eve (Midsummer) was just such an occasion, and in view of the antiquity of the custom and its widespread and enduring practice[78]—probably in celebration of the transformation of the Old Law into the New, for witches, elves, and fairies held sway until midnight—we can assume that leafy boughs and flowers were draped over houses and shops in towns and villages throughout England, that bonfires were lit in the streets about which the inhabitants sang and danced, and that officials paraded through the streets with minstrelsy, all singing and dancing processional carols. The night's revels might be dangerous for girls, as the song "A Midsummer Day's Dance" reveals,[79] for not all of them enjoyed the supervising wisdom of Shakespeare's Theseus. Meetings of merchant guilds and fraternities were probably also graced with song or the reading of poetical narratives like *Havelok the Dane,* which offered an appealing combination of slapstick humor and outrageously stated but ultimately genuine civic patriotism to the fishermen of Grimsby, or later the more obviously comic *Tournament at Tottenham,* probably composed for a civic celebration of some kind. It seems quite likely that much literature of this kind has been lost, and, further, that some of the other surviving "vernacular romances" (a contradiction in terms where English narratives are concerned), the humor of which has been often overlooked, were used for town festivities.

Monastic towns, like monastic manors, enjoyed less freedom of self-government than other towns. Thus at Bury St. Edmunds (a cloth center), except in those areas subject to the manor of Clare or tenements held by the Hastings family, the sacrist was lord of the town and the obedientiaries held the town property and rented it to the tenants. The manor of Bury, consisting of some 212 acres of arable land in addition to heath, wood, and pasture, was controlled by the cellarer, who had the View of Frankpledge, market rights, the right to forestall, the right to dig clay, fishing rights, the profits of mills, and miscellaneous rents. The sacrist appointed the town bailiffs, held the View there (which was extended in 1383–1384 to all residents), presided over the assizes of weights and measures and bread and ale, acted as archdeacon in the ecclesiastical court, collected tolls, and had the right of tronage.[80] It seems obvious that the sacrist and the cellarer were busy men, deeply involved in worldly affairs. But the monastery was also active in providing plays and pageantry for the entertainment and instruction of the citizens and their rural neighbors.[81] At Chester both the Abbey of St. Wearmouth and the nuns of St. Mary's held franchises in the town, so that part of it was under monastic jurisdiction, a fact that gave rise to some friction.[82] The town itself had two courts, the "Prentice" court, which was the sheriff's court, and the Portmoot, or mayor's court, which entertained pleas of land, cases of forestalling, purpresture and encroachment, and trespass, which was, in fact, considered in both courts.[83]

Town court rolls usually present us with more or less routine business, including land transactions; violations of the assize of ale (mostly by women, who often appear year after year for this offense, apparently paying fines as a sort of license), or bread (mostly by men); cases of debt or covenant; cases of negligence, like leaving dung in the streets; or the punishment of scolds (technically by means of the cucking-stool, but more frequently by the more profitable means of amercements). They nevertheless sometimes afford us interesting glimpses of the people and their behavior. According to the *Court Rolls of the Borough of Colchester,* in that city (as in London) a man might be fined for carrying a knife,[84] victimizing Flemings by summoning them and punishing them (2:171), or eavesdropping, a widely recognized trespass (3:162). A woman might receive a very heavy fine for adultery (13s. 4d.; 3:110), a fact that should dispel the notion that such fines were imposed only on manorial bond-women. Receiving or maintaining harlots could bring either a man or a woman before the court (2:24; 3: 49, 104). Harlots in Colchester were supposed to stay in Berislane, just as they were supposed to stay in Cock Lane outside the wall in London, and could be fined for seeking business elsewhere (3: 177, 186). Women consistently outnumbered men brought before the court for forestalling (2: 4, 13, 39, 76, 105, 130, 142).

The rolls sometimes reveal interesting characters, among whom at Colchester was one John Stanstede, appearing on the rolls first as a chaplain and later on one occasion as a rector. In 1372 the rector of St. Michaels of La Mylande, Colchester, was alleged to have wagered John Stanstede, chaplain, that if he could throw him he would give the spectators a gallon of wine and John two quarters of grain at Michaelmas. John threw him, but the rector refused the grain and denied the covenant. The rector failed to appear and was in mercy (3:11). Two years later it was agreed at Colchester market that if Master Nicholas, a doctor, could solve a question put to him by William Dentone, John Stanstede would pay a cordwainer a pair of boots worth 2s. But when Master Nicholas solved the question, Stanstede refused to pay the cordwainer (3:59). These last cases illustrate the validity of verbal covenants before witnesses in local courts, not to mention a taste for playful humor among townsmen. To get a hearing before the royal justices concerning contract or covenant without a written record, it was necessary to allege a breach of the peace, *vi et armis,* an expression often followed by the formula "to wit, with swords and bows and arrows," although no such weapons might be involved. An entry in the court roll for 1377 mentions a death's-head mask, a tunic with tails, and other apparatus for playing "miracles" (3:140). We can assume, therefore, that this form of entertainment was available at Colchester as elsewhere.

A few more cases from the *Records of the Borough of Nottingham* will illustrate the kind of justice administered as well as something of the mores of the people. In 1360 one John Shakespere alleged that a servant of John de Spondon "vi et armis insultum fecit, et ipsum vulneravit, verberavit, maletractavit, et sanguinavit et alia enormia ei intulit . . . contra pacem," committing 100s. damages. The court awarded him 40d.[85] In 1364 Thomas Hutton complained that on a day he was sitting in a tavern when Richard de Cobeley, shearman, "vi et armis ipsum Thomam insultum fecit, et ipsum verberavit, et quemdam ciphum plenum cervisiae in facie ejus jactavit . . . contra pacem," committing 20s. damages. For this enormity the court awarded him a ha'penny (pp. 183–85).

In Nottingham a chaplain might be hired to educate boys. Thus in 1395 a chaplain complained to the court that one William Tole had neglected to pay him 3s. 4d. for teaching his boy for five terms (p. 263). Other chaplains might engage in less commendable activities. Thus in 1389 John de Bilby complained that Roger de Mampton, chaplain, broke into his close and entered his chamber, where John found him under the curtains of a bed. When John asked what he did there, Roger replied that he did not come in any evil way. He promised not to enter John's premises again nor to be found with John's wife. Nevertheless, on a certain night, Roger broke John's wall and was with John's wife a long time "ubi secreta sua fuerunt." And so he did continually for a year to John's loss of two pairs of sheets, tablecloths, towels, a brass pot worth 13s. 4d., and the profit of four quarters of malt lost through Roger's coming and going to the damage of £100. Roger replied that he was simply making his rounds with holy water, a defense that may have produced laughter but won him small sympathy from the court (pp. 241–43). The peace rolls, incidentally, record many similar offenses on the part of chaplains.[86] The case reminds us a little of "A Midsummer Day's Dance," mentioned above, where the seducer is a holy-water clerk.

It is impossible to include "lords of manors" in a single social category, for they might include the king, the queen, greater and lesser noblemen or noble ladies, bishops, cathedral canons, abbots, priors, monastic obedientiaries, clerks, lawyers, merchants, tradesmen, parsons, self-perpetuating groups of trustees, colleges, town governments, or, in fact, almost any person or group of persons with sufficient wealth. The word *manor* is, moreover, a rather vague term, since a group of tenements in a town held by a single lord might be called a manor, and manors that were partly urban and partly rural were not unusual. Even in the countryside a manor might be chiefly residential, in some instances a place for monks to take their vacations from the routine of monastic life, and some agricultural manors were highly specialized. The modern historical vocabulary is here as elsewhere somewhat simplistic, especially where discussions of "the manorial system" are involved.

We do have some descriptions of manor houses and their appurtenances. An especially fine one was the home of the distinguished warrior Sir Nigel de Loring, who had been knighted at Sluys, became a Garter Knight in 1344, and served as chamberlain to Prince Edward. In his later years he retired to Chalgrave manor, although as a man of substantial wealth, he held other manors elsewhere.[87] The house at Chalgrave contained first a great hall, where Sir Nigel, his wife, his two daughters, the chaplain, his steward (when he was not on his rounds), and visitors took their meals on a dais, while the household servants and perhaps the local reeve at harvest time ate in the hall below. Conventionally, there would have been a gallery built on the wall above the dais for minstrels or reading clerks, who might furnish entertainment or instruction at dinner, and somewhere in the hall was a large fireplace. In all probability the walls were decorated with Sir Nigel's arms and armor and perhaps some tapestries or decorative hangings. At the western end, where the dais was set up, there were the usual pantry, buttery, wine cellar, larder, a chamber for wood, three upper chambers, one with a latrine, and a basement below, perhaps containing a kitchen. An outer court enclosed a garden for vegetables and herbs. Adjacent to the hall at the eastern end was a chapel with an enclosed rose garden on the outside. There was a guesthouse with a garden and a gatehouse at the entry. Other buildings included a dairy house, a bakery, a malt house, a kiln house, an alehouse, a well house, a cart house, a stable, and several barns, including a large barn with seven bays, a haybarn, a strawbarn, a peasbarn, and a granary. There were, in addition, two sheepcotes, a pigsty, a boarsty, a cowhouse, an oxhouse, a dovecote, and facilities for poultry, including geese. Within the grounds there were two orchards, one with two fishponds and one with three, as well as a nursery and a vivarium. A nearby field contained another pond. Altogether, Sir Nigel and his family must have lived in considerable comfort. We can assume a Bible and service books for the chapel, and probably prayer books, meditations, and devotional works, including a manual of penance, some of which were used when the family and their guests assembled in the chapel for evening prayers.

Many manor houses were, of course, far less elaborate than this one, which resembles the larger "inns" or residences in London except that it had more extensive grounds. Many lords among the nobility, like Thomas IV Lord Berkeley (1368–1417), were much given to the chase, hunting hares, deer, foxes, and badgers,[88] and some abbots maintained hunting dogs for the entertainment of their noble friends and benefactors, lesser monks being restrained from such pursuits. A bishop might have similar facilities.[89] Whether noblemen generally had literary interests has been the subject of some discussion. It was not necessary for a nobleman to be very literate to enjoy narratives, whether pious, historical, or jocular, read to him by a clerk or minstrel, or plays presented in a nearby town. It is quite likely also that active military men enjoyed songs and stories on festive occasions or at tournaments. Some of them had collections of books. Thus Guy de Beauchamp, Earl of Warwick, gave Bordesley Abbey some forty books, including some books of the Bible, meditations, saints' lives, romances and histories, a book of physic, one on surgery, a primer for children, an encyclopedia, and a miscellaneous anthology, all in French.[90] Clanchy has pointed out that by 1300 "an educated layman" was "probably familiar with three literary languages (Latin, French, and English)."[91] We do not know how many noblemen were "educated," but the proliferation of government documents of all kinds and the necessity for written records acted as a profound stimulus to learning. Chaucer, who was addressing a noble and clerical audience, employs frequent references (not all of which are obvious at first glance) to the Bible, the Latin classics, and to medieval works in both Latin and French. We must assume that he did so because his audience appreciated them.

Noblemen were naturally interested in historical writings, especially in writings, whether actually historical or fabulous, that concerned their ancestors. Indeed, those with long military careers might well acquire works that contained material about themselves. We sometimes forget that the *Chronicles* of Froissart were at one time "popular" reading for boys throughout England and that men with military experience or aspirations were likely to have been even more interested in them earlier. The subject of history appealed to abbots as well. Thus we learn that one abbot sought to borrow a book that "temporibus Godefridi de Bolon' aliorumque nobilium conquestum continet terre sancte."[92] One rather notorious abbot, Thomas of Pipe, of the Cistercian abbey of Stoneleigh, became noted as a local historian, so that Dugdale was led to observe that "his memory will be of good esteem to all that are lovers of history."[93]

His notoriety arises from the fact that during his administration the abbey—which, King Edward said, had been founded by his ancestors to provide chantries and other works of piety for his ancestors, himself, and his heirs—had neglected its chantries and had ceased both to give alms to the poor and to shelter pilgrims. He sent a commission to investigate in December of 1363. It was found that the abbot had alienated without any consideration or rent a messuage, a carucate of land, and ten marks in rents to his concubine, Isabella, and to their eldest son John, "de voluptuose affeccione quam habuit predicte Isabelle et filio eorumdem." He had also alienated a grange to some servants so that its income was used for the exclusive support of himself, Isabella, and her children, said to be "greater in number than his monks." Thomas had also disseized a tenant wrongfully through a false deed and then, to avoid discovery, reenfeoffed the holding to him in fee simple "to the disherison of the aforesaid abbey." The king seized the abbey until a new abbot was elected in 1365. Oddly, Pipe was abbot once more in 1381, but retired in 1382.[94]

Erring abbots like Thomas of Pipe or the unfortunate abbot of Missenden in Buckinghamshire who was drawn and hanged for forging and clipping the royal coinage—a treasonous offense[95]—were rare, although others might be simply inefficient. More influential abbeys did a great deal of entertaining, becoming in effect social centers for noblemen, merchants, or lawyers, who exchanged gossip concerning current affairs (a source of rumors) and enjoyed the food served to them. We may safely assume that at dinner some instructive and edifying material (like selections from *Piers Plowman,* for example) was often read before the company. Larger abbeys, friaries, and cathedrals often maintained extensive libraries, which sometimes contained works that might be called "popular" in a restricted sense, like Holcot's commentary on *Wisdom,* the *De regimine principum* of Aegidius Romanus, or even romances.

Generally, medieval people in all walks of life were alert to wit and humor, and, at the same time, thirsty for practical moral instruction, appreciating both the "solaas" and the "sentence" that might be found in a great variety of works ranging from sermons (not always without humor), historical works, romances, songs and poems on the evils of the time, instructive works on law,[96] medicine, or natural history, to mere fabliaux. No one thought that there was anything very odd about speaking the truth with a smile. Their assemblies, whether associated with meetings of parliament,[97] court sessions in counties, hundreds, or manors and towns, festivals at churches, friaries, houses of canons, or monasteries, or fairs, markets, processions and town festivals, offered them opportunities to hear and enjoy what we might call "popular" literature.

Lords could sometimes enjoy it in their manor houses, and, as the works of Chaucer attest, there were opportunities for literary entertainment at the royal court, and it seems quite likely that similar opportunities were available at the courts of prominent noblemen. However, I think that we should remember that there was then nothing like the large homogeneous audience available for writers today, when tastes are largely Epicurean in nature and when reactions to song and story are predominantly emotional. As has often been observed, medieval people were practical rather than sentimental, an attitude made more or less natural by the fact that life was then more difficult, a great deal shorter, and not very rich in opportunities for leisure, which was not regarded then as something to be cultivated in any event but as an invitation to irrational behavior. It will repay us when considering medieval popular literature (or any other kind of literature) to consider the question of the audience to whom it was addressed and, where possible, the kind of occasion for which it might have been used.

N O T E S

1. M.T. Clanchy, *From Memory to Written Record in England, 1066–1307* (Cambridge, Mass.: Harvard Univ. Press, 1979), p. 170.
2. Governmental structures were for the most part customary and had nothing to do with "political theory," which was then ultimately moral theory.
3. See the parliamentary complaint in the third year of King Richard (3 R II), *Rotuli Parliamentorum* (Record Commission, 1783, hereinafter *RP*), 3:80.
4. The situation is discussed at length by J.R. Madicott, *The English Peasantry and the Demands of the Crown*, Past and Present Supplement, vol. 1 (1975). It is reflected in an Anglo-Norman poem printed by Isabel S.T. Aspin, ed., *Anglo-Norman Political Songs* (Oxford: B. Blackwell, 1953), no. 10. There is an excellent analysis of the poem in G.L. Harriss, *King, Parliament, and Public Finance in Medieval England to 1369* (Oxford: Clarendon Press, 1975), pp. 250–52.
5. For the statute, see *Statutes of the Realm* (London, 1810–28, hereinafter, *SR*), 1:311–16.
6. For a discussion of the word *virgate* and related terms, see D.W. Robertson, Jr., " 'And for my Land thus Hastow Mordred Me?': Land Tenure, the Cloth Industry, and the Wife of Bath," *Chaucer Review*, 14 (1980), note 26, pp. 418–20.
7. 1 R II c. 6, *SR*, 2.2; cf. *RP*, 3.21.
8. *RP*, 3.46; cf. Nora Ritchie, "Labour Conditions in Essex in the Reign of Richard II," in E.M. Carus-Wilson, ed., *Essays in Economic History* (London: E. Arnold, 1954–1962), 2:93.
9. See, for example, the parliamentary complaint of 1391, *RP*, 3:296.
10. 12 R II 4, *SR*, 2:57. Generally, "reform" statutes were passed in the first

year of Richard's reign, when he was too young to be responsible and there was, in any event, a generally conciliatory policy on the part of the government; and in 1388 when the Appellants were in control. Richard was much less concerned about abuses than Edward had been during his best years.

11. The matter is actually somewhat complex. See, for example, Barbara F. Harvey, *Westminster Abbey and Its Estates in the Middle Ages* (Oxford: Clarendon Press, 1977), chs. 9, 10.

12. *RP,* 3:319.

13. See especially F.R.H. Du Boulay, *An Age of Ambition: English Society in the Late Middle Ages* (London: Nelson, 1970).

14. See most recently J.G. Hurst, "The Changing Medieval Village in England," in J.A. Raftis, ed., *Pathways to Medieval Peasants* (Toronto: Pontifical Institute of Mediaeval Studies, 1981), esp. pp. 38–44. Cf. Sarah M. McKinnon, "The Peasant House: The Evidence of Manuscript Illuminations," in the same volume, pp. 301–9.

15. For the Assize of Bread and Ale, see *SR,* 1: 199–200, 201–4.

16. For articles of the View, which might vary somewhat from place to place, see *SR,* 1:246–47.

17. E.g. see K.C. Newton, *The Manor of Writtle: The Development of a Royal Manor in Essex, c. 1086 – c. 1500* (Chichester: Phillimore, 1970), pp. 40–52.

18. R.H. Hilton, ed., *The Stoneleigh Leger Book,* Dugdale Society (Oxford: Oxford Univ. Press, 1960), p. 103.

19. Ritchie, "Labour Conditions," p. 97.

20. W.D. Peckam, ed. and trans., "Thirteen Customals of the Sussex Manors of the Bishop of Chichester," Sussex Record Society, no. 31 (Cambridge: W. Heffer and Sons, 1925), pp. 106–8. This customal was completed in 1374.

21. See Alexandra F. Johnston, "Parish Entertainments in Berkshire," in *Pathways to Medieval Peasants,* pp. 335–37.

22. See John V. Fleming, *An Introduction to the Franciscan Literature of the Middle Ages* (Chicago: Franciscan Herald Press, 1977), ch. 4; and David L. Jeffrey, *The Early English Lyric and Franciscan Spirituality* (Lincoln: Univ. of Nebraska Press, 1975), chs. 5, 6.

23. W.H.D. Longstaffe and John Booth, eds., *Halmota Prioratus Dunelmensis,* Surtees Society, no. 82 (Durham: Andrews and Co., 1889), p. 171.

24. Ibid., p. 166.

25. 12 R II 6, *SR,* 2:57.

26. For an illustration of debt cases on one medieval manor (Writtle), see Elaine Clark, "Debt Litigation in a Medieval English Vill," in *Pathways to Medieval Peasants,* pp. 247–79.

27. *Halmota Prioratus Dunelmensis,* p. 166.

28. See W.O. Ault, ed., *Court Rolls of the Abbey of Ramsey and of the Honor of Clare* (New Haven: Yale Univ. Press, 1928), p. 206 and note; and *Halmota Prioratus Dunelmensis,* p. 86.

29. Carleton Brown, ed., *English Lyrics of the Thirteenth Century* (Oxford:

Clarendon Press, 1932), no. 89. The speaker offers to get the hayward ("hedge-guard") drunk, take from him the "wed" or token payment the moon-man has given him, and with it placate the bailiff.

30. Frances M. Page, *The Estates of Crowland Abbey: A Study in Manorial Organization* (Cambridge: Cambridge Univ. Press, 1934), p. 143.

31. W.O. Massingberd, trans., *Court Rolls of the Manor of Ingoldmells in the County of Lincoln* (London: Spottiswood, 1902), pp. 19, 42, 53, 93.

32. Ault, *Court Rolls*, p. 256.

33. See F.W. Maitland and W.P. Baildon, eds., *The Court Baron*, Selden Society, no. 4 (London: B. Quaritch, 1891), p. 133.

34. *Halmota Prioratus Dunelmensis*, p. 42.

35. Ibid., pp. 33, 40, 40–41, 141.

36. Page, *Estates of Crowland Abbey*, p. 139, and J.A. Raftis, *Warboys: Two Hundred Years in the Life of an English Village* (Toronto: Pontifical Institute of Mediaeval Studies, 1974), pp. 250–51.

37. E.g., see *Halmota Prioratus Dunelmensis*, pp. 144, 154, 169, 171.

38. *Court Rolls of the Manor of Carshalton*, Surrey Record Society, 7, no. 2 (London: Roworth, 1916), p. 38.

39. *Halmota Prioratus Dunelmensis*, p. 101.

40. Clanchy, *From Memory to Written Record*, p. 32.

41. *Manorial Records of Cuxham*, Oxfordshire Record Society, no. 50 (1976), pp. 37–40. For labels on bundles of documents, see Hubert Hall, *The Antiquities and Curiosities of the Exchequer* (New York: A.C. Armstrong, 1891), pp. 54–58.

42. Clanchy, *From Memory to Written Record*, pp. 34–35.

43. "The Court and Court Rolls of St. Alban's Abbey," *Transactions of the Royal Historical Society*, 4th ser., vol. 6 (1924), pp. 68, 71–72.

44. For a monastic school, see H.P.R. Finberg, *Tavistock Abbey: A Study in the Social and Economic History of Devon* (Cambridge: Cambridge Univ. Press, 1951), p. 224. Some boys became priests; "others," Finberg tells us, "appear later as burgesses, portreeves, and members of parliament."

45. Cf. Nicholas Orme, *English Schools in the Middle Ages* (London: Methuen, 1973), esp. pp. 103–4, 146–49.

46. See Carleton Brown, ed., *Religious Lyrics of the Fourteenth Century* (Oxford: Clarendon Press, 1924), no. 28. This and related songs involving the Christ child are probably variants of a popular lullaby.

47. The peace rolls reveal that in Lincolnshire two men lurked in a churchyard covered with a white sheet, and then attacked one John Lockwood and his servant when they came to see who was there. See Elisabeth G. Kimball, *Some Sessions of the Peace in Lincolnshire 1381–96*, Lincoln Record Society, no. 56 (Hereford: Hereford Times 1962), p. 235.

48. For works dealing primarily with spiritual guidance, see P.S. Joliffe, *A Check-List of Middle English Prose Writings of Spiritual Guidance* (Toronto: Pontifical Institute of Medieval Studies, 1974). If we were to add to this list works in verse and related works not included in Joliffe's rather rigorous classification, the

volume of survivals would be impressive indeed. Some citizens of towns had sufficient training to appreciate similar books in French or Latin, and the same thing might be said of some noblemen.

49. The distinction between a sermon and a treatise, or what we should call a treatise (for the medieval term was looser), is a hazy one, for a lengthy exposition could readily be excerpted for use as a sermon. The Parson's Tale itself omits the Commandments, a fact of which the Parson is clearly aware; see *The Works of Geoffrey Chaucer,* ed. F.N. Robinson, 2d ed. (Boston: Houghton Mifflin, 1957), lines 956–57. Some penitential treatises also included treatments of the Sacraments.

50. See, for example, Derek Pearsall, "The *Troilus* Frontispiece and Chaucer's Audience," *Yearbook of English Studies,* 7 (1977): 73–74.

51. *West-Country Historical Studies,* (New York: A.M. Kelly, 1969), p. 105.

52. The best concise account is M. de W. Hemmeon, "Burgage Tenure in Medieval England," *Law Quarterly Review* 26 (1910): 215–30, 331–48; and ibid., 27 (1911): 44–59. For a very detailed account of tenurial arrangements in Bristol containing frequent comparisons with other boroughs, see E.W.W. Veale, ed., *The Great Red Book of Bristol,* Bristol Record Society, vol. 2, pt. 1 (1931).

53. See Hemmeon's book, *Burgage Tenure in Medieval England* (Cambridge: Harvard Univ. Press, 1914), pp. 59–60.

54. *City Government in Winchester* (Oxford: Oxford Univ. Press, 1923), p. 1.

55. See Mary Bateson, *Borough Customs,* Selden Society, nos. 18–19 (London: B. Quaritch, 1904–1906). Further details are often given in the histories and studies of towns listed in the bibliography supplied by Susan Reynolds, *An Introduction to the History of English Medieval Towns* (Oxford: Clarendon Press, 1977), pp. 202–23.

56. For the customs of Kent, see *SR,* 1:223–25, where they are described in terms of Kentish maxims.

57. Cirencester, a monastic town, had its own court until 1309, when the abbot outraged his tenants by forcing them to attend his manorial court. They eventually sought a remedy before the chancellor, but the abbot was able to purchase his privileges, and the town did not regain self-government until the nineteenth century. See H.P.R. Finberg, ed., *Gloucestershire Studies* (Leicester: Leicester Univ. Press, 1957), pp. 74–81.

58. For Beverley's government and customs, see Arthur F. Leach, ed., *Beverley Town Documents,* Selden Society, (London: B. Quaritch, 1900).

59. Margaret Aston, *Thomas Arundel: A Study of Church Life in the Reign of Richard II* (Oxford: Clarendon Press, 1967), p. 293.

60. For the relevant documents, see Alan H. Nelson, *The Medieval English Stage: Corpus Christi Pageants and Plays* (Chicago: Univ. of Chicago Press, 1974), pp. 88–89.

61. K.C. Newton, *Thaxted in the Fourteenth Century* (Chelmsford: Essex County Council, 1960), pp. 20–23.

62. For these and other details see Mary Bateson, ed., *Records of the Borough of Leicester*, 2 vols. (London: C.J. Clay and Sons, 1899–1923).

63. Dorothy Mary Owen, *Church and Society in Medieval Lincolnshire* (Lincoln: History of Lincolnshire Committee, 1971), pp. 130–31.

64. Ibid., p. 101.

65. The details here are from J.S. Furley, *City Government in Winchester*, passim.

66. The details concerning city government in the following discussion are from the excellent study by Colin Platt, *Medieval Southampton* (London: Routledge and Kegan Paul, 1973).

67. Other orders were prominent in other towns. Thus, for example, at Clare, Suffolk, the Augustinian friars were prominent, enjoying the patronage of Elizabeth de Burgh and Lionel, Duke of Clarence. See Gladys H. Thornton, *A History of Clare, Suffolk* (Cambridge: W. Heffer and Sons, 1928), pp. 84–88. In London the Dominicans and Carmelites enjoyed close association with the royal government and the Augustinians were promoted by the Bohun family.

68. The accusation was actually based on 2 Tim. 3:6, originally used against the friars by William of St. Amour. See D.W. Robertson, Jr., *Chaucer's London* (New York: Wiley, 1968), pp. 192–96.

69. William Hudson, "On a Series of Rolls of the Manor of Winton," Sussex Archaeological Society Collections, no. 54 (1911), p. 181.

70. Rossell Hope Robbins, ed., *Secular Lyrics of the Fourteenth and Fifteenth Centuries* (Oxford: Clarendon Press, 1952), nos. 25, 26, and 27.

71. Ibid., no. 49.

72. This absolution for understandable reasons has disappeared from the American version of the song as rendered by Burl Ives.

73. Brown, *Religious Lyrics of the Fourteenth Century*, no. 103, ll. 49–60, and no. 117, ll. 49–56.

74. For a discussion, see Rosemary Woolf, *The English Mystery Plays* (Berkeley: Univ. of California Press, 1972), pp. 174–75. Other plays contain somewhat less obvious but telling examples.

75. Bateson, *Records of the Borough of Leicester*, 2:161–62.

76. Margery K. James, *Studies in the Medieval Wine Trade*, ed. E.M. Veale (Oxford: Oxford Univ. Press, 1971), p. 131. On the relationship between trade and war, see especially Kenneth Fowler, "War and Change in Late Medieval France and England," in Fowler, ed., *The Hundred Years War* (London: Macmillan, 1971), esp. pp. 4–8.

77. Brown, *English Lyrics of the Thirteenth Century*, no. 74.

78. See Richard Axton, *European Drama of the Early Middle Ages* (Pittsburgh: Univ. of Pittsburgh Press, 1975), pp. 147–50, 183–84; Adam de la Halle, *Le Jeu de la Feuillé*; Dunbar's *Twa Mariit Wemen and the Wedo*. Shakespeare's *Midsummer Night's Dream* deftly reflects the tradition. There is some information about the custom in Robert Chambers, ed., *Book of Days* (London: W. and R. Chambers, 1888), 1:814–17. For the London observance see R.R. Sharpe, ed.,

Calendar of Letter Books Preserved among the Archives of the Corporation of the City of London (London: J.E. Francis, 1899 et seq.), *Letter Book H,* p. 232; and J. Stow, *A Survey of London,* ed. C.L. Kingsford (Oxford: Clarendon Press, 1908), 1:101–3.

79. Robbins, *Secular Lyrics,* no. 28.

80. See M.D. Lobel, *The Borough of Bury St. Edmunds* (Oxford: Clarendon Press, 1935), pp. 1–53.

81. See Gail McMurray Gibson, "Bury St. Edmunds, Lydgate, and the *N-Town Cycle,*" *Speculum* 56 (1981): 56–90.

82. Douglas Jones, *The Church in Chester 1300–1540,* Chetham Society, 3rd ser., 7 (Manchester: Butler and Tanner, 1957) 39–42.

83. See A. Hopkins, *Select Rolls of the Chester City Courts,* Chetham Society, 3rd ser., 2 (1950): xviii–xxiii. The introduction to this volume contains useful comparative notes.

84. I.H. Jeayes, ed. and trans., *Court Rolls of the Borough of Colchester* (Colchester: Town Council of the Borough of Colchester 1921–1941), 2:226.

85. W.H. Stevenson, ed., *Records of the Borough of Nottingham* (London: B. Quaritch, 1882), 1:177.

86. See for example, Elizabeth G. Kimball, ed., *Rolls of the Gloucestershire Sessions of the Peace 1361–98,* Transactions of the Bristol and Gloucestershire Archaeological Society (Kendal: T. Wilson, 1942), 62: 115–16, 122–23, 124–25, 130, 154; Elizabeth Chapin Furber, ed., *Essex Sessions of the Peace 1351, 1377–1379,* Essex Archaeological Society Occasional Publications (Colchester: Essex Archaelogical Society, 1953), 3:169; Bertha Haven Putnam, ed., *Proceedings before the Justices of the Peace in the Fourteenth and Fifteenth Centuries,* Ames Foundation (London: Spottiswood, Ballantyne and Co., 1938), pp. 112, 112–13, 139–40. Rectors, parsons, and vicars were sometimes similarly inclined. See ibid., pp. 113, 119, 120, 220, 369. Even an archdeacon might succumb. See Furber, *Essex Sessions,* p. 98.

87. Marian K. Dale, ed., *Court Rolls of Chalgrave Manor, 1278–1313,* Bedfordshire Historical Record Society (Streatley: The Society, 1950), 28: xviii. At his death Sir Nigel left bequests to the friars, to nunneries, and to churches in thirteen parishes where he held manors. For his manors in Devon and Cornwall, see *Calendar of Inquisitions Post Mortem,* vol. 16, 7–15 R II (1974), nos. 128–29, pp. 96–97; no. 326, p. 116.

88. See John Smyth, *The Lives of the Berkeleys,* Bristol and Gloucestershire Archaeological Society (Gloucester: J. Bellows, 1883–85), 2:12.

89. For a "chace of deer" held by the Bishop of Chichester, see Peckam, "Thirteen Customals," p. 124.

90. Clanchy, *From Memory to Written Record,* p. 60.

91. Ibid., p. 86.

92. W.A. Pantin, "The Letters of John Mason," in *Essays in Medieval History Presented to Bertie Wilkinson,* ed. T.A. Sandquist and M.R. Powicke (Toronto: Univ. of Toronto Press, 1969), pp. 216–17.

93. Sir William Dugdale, *Monasticon Anglicanum* (London: J. Bohn, 1846), 5:445.

94. See G.O. Sayles, ed., *Select Cases in the Court of King's Bench,* Selden Society (London: B. Quaritch, 1971) 7:133–35; Hilton, *Stoneleigh Leger Book,* xviii–xxi.

95. Sayles, *Select Cases,* 7:118.

96. For an example of humor in a law book, see the hypothetical case of a tenant who took a fish from his lord's pond in Maitland and Baildon, *The Court Baron,* pp. 54–55.

97. The mayor's accounts at Leicester for 1357–1358 include, among his expenses in London, 4d. paid to the King's fool. See Bateson, *Records of the Borough of Leicester,* 2:108. There is every reason to assume that diversions involving song and story were arranged by parliamentary representatives during their sojourns in London.

The Fourth Lateran Council
and Manuals of Popular Theology
by Leonard E. Boyle, O.P.

The Fourth Lateran Council of late 1215 is generally accepted as the most pastoral of all the general church councils of the Middle Ages. When Innocent III first announced it in April 1213, he stated that its aims were "to extirpate vices and foster virtues, correct abuses and reform morals, suppress heresy and strengthen the faith, settle disorders and establish peace, encourage princes and Christian peoples to aid and maintain the Holy Land."

Although concern with the Holy Land occupied the last and longest constitution of the council, the other seventy constitutions are, in one way or another, taken up with aspects of the pastoral care. The areas they cover include the holding of annual diocesan synods, clerical mores and apparel, annual confession, annual communion at Easter, the upkeep of churches, the custody of the Eucharist, the provision of proper salaries for parochial priests. In all or most of these constitutions there is a sensitivity to the needs of the pastoral care that has no parallel in previous councils. It is, for example, characteristic of the council that in denouncing the practice of underpaying parochial priests, it pointed to illiteracy as one of the consequences of this practice. Encouraging a literate clergy clearly was one of its several preoccupations. If those selected for ecclesiastical benefices "must not be wanting in uprightness and a knowledge of letters," each cathedral church was ordered to have a resident theologian who would educate priests for the pastoral care, and each bishop was to see to it that candidates for the priesthood were sufficiently informed on their sacred duties and on the nature and administration of the sacraments.[1]

Few if any of these pastoral constitutions were wholly innovative. By and large the package of constitutions with which Innocent III presented the four hundred and more bishops for their approval during the three weeks that the council lasted, simply summed up, on the one hand, some local practices which had proven themselves in various parts of Europe and, on the other, some of the theological and legal advances of the renaissance of the twelfth century. But in putting its stamp on a century or so of innovation and practice the council changed the face of the pastoral care. Among other things, it provided the parochial priest with a responsibility vis-à-vis his parishioners which he never had had in any explicit fashion before this, and it consolidated at large in the Church an identity which he had been slowly acquiring since the First Lateran Council of 1123. It is not an exaggeration to say that it was at the Fourth Lateran Council that the *cura animarum* came into its own for the first time ever. Before the council there was an entity called the *cura animarum* and there were priests known as parochial or parish priests ("presbiteri parochiales"), but it was the Fourth Lateran Council which gave both these parochial priests and the *cura animarum* or parishioners an identity and a self-awareness, and an honorable, recognized place in the church at large.

One important consequence of this new awareness of the *cura animarum* was a vast literature of the pastoral care, a literature to which, for want of a better or more generic word, I may assign the term *pastoralia*. As one may see from the annotated diagram accompanying this paper, the term embraces any and every literary aid or manual which may be of help to a priest in his *cura animarum,* whether with respect to his own education or that of the people in his charge. The movement towards the provision of pastoralia for the generality of the clergy (and laity) has its beginnings before 1215, but the council, and without even a word on the subject, not only gave an urgency to the movement but also encouraged it to blossom in a variety of forms, the slender with the large. Within fifty years of the council there was a profusion of episcopal or synodal constitutions all over Europe and a remarkable array of manuals of confession, *summae* of moral teaching, expositions of the Ten Commandments, compendia of vices and virtues, collections of sermons and sermon exempla, and general manuals of the pastoral care, in Latin and in various vernaculars.

From the point of view of pastoralia and the *cura animarum* in general, the most important as well as the most influential pastoral constitution of the Fourth Lateran Council is that known by its opening words as *Omnis utriusque sexus*. By this constitution the council endowed both the penitent's act of confession to a priest and the priest's role as confessor with a public and a definite identity for the first time ever in the history of the Church. All parishioners were ordered to confess all mortal sins once a year privately to their respective parochial priests and to no other. All confessors, on the other hand, had to be discerners of souls and not simply dispensers of absolution and penance.

If any one single thing occasioned the rash of aids for confessors and in respect of confession among the Latin and vernacular pastoralia of the thirteenth and later centuries, it was this last. When dealing with souls, the Council said, the confessor should know them as well as any competent medical doctor is presumed to know the bodies he treats for injuries or illnesses. The confessor should not only be able to assign a suitable penance to penitents but just as a doctor does in the case of his patients, should be in a position also to suggest to the penitent just what is the cause of his or her trouble, and how best to prevent its recurrence. If, on his or her side, the penitent had to confess all sins as completely as possible, the priest for his part had to be as discreet and understanding as any doctor, diligently probing the penitent's character and background in addition to the circumstances of each sin.

Needless to say, there was nothing startlingly new in this new approach: the concept of *medicus animarum* was an old and indeed hackneyed one. What makes the approach important in the history of the *cura animarum* and of pastoralia is that this is the first time that the precise role of the confessor in relation to the penitent was authoritatively set before the church as a whole. Now, officially, the confessor must not only be a dispenser of penances but also a counsellor of souls. He had to know something more than the old *canones poenitentiales* and their lists of appropriate penances. He had to know the ins and outs of sins, vices, and virtues. In other words he had to have a broad education in order to be the competent confessor envisaged by the council.

Because of *Omnis utriusque sexus* and these emphases, manuals of confession of all kinds and shapes form a large part of the pastoralia that the Fourth Lateran Council occasioned. In fact one may say in all seriousness that the bulk of the pastoralia in the accompanying diagram is largely taken up with penance and confession, directly or indirectly. In the long run, for example, the many manuals of virtues and vices, both in Latin and in the vernacular, are really aids to contrition and confession. Generally speaking so too are the various tracts on preaching and the ubiquitous collections of sermons and sermon exempla, since on the whole the end of preaching was seen not so much in terms of the proclaiming of the word of God in the scriptures as of the conversion of souls. To the Fourth Lateran Council in constitution 10, on preaching and preachers, confession and preaching went hand in hand—which is why the Dominicans, shortly after they had been recognized by the . papacy as an order of preachers-in-general in 1217, were also commissioned as confessors-at-large (and, consequently, entered and eventually dominated the field of manuals of confession).

This is not to say, however, that all of these forms of manuals of confession or of pastoralia in general came into being only after the Lateran Council of late 1215. There is clear evidence that most of them came into existence in the interconciliar period 1179–1215, between, that is, Third Lateran and Fourth Lateran, and that by and large they were the result of a combination of circumstances in that span of time. It was precisely in this period that the parochial clergy were beginning to make themselves heard as a body and were, as Robert Courson put it in 1207, "hammering at the gates of theology for solid food."[2] Because of the inroads of unorthodox movements within the Church and of the demands of the new social order, it was also in these interconciliar years that some attempt was made to arm the parochial clergy with the latest teaching of the schools, the better to stand up to the winds of change. And it was just then, too, at the tail end of the renaissance of the twelfth century, that the literary genres to accomplish this popularization were readily to hand in the new *summae, distinctiones,* and manuals of the schools of law and theology that had come into being during that renaissance.

On the morrow of the Fourth Lateran Council, confessors who strove to implement the new norms therefore had something to fall back on. Manuals of confession, perhaps a half-dozen or so, from which to supplement the old *libri* or *canones poenitentiales,* had been on the market for some fifteen or twenty years before the council. These were mainly from the circle of Peter the Chanter at Paris and, anticipating the council and the needs of confessors after it, they attempted precisely to provide confessors with information on contemporary theology, current law, and the social problems of the day.[3]

These manuals of the interconciliar period represent a new approach to penance and confession which had been gaining ground since the days of the Gregorian reform in the second half of the eleventh century, and which owes much to, first, the pseudo-Augustinian *De vera et falsa poenitentia* and its insistence that priests in confession should take the circumstances of each sin into account, then to Peter Abelard and his teaching on the place of interior penitence in the confession of sins. Unlike the old *libri poenitentiales* with their lists of stock penances and little else, these new manuals urged the priest to understand the penitent as a person according to his or her particular circumstances or calling (wife, husband, teacher, laborer, merchant, for example). The numb, almost passive role of the penitent in the old penitential literature disappears too under the influence of Abelard and his school. The act of confessing becomes more personal, more aware of self. Contriteness of heart is seen to be what matters in the long run, for it is by this that sins really are expiated. Sin, in the new view, is a diminishing of being. One therefore recovers one's integrity not by some long process of "physical" satisfaction for sin, as had been the practice for centuries, but by repentance, by a cleansing of the heart which one then presents to the priest as the representative of God and the Church.[4]

Two things are important here, and they animate both *Omnis utriusque sexus* and the pastoralia that that constitution inspired: the penitent not only had to confess sins but also had to be contrite, to present a clean heart; the confessor in turn now had to pay as much attention to the interior disposition of the penitent as he did to the penitent's sins.

To take the last point first as an illustration of the impact of *Omnis utriusque sexus,* in the period after the Fourth Lateran Council the first wave of manuals of confession—that up to about the year 1260—is largely concerned with educating priests to be the "prudent and discreet" confessors specified by the constitution. In general one may give the collective label *summae poenitentiae* to all of these, since it is wide enough to include anything from a leaflet on "How to confess" to a full-blown treatise on the sacrament of penance itself. Within this category the most important form was the *summa confessorum,* the best-known, though not necessarily the best example of which is the *summa* of Raymond of Pennafort. These *summae confessorum* were reflective rather than practical *summae* of the administrative type, and they were directed toward the intellectual preparation of priests for a prudent, discreet, and informed exercise of the office of confessor; they are academic works, providing the priest in his study with some help on how to discern souls and to evaluate their problems in the light of current theology, law, and society.[5]

The second wave of penitential pastoralia, however—that around or about 1260—has a broader basis and is more directly concerned with the penitent as such and with the education of the penitent. Since contrition and cleanness of heart—the personal efforts of the penitent rather than the formal role of the confessor—were now so important in confession and penance, it was of equal importance that the individual penitent, whether cleric or lay, should have some instruction not just in how to confess properly but in how to combat sin, how to build up the self, how to develop cleanness of heart. Here in this second wave there is much in Latin, but there is an appreciable amount too in the vernacular all over Europe.

Although in its vernacular aspect this second wave does not appear to have had much momentum before about 1260, the way was prepared by the many diocesan constitutions that began shortly after 1215 to promulgate the legislation of the Fourth Lateran Council and to put it into effect. At Salisbury in 1217 Bishop Richard Poore ordered that the Creed was to be taught in the vernacular and that the form of marriage was to be proposed and expounded to the contracting parties in either English or French. At Worcester in 1229 it was enacted that the lay person was to be instructed in the Creed "in the language known to him or her" before being admitted to confession. At Winchester some thirty years later it was ordered that parochial priests were to be examined in their ability to expound the decalogue, the sacraments, the seven deadly sins, and the articles of faith, "in lingua vulgari."[6]

Where the second wave is most evident is in the production in the vernaculars of manuals of virtues and vices. Like manuals of confession in general, the first such manuals of virtues and vices were in Latin and were meant for the education of the clergy, a prime example being the *Summa de vitiis et virtutibus* just before 1250 of the Dominican Guillaume Peyraut ("Peraldus"), some five hundred MSS of which are extant.[7] But it was not long before versions of this *summa* and of similar manuals were made available in the various vernaculars and with the laity chiefly in mind: the Anglo-Norman *Manuel des péchés* of William of Waddington, ca. 1260; the *Lumière as laïs* of Peter of Peckham in 1267; the *Somme le roi* of Laurent of Orléans, the Dominican confessor of Phillip III of France, in 1280; the *Miroir du monde,* a derivative of the *Somme,* a year or two later; not to speak of the English *Handlyng Synne* and *Ayenbite of Inwit* at the turn of the century, nor of the pioneering *Specchio della penitenza* and *Disciplina degli spirituali* of the Dominicans Jacopo Passavanti and Domenico Cavalca respectively, thirty or forty years later.

All of this literature is well known and its derivation from *Omnis utriusque sexus* generally accepted. Not less important is the effect of that constitution in itself and through these manuals and treatises on lay and clerical spirituality. This did not come about at once. Innocent III's program in 1213 of the proposed Lateran Council of 1215 included "the extirpation of vices and the fostering of virtues," but inevitably the first flush of manuals, both Latin and vernacular, concentrated more on vices than on virtues, and saw virtues more as a means of combating vices than as things to be cultivated for themselves and in their own right. One need only look at the various manuals of confession in this period to see this at once, or at the *De vitiis et virtutibus* of Peyraut, the model of all manuals of this type.

But this "negative" phase did not last forever. Although I do not think that he had any great influence in this matter, the fact that Thomas Aquinas in the "Secunda secundae" of his *Summa theologiae* (ca. 1270) treats of virtues-and-vices rather than of vices-and-virtues in the manner of Peyraut, surely suggests a more "positive" view of the person and a greater appreciation of his or her capacity for virtue.[8] For Aquinas it is the virtues that produce the cleanness of soul and contriteness of heart which the Christian should present to God and the Church in confession, and vices are put firmly in their place as departures from the virtuous condition which should be goal of the Christian.

Certainly it will be found that from the 1280s onward the theme of "the extirpation of vices" gives way to that of "the fostering of virtues," and the soul comes to be seen as something to be cultivated with virtues and not just to be kept clear of weeds. I am thinking here of the remarkable flowering of spirituality and mysticism and expressions thereof, largely vernacular, in poetry and prose in the latter part of the thirteenth century and in the whole of the fourteenth, to go no further. With its concentration on the relationship of the soul at its inmost to God, this flowering is the logical if rather tardy result of the shift of emphasis from exterior penance to interior penitence which the *De vera et falsa poenitentia,* Abelard, and others had brought about in the world of the parochial clergy and of clergy and laity in general in the century after the Gregorian reform. This shift also caused first theologians and then the laity to look closely into interior dispositions and, eventually, through the promotion of examinations of conscience and personal prayer, to look more closely at themselves as persons in the image of God.

While it cannot be said *tout court* that it was the Fourth Lateran Council and its constitution *Omnis utriusque sexus* that brought all of this about, the fact remains that it was through *Omnis utriusque sexus* and the consequent change of relationship between priest and penitent that the teaching of theologians and others on interiority reached every level of Christian life—in sermons, in collections of exempla, in pastoralia in general, and particularly in vernacular expositions of penance and penitence and of virtues and vices.

This is not to say that with all this increasing emphasis on penitence and contrition of heart, the preoccupation with vices disappeared around

1280 never to raise its head again. Not at all. Where, for example, Langland in *Piers Plowman,* with his exaltation of virtues, is somewhat in the new mode, Chaucer in the *Canterbury Tales* is firmly in the old with his almost exclusive preoccupation in the Parson's Tale with the seven deadly sins.

Langland, of course, does have a lot to say about these deadly sins toward the opening of his poem and is therefore, I suspect, in the long run in the tradition of vices-and-virtues rather than of virtues-and-vices. But both Langland and Chaucer are plainly in a line of pastoral literature that owes its inspiration to the Fourth Lateran Council. Each is a witness, as is so much of the vernacular writing of the thirteenth and fourteenth centuries, to the merging consciousness of self that underlies the legislation on priest and penitent in the constitution *Omnis utriusque sexus* of that council, and which gradually, through the prominence given to that constitution in episcopal legislation and in the generality of pastoralia, wrought a revolution in spirituality.[9]

N O T E S

1. A critical edition of these constitutions is in *Conciliorum oecumenicorum decreta,* ed. J. Alberigo et al. (Freiburg im Breisgau: Herder, 1962), pp. 203–47.

2. See V.L. Kennedy, "Robert Courson on Penance," *Mediaeval Studies,* 7 (1945): 294.

3. See J.W. Baldwin, *Masters, Princes, and Merchants: The Social Views of Peter the Chanter and his Circle* (Princeton: Princeton Univ. Press, 1970), 1:17–62.

4. See P. Anciaux, *La Théologie du sacrement de pénitence au XIIe siècle* (Louvain: E. Nauwelaerts, 1949); J.C. Payen, "La pénitence dans le contexte culturel des XIIe et XIIIe siècles," *Revue des sciences philosophiques et théologiques* 61 (1977): 399–428.

5. In general see P. Michaud-Quantin, *Sommes de casuistique et manuels de confession au moyen âge (XIIe–XVIe siècles)* (Louvain: E. Nauwelaerts, 1962) and the works listed below at nn. 16–17 of the diagram.

6. *Councils and Synods, with Other Documents Relating to the English Church,* vol. 2, *A.D. 1205–1313,* ed. F.M. Powicke and C.R. Cheney (Oxford: Clarendon Press, 1964), Part I, pp. 61, 172, 721.

7. See A. Dondaine, "Guillaume Peyraut: Vie et oeuvres," *Archivum Fratrum Praedicatorum* 18 (1948): 162–236.

8. See L.E. Boyle, *The Setting of the "Summa theologiae" of Saint Thomas* (Toronto: Pontifical Institute, 1982), pp. 21–22.

9. The annotations to the appended diagram are not meant to be exhaustive.

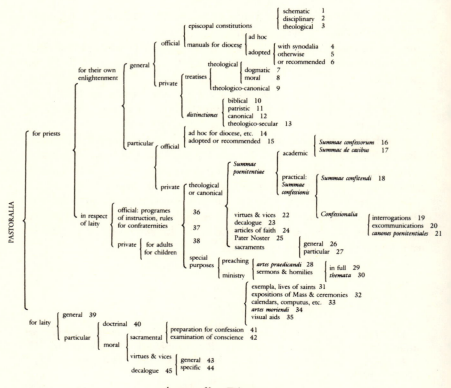

Appendix: Diagram

Notes to the Diagram, "Pastoralia"

1. For example, the syllabus "Ignorantia sacerdotum" of John Peckham, archbishop of Canterbury, at the council of Lambeth, 1281, in *Councils and Synods, with Other Documents Relating to the English Church*, vol. 2, *A.D. 1205–1313*, ed. F.M. Powicke and C.R. Cheney, (Oxford: Clarendon Press, 1964), Part II, 900–905 (hereafter cited as Powicke and Cheney, *Councils*).

2. Most episcopal constitutions were of this type, on which in general see C.R. Cheney, *English Synodalia of the Thirteenth Century*, 2d ed. (Oxford: Oxford Univ. Press, 1968); O. Pontal, *Les Statuts synodaux*, Typologie des sources du moyen âge occidental no. 11 (Turnhout: Brepols, 1975); and for bibliography, J.T. Sawicki, *Bibliographia synodorum particularium* (Vatican City: Biblioteca Apostolica Vaticana, 1967), with supplements in *Traditio* 24 (1968): 508–11 and 26 (1970): 470–78, and thereafter in *Bulletin of Medieval Canon Law* 2 (1972): 91–100; 4 (1975): 88–92; 6 (1976): 95–100.

3. Many constitutions carry useful theological reflections, e.g., those of

Richard Poore, Bishop of Salisbury (1217–1228); see Powicke and Cheney, *Councils*, 1:57–96.

4. For example, the *Summula* of Peter Quivil of Exeter, probably issued with his constitutions for the diocese in 1287: Powicke and Cheney, *Councils*, 2:1050–77; see also M.W. Bloomfield, B.G. Guyot, D.R. Howard, and T.B. Kabealo, *Incipits of Latin Works on the Virtues and Vices, 1100–1500 A.D., Including a Section of Incipits of Works on the Pater Noster* (Cambridge, Mass.: Medieval Academy of America, 1979), n. 0369 (hereafter cited as Bloomfield-Guyot, *Incipits*).

5. For example, the *Templum domini* (or *dei*) of Robert Grosseteste, Bishop of Lincoln (1235–53), for MSS of which see S.H. Thomson, *The Writings of Robert Grosseteste* (Cambridge: Cambridge Univ. Press, 1940), pp. 138–140; Bloomfield-Guyot, *Incipits*, nn. 5891–92.

6. A fine example is the manual of the canonist Peter Sampson for the diocese of Nîmes, on which see A. Artonne, "Le livre synodale de Lodève," *Bibliothèque de l'école des chartes* 108 (1949–1950): 36–74. Sampson's manual, which later was taken over by other dioceses such as Lodève, was published as though it were a composition of his own by Raymond, Bishop of Nîmes, in 1252.

7. Simple pastoral expositions of e.g. God, Trinity, and Incarnation are hard to come by. Most manuals are parenetic or "moral" rather than systematic or "dogmatic."

8. For example, the *Manipulus curatorum* of Guido de Monte Rocherii (Lyons: C. Lumsden, 1552), a work written in 1333 and dedicated to the then bishop of Valencia; or the *Instructions for Parish Priests* of John Myrc, ca. 1400, editions of which are available in the Early English Text Society (EETS), o.s., 31 (by E. Peacock, London: Keegan Paul, 1868) and in G. Kristensson, *John Mirk's Instructions for Parish Priests* (Lund: Gleerup, 1974).

9. Good examples are the *Oculus sacerdotis* of William of Pagula, ca. 1320–1326 (MSS in Bloomfield-Guyot, *Incipits*, n. 1088); and the *Pupilla oculi* of John de Burgh, ca. 1384 (ed. London: W. Bretton, 1510; MSS in Bloomfield-Guyot, *Incipits*, n. 2441), on both of which see L.E. Boyle, *Pastoral Care, Clerical Education and Canon Law, 1200–1400* (London: Variorum Reprints, 1981), section 4 (reprinting an article of 1955).

10. For example, the "Distinctiones super auctoritatibus sacrae scripturae" of the Franciscan Mauricius Hibernicus in the second half of the thirteenth century (Bloomfield-Guyot, *Incipits*, n. 0088); and the various biblical *distinctiones* noted by A. Wilmart, "Un répertoire d'exégèse composée en Angleterre vers le début du XIIIᶜ siècle," in *Mémorial Lagrange* (Paris: Gabalda, 1940), pp. 316–46; by R.H. and M.A. Rouse, "Biblical Distinctions in the Thirteenth Century," *Archives d'histoire doctrinale et littéraire du moyen âge* 41 (1974): 27–37; and by L.-J. Bataillon, "Intermédiaires entre les traités de morale pratique et les sermons: Les *distinctiones* bibliques alphabétiques," in *Les Genres littéraires dans les sources théologiques et philosophiques médiévales* (Louvain-la-Neuve: Institut d'études médiévales, 1982), pp. 213–25.

11. Particularly the *Manipulus florum* of Thomas Hibernicus at Paris, ca.

1306, with some 6000 extracts from patristic writers: see R.H. and M.A. Rouse, *Preachers, Florilegia and Sermons: Studies on the "Manipulus florum" of Thomas of Ireland* (Toronto: Pontifical Institute, 1979); and Bloomfield-Guyot, *Incipits*, n. 0091.

12. For example, the *Opus trivium* of John Bromyard, ca. 1330: MSS and editions in T. Kaeppeli, *Scriptores ordinis praedicatorum medii aevi*, vol. 2 (Rome: Istituto storico domenicano, 1975), p. 393 (hereafter Kaeppeli, *Scriptores*).

13. The best example is the ubiquitous *Catholicon* of John Balbi of Genoa ("Januensis"), published in 1286, for MSS and editions of which see Kaeppeli, *Scriptores*, 2:380–83.

14. For example, the *Tractatus de septem criminalibus peccatis* of Alexander Stavensby, Bishop of Coventry (1224–1238), printed in Powicke and Cheney, *Councils*, Part I, 214–20 (see also Bloomfield-Guyot, *Incipits*, n. 1183).

15. Thus the tract *De articulis fidei et ecclesiae sacramentis* of Thomas Aquinas *(Opera omnia* [Paris: L. Vives, 1875], 27:171–82; critical edition, *Opera omnia*, vol. 42 [Rome: Ad Sanctae Sabinae, 1979]), written between 1260 and 1268, was imposed on all parochial priests of the provinces of Mainz (1451), Cologne (1452), and Würzburg (1452): see *Concilia Germaniae*, ed. J. Hartzheim (Cologne: J.W. Krakamp, 1763), 5: 398, 413, 420.

16. The example that gives the name to the genre is the *Summa confessorum* of John of Freiburg, 1297–1298, for MSS and editions of which see Kaeppeli, *Scriptores*, 2:430–36. On the genre see J. Dietterle, "Die *Summa confessorum*," *Zeitschrift für Kirchengeschichte* 24 (1903): 353–74 and following volumes to 28 (1907): 401–31; L.E. Boyle, *"Summae confessorum,"* in *Les Genres littéraires*, pp. 226–37, where the present diagram (but without annotation) first appeared.

17. The best known is the *Summula de poenitentia* of Raymond of Pennafort, written first in 1224–1225, then revised a decade later: see S. Kuttner, "Die Entstehungsgeschichte der *Summa de casibus poenitentiae* des hl. Raymund von Pennafort," *Zeitschrift der Savigny-Stiftung für Rechtesgeschichte* 83, *Kanonististische Abteilung* (1953): 419–48; and, for MSS and editions, Kaeppeli, *Scriptores* 3:283–87. A good example also is the *Summa de casibus Astesana* (Cologne: H. Quentell, 1479) of the Franciscan Astesanus of Asti, written ca. 1316. In general see P. Michaud-Quantin, *Sommes de casuistique et manuels de confession au moyen âge (XIIe–XVIe siècles)* (Louvain: E. Nauwelaerts, 1962).

18. See e.g. the *Aureum confessorium et memoriale sacerdotum* of William Duranti the Elder, ca. 1280, printed as an appendix, with separate pagination, in editions of his *Speculum iudiciale* (e.g., Frankfurt: Sumptibus Heredum A. Wecheli et J. Gymnici, 1592).

19. See the various tracts on confession recorded by Thomson, *Writings of Robert Grosseteste*, pp. 125–26, notably the *De modo confitendi* from ca. 1230–1240, and the tract "Deus est" which has been edited by Siegfried Wenzel in *Franciscan Studies* 30 (1970): 218–93.

20. Most manuals carry a section on excommunication. The most detailed medieval work on excommunications as such is that of Berengarius Fredoli, ca.

1300, ed. E. Vernay, *Le Liber de excommunicatione du Cardinal Bérengar Fredoli* (Paris: Rousseau, 1912).

21. A list of *canones poenitentiales* is to be found in many manuals, e.g. John of Freiburg, *Summa confessorum* (any edition), 3.24, q. 124; *Summa astesana* (any edition), 5.32; William of Pagula, *Oculus sacerdotis*, MS Hatfield House, Herts., fols. 21v–25r (Prima pars, c. 32, in this and most MSS). In general see H.J. Schmitz, *Die Bussbücher und die Bussdisciplin der Kirche* (Mainz: F. Kirchheim, 1883), pp. 792–808.

22. The classic manual is the *Summa de vitiis et virtutibus* of Guillaume Peyraut ("Peraldus"), written 1236–1248. For MSS and printed editions see Kaeppeli, *Scriptores*, 2:133–42; and Bloomfield-Guyot, *Incipits*, n. 1628.

23. Most manuals of a general kind treat of the Ten Commandments. There are many special treatises on the topic, for example the influential *De decem mandatis* of Robert Grosseteste, for which see Thomson, *Writings of Robert Grosseteste*, pp. 131–32, and MSS listed there.

24. Again most manuals of a general nature deal with the articles of faith. Several specific treatises are noted by Bloomfield-Guyot, *Incipits*, nn. 0831, 1242, 4916, 5012.

25. The Pater Noster was the subject of many treatises, a comprehensive list of which by B.-G. Guyot is in Bloomfield-Guyot, *Incipits*, pp. 567–686 (nn. 8001–9261).

26. For example, the *Summa de administratione sacramentorum* of William of Paris, ca. 1300, analysed by A. Teetaert, "Un compendium de théologie pastorale du XIII^c–XIV^c siècle," *Revue d'histoire ecclésiastique* 22 (1930): 66–102; see also Kaeppeli, *Scriptores*, 2:130–31. Perhaps the most influential work in this area, though its nature is more general, is the *Compendium theologicae veritatis* of Hugh of Strasbourg, a little before 1265. It is printed among the works of Albert the Great in *Albertus Magnus, Opera omnia*, vol. 33 (Paris: L. Vives, 1893), pp. 1–261, and is extant in some 600 MSS according to the list in Kaeppeli, *Scriptores*, 2:260–69.

27. On, e.g., the Eucharist, see the *Speculum ecclesiae*, ca. 1230, of Hugh of St. Cher, ed. G. Sölch (Münster in Westphalia: Aschendorff, 1940), some 220 MSS of which are listed in Kaeppeli, *Scriptores*, 2:276–80; or, on Matrimony, Tancred of Bologna, *Summa de sponsalibus et matrimonio*, ed. A. Wunderlich (Göttingen: Vandenhoeck and Ruprecht, 1841), written in 1210–1214, on which Raymond of Pennafort relied heavily when adding a fourth book *(De matrimonio)* to his *Summula de poenitentia* in 1234–1235.

28. See the treatises of Robert Basevorn and Thomas Waleys, edited in T.-M. Charland, *Artes praedicandi: Contribution à l'histoire de la rhétorique au moyen âge* (Paris: J. Vrin, 1936), pp. 227–403, and the general discussion of the genre at pp. 1–226.

29. For example, the sermons of Stephen Langton, Archbishop of Canterbury (1206–1228), printed by P.B. Roberts, *Selected Sermons of Stephen Langton* (Toronto: Pontifical Institute, 1980). See also for a full list of Langton's ser-

mons, P.B. Roberts, *Stephanus de Lingua-Tonante: Studies in the Sermons of Stephen Langton* (Toronto: Pontifical Institute, 1968). For a fine survey of MSS containing sermons see J.-B. Schneyer, *Repertorium der lateinischen Sermones des Mittelalters für die Zeit von 1150 bis 1350*, 9 vols. (Münster in Westphalia: Aschendorff, 1960–1980), and his *Wegweiser zu lateinischen Predigtreihen des Mittelalters* (Munich: Verlag der Bayerischen Akademie, 1965).

30. A collection of *themata* for every Sunday, feast, and possible occasion is in William of Pagula's *Speculum praelatorum* (written 1320–1326) in Merton College, Oxford, MS 217, fols. 180r–248r (followed, fols. 248r–441r, by a set of *distinctiones* from "Aperire" to "Zelus" for the use of preachers).

31. For a Franciscan collection, probably compiled in Ireland ca. 1275, see A.G. Little, *Liber exemplorum ad usum praedicantium* (Aberdeen: Aberdeen Univ. Press, 1908), and, for some other collections of exempla, Bloomfield-Guyot, *Incipits*, nn. 0476, 0956, 2813, 4615. The standard work on exempla is J.-T. Welter, *L'Exemplum dans la littérature religieuse et didactique du moyen âge* (Paris: E.H. Guitard, 1927).

32. The classic work is the *Rationale divinorum officiorum* of William Duranti the Elder (ed., for example, Venice: M.A. Zalterius, 1599), composed 1285–1296.

33. Generally found at the beginning of missals and breviaries.

34. See M.C. O'Connor, *The Art of Dying Well: The Development of the Ars moriendi* (New York: Columbia Univ. Press, 1942).

35. Wall-charts or rolls of the virtues and vices such as the small roll in the Bodleian Library, Oxford, MS Lat. theol. c. 2 (R). In general see F. Saxl, "A Spiritual Encyclopedia of the Later Middle Ages," *Journal of the Courtauld and Warburg Institutes* 5 (1942): 82–134, esp. 107–8.

36. For example the "catechism" of John de Thoresby, Archbishop of York (1352–1373), based on Pecham's "Syllabus," printed in T.F. Simmons and R.E. Nolloth, *The Lay Folks' Catechism; or, the English and Latin versions of Archbishop Thoresby's Instruction for the People*, EETS, o.s. 118 (London: Keegan Paul, 1901). For rules of confraternities see G.G. Meersseman, *Ordo fraternitatis: Confraternite e pietà dei laici nel medioevo*, 3 vols. (Rome: Herder, 1977).

37. A good example is the *De ludis scaccorum* or "Libellus de moribus hominum et de officiis nobilium super ludo scaccorum" of Jacobus de Cessolis, written ca. 1290, which is extant in numerous MSS and has versions in practically every vernacular of the fourteenth and fifteenth centuries: see Kaeppeli, *Scriptores*, 2:311–17; and J.M. Mehl, "L'exemplum dans Jacques de Cessolis," *Le moyen âge* 84 (1978): 227–46.

38. See the *De instructione puerorum* of William of Tournai, ed. J.A. Corbett (Notre Dame, Ind.: Mediaeval Institute, 1955), which was recommended to the Dominican Order at large by the General Chapter at Paris in 1264: see Kaeppeli, *Scriptores*, 2:167; and R. Fluck, "Guillaume de Tournai et son traité *De modo docendi pueros*," *Revue des sciences religieuses* 27 (1953): 333–56. A little later, but before 1268, the Franciscan Gilbert of Tournai wrote a similar *De modo addiscendi* as the third part of his *Rudimentum doctrinae*: see A. Matami, "Gilbertus Tor-

nacensis (de Tournai) ac eius *Rudimentum doctrinae," Antonianum* 32 (1957): 431–33.

39. Thoresby's "Catechism." See also P. Hodgson, *"Ignorancia sacerdotum:* A Fifteenth-Century Discourse on the Lambeth Constitutions," *Review of English Studies* 24 (1948): 1–11; *Speculum Christiani,* ed. G. Holmstedt, EETS, o.s. 182 (London: Oxford Univ. Press, 1933).

40. See the various writings listed by P.S. Jolliffe, *A Check-List of Middle English Prose Writings of Spiritual Guidance* (Toronto: Pontifical Institute, 1974), pp. 104–14 (Class I: "General positive teaching").

41. Class E ("Confession and Penance") in ibid., pp. 76–79.

42. For example, Robert Mannyng of Brunne, *Handlyng Synne,* ed. E.J. Furnivall, EETS, o.s. 119, 123 (London: Keegan Paul, 1901, 1903); Michael of Northgate, *Ayenbite of Inwit,* ed. R. Morris, EETS, o.s. 23 (London: N. Trübner, 1866); and Class C ("Forms of confession") in Jolliffe, *A Check-List,* pp. 67–74. See in general D.W. Robertson, Jr., "The Cultural Tradition of *Handlyng Synne," Speculum* 22 (1947): 162–85.

43. See E.J. Arnould, *Le Manuel des péchés: Etude de littérature religieuse anglo-normande* (Paris: Droz, 1940), for a general survey of vernacular tracts in this area; *The Book of Vices and Virtues,* ed. W.N. Francis, EETS, o.s. 217 (London: Oxford Univ. Press, 1942); Bloomfield-Guyot, *Incipits,* passim.

44. Classes G ("Specific virtues") and K ("Temptations") in Jolliffe, *A Check-List,* pp. 85–90, 119–26. See also G.H. Russell, "Vernacular Instruction of the Laity in the Later Middle Ages in England: Some Texts and Notes," *Journal of Religious History* 2 (1962): 98–119.

45. For example in the tract *Dives et Pauper:* see H.G. Pfander, "Dives et Pauper," *The Library,* o.s. 14 (1934): 299–312; and in MSS of the *Pore Caitiff* collection in Jolliffe, *A Check-List,* pp. 65–67.

The Influence of Canonical and Episcopal Reform on Popular Books of Instruction

Judith Shaw

Pope Innocent III chose a passage from Luke as the text for his opening sermon to the Fourth Lateran Council delegates: "Desiderio desideravi hoc pascha manducare vobiscum, antequam patiar, id est antequam moriar (Luc. xxii)."[1] Innocent hoped that his choice would prove prophetic and that the Church's present difficulties, like Christ's sufferings following the paschal feast, would prove to be merely a passing phase, a "transitus" he called it, that would give way to a better time. It was to these difficulties, then, and their eventual amendment that he urged the delegates to address themselves. Innocent's hopes for the Church were threefold:

> Triplex autem Pascha sive Phase desidero vobiscum celebrare, corporale, spirituale, aeternale: corporale, ut fiat transitus ad locum, pro miserabili Jerusalem liberanda; spirituale, ut fiat transitus de statu ad statum, pro universali Ecclesia reformanda; aeternale, ut fiat transitus de vita in vitam, pro coelesti gloria obtinenda.[2]

The forces opposing the recovery of the Holy Land were at least recognizable. Less palpable but even more pernicious, according to Innocent, were the enemies within, namely those evils "in populo Christiano" "ignorantiam, negligentiam, et concupiscentiam"[3] through which "perit fides, religios deformatur, libertas confunditur, justitia conculcatur, haeretici pullulant, insolescunt schismatici, perfidi saeviunt, praevalent Agareni."[4] It was these internal concerns, not the infidel, that finally became the focus of the Lateran directives and that gave rise to the popular books of instruction. In turn, these vernacular manuals became one of the most effective means of combating the ignorance and vice that gripped the Church, threatening its dissolution.

The confession of faith with which the body of constitutions opened insisted upon the Church's complete control over man's spiritual life. No man, it was said, would be saved outside the body of the one true Church. The sacraments were seen as the channel through which this grace was dispensed. This reassertion of the importance of the sacraments in the opening canon of the Council takes on particular significance in light of the central role that the sacrament of penance was to play in the spiritual reform of the laity. Penance was seen by many as a fitting cure for those evils which threatened the Church's existence. At the very least, it encouraged the individual Christian to participate in the sort of self-reflection in which the Church herself was presently engaged. Then, too, the confessional offered a ready forum for the education of the laity in the new moral theology, while the power of priests to bind and loose provided the needed impetus to learn. The sacrament was given added prominence with the passage of constitution 21, *Omnis utriusque sexus,* which required that every Christian confess privately to his own priest at least once a year upon pain of minor excommunication.

By the thirteenth century, the practice of public penance had largely given way to that of private confession—a custom to which the twenty-first decree gave official sanction.[5] However, with the official institution of penance as a yearly obligation, the Church felt a renewed responsibility for creating in the average Christian that tenderness of conscience that would lead to true contrition and a complete confession. The added awareness that this knowledge could be of assistance in the broader program of Church reform undoubtedly helped fuel this effort. Robert Mannyng describes the degree of forethought necessary for a good confession in his discussion of penance in *Handlyng Synne:*

> Every man shulde have a-fore þoʒt
> How and whan hys synne was wroʒt,
> And beþenke hym weyl on every dede,
> Fyrst are he to shryftë ʒede;
> Elles, asoyled may he nat be clene,
> Of forʒetë synnes, y mene.
> Over lytyl fors certys he ʒyveþ
> Of any penaunce, or how he lyveþ;
> Swychë men, here synne þey synke,
> Þat recchë nat þer-on to þynke.
> Some men, whan here synne ys wroʒt,
> Hyt no more cumþ yn here þoʒt,
> And ʒyveþ no fors, þat he forʒeteþ
> Hys synne; and hym þe fend eteþ.[6]

Since few laymen possessed either the self-awareness or the moral lexicon necessary for such a full examination of conscience, it became the duty of the confessor to assist the penitent in this inquiry while administering the sacrament. Constitution 21 compares the confessor in this role to a physician, who must diligently inquire concerning symptoms so he can prescribe the proper cure for the disease.

> Sacerdos autem sit discretus et cautus, ut more periti medici superinfundat vinum et oleum vulneribus sauciati, diligenter inquirens et peccatoris circumstantias et peccati, quibus prudenter intelligat, quale debeat ei praebere consilium, et cuiusmodi remedium adhibere, diversis experimentis utendo ad salvandum aegrotum.[7]

The medical analogy is apt if only because it emphasizes the skill and learning necessary for the practice of both professions. Innocent, however, had already questioned the efficacy of the clergy in his opening address to the delegates. It was his belief that "omnis in populo corruptela principaliter procedit a clero."[8] As a necessary prelude, then, to the spiritual reform of the laity, the Council passed several measures aimed at correcting clerical abuses. These ranged from the two clauses requiring that priests be properly instructed (27 and 30) to those forbidding clerks from marrying, keeping concubines, frequenting taverns or games, and donning worldly attire (14, 15, 16, 17).[9] But even those confessors who were not given to the frivolities warned against in the canons were unfamiliar with the rigors of the new moral theology, with its more casuistic approach to sin and redemption, and understandably so, since the new theology was itself a recent product of the Schools.[10] As one critic rightly concludes, "a confessor needed to be something of the artist since the doctrine of the circumstances of sin developed in the Faculty of Arts; a theologian if he were to have knowledge to instruct and guide his penitent; a canon lawyer in order to be able to deal with sins that were also offences against church law; a civil lawyer since Roman law provided principles for those cases not covered by the canons and decretals."[11]

It was in order to prepare priests for these new roles that the first *summae confessorum* were produced. As the name implies, these manuals attempted to summarize the information necessary for a priest to carry out his duties in the confessional. The handbooks varied in emphasis from those which dealt with the casuistic aspects of penance to those which evidenced a more theological bias, concentrating on moral problems and the theory of the sacrament.[12] The seminal manuals in the tradition were dry and academic. The author of one of these, Raymund of Pennaforte, a penitentiary to Gregory IX and the compiler of book 5 of the *Corpus iuris canonici*, speaks with good reason of the "diversis auctoritatibus" which he makes use of in his *Summa de casuum*.[13] However, by the fourteenth century manuals were being written in the vernacular that were more practical in nature and had a much wider appeal. These popular manuals were addressed to "lewed" folk and priests of "mean lore." The term *lewed* is somewhat misleading since it suggests an illiterate audience when, in fact, the distinction being made is between those who could read and understand Latin and those who could not. Since some priests fell into the latter category, manuals in the vernacular were also written for priests. So useful was this vernacular didactic literature and so popular did it become during the two centuries following the Council that E.J. Arnould was led to refer to these years as "l'âge d'or de la littérature religieuse didactique."[14] It is no wonder that Payen credited the proliferation of confessional manuals with making "pénitence le plus grand des sacrements, celui qui est au centre même de la vie chrétienne."[15]

Although the General Council laid down the guidelines for reform, it was left to the bishops to implement these changes in their local dioceses. The promulgation of the Lateran decrees was assured by the passage of Constitution 6, which required bishops to convene provincial synods once a year, at which they were to publish all general and provincial canons. However, as the result of the episcopate's recently awakened sense of their pastoral duties, these provincial synods became the setting for additional legislation, rather than a mere rubber stamp for Rome. The English bishops were particularly fervent in this respect. Richard Poore, for example, who had attended the Council and who was the first English bishop to publish its decrees, nevertheless required his own parishioners to confess three times a year rather than the once yearly required by the Council. Gibbs and Lang note that even in those instances where the Lateran directives form the backbone of English statutes, "main principles are clothed in localized and particularized detail."[16] This same tendency toward expansion and practical application can be seen in the bishops' treatment of the problem of penance, where it accounts for their unique contribution to the popular books of instruction.

With regard to penance, the bishops were most concerned with instructing the clergy on how to hear confessions. It was in order to meet this need that several English bishops either appended books of instruction for confessors to their local diocesan statutes or else included the necessary information in the statutes themselves.[17] In addition to offering instructions for confessors, replete with explanations of the vices that were designed to aid priests in their inquiry into the circumstances and nature of the sins committed, these bishops' books contained brief discussions of the rudiments of faith, that were intended as outlines for vernacular sermons to be delivered at set intervals to the faithful. The *Summula* of Peter Quivil, Bishop of Exeter (ca. 1287), was typical in this respect, for in addition to a treatise on the sins and confession, it contained a brief commentary on the Ten Commandments and the articles of faith along with an injunction to teach the people the Creed, the Pater Noster, and the Ave Maria: "Debet etiam sacerdos docere laycum quod credat et sciat symbolum, scilicet Credo, saltem in lingua materna, et quod sciat orationem dominicam, scilicet Pater Noster, et salutationem beate Marie virginis, scilicet Ave Maria."[18] The purpose of this compilation of materials was to help confessors prepare penitents for the confessional, as the bishop makes clear in his dedication. "Hec igitur ego Petrus Exoniensis presbiter intime considerans, et insufficientie presbiterorum secularium confessiones audientium compatiens, quorum ignorantiam protho dolor sepissime sum expertus, presentem summulam eisdem assigno ut eam sciant ad utilitatem suam et confitentium."[19] At the conclusion of the *Summula* Bishop Quivil orders all parish priests in his diocese to copy and study his treatise sometime within the next six months. Similar injunctions were appended to the *summula* of other bishops.

Alexander Stavensby adjured the priests in his diocese, "simul cum sermone de septem criminalibus peccatis, que ad vos mittimus, et hoc cum quodam tractatu modico de confessione. Hec serventur et scribantur, sicut vultis quod ecclesie vestre non suspendantur, cum ad ecclesias vestrat accesserimus vel per nos vel per nuntium nostrum."[20] And Walter de Cantilupe wrote, "Quendam tractatus de confessione fecimus, quem sciri ab omnibus capellanis precipimus et etiam observari in confessionibus audiendis, quia longum esset ipsum in presenti synodo publicare."[21]

Considering these injunctions, it is not surprising that the bishops' tracts served as models for other manuals, particularly since the bishops themselves seemed to invite such imitation. Chief among these models was the ninth constitution of John Pecham, Archbishop of Canterbury, which despite its limited focus formed the basis of numerous manuals, written in both Latin and English, for the use of the laity and priests. Unlike the *Summula* of Bishop Quivil, which provided summaries of the information necessary for hearing confession and instructing the laity, the Lambeth Constitution provided little more than an outline of sermon materials necessary for the education of the faithful. This syllabus for preachers included the "quatuor decim fidei articulos, decem mandata decalogi, duo precepta evangelii, scilicet, gemine caritatis, septem etiam opera misericordie, septem peccata capitalia, cum sua progenie, septem virtutes principales, ac septem gratie sacramenta."[22] One section of the *Oculus sacerdotis*, William of Pagula's influential Latin manual for priests, was an expansion of the Lambeth syllabus, which John Mirk then rendered into English in his *Instructions for Parish Priests*.[23]

Some seventy-six years after the Lambeth Congress, Archbishop Thoresby of York issued his own version of Pecham's constitution for the edification of the York clergy. His instructions for priests were subsequently expanded and rendered into rude English verse for the use of layfolk. A Wycliffite adaptation followed; also in English it betrayed its bias by perorations on such subjects as the right of parishioners to withhold tithes from underserving priests and the need for the secular clergy to work among the poor.[24] Unlike the *Oculus* and its imitators, which placed Pecham's syllabus within the context of pastoral care as a whole, these northern adaptations concentrated on the syllabus alone. The limited focus of these manuals can be understood when we realize that they were written to help priests to teach and laymen to learn their catechism. The vernacular expansion of Thoresby's instructions, *The Lay Folks' Catechism*, was clearly intended as a supplement to the sermons on the "sex thinges"; it ends suitably with the promise of forty days' pardon to anyone who learns his catechism.[25] This reappearance of essentially the same material in several manuals, albeit in varying forms, in different languages, and for disparate audiences, illustrates quite graphically the interrelatedness of the Latin, vernacular, and bishops' manuals. The reissue of Pecham's syllabus by another bishop points to one other interesting phenomenon that accounts in large part for the homogeneity of the manuals—that is, the tendency of the bishops to borrow from each other. This tendency is all the more evident when we consider canon law borrowings from the bishops' statutes.

The vernacular manuals frequently quoted the bishops' statutes and those of the General Council on matters pertaining to canon law, since church law figured prominently in the daily life of the average Christian. Priests, in particular, needed to know at least the rudiments of the law in order to perform their duties. The most obvious point at which canon law and daily life intersected was in the sacrament of marriage. Constitution 50 of the General Council forbids marriage within the first four degrees of kinship or affinity. It was obviously this decree that Richard Poore was referring to in his statues for Salisbury. "In generali concilio statutum est quod prohibitio copule coniugalis quartum consanguinitatis et affinitatis gradum decetero non excedat, quoniam sine gravi dispendio animarum huiusmodi prohibitio (copule coniugalis) non potuit in ulterioribus gradibus generaliter observari."[26] Since the penalty for contracting such an illegal marriage was excommunication, Poore's warning was often repeated. The author of *Jacob's Well* devotes an entire section of his manual (chapter 8) to explaining, in terms understandable to a layman, how to determine degrees of affinity and consanguinity and what degrees were acceptable. An even more troubling problem was determining whether a "goostly" affinity existed between a man and woman who wished to marry. That such spiritual affinity was considered just as much an impediment to marriage as blood ties was made clear by Chaucer in his discussion of these distinctions in the Parson's Tale: "And certes, parentele is in two maneres, outher goostly or flesshly; goostly, as for to deelen with his godsibbes. / For right so as he that engendreth a child is his flesshly fader, right so is his godfader his fader espiritueel. / For which a womman may in no lasse synne assemblen with hire godsib than with hire owene flesshly brother."[27]

In addition to an intimate knowledge of the marriage laws, priests needed to know which sins lay within their jurisdiction and which sins only the bishop could absolve. In his manual for parish priests, Mirk advises priests to send the following offenders to the bishop: "All that smite priests or clerks, houseburners, murderers, mothers that overlie their children; a man cursed with book and bell; heretics, vowbreakers, coin-clippers, usurers, false witnesses, and folk that have been unlawfully wedded; those who have lain with sisters or cousins; and all that are cursed by the great excommunication."[28] These are the chief offenses for which excommunication was pronounced, to which might be added those who commit sacrilege, false tithers, simoniacs, and those who interfere with church justice. Constitution 47 required that all excommunications be preceded by a warning. In keeping with this injunction, the author of *Jacob's Well* requires that all priests show the articles of the Great Curse to their parishioners four times a year, once in each quarter. In his own list of the articles, which follows and which is amazingly complete, comprising seven chapters of the manual (chapters 3–9), this author cites general and episcopal authorities directly, a fact which led his editor to surmise, somewhat erroneously, that he was "well versed in Canon law and in the decrees of councils, especially those held in England."[29] Actually, the list in *Jacob's Well* was a commonplace that appeared frequently in the bishops' statutes in various stages of abbreviation and with various attributions.[30] The list was usually accompanied by the injunction to preach on these subjects four times a year. Undoubtedly, the author of *Jacob's Well* copied one of these statutes or made use of a canonical compilation in putting together his list, rather than gleaning statutes from individual episcopal authorities, as his editor suggests.

Canonical distinctions also made their way into the confessional inquiry, where the various species of homicide appear under the Fifth Commandment and the sin of Wrath. Similarly, the degrees of "goostly" and "flesshly" affinity fell under the sin of incest, while the Eighth Commandment naturally lent itself to a discussion of false witness and perjury. In this way, the confessional became a forum in which priests could instruct and question the faithful on the principles of canon law. The warnings against overlaying children that appear frequently in discussions of homicide under the sin of Wrath show an awareness of how violations of the law could be fitted into the various classifications of sins.

In addition to influencing the choice and arrangement of subject matter in the vernacular manuals, the bishops offered certain prescriptions concerning the appropriate style in which to address the people. Although these remarks, which borrow from Franciscan rhetoric and the *artes praedicandi,* were directed at preachers, they apply to the manuals as well. The need to address the people in their own tongue is universally acknowledged. Bishop Poore urges priests to expound the articles of faith "frequenter domestico ydiomate."[31] Archbishop Pecham, writing approximately fifty years later, maintains that a priest should preach at least four times a year on the tenets of faith. These sermons were to be delivered "vulgariter, absque cujuslibet subtilitatis textura fantastica."[32] Roger Weseham, Bishop of Coventry, expands upon these suggestions for a popular style in his *Instituta.*

> Nos igitur qui racionem reddituri sumus de animabus subditorum nostrorum vocati sicut credimus et speramus per conspiracionem divinam et ad curam et regimen animarum ipsarum, volumus, in visceribus Iesu Christi obsecramus, et desideramus quod fides Iesu Christi operans per dilectionem, sine qua quasi mortua est fides, per nos ac per vos pure, integre, et expresse subditis nostris innotescat, non solum in ydiomate latino, immo in proprio ydiomate sub verbis magis notis ac congruis prout deus vobis ac nobis inspiraverit. Volumus eciam quod de fide et de suis articulis fiant frequenter menciones in ecclesiis ad populum et predicaciones aliquando simpliciter et sine discucione, magis initentes exemplis quibus congrue possunt quam racionibus subtilibus vel inquisicionibus vel discucionibus.[33]

The vernacular was to play an important role in the reform of the laity, as the bishops here acknowledge. Not only did it help the "lewed" better to understand the basic tenets of faith, but more importantly it helped in the delicate process of interiorization that must necessarily accompany a full examination of conscience. The author of *The Lay Folks' Mass Book* relates the comforting example of the adder, who, though he does not understand a word of the charm he hears, still knows what it means, as an illustration of how the "lewed" benefit from hearing the Latin service.[34] Yet the same author goes on to render the mass into English so that "lewed" men can participate in the service. The author of a fifteenth-century mass book for the Sisters of Sion argues that participation is not enough. The nuns need to understand the service, he says, and it is for this reason that he has drawn it into English.

> But forasmoche as many of you, though ye can synge and rede, yet ye can not se what the meanynge therof ys: therefore to the onely worshyp and praysyng of oure lorde Iesu chryste and of hys moste mercyfull mother oure lady and to the gostly comforte and profyte of youre soules I have drawen youre legende and all youre servyce in to Englyshe, that ye shulde se by the understondyng therof, how worthy and holy praysynge of oure gloryous Lady is contente therin, & the more devoutely and knowyngly synge yt & rede yt and say yt to her worshyp.[35]

As this author realizes, a deeper understanding of the service is a prerequisite to more active participation. So too a deeper understanding of the tenets of the faith and the new moral theology was seen as essential to participation in the sacrament of confession. It was for this reason that these subjects were treated in the vernacular.

Nowhere is the role of the vernacular in this process more clearly defined than in the directions for learning the catechism. Both the sermons that were intended to teach the faithful the basic tenets of the faith and the yearly examination on these catechetical subjects were administered in English. As preparation for the examination, priests were enjoined to preach "Openly on Inglis opon sononndaies" on the "sex thinges."[36] The author of the *Lay Folks' Catechism* explains why these sermons were to be delivered in English.

> And forthi that nane sal excuse tham
> Thurgh unknalechyng for to kun tham,
> Our fadir the Ercebisshop of his godenesse
> Has ordayned and bidden that thai be shewed
> Openly on inglis o-monges the folk.   (p. 22)

During the course of the examination, which was usually administered before the Lenten confession, the priest was supposed to ascertain "whethir thai kun this sex thinges" (p. 22). If any parishioners were found ignorant, they were set to learn their catechism as part of their penance.

Mirk outlines the actual form that this examination was to take in his *Instructions to Parish Priests*. According to this account, the examination on the catechism was supposed to proceed the inquiry into sins. Indeed, immediately upon settling the penitent in and assuming his own position, which incidentally varied according to the sex of the penitent, the priest was supposed to ask, "const þow þy pater and þyn ave / And þy crede, now telle þow me."

> 3ef he seyth he con hyt not,
> Take hys penaunce þenne rrot.
> To such penaunce þenne þou hym turne.
> Pat wole make hym hyt to lerne. (p. 25)

The ensuing examination on the articles of faith and the Ten Commandments took the form of questions and answers, much like the inquiry into the "peccatoris circumstantias et peccati." Thus, in regard to the first article of faith, the penitent was asked, "be-levest þow on fader & sone & holygost, / As þou art holden?" (p. 26). Similarly, regarding the first commandment he was asked, "hast þow worschypet any þynge / More þen god, oure hevene kynge?" (p. 27). These questions were designed to help the penitent probe his conscience regarding adherence to the fundamental matters of faith in the same way that the ensuing inquiry on the sins was intended to encourage an examination of moral conduct.

When it comes to the actual memorization, we have some idea of the degree of accuracy expected when reciting the catechism from some remarks made in connection with another passage that midwives were supposed to commit to memory. In the event that a newborn infant's life was in danger and a priest was not available, midwives were supposed to administer the sacrament of baptism. For this purpose, they were required to learn a simple baptismal formula in the vernacular. Indeed as Mannyng makes clear in *Handlyng Synne,* it was the duty of the parish priest to teach and examine midwives on this formula.

> Mydwyvës þat wyþ wymmen wone,
> Alle þe poyntes, behoveþ hem kone;
> Prestes shuld teche hem þe ordynaunce,
> what þey shuld sey and do yn chaunce,
> And examyne her what she couthe,
> what she shuld do, and seye with mouþe. (p. 300)

Mannyng goes on to relate an exemplum about a midwife who mistakenly baptizes a child in the name of "God and seynt Ione," thereby damning him (p. 301). The fate of the child and the subsequent punishment of the midwife gives poignancy to the *moralite* of the story.

> Mydwyves, y tolde thys tale for 3ow,
> Pat 3yf 3e kunnat, lerneþ how
> To savë þat, God bo3t ful dere,
> Pe poyntes of bapteme y rede 3ow lere;
> Mydwyfe ys a perylus þyng
> But she kunne þe poyntes of crystenyng. (pp. 301–2)

Not only could one err by substituting other names for those of the trinity but also by confusing the order of the names. It is evidently to uncover this error that in *Instructions for Parish Priests* Mirk advises priests to inquire "slyly" when a child has been baptised at home "ȝef þe wordes were seyde on rowe" (p. 18). In regard to the priest's use of the Latin ordinance for baptism, he warns that confusing the order of names invalidates the sacrament.

> But ȝef cas falle thus,
> Þat he þe wordes sayde a-mys,
> Or þus In nomine filij & patris & spiritus sancti. Amen
> Or any oþer wey but þey set hem on rowe,
> As þe fader & þe sone & þe holy gost.
> In nomine patris & filij & spiritus sancti. Amen.
> ȝef hyt be oþer weyes .I.-went,
> Alle þe folghþe ys clene I-schent.   (p. 19)

In contrast, Mirk maintains that bad Latin—of which he gives an example: "in nomina patria & filia spiritus sanctia" (p. 18)—does not invalidate the baptism. Undoubtedly, a similar latitude was allowed the laity in their recitation of the Creed, the Ave, and the Pater Noster. Indeed, Chaucer's Parson recommends the Pater Noster as the ideal prayer specifically because it allows for such shortcomings.

> Certes, it is privyleged of thre thynges in his dignytee, for which it is moore digne than any oother preyere; for that Jhesu Crist hymself maked it; / and it is short, for it sholde be koud the moore lightly, and for to witholden it the moore esily in herte, and helpen hymself the ofter with the orisoun; and for a man sholde be the lasse wery to seyen it, and for a man may nat excusen hym to lerne it, it is so short and so esy; and for it comprehendeth in it self alle goode preyeres.   (ll. 1039–41)

Clearly, the leniency allowed in these matters is a measure of the Church's concern with the education of the laity, as are the injunctions to address the people in their own tongue. The word that is used to describe both the mastery of the question-and-answer section of the examination and the actual memorization is *kun*. The word has a double meaning in the *MED*, where it is defined variously as (1) knowing or having mastery of a field of learning or a body of doctrine and (2) knowing by heart. Both types of learning were, of course, necessary for the practice of penance, hence the concern for catechetical matters in the penitential manuals and the association of the catechetical examination with the sacrament itself. But the word *kun* is used more generally in the manuals to describe the hoped-for effect of the Church's program of education on the laity. In an obvious echo of Innocent himself, the author of the *Speculum Christiani*, a fourteenth-century devotional tract written in both Latin and English, equates *unkunynge* with vice and learning with virtue: "Vnkunynge es moder of erroures and noryscher of vices."[37] The author of the *Lay Folks' Catechism* ends his treatise with a play on the word, which highlights the role that learning was seen to play in the scheme of salvation since the Council.

> For if ye kunnandly knaw this ilk sex thinges
> Thurgh thaim sal ye kun knawe god almighten.   (p. 98)

Among his prescriptions for assuming a style appealing to the people, Roger Weseham recommends the use of plain words, "verbis congruis et simplicibus," and "exempla quibus congrue."[38] This practice of speaking to the people in their own idiom—a practice for which the word *congrue* is a fitting description—accounts for the most obvious features of the popular style. One of the most striking examples of this type of accommodation is the use of exempla in the manuals to illustrate moral truths. Mannyng describes the desired "affekt" of these "talys" in his *Handlyng Synne*.

> For lewdë men y vndyr-toke
> On englyssh tunge to make þys boke.
> For many ben of swyche manere,
> Þat talys and rymys wyl bleþly here;
> Yn gamys, & festys, & at þe ale,
> Love men to lestene trotëvale:
> Þat may falle ofte to vylanye,
> To dedly synne, or oþer folye;
> For swyche men have y made þis ryme
> Þat þey may weyl dyspende here tyme,
> And þere-yn sumwhat for to here,
> To leve al swychë foul manere,
> And for to kunnë knowe þerynne
> Þat þey wene no synne be ynne.   (pp. 2–3)

According to Chaucer's Pardoner, such tales had a particular appeal to "lewed" folk, making them a standard accompaniment in popular manuals: "For lewed peple loven tales olde; / Swiche thynges kan they wel reporte and holde" (Pardoner's Prologue, ll. 437–38).

Another of Chaucer's preachers, the Parson, abjures such devices, fearing that they will lead to sin; however, he uses other rhetorical devices that are equally designed to appeal to the people. The most obvious example of this lapse into the popular style in the Parson's Tale is the description of the superfluously dressed man that appears under the sin of Pride (ll. 416–31). The piling-on of observable detail, the use of natural and medical analogies, and the many references to the various estates with their respective duties and shortcomings that make up this portrait are typical means by which authors attempted to bring abstractions within the understanding of the people.[39] Significantly, this section of the tale has no parallel in its rather academic source.[40] The Parson himself offers a justification for these devices of the popular style in the passage preceding his description. Here, he maintains that although "now been ther two maneres of pride, that oon of hem withinne the herte of man and that oother is without . . . oon of thise speces of pride is signe of that oother, right as the gaye leefsul atte taverne is signe of the wyn that is in the celer" (ll. 409–11). However, as Siegfried Wenzel noted in the case of Sloth, this externalization of inner states in terms of observable detail can result in a shift in meaning. In Scholastic thought, Sloth was a state of mind, referred to by Aquinas as a "taedium de bono" or boredom with good. The popular rendering of the sin "emphasizes not the emotional disorientation of disgust for the divine good, but rather the numerous observable faults which derive from such a state."[41] As a result, the popular image of Sloth is much closer to the modern interpretation of the sin as laziness.

A similar shift in meaning is evident in popular definitions of spiritual homicide. The canonists defined the sin broadly as "omnem iniquum motum ad nocendo fratris,"[42] a classification which they divided into such categories as "odiendo, detrahendo, opprimendo, male consulendo, nocendo, victum subtrahendo."[43] In the vernacular manuals, however, the emphasis has shifted to the last of these categories. As a result, spiritual homicide emerges as a crime against the poor and oppressed. As in the case of Sloth, the bishops' treatments of the sin stand midway between these two conceptions. Alexander Stavensby and John Pecham, for example, add such additional categories as "per calumpniam opprimere vel pecuniam suam auferre, qui non reficiunt indigentes," and "qui innocentes opprimunt et confundunt" to the traditional classifications to effect a change in meaning.[44] The question of sustenance for the poor is even more at the heart of the vernacular definitions. Mannyng defines spiritual homicide solely in these terms.

> Ȝyf þou þurgh wykked ordynaunce
> Fordost pore mannys sustynaunce
> Pat aftyrward he may nat lyve,
> Þou art coupable,—a ȝyfte y ȝyve.
> Ȝyf a porë man þe crave
> A melys mete, hys lyfe to save,—
> Ȝyf þou mayst ȝyve hym, & nat wylt,
> Beforë god þou hast hym spylt.
> Seynt Ambrosë seyþ hardly,
> Pat hyt ys slaghtyr gostly.   (p. 119)

John Wycliffe goes one step further, defining the sin not only as the deprivation of bodily but also of spiritual sustenance, a definition which lays heavy stress on man's pastoral duties and which is specifically aimed at lapses in the priesthood.[45]

This tendendcy toward defining the vices in terms of social abuses was typical of the manuals. Like the tendency toward externalizing inner states, it was a function of the confessional and the need to bring abstractions within the understanding of the laity. The *forma confitendi* required priests to question the penitent about his social position. According to the formula—quis, quid, ubi, per quos, quociens, quomo-do, quando?—this was the first question to be asked. Thus, Mirk advises priests when hearing confession to "bear in mind who the penitent is; whether young or old, bond or free, poor or rich, single or married, clerk or secular person."[46]

Such determinations, of course, bore on the nature and severity of the penance levied by the confessor. As in the estates criticism, certain vices came to be associated with certain social classes in the manuals. The exempla in *Handlyng Synne,* where Pride is a knight, Envy a monk, and Wrath a parson, betray these prejudices. The popular manuals betrayed an additional prejudice that was a function of their audience. Thus, after defining simony generally, the author of *The Book of Vices and Virtues* includes a special definition of the sin tailored to "lewed" folk.[47] Similarly, the author of *Jacob's Well* speaks at great length about the intricacies of calculating farming tithes in his discussion of tithing.[48] Not only do these intrusions presume certain sympathies among the audience, but as in the case of spiritual homicide, they can effect a shift in the meaning of the concepts that makes for a popular definition.

Finally, we can speak briefly, and rather broadly, about the literary implications of the reform movement. It is significant in this context that Chaucer chose to conclude his *Canterbury Tales* with a treatise on confession, which stands not only as the terminus of the pilgrimage itself but also as the final comment on the tales that have gone before. So too the literature of the reform serves as a commentary on the major poetry of the period. From this perspective the confessions of Gawain, Piers, and the Lover in the *Confessio amantis* become part of a larger pattern. Their quests take on clearer dimensions, as do the characters of their interrogators.

From this perspective, too, the vexing question of the relation of the estates to the moral character of the pilgrims assumes a sharper focus. Indeed, the idea of character that emerges in the poetry borrows from the conceptions of human psychology taught in the confessional. Perhaps this is why so many characters reveal themselves through self-confession. The false revelations of such characters as the Pardoner lead us to the question of intent, which Mannyng said was the key to any good confession. The question is raised again in certain tales, such as the Friar's, where intent is at the heart of the debate between the devil and the summoner.

There is also the troubling question of the effects of literary intent on both texts and their authors. In the case of the Reeve, for instance, we find that the motivation behind his tale, the desire for revenge, is responsible for its eventual backlash. Thus a man's moral character becomes a measure of his literary fortunes, a thought which obviously troubled Chaucer as he considered the moral implications of his own art. It is evident from these few examples that Innocent's advice to look within, as given form in the confessional and the manuals, affected the literature of the period as profoundly as it affected man's view of himself.

NOTES

1. "Sermo VI," *PL,* 217.673.

2. "Sermo VI," *PL,* 217.675.

3. "Sermo VII," *PL,* 217.680.

4. "Sermo VI," *PL,* 217.678.

5. For the history of penance, see O.D. Watkins, *A History of Penance* (London: Longmans, Green, 1920); R.C. Mortimer, *The Origins of Private Penance in the Western Church* (Oxford: Clarendon Press, 1939); John T. McNeill, *A History of the Cure of Souls* (New York: Harper and Row, 1951); Bernard Poschmann, *Penance and the Anointing of the Sick,* trans. Francis Courtney (New York: Herder, 1964).

6. Robert Mannyng, *Handlyng Synne,* ed. Frederick J. Furnivall, EETS, o.s. 123, (London: Kegan Paul, Trench, Trübner, 1903), pp. 335–36.

7. *Corpus iruis canonici,* ed. Aemilius Friedberg, vol. 2 (Graz: Univ. Verlagsanstalt, 1959), col. 887–88.

8. "Sermo VI," *PL,* 217.678.

9. C.J. Hefele and H. Leclercq, *Histoire des conciles* (Paris: Letouzey et Añe 1907–1938), 5:1340. For the English reception of these decrees, see Marion Gibbs and Jane Lang, *Bishops and Reform, 1215–1272* (Oxford: Oxford Univ. Press, 1934), pp. 94–129.

10. See Linda Georgianna, *The Solitary Self: Individuality in the Ancrene Wisse* (Cambridge, Mass.: Harvard Univ. Press, 1981), pp. 79–119.

11. Thomas Chobham, *Summa confessorum,* ed. F. Broomfield (Louvain: Editions Nauwelaerts, 1977), p. xiv.

12. For various systems of classifying the manuals, see F. Broomfield, pp. xi–

xl; Siegfried Wenzel, *The Sin of Sloth: Acedia in Medieval Thought and Literature* (Chapel Hill: Univ. of North Carolina Press, 1960), pp. 68–83; D.W. Robertson, Jr., "The Cultural Tradition of *Handlyng Synne*," *Speculum* 22 (1947): 162–85; H.G. Pfander, "Some Medieval Manuals of Religious Instruction in England and Observations on Chaucer's Parson's Tale," *Journal of English and Germanic Philology* 35 (1936): 243–58.

13. Raymund de Penaforte, *Summa de poenitentia, et Matrimonio cum glossis ioannis de Friburgo* (1603; rpt. Gregg Press Limited, 1967).

14. E.J. Arnould, *Le Manuel des péchés: Etude de littérature religieuse anglo-normande* (Paris: E. Droz, 1940), p. 28.

15. Jean-Charles Payen, *Le Motif du repentir dans la littérature française médiévale: Des origines à 1230* (Geneva: Droz, 1967), p. 561.

16. Gibbs and Lang, *Bishops and Reform*, p. 122.

17. In F.M. Powicke and C.R. Cheney, *Councils and Synods, with Other Documents Relating to the English Church* vol. 2, *A.D. 1205–1313* (Oxford: Clarendon Press, 1964), see Alexander Stavensby, pp. 214 ff.; Grosseteste, pp. 265 ff.; Pecham, pp. 886 ff.; Quivil, pp. 982 ff. and 1059 ff. Also, see C.R. Cheney, *English Synodalia of the Thirteenth Century* (Oxford: Oxford Univ. Press, 1941); and Arnould, *Manuel des péchés*, pp. 9–27.

18. Powicke and Cheney, *Councils*, 2:1076.

19. Ibid., pp. 1061–62.

20. Cheney, *English Synodalia*, p. 42.

21. Powicke and Cheney, *Councils*, 1:669b.

22. Ibid., 2:901.

23. Leonard E. Boyle, "The *Oculus sacerdotis* and Some Other Works of William of Pagula," *Pastoral Care, Clerical Education and Canon Law, 1200–1400* (London: Variorum Reprints, 1981), p. 88.

24. John Thoresby, *The Lay Folks' Catechism*, EETS, o.s. 118 (London: Kegan Paul, Trench, Trübner, 1901), pp. 5, 45. This edition contains all three versions as well as the text of Pecham's constitution.

25. Ibid., p. 98.

26. Powicke and Cheney, *Councils*, 2:89.

27. *The Works of Geoffrey Chaucer*, ed. F.N. Robinson, 2d ed. (Boston: Houghton Mifflin, 1957), p. 258.

28. John Mirk, *Instructions for Parish Priests*, ed. Edward Peacock, EETS, o.s. 31 (New York: Greenwood Press, 1902), p. 51.

29. *Jacob's Well: An English Treatise on the Cleansing of Man's Conscience*, ed. Arthur Brandeis, EETS, o.s. 115 (London: Kegon Paul, Trench, Trübner, 1900), pp. ix–x.

30. For similar lists, see David Wilkins, *Concilia Magnae Britanniae et Hiberniae* (London, 1737), 1: 506 (abbreviated list), 585, 601–2 (Richard Poore), 613, 618 (abbr. list), 661–62, 693 (abbr. list), 862 (abbr. list); 2: 33–35, 56 (John Pecham), 161 (Peter Quivil), 172 (abbr. list), 413–15, 749 (abbr. list).

31. Powicke And Cheney, *Councils*, 1:61.

32. Ibid., 2:901.

33. Cheney, *English Synodalia*, p. 150.

34. *The Lay Folks Mass Book: or The Manner of Hearing Mass*, ed. Thomas Frederick Simmons, EETS, o.s. 71 (London: Oxford Univ. Press, 1879), p. 140.

35. *The Myroure of Oure Ladye*, ed. John Henry Blunt, EETS, e.s. (London: N. Trübner, 1873), pp. 2–3.

36. Thoresby, *Lay Folks' Catechism*, p. 6.

37. *Speculum Christiani: A Middle English Religious Treatise of the Fourteenth Century*, ed. Gustaf Holmstedt, EETS, o.s. 182 (London: Oxford Univ. Press, 1933), p. 4.

38. Cheney, *English Synodalia*, p. 150.

39. For a discussion of these devices as they are used in the popular sermons, see Siegfried Wenzel, *Verses in Sermons: Fasciculus Morum and Its Middle English Poems* (Cambridge, Mass.: The Medieval Academy of America, 1978), pp. 50–59.

40. Siegfried Wenzel, "The Source of Chaucer's Seven Deadly Sins," *Traditio* 30 (1974): 362.

41. Wenzel, *the Sin of Sloth*, p. 88.

42. *Corpus iuris canonici*, vol. 2, col. 1164.

43. Bernard of Pavia, "Select Passages from the Works of Bracton and Azo," ed. Frederic W. Maitland, *Selden Society*, VIII (1895), 227.

44. Powicke and Cheney, *Councils*, 2:216–17; 1:902.

45. John Wycliffe, *Þe Ten Comaundementis*, in *Select English Works*, ed. Thomas Arnold, vol. 3 (Oxford: Clarendon Press, 1869), p. 87. See also Judith Shaw, "Corporeal and Spiritual Homicide, the Sin of Wrath, and the Parson's Tale" for a fuller discussion of this shift in meaning.

46. Mirk, *Instructions for Parish Priests*, p. 44.

47. *The Book of Vices and Virtues*, ed. W. Nelson Francis, EETS, o.s. 217 (London: Oxford Univ. Press, 1942), p. 38.

48. *Jacob's Well*, pp. 37–43.

Medieval Popular Literature: Folkloric Sources

Bruce A. Rosenberg

Every culture in every age and at every time has a folklore, which for simplicity we shall define as any aspect of culture transmitted orally. Folklorists have found certain aspects of culture more interesting, or more important, than others, and so certain genres have received more attention than others: the folktale, the ballad, riddles, proverbs, and legends, for instance, have garnered far more attention than have beliefs in weather lore and folk medicine. When we turn our attention to the folklore of the Middle Ages, this imbalance is in our favor. Narratives which are closely related to certain folktales—are episodically analogous—have been written down, providing documentary evidence of their existence. Folklorists have devised methods which enable us to establish the approximate structure of folktales current during the Middle Ages, and with such reconstructions we can see how folktale and literary tale are related. Folk beliefs and practices may be harder to establish, unless we are very lucky in finding a text that makes such items clear. More commonly, however, when we find a writer such as Chaucer employing a folk belief, his assumption is that every reader and listener will understand its significance immediately, and so he does not bother to explain it. We would not expect Saul Bellow to digress to explain why one of his characters knocks on wood, or "blesses" a sneeze; and Chaucer does not say why Aurelius is invited to dinner by the magician in the Franklin's Tale; nearly a dozen lines are devoted to this act. Why? What does it mean?

Folk literature in the Middle Ages was "popular," though not—obviously—in the contemporary sense of that word. To distinguish more precisely among these categories that comprise a culture's narrative output, we should first isolate three critical components in any artistic production: the artist/performer, the medium through which the work is expressed, and the audience. The relationship among these closely entwined components is symbiotic; and each of those culturally defined "levels" of literary production—elite, popular, and folk—can be usefully defined by describing this relationship, particularly in terms of the distance between each element and the others.[1]

The anthropologist's conception of popular culture is the one most useful to this discussion—that is, all of the produced items—the "things"—of a society, physical and cognitive. Literature, drama, film, television, and comic books are only a minute segment of a people's culture, despite most critics' associations of popular culture exclusively with movies, television programs, and trashy novels. The Middle Ages, of course, had none of these entertainments which a more advanced technology has made possible. There was some form of popular culture in the twelfth, thirteenth, and fourteenth centuries, but it was a very minor part of life. The fundamental task of folklore and popular culture studies is to evaluate an item or genre in society with the aim of making a statement about that society. Popular culture contributed little to medieval life. Folklore, on the other hand, was a major expressive medium of much that was deeply embedded in the medieval grain. Its evaluation reveals a great deal about that society and its collective life.

In contemporary artistic transactions, an important mediator intervenes in the artistic chain of creator/performer–audience: the producer. This agent, single or collective, assesses the tastes and desires of the consumer of art, and guides the creation as well as the performance of that art according to what is perceived as the current canons of taste. The producer—whether literary agent, gallery proprietor, film distributor, or the like—is, today, in the important position of being able to support the artist by marketing the artist's products to an audience. Thus the producer can also influence the taste of an audience through the control exerted over what is offered to them; and even more significantly, the producer can importantly influence what the artist produces because of the producer's access to and persuasiveness over available markets.

The professional producer widens the distance between artistic creator and audience, a relationship which, in the instance of the making of folk art, is quite close. The folk artist performs for a community whose tastes and aesthetic preferences are known directly; commonly, the folk artist lives in the same community as the audience. The distance between performer and audience in such a world is slight; often the audience knows the artistic product as well as does the performer because it is a part of its tradition as much as it is of the artist's. In such a milieu the original creator is probably anonymous, even to the performing artist, who usually interprets his/her role as perpetuating a tradition, and less so of exercising his/her indivdual talent. Few medieval authors signed their works because they also viewed themselves as perpetuators rather than as originators. When this attitude wanes, the author not only seeks to be identified in the public's mind with his/her own original works, others are discouraged from exploiting the original contribution. Copyrights come into existence.

In the late Middle Ages in England, a greater distance separated the audience from the literary artist than it did from the folk performer, but the writer/minstrel was closer to the consumer than is the commercial writer in the modern world with its intermediary link in the artistic chain, the producer. Many popular narratives were at that time performed by minstrels, who seldom were the creators of their texts and who had to judge for themselves what would "sell." The minstrels who sang the ballads and recited the romances to thirteenth- and fourteenth-century English audiences were rarely, if ever, aristocrats. The subjects of their narratives were frequently aristocratic, but the social class of the audience cannot be deduced from these facts. Although such scholars of medieval narrative performance as Donald B. Sands unhesitatingly assert (p. 1) that "not lords, knights, and franklins, but coopers, brewers, and tavern keepers" made up the audience—the orthodox understanding of the medieval performance situation for the romances—the question is complex.

We know, by way of contrast, that some popular songs were composed quite apart from a learned, international, aristocratic tradition. The conditions of composition and performance are like those of folksongs, though they did not necessarily enter a folk tradition. We are fortunate that Boccaccio seems to have recorded the genesis of such a song, and a few of its words. The fifth story on the fourth day of *The Decameron* (p. 258) relates how a young woman lost the vase that held her beloved's ashes (the Pot of Basil motif, T 211.4.2):

> The girl did not cease mourning, still crying for her pot. And weeping, she died. So her unhappy love came to an end. But after a while the story became well-known to many, and one of them composed the song which is sung to this day:
> > Who can the heartless Christian be
> > That took my pot away from me?

As seemingly explicit as is this account and its illustration, it does not prove that such a song as this was really current in Boccaccio's time, or a little before; the remark is in a fiction, and an improbable fiction at that. But it is clear that popular (folk?) songs were composed during this time on various occasions—here at the death of a young woman because of a broken heart.

Francis J. Child thought that "Judas" (no. 23) was one of the "popular ballads" of the English Middle Ages; however, as this song is structured, it is not like any ballad we now know of. And so, while it may have been sung during the Middle Ages, it was not in a form we can identify as popular nor was it performed under circumstances which we can reconstruct; and we do not know how popular it was.[2]

The Middle English romances are known to have been current in England at least as early as the first quarter of the thirteenth century. We have the manuscripts which internal evidence dates that early. *King Horn,* for instance, was probably written down ca. 1225, and so was likely to have been in oral currency for a time before that; how long is not known. Episodic similarities with the Anglo-Norman *Horn et Rimenild* (ca. 1170–1180) suggest that this story, at least, was known about fifty years before composition in the Southwest or South Midlands, though it was probably in existence even before that, possibly as the narrative of a different character entirely. Dating, by the use of bibliographical and philological methods, gives scant clues to the actual age of any traditional composition, since its oral life is rarely noted or recorded. The "Ballad of Hind Horn" was collected in the nineteenth century, nine versions having been published by Child. Charles W. Dunn thinks that "the age of the folk tradition may well reach back to the fourteenth century"; the vagueness of his wording reflects, with unusual candor, our inability to make such a temporal judgment (in Severs, p. 21). "The Ballad of Hind Horn" has been popular in recent times; but during the late Middle Ages? Nothing can be known with certitude.

The characters in the romances are mainly aristocratic; does that mean that the audience was aristocratic or that a laboring class identified with the lives and problems of their social superiors? That is still being argued, though the greatest weight now favors the latter possibility. Nearly all of the Middle English romances are considered "popular" because they were often performed for nonaristocratic audiences, were well known to contemporaries (Chaucer knew of at least a few), and in several instances more than one manuscript copy has survived. These romances do not seem to be in a learned, aristocratic tradition. Most romances are close, episodically, to folktales, a further indication of their social provenience.

But "popular" for many scholars means "inferior." The bases for this evaluation are three. Aesthetic criteria are most commonly invoked. W. Edson Richmond remarks (in "Textual Transmission," p. 173) that "with only a few exceptions" the ballads "were held to be too crude for the appreciation of a man of any literary taste." In order to assert the aesthetic excellence of *The Song of Igor's Campaign,* the translator, Vladimir Nabokov, denied its folklore elements and insisted on its artistic creation: "The structure of The Song shows a subtle balance of parts which attests to deliberate artistic endeavor and excludes the possibility of that gradual accretion of lumpy parts which is so typical of folklore. It is the lucid work of one man, not the random thrum of a people" (p. 6).

Less commonly, a scholar denigrates the class from which folklore is thought to originate: the most frequently quoted denunciation of the possibility of folkloric sources for the romances is that of Roger Sherman Loomis, who called the folk "plowmen, goose-girls, blacksmiths, midwives, or yokels" ("Arthurian Tradition," p. 2). How could great literature ever come from the likes of them? Elsewhere Professor Loomis ridiculed the folk as "swineherds, clodhoppers, fishermen" ("Objections," p. 63).

Third, a critical evaluation of folklore may have a generic bias; e.g., the epic is inherently worthy, while the folktale is innately crude and inferior in form. All three rationales are interrelated.

Popular culture is also a frequently denounced target of many intellectuals and academics. In 1981 professors Kastan and Gaylord of Dartmouth College blamed the low level of undergraduate writing on "the continuing presence of popular culture"; Kastan, as cited by Dartmouth's student newspaper, asserted that in a world that is becoming increasingly visual because of the popularity of television, a way of life develops which tends to hinder the improvement of writing as well as of thinking (Gill, p. 1).

One outcome of such attitudes may be the belief that the courtly romance genre is, in genesis and development, upper-class. The romances were favorites of the artistocracy but were not their exclusive property; all audiences cannot be inferred merely from the performance of a specific genre. The Anglo-Saxon riddles provide a useful lesson against such assumptions. Riddles are commonly an oral form, yet most of those in Old English are written and may be found in the *Exeter Book.* A few have been interpreted by scholars as dealing with philosophical subjects, though several are obscene. Frederick Tupper therefore assumed that the characters in the riddles must have been from the lower classes, but a recent analysis by Ann Harleman Stewart of several of their terms for men and women—and a comparison with their usage in other Old English poems—shows that when the riddles refer to classifiable human characters, their social stations are usually noble.

The English romances, then, are less formal and elevated in style than their French originals, usually closer in style and episodic development to analogous folktales. The minstrels who performed them would have been slightly less sure of the taste of the audience because—as we think—by the late fourteenth century and later their listeners were more varied, socially, than at court. Though corroborative evidence is quite scarce in England, we nevertheless feel that the romances were often performed for a traditional, unschooled audience. In these ways they can be classified and analyzed as popular literature, nearly as close to a folk, communal milieu as to its alleged aristocratic origins.

The varieties of folklore being so great ("any aspect of culture . . ."), it is important to decide prior to a survey of folklore in literature which aspect will be the most helpful. Investigations have been made of riddles and literature, the literary use of proverbs (Chaucer's narratives abound in them), custom and belief. For the literary historian the most profitable aspect of folklore study has been the relation of authentically oral narratives, such as the folktale and the legend, and analogous literary products.

Since we never assume that any medieval author invented his own story, but always borrowed it from tradition, the study of the folktale as it exists in society is as important as are other analogues within an author's milieu. If we know an author's source, we can evaluate his intentions by the ways in which he departs from (abridges, amplifies, alters, etc.) it. Or by what he retains. If that source is oral, it must be reconstructed from its contemporary reflexes, making any comparison less precise than if it were written, but evaluations are nevertheless possible. The folktale's existence in oral currency in the Middle Ages is a hypothetical reconstruction but no less real for that; no less real than putative "lost French originals"— the retreat of many medievalists who cannot locate sources they want to exist. It is also no less real than the quark, which has never been seen but whose reality is now assumed.

The Finns gave us the methodology for reconstructing folktales which were current centuries ago.[3] They were initially interested in analyzing their national epic, the *Kalevala,* in turn a construction by the Finnish poet and folklorist Elias Lönnrot. He had collected a great many short poems, *runot,* and assembled them in a form thought to be similar to a (hypothetical) medieval epic. During the middle of the nineteenth century the Finns' study of the *runot* and related folk narratives led them to understand that nearly all of the stories had analogues in other nations, and that the reasons for these similarities were not independent creation (polygenesis), but cultural diffusion (monogenesis). They further concluded that polygenesis was an all but impossible explanation for the origin of folk tales, so pervasive was the diffusion of these narratives in their field experience.

The researcher employing the Finnish Method (also called the Historic-Geographic Method) collects as many specimens of a particular type as he can locate. He then attempts to reconstruct the life history of his tale, paying special attention to those versions with traits which seem to be characteristic of a particular region or subculture (*Oiko*types). One of the important goals will be to establish the original form of the tale (the Archetype), though that be millenia old.

American folklorists almost never involve themselves with studies of this type and scope any more, for several reasons. To amass all of the known specimens of a particular Type may be the labor of years, and the subsequent necessary analysis of those narratives—frequently more than a thousand in number, recorded in dozens of languages, many of which may be obscure—would be the work of an additional decade or more. And in the end the results have not turned out to be as interesting or as important as had been hoped. The reconstruction of the hypothetical Archetypes, for instance, has dubious validity and often almost as slight a value. In the end, the folklorist using the Finnish Method does not "have" the original, but only something (theoretically) like it. This may not be detailed enough for rigorous analysis.

The Finns developed their rationales and their methods under the influence of Darwinian positivism, which they interpreted to mean that each tale had to be studied as an individual specimen as well as part of a world-wide genre. Literary use of folktales was especially important, because the extensive distribution likely in printed texts made folktales embedded within them more influential. A comparable situation exists in the Walt Disney movie versions of "Snow White" and "Cinderella," whose traits many Americans now think of as standard.[4] The speed with which the cinema has disseminated narrative traits, and the influence it has had on the perceptions of millions, make it even more important to folklore study than print.

The Finns began to assemble extensive dictionaries of all of the narrative episodes from the tales they were collecting; these became the *Motif Index*. Assuming a great stability of narrative episodes, even through repeated retellings, the Finns compiled indexes of tale types which they hoped would be identifiable and thus classifiable; this compilation became *The Types of the Folktale*.

Both indexes have serious faults. The motifs included in them are not exclusively narrative but often descriptive. Many are not easily classifiable, but spill over into two or more of the Finns' categories: for instance, a revenant can be magical or simply a returnee from the dead. If the revenant performs a special function in the tale being studied, it can be classified in yet other ways. And some motifs, in theory components of oral narratives, can themselves be independent tales. The folktales—those narratives which we would all concede to be folktales—do not always exhibit the stability the Finns had hoped for. Human characters can be replaced by animals, and vice versa; details are commonly added or deleted; names, places, artifacts constantly change, and the deletion or alteration of a trait early in the tale may cause the teller to alter or add others to maintain consistency.[5] So many traits may mutate that in some cases the tales are barely, if at all, recognizable as belonging to their supposed Type.

Yet after all of this has been said, after all the quibbles have been made, all the objections registered, all the flaws in the assumptions of the Historic-Geographic method pointed out, most folklorists have found that the method is nevertheless usually valid.[6] In many cases folktales hypothetically reconstructed bear a striking resemblance both to medieval narrative and to folktales collected today in the field, centuries after analogues have appeared in medieval manuscripts. If one has read (ideally, if one has heard) the text of a modern/medieval tale, its stability—within the predictable parameters of variability—will be unquestioned. Friedrich Wilhelm Panzer's comparison of *Beowulf* to the more than 200 versions of the folktale called "The Bear's Son" is one of the earliest of such studies, and despite its faults is still a valuable work of scholarship. Fr. Paul Beichner's analysis of Chaucer's intentions in the Miller's Tale is based on the folklorist's reconstruction of a type of "The Flood" (Aarne-Thompson Type 1361), instantly recognizable, as are the Turkish folktales used in Utley's and Bettridge's outstanding study of the Clerk's Tale and some Mediterranean tellings of the Griselda story (*not* a specimen of A-T 887, "Griselda," but a closely related variant, "The Patience of a Sultaness" [Turkish Archive Type 306]).

Literary historians of English medieval literature know, for instance, that the Middle English *Sir Launfal* derives from the *Lai de Lanval* of Marie de France. In this narrative matrix also is the Old French *Graelent*. Folklorists have found that the most remarkable trait in this cluster of narratives is the figure of the supernatural wife. Thompson describes the cluster as follows:

Occasionally we are merely told that a prince is on a hunt and encounters the supernatural woman. . . . The hero marries the supernatural woman and lives happily with her. On one occasion he wishes to go home on a visit. She consents, and gives him a magic object, usually a wishing ring, or else the power to make three wishes come true. But she warns him in the strongest terms against breaking certain prohibitions. He must not call for her to come to him or utter her name. . . . When he goes home he tells of his adventures and is induced to boast of his wife. He calls upon her to come, so that they may all see how beautiful she is. . . . She does come, takes the ring, and disappears. . . . In whatever way the wife is lost, the narrative now proceeds with his adventures while he seeks for and eventually recovers her. . . . Sometimes she is about to be married to another man. A ring hidden in a cake, or some other device, brings about recognition, and the couple are reunited. Some versions proceed from this point into the story of The Girl as Helper in the Hero's Flight (Type 313). . . .

Despite some discrepancies (the magic object, the altered ending), *Sir Launfal* is of this narrative matrix. Polygenesis is not considered a serious possibility; *Launfal* and its French early analogues are thus part of this folktale matrix. So too is Chrétien's *Yvain,* though which are sources and which are derivatives has not been established.

Sir Launfal's relationship to Type 400 is easily demonstrated, as structurally analogous as it is to its oral brothers. Details may differ (a magic purse for Launfal, a magic ring for the folktale hero) and the ending has been interpreted liberally by Thomas Chestre (yet note the several possible endings in oral versions); nevertheless the many important similarities are unmistakable.

More challenging are those literary works in which the borrowing (in whatever direction) is not superficially apparent. *Sir Degaré,* an early fourteenth–century romance from the South Midlands, readily lends itself to the demonstration of how complicated narratives are related to simpler components.

A king in Brittany has offered his daughter to anyone who can defeat him in combat. For several years no one is successful. Then, one day, the princess becomes separated from her party in the woods and is ravished by a knight from fairyland. As he leaves, he gives her a pointless sword with which their son is to identify him; he keeps the broken point. When the child is born, his mother abandons him, leaving in his cradle a pair of gloves and a letter identifying the noble heritage of the infant, who is to love only her whom the gloves fit. The child is raised by a hermit and his sister; when he is twenty years old he sets out on a search for his parents. Degaré, so named by his foster parents, is knighted when he saves an earl from a dragon; later he unknowingly unhorses his grandfather, thus winning his own mother as a prize. He shortly discovers who she is—in time to avoid incest—through an exchange of gloves, and of his birth from her. With the pointless sword, he seeks his father. His quest takes him to a castle in a deep woods, all of whose inhabitants are enchanted. He breaks the spell, is promised the castle maiden's hand, but delays marriage to her until he finds his father. Soon after, a knight in the woods challenges him for poaching, but when he sees the sword without a point he identifies himself as Degaré's father. They return to Degaré's home where his father is properly married to his mother; Degaré then returns to the enchanted castle to marry the lady to whom his prowess had gotten him be-trothed. (Severs, pp. 140–41)

A folklorist's first step in an analysis of this romance is to identify the salient narrative elements in it, and then to see what patterns, if any, are present (see Rosenberg, "Three Tales"). The situation at the beginning of the story describes a marriage test (motif H 1310): the daughter who can only be won by the man who can defeat her father. However, it is the knight from fairyland who seduces her without bothering about a tournament—Prince Finds Heroine in Woods (N 711.1). A sword token is left (T 645) for the child who is subsequently abandoned or "exposed" (R 131); as a young man he wins a bride in a tournament (H 331.2). The consummation of this Oedipal marriage is avoided and Degaré sets out once more on his quest to find his father. First, his bravery and skills earn him the possession of a bride as prize (T 68), but he temporarily refuses to marry her (L 225). A little later, a fight between unknowns (N 731.2), which is potentially a parricide (N 323), is averted because of the recognition token (N 731); he brings about the marriage of his parents (L 161).

Sir Degaré has three salient narrative features ('subplots' is not quite accurate): the incipient Oedipal relationship between Degaré and his mother, his abandonment while an infant, and his search for his father. His search is for both parents, but he finds her early in his adventures and the narrative does not conclude until he has found his father as well. When his parents have been reunited, the purpose of the quest stated at the story's beginning has been fulfilled; Degaré quickly returns to his own fiancée, and the narrative is concluded.

All of the motifs mentioned above are found significantly in three folktales, and once this identification has been made, the researcher has a working hypothesis against which several supportive criteria can be tested. One of these constituent tales, best known to us in Sophocles' most haunting myth, has an oral life as a folktale, "Oedipus," A-T Type 931. *The Types of the Folktale* gives the following summary: "As foretold by the prophecy, the hero kills his father and marries his mother." Collectors of the folktales of this Type most commonly encounter several motifs associated with it: parricide prophecy (M 343); mother-incest prophecy (M 344); exposure of child to prevent fulfillment of parricide prophecy (M 371.2); the compassionate executioner (K 512); the exposed or abandoned child (R 131); exposed infant reared at a strange king's court (S 354); parricide prophecy unwittingly fulfilled (N 323); and mother-son incest (T 412).

Degaré, like the hero of the folktale, is abandoned. Like him, he is raised in a strange home, though a hermit's and not a king's. The folktale hero commonly does sleep with his mother, but Degaré recognizes her in time. The romance does not permit the parricide, though its echoes are strong: near the end of the romance Degaré encounters his father and, not knowing who he is, prepares to respond to his challenge to fight. Fortunately, here too the hero recognizes his parent in time—again through the agency of the recognition token—to prevent committing an unpardonable sin. But this is the second near-parricide in this story; earlier he had unhorsed his grandfather in order to win his mother as his bride. The position of this episode—just after he has returned home from his adolescence abroad and just before his near-incest—is in the romance as it is in the folktale, and in the myth.

A second folktale, "The King Discovers His Unknown Son" (A-T Type 873), is of a father who has never seen his son, until one day when he is recognized because he carries a token earlier left with his mother. The motifs most frequently found attached to this tale are: a king in disguise leaves a token with a girl to give to their son if one is born (T 645); the boy is teased because he is a bastard and goes in search of his unknown father (H 1381.2.2.1.1); the son is subsequently identified (N 731 or H 80); and the king marries the boy's mother (L 162). In the folktale the king at one point orders, unwittingly, the boy's execution, but this element was either disregarded by the romance writer or incorporated in sublimated form, as the fight of unknowns in the woods.

Two of the three major elements still not accounted for are found in another folktale, "The Maiden without Hands" (A-T Type 706), the narrative which is closely related to Chaucer's Man of Law's Tale and to Trivet's *Chronicle* before him. Yet in Chaucer the heroine (Custaunce) is not mutilated as is the folktale heroine—the title shows just how important this motif is—and of course cannot get her hands miraculously restored. This seems to be just the kind of alteration that Trivet, and Chaucer after him, would make to retain the credulity of their audiences. The folktale heroine's hands are cut off, often because she will not marry her father; *Degaré*'s writer deletes this motivation (though we have another echo of it in the line "Þis maiden he loued als his lif" 1.21), and some of the folktale versions do also. Laura Hibbard argued that this incest motif has an analogue in stories in which the father insists on marrying his daughter because no one can be found to match her beauty. In another Middle English romance, *Emaré,* the incest is not concealed.

Neither Custaunce nor Degaré's mother is mutilated, though the romance retains strong hints of its source: the maiden is recognized not by the folktale's amputated hands, but by gloves. In the romance gloves are presumably taken off and left with the infant, and later become the sign by which he will identify his mother. The harshness of some tales, as they circulate in oral tradition among peasants, is plausibly sublimated as the tale moves to court, with its pretensions of delicacy. The metonomous proximity of gloves and hands is evidence of the refinement that fits *Degaré* for aristocratic tastes.

The three folktales—types 873, 931, and 706—account for nearly all of the motifs in *Degaré.* Left over is that portion of the romance which concerns the hero's winning a bride for himself; but that sequence, involving as it does the maiden held in an enchanted castle and the hero's defeat of a giant to secure her disenchantment, is so common throughout romance literature (as well as folk narrative) that one would be hard put to identify a specific source. It is an element not present in any of the three tales, but was added out of the pool of narrative materials available in either romance literature or oral tradition, or both—they are not exclusive.

The relevant motifs having been identified, at least three more tests need to be applied to the romance to convincingly establish its folktale composition: do oral tellers actually compose such complicated plots, fusing together three or more simpler yet discrete narratives? Do the motifs appear in the same order in the romance as they do in the oral tales? Historically, were the folktales current at the time of the romance's composition?

The first question is easily answered. Yes. Quite a number of conflated narratives have been recorded, many of these on the Continent, where most of the romances are said to have originated. And in all but a very few cases the constituent folktales are closely related by the actions of the heroes. Ranke's *Folktales of Germany* contains such a narrative, blending Tale Types 300, 303, and 304. The closeness of their numbers is one clue to the similarity of plots in all three tales.[7] In all three a hero (sometimes with his brothers) sets out into the world, has several adventures, and in the end marries a maiden (occasionally she is a princess). The adventures of the hero are noticeably similar from story to story, and sometimes can be used interchangeably. The presence of such similar episodes probably produced an association of different tales in the mind of the teller to begin with; they simplify the task of conflation once the association has been made.

The biggest danger in this kind of analysis is to find a single motif and on the basis of it to assume that one has identified the entire source tale. Constituent motifs seldomly float freely and independently; they do occasionally become detached from one Tale Type and affiliated with another. When the constituent motifs of a tale are identified, the researcher's first task is then to establish their relationship within a narrative framework. It is insufficient and usually misleading to treat constituent motifs as discrete and autonomous entities; the following analysis of *Sir Eglamour* relates each of several episodes to other romances, but sees no connection between them:

> The second part—the adventures of the cast-out Christabelle—is a "patchwork" of equally well-worn incidents: the calumniated wife (see Chaucer, *Man of Law's Tale; Emaré* [87]; *William of Palerne [Guillaume d' Angleterre]* [11]), the loss of children (see Eustace legend, above) by robber animals (see *Isumbras, Torrent, Octavian, Valentine and Orson* [103], *Bevis* [6]), the griffin as robber beast (*Octavian, Torrent*), the recovery of treasure (*Isumbras*), the reconitions *(Torrent)*. *Sir Degaré* (see [92]) may have given the hint for the Oedipus-like episode; and a popular theme (Sohrab and Rustum) inspired the combat of father and son. (Severs, pp. 124–25)

Analyzed as though it were a patchwork, this romance becomes a patchwork. But is this the way narratives are constructed? To take just one instance from the above list, the "popular theme" of the combat of father and son also occurs in *Sir Degaré*, which may have provided "the hint" for the Oedipus-like episode. What is gained by further fragmenting *Sir Eglamour* when one source will account for more than one episode? If the second part of this romance does derive, coherently, from a single narrative, that provenience would certainly be obscured in such an analysis.

"We must therefore be careful," Francis Utley once sagely warned, "when pleading genetic relationship between two widely separated parallels, to trace complexes of motifs rather than single motifs, however central they may be to the main story" (p. 605). No less an authority than Kittredge claimed that the Middle English *Sir Orfeo* derived from the Celtic *The Wooing of Etain,* a relationship which was based on one similarity only—that in both stories the wife of a king is abducted from amidst a company of knights. But Kittredge could not identify any other portions of the narratives that were alike. Utley concluded his cautionary remarks with the observation that "Arthurians will surely be interested in this warning, since their study has been plagued with those who turn such *catenae* of varying but overlapping motifs into the pseudo-history of a tale" (p. 605).

One of the safest methods of deciding that motifs in a literary work correspond to an oral one by intention is to see whether the motifs are present in both narratives in the same order. It is extremely unlikely that two or more motifs will become attached to an alien narrative in a coherent, recognizable, known manner by accident. The motifs of the "Misplaced Kiss" (the lover who presents his rump to be kissed by his rival) and of the husband asleep in a tub in the rafters (so that he may escape the flood he has been told is imminent) are presented in the same sequence in both the Miller's Tale and the folktale, "The Flood." That sequence certifies the close relationship between these two different tellings of what is basically the same story. The presence of just one overlapping motif would be interesting, but would not by itself demonstrate a genetic relationship.

For the final test one must resort to history: was the claimed folktale available to the writer—of a romance or of any other genre? Folklorists feel that a great many of the folktales in circulation today were first composed during the early Middle Ages, though incontrovertible proof is lacking. We cannot always show, positively, that folktales existed unless they appear in written narratives, and their appearance says nothing about the extent of their life apart from that manuscript.

With *Sir Degaré* we can be fairly certain that all three folktales had already been composed: "Oedipus," Type 931, without question, since the classical play and the myth—a very popular one—had been known for more than a millenium before the date of *Degaré*. We know also that "The Maiden without Hands" has the requisite antiquity, dating from at least the time of Trivet. The tale's distribution all over Europe, the New World, and the Balkans further suggests its age as well as its popularity. As for Type 873, "The King Discovers His Unknown Son," there is, regrettably, little evidence to suggest its age. This tale has been collected in Scandinavia, central Europe, Russia, the Balkans, India, and the New World, but it has not been collected in the numbers or over the area one would hope to feel comfortable with in assuming a medieval genesis. The age of this tale cannot be accurately demonstrated one way or another; it was only probably, not positively, known during the Middle Ages.

Much simpler in their compositions are several other romances, though their relationship to analogous folktales is by no means simple. The Middle English *Ywain and Gawain* is an abbreviated retelling of

Chretien's *Yvain*. Both are of the same narrative matrix as the folktale "The Man On A Quest For" (Type 400), with its salient motif of the "Forgotten Fiancée." The relationship between these literary and oral tales has never been worked out, and medievalists have never considered any possibility other than the chronological primacy of Chrétien's story. The folktale could well come from the more complicated and sophisticated French romance; the genesis and literary relations of *Emaré* are also uncertain, though its story of the calumniated bride, persecuted at first by her lecherous father and then by a wicked mother-in-law, relates it to the Man of Law's Tale (and thus to Trivet's *Chronique anglo-normande)* as well as to another Middle English romance, *Sir Eglamour.*

The romances also lend themselves readily to folktale morphological analysis, by the system formulated by Vladimir Propp to analyze the popular tale. The idea here is not to demonstrate further the genetic relationship between folktales and a variety of literary works—that should not be necessary—but to draw some conclusions about the meaning of several romances to which their plots give hints.

The Middle English romances fall into one of three structural groups. Classification by structure is a far more useful mode of analysis than by the "Matters"—of England, France, and Rome—a taxonomy given us during the thirteenth century, and barely modified since. The three types are stories of crime and punishment, of lovers united after one or more separations, and of tests posed and successfully passed.[8]

Typical of the first type is the mid- to late-fourteenth-century *Athelston,* in which one of four sworn brothers becomes king of England. Shortly after, another, Egelond, is falsely accused of treason and is jailed by Athelston. After protests and an appeal to the Archbishop of Canterbury, the accused and his accuser, Dover, are subject to trials by fire. Egelond passes handsomely, but Dover fails and is executed. The crime in this narrative is the improper imprisonment of Egelond; the punishment is Dover's execution and Egelond's reinstatement. During the course of the narrative Athelston kicks his pregnant wife in the womb, killing their unborn child, but this event is secondary to the false accusation and jailing: Athelston's rage is not the event that begins the narrative, and the death of their unborn has no further repercussions in the romance. It is present only to illustrate Athelston's furious anger. He has become a dangerous fool who has, primary to this narrative, jailed one of his sworn brothers.

Other romances of this type include *Gamelyn,* in which the hero named by the title is cheated of his rightful inheritance by a greedy older brother, Johan. After several adventures, including a stint as an outlaw in the forest, he succeeds in having Johan condemned, is himself appointed Chief Justice of the Free Forest, regains his inheritance, and marries. The very young Havelok is given to a fisherman to be killed in order that his lands may be confiscated; years later, Havelok (kept alive by the Compassionate Executioner) returns to his native Denmark, defeats his treacherous foster parent, and regains his throne.

In stories of the second type two lovers meet (and, of course, love each other), and are separated one or more times before they are finally reunited. In a reunion typical of the Middle Ages, they may vow to spend the rest of their lives in a convent and monastery. *King Horn* is one of the earliest examples of this type in England. *Sir Launfal* follows this general narrative thrust, as do *Parthenope of Blois, Bevis of Hampton,* and *Guy of Warwick. Sir Eglamour* also has more than one separation. *The Squyr of Lowe Degre,* one of the latest of the romances (ca. 1500), does not survive in any medieval manuscript, but whether as a sentimentalized imitation of "real" medieval stories or not, it embodies the very popular separation-reunion sequence.

Stories of test and fulfillment include that most famous of English romances, *Sir Gawain and the Green Knight,* but also a number of several lesser stories—the *Wedding of Gawain and Dame Ragnell, Sir Gawain and the Carl of Carlisle, William of Palerne,* and *Sir Isumbras,* among others. The test in *Sir Degaré* is not formally imposed—Degaré decides on his own initiative that he must find his mother and father—and his perseverance, strength, and native abilities win for him in the end.

What does all this mean? What is the importance of rearranging the orthodox taxonomy of the romances from "Matters" to structural types? The value of the shift in methodology lies not in arguing that folktales and romances are genetically related, though morphological analysis does draw our attention to similarities in the characters of both genres. The conniving steward, the greedy guardian, and the treacherous companion knight all have folktale counterparts. The wicked stepmother or mother-in-law and the lecherous father are characters from both kinds of narratives. So too is the father in *The Squyr of Lowe Degre* (a king in the romance), a frequently encountered character in folktales, where his function is (also) to impose tasks on the hero in order to test his worthiness to marry his daughter. That both romances and folktales are morphologically compatible does not demonstrate their genetic relationship; even Propp (p. 100) noted that "certain novels of chivalry" could be accurately described by his system, and they certainly were not folk tales.

This comparative decomposing does facilitate a tabulation and analysis of several important functions. For instance, the romances of test and reward pose difficulties for the hero which, seemingly, are resolved by aristocratic qualities. *Sir Gawain and the Green Knight*, with its strong folkloric motif of the beheading contest, is nevertheless almost assuredly aristocratic. The other romances in this group test the hero's courtesy (and his care of horses), his courage, his sense of honor, his piety, his determination to find his parents.

While a number of these tests are not exclusively the property of one class, at first glance the crimes committed against several other heroes do seem to be class-related. Gamelyn and Havelok are cheated of their inheritances, including lands—crimes not normally committed against peasants. Egelond is falsely accused of treason (in *Athelston*), by itself not a crime limited to one social estate (no more than is false imprisonment), but the immediate narrative situation of this romance—the characters have become high-ranking nobles—suggests an aristocratic concern. Are these tales, then, popular with the nobility, or with the lower and middle classes, who have interiorized the concerns of their social betters? Kings, queens, dukes, princesses, and knights are frequently found in folktales collected from the peasantry. Neither their content nor the social position of the characters reveals who the audience of the romances was, if there was only one audience.

As a matter of fact, characters of the lower classes are presented favorably. A fisherman helps Havelok, a cowherd helps William of Palerne, Adam the Spenser is Gamelyn's good and trusty companion, a servant in the *Chevalere Assigne* saves the children he is ordered to kill. But in *Sir Gawain and the Carl of Carlisle* the destructive force appears as a carl, yet when he is disenchanted he resumes his everyday role of knight. Stewards were in the social interstices between their masters and the peasants with whom they often had to deal.

If the romances were written for the unlanded, the steward, as a character, might be portrayed unfavorably. And in a number of romances he is: in *Roswall and Lillian, Amis and Amiloun, in Sir Degrevant*. But the steward can also be a faithful and trustworthy friend and servant, and he is depicted this way in *King Horn, Sir Orfeo, Bevis of Hampton*, and *Sir Tristrem*, among others. No clear-cut pattern emerges. The kings in the romances are also neither all good nor all bad, often occupying a role similar to that of the maiden's father in folktales: they perform this function in *Horn, Duke Huon of Burdeux, Sir Torrent of Portyngale*, and *Sir Eglamour of Artois* (where the ruler is an earl). And knights are hostile to the hero (or heroine) as often as they are helpful. Only in the *Taill of Rauf Coilyear* do we have a plot and a sympathetic, pivotal character that the untitled classes can identify with. Nearly all of the other romances make use of narrative materials common to folk stories, but that use is in a setting redolent of the concerns of the minor aristocracy. The author of *Sir Launfal* has been criticized for his undiluted concern with money, the major and disconcerting flaw of its hero. The orthodox interpretation is that such greed reveals the lusts of the lower classes; but is rapacity the exclusive possession of one class? In the late Middle Ages a great many of the nobility were impoverished, and coveted the wealth they felt should be theirs as befitting their birth.

Whether the romance begins with some crime, insult, or deprivation which the hero (or heroine) suffers and then resolves, whether lovers are separated one or more times before they are finally united, whether the hero is tested for some virtue or quality that he must elaborately demonstrate, one overarching pattern informs all of the romances: the hero is in the beginning young or unmarried (or both) and at the end of the story he is mature and the head of his own family. If he has been deprived of his inheritance (his lands, his kingdom, his wealth), he will regain them in the end, and with them begin his own dynasty. He begins, usually, as someone else's child; he ends as the husband and father of his own family. The separation of lovers seems to serve mainly the purpose of artistically frustrating our hopes that the lovers can at once begin their own family.

"Test and reward" stories begin with a character who may not change during the course of the narrative, but whose admirable qualities are known to the audience. Character development may not occur (*Sir Gawain and the Green Knight* is a notable exception), but the episodes are such that our perceptions of the hero alter—toward respect and admiration—because of what he has done. The romance, in this respect, is a parable of the young adult who leaves home, makes his or her way in the world, and returns to begin life anew as a mature adult. Having been put to the test, the protagonist can then live happily ever after. This life pattern does not seem to be the exclusive experience of one class; both noble and peasant have to "grow up," have to learn the ways of the world and how to cope with it, and are encouraged to begin their own socialization process with their own families. The romance thus reinforces an essential and universal life pattern of maturation, but also offers encouragement to those who must set out on that perilous road to kill dragons, giants, trolls, and so forth, by showing them stories in which the heroes invariably accomplish these tasks.

The folktale embodies that same structure—the movement from lack to elimination of lack—and also describes the adolescent's maturation.

And not in an entirely different sphere of action: the folktale hero's adversaries are also monsters and dragons and destructive giants and demons, which are also taken as symbolic representations of a variety of vicissitudes in life. The maturation and self-fulfillment are retarded by obstacles and obstructions; to develop as completely as one can, the dragon must be slain, the quest undertaken. Then will the princess be ripe for the taking.

Folktales, those narratives in oral circulation among traditional groups, have been adapted by a considerable number of romance writers and minstrels, and have loaned motifs to a great many others. When the folktale can be found in a literary work, we can usually ascertain its entire trajectory, a great deal about its structure, and a little of its genesis. Other aspects of folklore in literature—folk custom and belief—can shed light on the author's assumptions and those of his fictional characters. Often the revelations are minor—why does Chaucer's Canon wear a burdock leaf under his hood?—but occasionally they are important elements in interpretation.

Usually folk beliefs and customs are difficult to interpret—for one reason, because no international, comparative, taxonomic indexes exist; for another, because beliefs and customs frequently change and may disappear without a trace, or the belief may evaporate, leaving only a survival custom. Often it is hard to know whether a custom appearing in literature ever had a life of its own or was invented by the author.

To grapple with such problems, Richard Dorson in the mid-fifties worked out a methodology for establishing the authenticity of folklore in literature. First, one would want to show, through one's knowledge of the author's life, that the author has been exposed to the folklore that appears in the writing. With medieval authors such a demonstration can be very difficult indeed, and the researcher will deal almost entirely with probabilities. The burdock leaf is used in folk medicine to cool the skin in hot weather, but is also known—with the nettle and the thistle—as the devil's vegetable (Rosenberg, "Alchemist," pp. 566–80). Both of these uses and associations were known in Great Britain, and Chaucer probably was acquainted with them.

Secondly, the folklorist–literary critic should examine the work itself for a patterned evidence of the author's knowledge of lore. Modern authors frequently learn their folklore through their reading, as did D.H. Lawrence and John Steinbeck; the medieval author did not read folklore (the science that isolated people from their lore so that it could be studied is a recent one) so his use of it is very likely authentic, that is, incorporated in literature as an unreflecting portion of his life. If a medieval author borrows the plot of a folktale, one can only make that evaluation by the methods already discussed.

Finally, we will want corroborative evidence, which meant for Dorson that the folkloric item being considered (folktale, proverb, custom, etc.) had an independent existence in oral tradition. Unlike the other two elements in this proof, this one concerns itself with the nature of the folkloric material and not with the author's knowledge. This can be the most difficult proof of all, since even if an item can be shown to have an authentic existence when it was collected (most likely during the past one hundred and fifty years), that does not guarantee its existence during the Middle Ages.

In the Franklin's Tale when Aurelius goes to the magician to have him make rocks off Brittany's shore disappear, he is given a spectacular display of his host's powers, and is then invited to join him for dinner (Fisher ed., V 1209 ff.) This is more than just a realistic detail (though it is that also). The Franklin makes much of this dinner; eleven lines are devoted to it, while one or two would certainly get the point across, and it need not have been mentioned at all:

> To hym this maister called his squier
> And seyde hym thus: "Is redy oure soper?
> Almoost an houre it is, I undertake,
> Sith I yow bad oure soper for to make,
> Whan that thise worthy men wenten with me
> Into my studie, ther as my bookes be."   (V 1209–14)

"Sire," the servant replies, "it is al redy," and they all go in to eat. At "after-soper" (V 1219) they discuss the magician's fees for making the rocks of Brittany disappear, from the Gerounde to the mouth of the Sayne (V 1222).

The dinner, in established and recorded folk practice, could mean at least two things: first, the food of the magician puts those who ingest it in his power, and second, dinners are customarily convened to consummate transactions, particularly business agreements. The first possibility fits the situation in the tale of Rip Van Winkle, who ran afoul of his drink in the mountain retreat and fell into the power of the bowlers for twenty years after. It would be in the interest of the Franklin's magician to gain control over his guest; in later relinquishing Aurelius from his pledge of a thousand pounds, his nobility would be all the greater. Sitting down to supper merely to agree to a business transaction is not as dramatic, and Aurelius and the magician do not begin to discuss terms until after dinner. What did the practice mean in the Middle Ages? Or in the

Franklin's Tale is it, after all, just a dinner, an interruption after the magic show prior to hard negotiations?

Again, *The Decameron* gives us a clue. The eighth story on the eighth day concludes satisfactorily for all of the characters, and Boccaccio tells us that "the four had a good dinner together to seal the pact" (p. 504). In Chaucer's narrative the dinner comes before the negotiations, but this variation is not important to the function of the dinner. The magician apparently thinks that the meal will prepare his guest for the high price he is about to ask, but Aurelius needs no cajoling; he would give the world if he were master of it. That much is interpretation. The practice has been recorded in oral tradition, and Boccaccio's use of it and his explicit description of its purpose strongly suggest that Chaucer made so much of this meal, and put it where he did, to indicate to his audience that the deal's conclusion was foregone. Aurelius has to be shown to be not only anxious to have the rocks disappear but willing to give whatever the magician asks for his services. His lust for Dorigen must be shown to have no limits. The dinner is served before the agreement because in this case there are no negotiations; it would serve very little purpose if Chaucer had placed it later. Where it is now indicates that Aurelius has already, in his own mind, agreed in advance to whatever the magician will ask.

Not all folklorists are interested in literature; few scholars of literature care about folklore. Yet at the intersection of these disciplines there is a lot of foment and light. A disproportionate number of teachers of literature who are also folklorists teach medieval literature. The two disciplines are not remote from each other, as nearly all people who are not in these fields seem to think. It is merely that since nearly all medieval narrative was in oral circulation at one time or the other during its life history, its study is interesting to the folklorist; to study it perceptively, the medievalist must know a lot about folklore, particularly about folk narrative and the way it performs in oral circulation. In nearly all phases of the creative process in literature, from composition to finished text, the folklorist—or the literary critic's knowledge of the theories and methodologies of folklore—enables him to make a distinctive evaluation of the subject. The knowledge of folklore is quite valuable to an understanding of medieval literature; in many cases it is invaluable.

N O T E S

1. This analytical scheme was suggested to me by Professor John G. Cawelti at a National Humanities Institute seminar at the University of Chicago during

1976. It will be incorporated in a forthcoming book-length study of folk, popular, and elite aesthetics.

2. No less an authority than Kittredge assumed the antiquity of the folk ballad: see his introduction to *English and Scottish Popular Ballads,* p. xiv. This has been questioned by Richmond, "New Look," pp. 86–97.

3. A full discussion of this methodology is found in Krohn's *Folkloristische Arbeitsmethode;* this book is more conveniently available in Roger L. Welsch, trans., *Folklore Methodology* (Austin: Univ. of Texas Press, 1971).

4. The Walt Disney variants delete or alter certain unpleasant details found in many of the authentic versions: the amputated finger as token of recognition; the punishment of the wicked queen, who was forced to dance herself to death in red-hot iron shoes.

5. Fifteen of the most common variations are briefly described in Thompson, *Folktale,* p. 436. These were elaborated in Krohn, *Arbeitsmethode.*

6. Since literary historians are not interested in all the known versions of a type, but (usually) in only a few of the relevant ones, their comparative studies are relatively uncomplicated.

7. Unfortunately, the numbering system is not always consistent and logical: "Griselda," for instance (Type 887), is in its plot quite similar to "Crescentia" (Type 712).

8. This taxonomy has been suggested by Rosenberg, "Morphology," pp. 63–77.

WORKS CITED

Beichner, Fr. Paul E. "Characterization in the *Miller's Tale.*" In *Chaucer Criticism.* Vol 1. ed. Richard Schoeck and Jerome Taylor. Notre Dame: Notre Dame Univ. Press, 1960.

Bettridge, William, and Francis Lee Utley. "New Light in the Origin of The Griselda Story." *Texas Studies in Language and Literature* 13 (1971): 153–208.

Boccaccio, Giovanni. *The Decameron.* Trans. Frances Winwar. New York: Modern Library, 1955.

Child, Francis J., ed. *The English and Scottish Popular Ballads.* 5 vols. Boston: Houghton, Mifflin, 1886–98.

Dorson, Richard M. "The Identification of Folklore in American Literature." *Journal of American Folklore* 70 (1957): 1–8.

Finnegan, Ruth. *Oral Poetry.* Cambridge: Cambridge Univ. Press, 1977.

Fisher, John Hurt, ed. *The Complete Poetry and Prose of Geoffrey Chaucer.* New York: Holt, Rinehart, Winston, 1977.

Gill, Chris. "Profs Say Writing Skills Need Work." In *The Dartmouth,* 9 (Nov. 1981), p. 1.

Kittredge, George Lyman. "Sir Orfeo." *Journal of American Philosophy* 7 (1886): 176–202.

———, and Helen Child Sargent, eds. *English and Scottish Popular Ballads*. Boston: Houghton Mifflin, 1904.

Krohn, Kaarle. *Die folkloristische Arbeitsmethode*. Oslo: H. Aschehaug, 1926.

Loomis, Roger Sherman. "Arthurian Tradition and Folklore." *Folklore* 69 (1958): 1–25.

———. "Objections to the Celtic Origin of the 'Matière de Bretagne.'" *Romania* 79 (1958): 47–77.

Nabokov, Vladimir, trans. *The Song of Igor's Campaign*. New York: McGraw-Hill, 1975.

Panzer, Friedrich Wilhelm. *Studien zur germanische Sagengeschichte*. 2 vols. Munich: C.H. Beck, 1910–12.

Propp, Valdimir. *The Morphology of the Folktale*. Trans. Louis A. Wagner. Austin: Univ. of Texas Press, 1968.

Ranke, Kurt, ed. *The Folktales of Germany*. Chicago: Univ. of Chicago Press, 1966.

Richmond, W. Edson. "A New Look at the Wheel: An Essay in Defining the Ballad." In *The European Medieval Ballad: A Symposium*. Otto Holzapfel, et al., eds. Odense: Odense Univ. Press, 1978.

———. "The Textual Transmission of Folklore." *Norveg* 4 (1954): 173–96.

Rosenberg, Bruce A. "Swindling Alchemist, Antichrist." *Centennial Review of the Arts and Sciences* 6 (1962): 566–80.

———. "The Morphology of the Middle English Metrical Romance." *Journal of Popular Culture* 1 (1967): 63–77.

———. "The Three Tales of *Sir Degaré*." *Neuphilologische Mitteilungen* 76 (1975): 39–51.

Sands, Donald B., ed. *Middle English Verse Romances*. New York: Holt Rinehart, Winston, 1966.

Severs, J. Burke, ed. *A Manual of Writings in Middle English 1050–1500*. Vol 1. New Haven: Connecticut Academy of Arts and Sciences, 1967.

Steenstrup, Johannes, C.H.R. *The Medieval Popular Ballad*. Trans. Edward Godfrey Cox. Seattle: Univ. of Washington Press, 1968.

Stewart, Ann Harleman. "Double Entendre in the Old English Riddles." In *Lore and Language*, forthcoming.

Thompson, Stith. *The Folktale*. New York: Dryden Press, 1946.

———, and Antti Aarne. *The Types of the Folktale*. FFC 184. Helsinki: Academia Scientiarum Fennica, 1964.

————, ed. *The Motif-Index of Folk Literature*. 6 Vols. Bloomington: Indiana Univ. Press, 1955–58.

Tupper, Frederick, Jr. *The Riddles of the Exeter Book*. New York: Ginn, 1910.

Utley, Francis Lee. "Arthurian Romance and International Folktale Method." *Romance Philology* 17 (1964): 596–607.

Secular Life and Popular Piety in Medieval English Drama

Stanley J. Kahrl

$\mathcal{A}$t a recent colloquium convened to discuss the *Ancrene Wisse,* one of the medievalists present asked the sort of question that brings everyone up short. "In what way," he asked, "can we think of the *Ancrene Wisse* as literature?" The answers came lame and halting. "It offers a keen sense of medieval religious life." "It was widely read. We know this from the number of surviving manuscripts that are recorded." "It offers a good example of the handling of narrative materials for religious instruction." One member of the group noted that the text, because it could be precisely located in space and time, appealed strongly to the Oxford school for language study. But did this, or did any of the other defenses offered, make it "literature"?

As people in the fourteenth and fifteenth century first used the term, this text is indeed literature. Both the *Oxford English Dictionary* and the *Middle English Dictionary* define the term, using medieval examples, as meaning "an acquaintance with 'letters' or books, . . . book learning." In the day of its greatest influence, the *Ancrene Wisse* existed principally as a book, instructing its readers in the practice of godly life. We, with our rather different sense of the term *literature,* however, find works of moral instruction hardly the sort of thing to assign as required reading in a course, say in Modern American Literature. For us, the term *literature* carries most often a later sense of 'writing which has claim to consideration on the ground of beauty of form or emotional effect.' As such, works of religious instruction fall outside the pale.

When that religious instruction takes the form of drama, the question of definition becomes even more problematic. In the first place, no one in the medieval period experienced drama as "literature," i.e., as matter to be read. Virtually no text we have of a medieval play survives in more than one copy.[1] For example, most of the single texts we do have of the plays produced by and for the townspeople of Medieval England were official registers maintained by a city official, such as the town clerk, and used as the "original" from which scenes, or even parts, were copied as needed by the people responsible for producing the individual scenes. At York the town clerk sat at the first station with the register to ensure that each play was performed properly, according to the official text. But for the individual citizens of any town or village we care to name, in which plays were performed annually by citizens of that town for their delight and instruction, no member of any audience was ever able to read the play once the actors had moved from the stage back to their ordinary lives as members of that town's citizenry. There were no quartos of the *Second Shepherds Play* to analyze once the Wakefield Cycle had come and gone.

Medieval drama existed primarily as an oral medium, at least as it was experienced most directly by those influenced by this form of "literature" in the Middle Ages. Not only were the annual civic religious plays an oral event, but also the plays performed from the fourteenth century on into the eighteenth century by troupes of strolling players were experienced almost entirely by their audiences in performance only. Scattered single texts of the short plays known as interludes do survive, suggesting somewhat the nature of these plays, but for the most part the repertory of the traveling companies exists only as occasional long-vanished titles.[2] We would like to know what Gawain saw performed in Arthur's court at Christmas after the departure of the headless Green Knight, as we would like to know the content of the "interludium Sancti Thome Martiris" performed in King's Lynn sometime in 1384–1385 by the players who received 3s, 4d. for their pains.[3] The sole surviving interlude text contemporary with these two early uses of the term, the *Interludium de clerico et puella,* demonstrates that at least some of these plays were farces, adapting to dramatic purposes certain traditional comic material from such other popular oral genres as the fabliau. The scarcity of such material is understandable, of course, for as Richard Axton notes in discussing the three surviving early farce texts, "It is not surprising that literary texts of secular plays are scanty; no doubt unscripted improvisation upon routine roles was common; but it is obvious that a performer's role in constant use would have little chance of survival into the post-medieval world."[4]

Interlude texts on sacred subjects survive from the medieval period in a slightly greater number. However, they present even greater difficulties for those interested in assessing the nature of medieval drama as a form of popular literature in medieval England. None of the plays contained in the most famous collection of fourteenth-century interlude texts can be certainly connected with any tradition of traveling players. *The Castle of Perseverance* is far too long and requires far too many players, far too complicated scenery ever to have been the stock in trade of the typical "four men and a boy." Where and how it was ever performed is still a mystery. *Wisdom Who Is Christ*, a talky, static, didactic piece may well have been performed at Lambeth Palace, and there alone. *Mankind*, certainly in its length, pattern of action, and dramatic liveliness a play probably more typical of the repertory of strolling players, may, in fact, have been a university adaptation of the traditional form.[5] The most famous fifteenth-century interlude text, the play of *Everyman*, now generally understood to be a translation of a Dutch original, like the plays of the Macro manuscript cannot be associated with any tradition of performance, and may, indeed, never have been performed at all.[6] The interlude texts which can be connected with the acting traditions of the strolling players in fact all fall outside the limits of this study. As David Bevington suggests in the subtitle to his useful survey of the genre, *From Mankind to Marlowe: Growth of Structure in the Popular Drama of Tudor England*, the period of greatest creative growth in the development of the interludes is properly the Tudor age.[7]

Most difficult of all is the situation we find when we turn to the most widespread dramatic form of all in medieval England. Current research being conducted by scholars editing the Records of Early English Drama indicates that in the counties south of the Thames, a form of mumming play known as *The Robin Hood Play* was performed in villages annually throughout that part of England. In the East Midlands, mumming plays of a different sort were performed on Plough Monday. Further north sword-dance plays seem to have been practiced. However, in this case we have the least call to speak of literature at all. Alan Brody, in his thorough study, *The English Mummers and Their Plays*, stresses the fact that the men's dramatic companies, as he calls the groups who performed the so-called folk plays, operated throughout their period of greatest vitality entirely with an oral tradition.[8] Here there can be no question, then, of literature, of texts to be read and studied by any members of the original audience. Here we can never expect to have a book.

At the same time, such plays raise, in a particularly acute manner, the difficulties we have when using the term *popular* to refer to any genre of literature in medieval England. Given the fourteenth- and fifteenth-century writers' use of the term *literature* as referring to an acquaintance with books, one must conclude that the expression *popular literature* would have seemed to them a total contradiction in terms. For as I have already indicated, and as, no doubt, other contributors to this volume will indicate as well, book learning reached the common people, the *populus,* almost always orally. The obvious reason, of course, is the widespread inability to read and write. Those able to save themselves from the civil courts by reciting their "neck verse" cannot ever, even in the late Middle Ages, have comprised a large portion of the general populace. However, we must not think of this unlettered populace as necessarily poor in artistic entertainment. Minstrels' songs, the plays of the strolling players, the annual mumming plays which circulated through a village on Plough Monday, or even the narrative elements of such sermons as the one Chaucer's Pardoner tells all form a broad popular foundation upon which much of the artistic expression of the lettered was built. C.L. Barber's seminal study of the influence mumming plays exerted on Shakespeare's festive comedy should remind us as well of the fact that such plays, too, continued to influence the succeeding great age of drama.

Medieval drama was "popular" in the larger sense as well; that is, it appealed to all levels of the population, regardless of class. On a given festival, be it Corpus Christi, Whitsun, or the saint's day of a particularly important local guild, every member of a given locality would take part in the celebration. At major cities, such as York, Lincoln, Conventry, or Chester, town councils regularly enacted statutes governing the form of attendance at the religious processions which were a part of those feasts. A set of sixteenth-century watercolors, recently rediscovered at Louvain by Meg Twycross, depicts such a procession, with each trade guild marching in a body, in holiday finery, each guild carrying torches, banners, and symbolic standards, the feretory for the Host borne at the center of a crowd of ecclesiastics, and, in the position of honor at the end of the procession, the town governing body in full regalia.

In 1419 Bishop Repingdon ordered the cathedral clergy in Lincoln to be more diligent in attending just such a procession, which annually on Corpus Christi day wound its way from the suburb of Wickford to the cathedral.[9] While we have no records of a play being performed in conjunction with that procession in 1419, we do know that in Lincoln between 1472 and 1496 civic religious drama was presented in the cathedral close at least nine times. Among others who watched the play were the canons of the cathedral, whose payments for a "prandium," or noon meal, taken in the room of a Thomas Sharp on that occasion, tell us that the plays were in fact performed.[10] Later, in the early sixteenth century, as the town's finances became straitened, following the shift of the wool staple to Boston, that cycle of plays seems to have been performed no longer. However, Lincoln's major civic guild, dedicated to Saint Anne, continued to produce religious plays on 26 July, the feast of Saint Anne, well into the sixteenth century. To ensure that these plays continued to receive adequate financial support, the city council enacted a statute in early 1519 stating that "euery man And woman w⁺ in this Citie beyng Able Schall be Broder & Syster in Scaynt Anne gyld & to pay yerly iiijᵈ Man & wyf at the lest."[11] Thereafter the collection of this annual guild membership tax was farmed out at a discount, guaranteeing the council the revenue they desired to ensure continued performance of at least one medieval play cycle well into the sixteenth century. But the major point, of course, is that they saw nothing extraordinary in having everyone in the city taxed to pay for this play. After all, everyone benefited; everyone saw it. And the same can be said of every other village, town, or city where we know that civic religious drama was performed.[12]

Those who saw the plays were not just the townsfolk of medieval England. By the later fifteenth century it had clearly become a custom for royalty, when staying at Kenilworth, to attend the performance of civic religious drama performed in the neighboring city of Coventry at Corpus Christitide. The visit of Queen Margaret of Anjou to Coventry on 16 June 1457 has long been known to theater historians from the fact that on that occasion "she sygh then alle the Pagentes pleyde saue domes day which myght not be pleyde for lak of day."[13] Not always noted are the visits of Richard III shortly before the battle of Bosworth Field in 1485, or Henry VII thereafter, in 1487 and again in 1492. Apparently because of this interest, the citizens of Coventry elected Henry and his queen brother and sister both of the Corpus Christi and the Trinity Guilds in 1500. Henry VIII saw the play in 1511, Mary Tudor at least a pageant in 1526, and Elizabeth saw plays in 1567.[14] This tradition of royal visits should alert us, parenthetically, to the difficulties of separating too sharply medieval artistic forms from those enjoyed by people living in England in the Tudor Age. Medieval plays had a vigorous life well into the reign of Elizabeth, at which time they were forcibly stamped out by Protestant divines, who saw them as remnants of the old religion, as politically dangerous survivals of the Catholic faith.

The visits of the Tudors to Coventry should not be thought of as isolated instances of nobility attending civic religious plays. In the mid-fifteenth century the citizens of King's Lynn mounted a civic religious play of their own. At Christmas 1445 the town laid out over two pounds to take their nativity play out to Middleton, the home of Lord Scales, where the play was performed with special scenic effects provided for the occasion.[15] From a subsequent entry in the town chamberlains' accounts for 1465–1466 noting repairs to "le Gesyn pro processione in ffesto Corporis xpi hoc anno" it seems likely that the nativity play taken to Middleton in 1445 (for performance at Twelfth Night?) was a regular part of a more complete Corpus Christi play performed in the Tuesday Market (Lynn's market square then and now, and still so called) in 1448, when Lord Scales brought Thomas, Earl of Oxford, to see the play.[16] The word *gesine* is Old French for "childbed." In the parish church of Lynn, dedicated to Saint Margaret, there was located the Gesine Chapel, named for a cult image of the Nativity which was kept there. Margery Kempe tells us that officials of the Guild of Holy Trinity carried this "Gesyne" image in procession through the streets of the town on other feast days.[17] It thus seems reasonable to infer that the play presented to Lord Scales at his home was a direct outgrowth of local popular cultic worship patterns of the citizens of Lynn. Those of us familiar with the response of Theseus's courtiers to Bottom and his troupe would do well to focus also on the rebuke Theseus delivers them for their supercilious attitude: "The best in this kind are but shadows; and the worst are no worse, if imagination mend them" *(Midsummer Night's Dream,* V, i, 209–10). The plays that were popular in Coventry or King's Lynn drew nobility to see them because these plays fulfilled needs felt throughout medieval society.

The medieval playwrights themselves thought of their plays as appealing to all levels of society. Mercy, in the opening address to the audience of *Mankind,* speaks to "3ᶜ souerens þat sytt and 3ᶜ brothern þat stonde ryght wppe."[18] The first *vexillator,* beginning the banns of the N-Town Cycle, states that the purpose of those performing that cycle is

> þe pepyl to plese with pleys ful glad
> now lystenyth us louely bothe more and lesse
> Gentyllys and 3emanry of goodly lyff lad þis tyde.[19]

The first vexillator delivering the banns for the *Castle of Perseverance,* however, specifies the core audience for the plays.

> Glorious God, in all degres lord most of myth . . .
> Save oure lege lord þe kynge, þe leder of þis londe,
> And all þe ryall of þis revme and rede hem þe ryth,
> And all þe good comowns of þis towne þat beforn us stonde
>   In þis place.[20]

"The commons of this town" indeed are the primary audience for the vast majority of the drama of medieval England.

One might object that England's townsfolk hardly constituted the majority of the population in a period when the majority lived on the land. Townsfolk might be the common people of the future, but they were not a sufficiently large percentage of the population to warrant calling their plays a form of "popular literature," if by popular we mean "of, pertaining or consisting of the common people, or the people as a whole as distinguished from any particular class." Close study of the surviving records of dramatic activity in a county like Lincolnshire, however, soon demonstrates that it was not just the nobility who traveled to see the plays. For example, we have no internal indications in the texts of *The Castle of Perseverance* or the N-Town Cycle to tell us how the banns which precede those plays were used, but a series of sixteenth-century entries from Long Sutton makes their use clear. At Long Sutton the churchwardens provided more detailed accounts than was normally the case, making it a practice to name the place of origin of actors receiving stipends from the church accounts on the occasion of their visits to the village of Long Sutton. In 1542–1543 Thomas Holbiche paid the "Bayne of freston in Bred and ale" ninepence, while his co-warden paid the "freston players whan thay cryed ye bane here" five shillings. Five shillings was, at the time, a fairly standard payment for a dramatic performance. There is no additional payment to the Frieston players in that year, though a further entry does record a payment simply to the "framton players whan they were here" of five shillings. It thus seems fair to assume that the banncriers from Frieston were actors advertising a play to be performed at their home village, hoping that people from Long Sutton would attend.[21] Banncriers also came to Long Sutton from Donington, Leake, Boston, and Kirton.

Now Frieston is a tiny village over twenty miles from Long Sutton. To get there one must either cross the River Welland at Fosdyke, where the modern bridge crosses the river, or go an even longer way around, through Spalding. Donington is on the old road from Boston to Spalding, and Leake is even further beyond Boston than Frieston, on the same line. The more one studies the map using the list of payments from Long Sutton, the more one is inclined to suppose that a highly developed network of dramatic activity, involving a great many of the towns and villages around the Wash, had built up by the close of the period when medieval plays were being performed. As the county volumes in the REED series begin to supplement those already published by the Malone Society, it seems probable that other networks, involving the towns and villages of medieval England in regionally shared dramatic activity, will increasingly emerge. And once one establishes the fact that the villagers

of medieval England were actively involved in the production of plays, it seems reasonable to state that those same plays were popular in the largest sense of the term.

Virtually nothing is known of the medieval playwrights, or the conditions which brought their plays into being. The civic religious plays performed on or around the feast of Corpus Christi survive in manuscripts which show evidence that the surviving play texts are collections of the work of several different hands. The "York Realist" has been identified for years as only one of several writers whose plays are contained in the official register of the plays of York.[22] Arthur Cawley's separate edition of the plays of the so-called Wakefield Master, which has influenced so much of the criticism of medieval drama by presenting in a readable form the collected dramatic "works" of one of the finest writers of the fifteenth century, likewise underlines the fact that the Wakefield Cycle is a collection of plays of widely differing quality. The collection of plays is often referred to as the Towneley Cycle because the manuscript containing those plays once belonged to the Towneley family in Lancashire. That manuscript was, like the manuscript containing the York plays, apparently once an official register.[23] Such registers represent the end of a process, show how the full collection of plays for a single locality appeared, but tell us nothing of the process by which that collection came into being. In the case of the work of the Wakefield Master, for example, we have two plays for a single subject, two treatments of the visit of the shepherds to Bethlehem at the time of the Nativity. One of these, the *Second Shepherds Play,* appears in almost all anthologies of medieval drama. Because of its length and complexity it is not, in fact, a good example of the average play in the long civic cycles. It does, however, seem to represent the last best thoughts of one playwright on the subject of the Nativity. No surviving record suggests that two plays on a single subject were ever performed in a given locality in the same year. So why do we have two treatments by a single author of a single subject in one manuscript? Probably because the manuscript was a collection of *all* the plays for one locality, all the plays they ever used. The manuscripts which are civic registers tell us what a given locality had at its disposal at the end of the life of the cycles, but do not tell us how such cycles came into being.

Not all the surviving manuscripts were used as official civic registers, however. In the early seventeenth century Sir Robert Bruce Cotton's librarian acquired, from the library of a fellow of Corpus Christi College, Oxford (one Richard Hegge), a manuscript collection of plays subsequently identified as MS Cotton Vespasian D. viii. Now in the British Museum, this composite manuscript appears, on first inspection, to have been some sort of official register as well. All the plays in the manuscript save one have been copied neatly in a fair hand, typical of the period ca. 1450–1475 when the manuscript was written.[24] However, close examination of the manuscript reveals that the scribe was apparently copying out a pile of individual plays before him which did not entirely make sense. The confusions suffered by the scribe begin with the inconsistent numbering of the banns, which does not correspond to the sequence of plays in the manuscript, particularly in the section dealing with the life of the Virgin Mary. Careful collation of the manuscript reveals also that the scribe both was copying a set of plays which must have existed as separate manuscripts lying before him, and that either he or someone copying those plays one step before him (particularly in the series of plays presenting the Passion) was altering the texts in the process of copying them out.[25] Because the stage directions in the plays dramatizing the Passion show a strong theatrical sense, and because the alterations in the Passion scenes—such as the addition of lines providing for a highly theatrical exorcism of the devils possessing Mary Magdalene— also show a strong sense of theater, it might be assumed that the scribe copying the manuscript was in fact the author of some of the changes in the text. But even that is a guess. Certainly whoever he was, he was not the sole reviser of the texts. Several other hands have been identified making small changes in the text copied by the main scribe. All of them appear to be the sort of changes one would expect of prompt copy.[26] This text, then, seems to have been the property of someone or some group who used it over a considerable period of time not so much as a civic document of control, but as the basic acting text from which the plays were to be produced.

Other surviving texts had other uses. One of the better-known single plays treating a subject also treated in the full-scale civic cycles is the play presenting the story of Abraham and Isaac found in a manuscript once the possession of Sir Edward Kerrison of Brome Hall in Suffolk.[27] Anthologized almost as often as the *Second Shepherds Play,* the Brome *Abraham and Isaac* is marked by its heavy pathos and its emphasis on the agony Abraham suffers as his son, Isaac, pleads to be spared. Of particular interest, however, is the fact that the play, which was apparently adapted from the play on the same subject in the Chester cycle, may never have been intended for performance at all. The text, as copied, contains no stage directions, nor any other indications that the scribe who copied it out thought of it as a play intended for performance. As Norman Davis, the play's editor, puts it, "The compiler [of this manuscript] began with the intention of collecting short moral pieces and trivial sayings as well as the edifying longer poems which are more appropriate company for the play."[28] This intention seems to have trailed off, as the bulk of the manuscript wound up as an account book for a Sir Robert Melton, whose name appears extensively in the accounts. His ownership of the book can be dated to the end of the fifteenth century. Whether he or a predecessor commissioned the commonplace book, of which the play is a part, cannot be determined. But what is clear is that whoever copied the play thought of it not as a piece for the theater, but as an object of contemplation.[29]

The great composite manuscripts already described, as well as a number of the individual scenes like that of the Brome *Abraham and Isaac* all point to the early fifteenth century as the major period of creative activity in the growth of civic religious drama in England. This is only to be expected. If we remember that it was only in the last quarter of the fourteenth century that English was made the official language of the schools, if we recall that Chaucer and his contemporaries were the first major writers to develop appropriate forms of literary expression for the high culture in England that used as their medium their native language, it is not surprising that the writers developing a literary form appealing to a wider, more popular audience would be found doing so in the generation following Chaucer, Gower, and Langland. Because no medieval writer regarded a story or poem as any one person's exclusive property, borrowing and adapting existing texts was a common practice.

The writers creating the dramatic texts in the early fifteenth century were no exception. Five plays in the Towneley manuscript—the scenes of Pharaoh, Christ and the Doctors, the Harrowing of Hell, the Resurrection, and the Last Judgment—were all borrowed from the York Cycle, virtually intact. Other plays in the Towneley manuscript may have been adapted from the York Cycle as well.[30] How or why this process took place, how the plays in the York Cycle were transmitted to someone, possibly from Wakefield, who wished to construct a new cycle for a different locale, we cannot say. The most obvious suggestion, that the person responsible for the original composition of the Wakefield Cycle knew of the play performed in the nearby great cathedral city of the North and simply borrowed the manuscript for awhile to copy out some of the plays during that part of the year when the plays were not in rehearsal, is not, in fact, as probable as it might seem. Borrowed books, then as now, have a habit of staying in the home of the borrower. Given the absolute necessity of having the "hole regenall" in the hands of the town clerk at the time the plays did go into rehearsal in York, it seems much more likely that some other form of borrowing was employed.

A second plausible suggestion would be to posit a visit by a writer from Wakefield, who would travel to York, sit down there in the clerk's office, and write out the plays he wished to copy. That is what we might do ourselves, in a similar situation. And indeed the text may have been transmitted in that fashion. However, a third possibility also must be considered, one that corresponds, in fact, more closely both to later modes of transmitting dramatic texts and to medieval practices in transmitting popular vernacular texts of all sorts. Remembering that the primary existence for all dramatic texts in the medieval period was as an oral event, at least as those texts were experienced by their original audience, it seems equally plausible to suggest that the borrowing of dramatic texts in the fifteenth century was often by means of memorial transcription. Look, for example, at two contrasting speeches from the opening lines of the York Hosiers' play, *Pharaoh,* and the play by the same name in the Towneley manuscript:

TOWNELEY

Primus Miles. My lord, if any here Were,
    That Wold not wyrk youre Wyll,
    If We myght com thaym nere,
    ffulle soyne we shuld theym spylle.

Pharao. Thrugh out my kyngdom Wold I ken,
    And kun hym thank that wold me telle,
    If any Were so Waryd men
    That wold my fors downe felle.   (ll. 25–32)

YORK

i.Cons sol. My lorde, yf any were
    þat walde not wirke your will,
    And we wist whilke thay were,
    Ful sone we sall þaym spill.

Rex. Thrugh-oute my kyndgdome wolde I kenn,
    And konne tham thanke þat couthe me tell,
    If any wer so weryd þen
    That wolde aught fande owre forse to fell.   (ll. 21–31)

On cursory reading, the two passages appear quite similar. On closer inspection one begins to see the small changes that generations of scholars have listed, in such parallel texts, as "variant readings." Because medieval writers constantly adapted earlier texts, editors of medieval texts have since the nineteenth century tried to work out patterns of transmission, comparing variants to establish wholly hypothetical earlier versions of the differing texts before them. The effect of this activity, of course, was to focus attention away from the texts before us, onto texts that do not and may never have existed, the whole activity of reconstruction serving only to denigrate the value of the texts that survive. This approach also treated the revisions as a literary process, as an activity in which one intelligence looked at a book composed by another intelligence, and copied it down with changes that the second writer imposed on the original in the process of transcription.

Looking at these two short parallel passages, however, from the perspective of a memorial transcription, one sees another process at work. In the first place, the loss of strongly northern dialectal features, such as *walde, sall,* is to be expected, though this could as easily be a mental process taking place in the mind of the scribe. Substituting *hym* for *tham* in the second line of Pharaoh's speech is probably not a substitution of a southern for a northern form, however, as the "th-" form of the third person plural accusative pronoun is fairly common in the rest of this play. The only reason to make the change would appear to be bad memory. *Wold,* likewise, seems to have been substituted as the commoner form, easier to remember than *couthe.* One can see, as well, how *men* was substituted for the adverb *then,* having been pulled into place by the unusual past participle form *weryed/waryd* ("accursed"). Finally, *aught fande* is lost from a four-beat line in a context where a three-beat line is certainly wrong. The York play is written in a complicated stanza of eight four-stress lines rhymed abababab followed by four three-stress lines rhymed cdcd, one of the major stanzaic patterns employed in that cycle. The Towneley scribe is following that pattern, as can be seen by the other lines in the quoted passage, as he does elsewhere in the play. The only reason to drop the two syllables, which make perfect sense in the original and are necessary to create a metrically regular line, is because they were forgotten.

The same situation can be seen in another case of borrowing involving the York Cycle. For a long time the so-called Shrewsbury Fragments, a set of lines for a single actor which survive in a manuscript in the library of the Shrewsbury School, have been known to contain lines also found in the York Cycle.[32] Here, too, a comparison of two stanzas demonstrates as well the probability of oral transmission rather than inaccurate copying from one text to another. The speech in question is the last speech in the York play of the Chandlers, the old liturgical *Pastores,* or Shepherds' play. The two versions of this speech are as follows:

YORK

iii Pastor. Nowe loke on me, my lorde dere,
Þof all i putte me noght in pres,
Ye are a prince with-outen pere,
I haue no presentte þat you may plees.

But lo! an horne spone, þat haue I here,
And it will herbar fourty pese,
Þis will I giffe you with gud chere,
Slike novelte may noght disease.
Fare wele þou swete swayne,
God graunte vs levyng lange.   (ll. 120–31)

SHREWSBURY

III. Pastor. A, loke on me, my Lord dere,
All if I put me noght in prese!
To suche a prince without[en] pere
Haue I no presand þat may plese.
But lo! a horn-spone haue I here
Þat may herbar a hundrith pese:
Þis gift I gif þe with gode chere,
Such dayntese wil do no disese.
Farewele now, swete swayn
God graun þe lifyng lang!   (ll. 39–46, p. 2)[33]

The Shrewbury Fragment, written in what Davis describes as a northwest Midland dialect, probably for performance within the diocese of Lichfield (an area somewhat to the south of York), was apparently composed early in the fifteenth century, and probably predates the version at York. Both versions seem metrically regular, none of the variations being of the sort we can ascribe particularly to a poor memory—except one. The horn spoon holds one hundred peas in the Shrewsbury version because that word alliterates with *herbar*. *Fourty* is certainly wrong, a slip which makes no sense as an editorial change, but could well come from a faulty memory of the original part. Once we grant that the error was made by the person recalling the text used at Lichfield, we can also see that the other small changes in the York text create looser lines, a less tightly constructed speech. They too are the sort of changes made by the memory. We cannot establish how such memorial transcriptions might have been made, but the mere possibility that they existed should cause us to treat the whole question of borrowing from a different perspective than that pursued so often in the past.

Who the Wakefield Master was, or what the York Realist did when he was not composing dramatic verse we cannot tell. To posit any suggestions as to the station of these writers we must suppose that the people we find involved in the writing and production of medieval plays in the sixteenth century were conservatives, seeking to maintain vitality in an old literary form, and that they were people much like those who wrote during the earlier vital period, the first half of the fifteenth century. Of these certainly the best known, and most often referred to, is the puzzling Robert Crow, Capper, of Coventry. A Robert Crow first appears in the

records of the Cappers "paying wax silver to mark the end of his appren-
ticeship in 1510," is named reviser of the Weavers' and Shearman and
Taylor's pageants in 1534, and appears frequently in the 1550s and
1560s doing everything from preparing the three worlds burned up at
the conclusion of the Drapers' Doomsday play to acting the part of
God.[34] Having studied the records listing Crow's activities, R.W. Ingram is now certain that the man playing the part of God in 1562 is not the
man first enrolled as a Capper in 1510, the span of time being much too
great. That we are dealing here with a father and son both bearing the
same name seems most probable. I myself am inclined to the opinion that
the Crow who was paid the extraordinarily large sum of 20s. by the
Cappers for "the Goldenflecc" which was part of their "solteltys on
Candelmase daye" [2 February] in 1525 was the father, and that he was
as well the author of the surviving Coventry pageants, revised in 1534.[35]
As Ingram remarks in discussing the extravaganza produced by the
Cappers on the occasion when one of their members, Nicholas Heynes,
assumed his duties as newly elected mayor on 2 February 1520, "The
Cappers, seemingly, celebrated this, and apt enough symbolism in their
subject of the Golden Fleece could be found for the occasion."[36] An
additional payment for players in the same accounts makes it virtually
certain that this Crow arranged some form of dramatic entertainment for
the triumph of his fellow guildsman.

Robert Crow's name does not reappear in the records of the Cappers.
All further occurrences of the name, too numerous to detail here, are
found in such other guild records as those of the Weavers or Drapers. Of
greatest importance for our current concern are the payments for the two
surviving pageants already referred to, in 1535, and an additional payment of again, 20s., made by the Drapers to a Robert Crow for "makyng
of the boke for the paggen."[37] The revision commissioned by the Drapers was extensive, increasing the annual payments substantially once the
revision had been made. A Robert Crowe also may have revised the
Smith's pageant in 1563, for at that time he was paid 8d. "for 2 leaves."
However, as the standard fee for an author seems to have been 5s., this is
more probably a payment for copying a part or parts. Because there is so
much evidence of Crow's other dramatic activity in the 1550s and 1560s,
and because there is a full twenty-year gap between the writing of the two
surviving pageants and the later revisions, it seems safest to assume that
the Elizabethan Crow was seeking to emulate his no-doubt illustrious
father at a time when major changes in the cycle were required to please
the new Protestant hierarchy.

Whether there were one or two men involved, however, the most important point to note is that a member or members of the mercantile class in sixteenth-century Coventry can be documented as the writer of dramatic texts on several different occasions. Hardin Craig, the editor of *Two Coventry Corpus Christi Plays,* scatters disparaging remarks about Crow's abilities as an author through his notes to the plays, but Ingram, who has had some experience producing medieval plays for modern audiences, states dryly that "Crow's abilities are proved by the natural-ness of the play as a stage-piece."[39] Where would a layman have obtained the education necessary to write such a play? The answer, of course, is at the local grammar school. In his thorough survey, *English Schools in the Middle Ages,* Nicholas Orme notes that "at Coventry the corporation took the initiative in inviting a schoolmaster to the city in 1425, and in 1439 they sent the mayor and six of the council to remonstrate with the prior of the cathedral against imposing a monopoly of education in the city, urging the right of any citizen to put his child in school where he pleased."[40] Orme's "List of Medieval English Schools, 1066–1530" demonstrates persuasively his contention that during the fifteenth cen-tury in every major English city it was possible for laymen to obtain a good basic education in a grammar school whether or not they intended to proceed to religious orders.[41]

But clergy would also have been involved in the writing of such plays. We have no author's name, nor any direct evidence of clerical involve-ment, as we have in the case of the Crow family, but there is the indirect evidence of extensive learning behind all of the major dramatic texts. One scrap of sixteenth-century evidence suggests who the clerical writers might be, however. During the early sixteenth century the citizens of Lincoln, apparently as a consequence of increasingly difficult economic times, gradually abandoned their practice of performing a cycle of reli-gious plays at the feast of Corpus Christi. The old city-wide guild of Corpus Christi continued to exist into the sixteenth century, for there is one single act in the town records dated 21 March 1530, calling on all citizens to contribute "to yᵉ bryngyng Fourthe of Corpus Christi gild and nott to deny the payment that they shalbe Sessed."[42] However, this seems to have been an act of futility. The real energy of the Council went to ensuring that someone ran the St. Anne's day procession and pageants. Beginning in 1515, and continuing for several years thereafter, the Com-mon Council passed a series of acts designed to guarantee the continued survival of at least one of the old religious dramatic festivals developed in Lincoln during the fifteenth century.

A brief review of the significant events will suggest both how the Common Council's purposes were accomplished, and how this activity may throw light on the role of clergy in the creation and management of the civic religious drama of medieval England.[43] The story opens on 27 July 1515, the day after St. Anne's day. That year the celebration must have been so mismanaged that the council decided to step in to manage affairs itself. Three of the members of council held a conference with a Mr. Dighton, the subject being two proposals for the endowment of the position of chaplain to the guild of St. Anne. Dighton had proposed that the guild chaplain be located in the church of St. Michael on the Mount (the old church of the Corpus Christi guild, now, as noted, apparently largely defunct), whereas a Mr. Chambers had offered to endow the same chaplaincy in the church of St. Mark's. The guild of St. Anne did have a chantry of its own, in the parish church of St. Andrew. Both St. Andrew's and St. Mark's were in the suburb of Wigtoft, whereas St. Michael's on the Mount is located immediately outside the Exchequer Gate, the main, western entry to the cathedral close. To have the St. Anne's priest located within the city, near the cathedral, was certainly desirable, and those who visited Dighton worked out an agreement with him as follows. In return either for agreeing to endow the chaplaincy with forty pounds "in redy money orels to gyf to yᵉ Seyd gyld iiij Markes yerly rent for euer," Dighton was granted the right to name the priest, who was "to Syng in yᵉ Churche of Scaynt Mychell vppon yᵉ hyll for hym & hys Fadur Moder and other wᵗ All the brether & Systers of Scaynt Anne Gyld." What the priest was to sing, of course, was masses for the souls of the departed. Dighton was following a common medieval practice, providing spiritual insurance through endowing a chaplain to sing masses for himself and his family, thereby ensuring that their days in Purgatory would be less.

But that was not all that the St. Anne's priest was to do. The council's aim in agreeing to the endowment was to obtain a producer for the annual performance and plays. Dighton apparently made his deed of gift, after a bit of pressure, sometime in late 1516 or early 1517, for on 10 June 1517 the Common Council agreed that

> Sir Robert Denyas Schalbe Sent Anne preste & he to haue to yᵉ ӡerly Sawde [i.e., income] of the same vˡⁱ And to begynne & entre in to the Same at Michelmes next Comyng & he to haue it for terme of hys lyfe of a gud and lawfull beryng vnder the Comyn Seale And he promysyth in this presentes ӡerly to helppe to yᵉ Bryngyng Foorth & preparyng of the pageantes in Scaynt Anne gyld.

Denyas at the same meeting of council paid a mark for the use of the Common Seal, suggesting that he got right to work. His appointment was reaffirmed on 22 September 1517, once St. Anne's Day had passed, with the additional provision that he was to sing mass for the souls of the brothers and sisters and benefactors of the guild of St. Anne. Dighton had what he wanted, and so did those running the affairs of Lincoln. Incidentally, the council also stipulated that the graceman of St. Anne's guild was to be the retiring mayor of the city. Since the act of 22 September stipulated that the St. Anne's priest was to receive his stipend from the graceman of the guild, it is clear that the council regarded the priest as working, in part, directly for them.

The choice of the St. Anne's priest to produce the procession and pageants made excellent sense. Chantry priests were not just found at St. Paul's London, as Langland sourly complains, but were located in every major settlement in England. By the sixteenth century the assets assigned for their support were so large that they became the target of Henry VIII's expropriators after they had absorbed the assets of the monasteries. When the chantries were dissolved in 1548, many local communities retained control of those assets, however, claiming that the chaplain was not only a priest singing mass for the souls of the departed, but a schoolmaster as well. And in many cases they were right. Orme notes that "most of the interest in education in the fifteenth century found expression in the . . . foundation of chantry schools," which their benefactors found "cheaper and more modest" than the founding of a college of secular priests.[44]

Virtually every major guild had its own chantry priest, for whether a guild was an association of tradesmen or a city-wide religious guild, such as the guild of Corpus Christi or St. Anne, one of the major purposes of the association was to provide for the burial of its members and for prayers for the souls of the departed on the anniversaries of their death. Guild charters all speak of annual meetings of the guild at which the members took part in a religious ceremony conducted by their own priest before taking part in the annual feast, a feast of the sort at which Robert Crow provided a pageant of the Golden Fleece as entertainment. One can visit the great fifteenth-century hall of the Merchant Adventurers today in York, where players rehearsed their parts in the climactic pageant of the Last Judgment, and see the guild chapel where the Mercers observed the feast days of the Annunciation and Assumption of the Blessed Virgin as well as the feast of the Holy Trinity, all celebrated by the chaplain of the leading guild in York. Is it not reasonable to assume that the men who played a major role in the religious life of the guilds, who were often the schoolmasters for the children of the members of the guild, would also have been the writers the same guildsmen turned to, as did the councillors at Lincoln, for help in writing, producing, and staging the civic religious plays of medieval England?

The plays produced by such writers, for such patrons, are an integral part of lay piety throughout late medieval England. To experience the plays at first hand, as one increasingly is able to do both in the British Isles and in North America, is to experience at first hand a religious life largely lost to English-speaking people after the Reformation. At one time scholars studying medieval drama, such as Chambers, Young, or Hardin Craig, saw the dynamic force within the plays as an attempt to move away from the control of the Church, to "secularize" the texts being created, and to introduce a strongly anticlerical spirit into material once liturgical, solemn, and dull. A.P. Rossiter saw clearly the parallels between the characters who mock and torture Christ in these plays, and the grotesque, leering faces we see in the paintings of Breughel and Bosch. For him, however, these faces were "an expression of the devilish as the inversion, reversal, and parody of the divine."[45] Rossiter was unable to see, no doubt because he was himself a tortured spirit haunted by the horrors of World War II, the deep reverence for the life and works of Christ that stands behind the foreground of lost souls we find peopling the medieval plays. Abiachar, Mary's uncle, stands helpless as her judge in the N-Town *Trial of Joseph and Mary* in a world where the laws of evidence are still primitive, and where only a miracle can save her from the spite of her accusers. But before the play is over, every doubt we ourselves may have had about the truth of the Virgin Birth has been objectified in the responses of the different characters in this play. We are urged to acknowledge our lack of faith, and we too are forgiven as the play draws to its end, as are those who first doubted her word. As the N-Town Passion play opens, a Demon moves into the audience, wearing contemporary clothing of the very latest cut. He identifies his friends in the audience, and urges them to

Gyff me ʒour love, grawnt me by Affeccion
And I wyl vnclose þe tresour of lovys Alyawns
And gyff ʒow ʒoure desyrys afftere ʒoure intencion.[46]

He is followed by John the Baptist, whose task it is to remind that same audience of the straight and narrow path to eternal life. Watching the action that follows, the audience has no excuse to say, when the Day of Judgment follows, "I did not know. Nobody told me." Particularly in the figure of Judas we see the choice consciously made. Christ directly addresses him during the Last Supper, asking him if he really wants to take the bread from Christ's hand. "Judas, art þou Avysyd what þou xalt take?" he asks, and Judas replies "Lord, þi body I wyl not forsake."[47] He has made his choice, a choice that will lead him to the halter and eternal damnation before the play is over.

Some of the clerical figures are, to be sure, monsters. Annas and Caiaphas, in the Wakefield Master's *Coliphizacio,* can be taken as examples of Establishment figures abusing power to retain power. They are as frightening as the Turkish officer who tortures Lawrence in *Lawrence of Arabia,* or the "prince of darkness," Concannon, in *The Verdict.* But the actual physical violence is carried out by ordinary people, the soldiers who are supporting the status quo, blood brothers of Herod's minions who perpetrate the slaughter of the Innocents or the soldier-carpenters who nail Christ to the Cross. In a world where the ordinary citizen was told that he or she crucified Christ daily with his or her sins, identification with the evil characters on stage must have occurred as often as did a sympathetic identification with the sorrows of Mary. The Wakefield Master took great pains to create Cain as a fifteenth-century yeoman of some means—one of the stingy, money-grubbing farmers of that time who got ahead by meanness and selfishness, who beat their servants and refused to grant that any of their good luck came from the grace of God. As V.A. Kolve amply demonstrated, the attempt to anchor the plays in medieval time and space serves admirably to objectify abstract didactic doctrines for a popular audience.[48]

The plays came into being in the first place to educate the general populace in the articles of the faith.[49] They are a part of the world of the *Lay Folks Mass Book,* the Northern Passion, South English Legendary, the world of the saints' lives and "the late medieval cult of Jesus."[50] Meg Twycross has recently explored in considerable detail the influence of the popular narrative lives of Christ, particularly Bonaventure's *Meditationes vitae Christi,* on the form taken by the English Passion plays.[51] To approach the plays as they were approached in their heyday one should probably reread the *Meditations* in Nicholas Love's translation. One should also visit the Victoria and Albert Museum to contemplate there the remarkable Hildburgh collection of fifteenth-century alabasters depicting scenes from the Passion of Christ, the Life of the Virgin, and the martyrdom of the saints. As the catalogue expresses it, "The alabaster carvings produced by the workshops of the Midlands constitute an essentially popular art form and illustrate how scenes from the New Testament and the Legends of the Saints were visualized by ordinary people in the fourteenth and fifteenth centuries."[52] One should walk the naves and aisles of the wool churches of East Anglia to absorb the look of the physical space in which the audiences worshipped when they were not attending the plays, visit the parish churches of Norwich, of King's

Lynn, or Lavenham to feel at first hand the world of the plays.[53]

For the plays, finally, are one of the most assuredly popular forms of literature to survive from the Middle Ages. We need not define them so merely because they include early examples of jests, such as the tale of the Fools of Gotham upon which the Wakefield Master built *The First Shepherds Play,* nor are they popular because we find in *Mankind* or *The Play of the Sacrament* tantalizingly oblique uses of folk-play elements as part of the stage action. They were popular because they were written to reach as wide an audience as possible, and in that they succeeded. No other art form surviving from that period reached more people in its day; no other can give us as clear a picture of popular literature in medieval England.

NOTES

1. The plays performed in Chester survive in seven full, or nearly full, copies, and one fragment. Only one, Peniarth 399, appears to have been written during the period when the plays were performed. Lumiansky and Mills date it "c. 1500 (?)," and suggest that it may have been a producer's copy. All other manuscripts were either copied for reading or for antiquarian purposes. For a complete discussion of the manuscripts, see *The Chester Mystery Cycle,* EETS, s.s. 3 (London: Oxford Univ. Press, 1974), ix–xxvii.

2. Because the term *morality play* is not a term in use in the medieval period to describe the plays performed by such companies of players, and also because the term *morality* carries with it too often the sense of dull, preachy allegorical plays, the term *moral interlude* is now preferred when referring to the plays performed by the traveling companies. For a discussion of the terminological problem, see Stanley J. Kahrl, *Traditions of Medieval English Drama* (London: Hutchinson, 1974), pp. 103–4.

3. *Sir Gawain and the Green Knight,* ed. J.R.R. Tolkien and E.V. Gordon, 2d ed., rev. Norman Davis (Oxford: Clarendon Press, 1967), p. 14, ll. 471–72: "Wel becommes such craft vpon Cristmasse, / Laykyng of enterludez, to laȝe and to syng"; *Collections XI,* Records of Plays and Players in Norfolk and Suffolk, 1330–1642, ed. David Galloway and John Wasson (Oxford: Malone Society, 1980–1981), p. 38.

4. Richard Axton, *European Drama of the Early Middle Ages* (London: Hutchinson, 1974), p. 19.

5. For the texts of these plays, see *The Macro Plays,* ed. Mark Eccles, EETS, 262 (London: Oxford Univ. Press, 1969).

6. For a full discussion of the relations between the English text of the play *Everyman,* and the Dutch play *Elkerlijc,* as well as the staging of the English

version, see *Everyman,* ed. A.C. Cawley (Manchester: Manchester Univ. Press, 1961), pp. ix–xiii, xxix–xxxi.

7. David Bevington, *From Mankind to Marlowe: Growth of Structure in the Popular Drama of Tudor England* (Cambridge: Harvard Univ. Press, 1962).

8. See especially Brody's chapter, "Performing the Action," in *The English Mummers and Their Plays* (Philadelphia: Univ. of Pennsylvania Press, 1969), pp. 14–32.

9. *Collections VIII,* Records of Plays and Players in Lincolnshire, 1300–1585, ed. Stanley J. Kahrl (Oxford: Malone Society, 1969 [1975]), p. 29.

10. Ibid., pp. 35–38.

11. Ibid., p. 47.

12. For an extensive list of towns and villages known to have produced religious plays in the British Isles in the medieval period, see Appendix W. "Representations of Medieval Plays," pp. 329–406 in E.K. Chambers, *The Medieval Stage,* vol. 2 (London: Oxford Univ. Press, 1903). Those wishing to gain a more complete sense of how English townspeople managed their plays in the fourteenth, fifteenth, and sixteenth centuries are particularly encouraged to consult the volumes published by the Toronto University Press for the Records of Early English Drama. The records of York, Chester, Coventry, and Newcastle are in print, those of Norwich are following, and a great many more are either in preparation or in pgrogress.

13. *Coventry,* ed. R. Ingram, Records of Early English Drama (Toronto: Toronto Univ. Press, 1981), p. 37. Hereafter referred to as REED.

14. Ibid., pp. 66, 67–68, 95, 107, 125, 243.

15. See *Collections XI,* pp. 48–52 for references to this play, and to performances of the Corpus Christi play. In this period a typical priestly stipend would be around five pounds per annum.

16. Ibid., p. 52 for the reference to the *gesine,* p. 49 for the performance in 1448.

17. *The Book of Margery Kempe,* ed. Sanford Brown Meech and Hope Emily Allen, EETS, 212 (London: Oxford Univ. Press, 1940), pp. 324n and 359. I am particularly indebted to Dr. Gail Gibson for calling my attention to this reference.

18. *Mankind,* l. 30, p. 155, in Eccles, ed., *Macro Plays.*

19. *Ludus Conventriae,* ed. K.S. Block, EETS, e.s. 120 (London: Oxford Univ. Press, 1922), ll. 5–9, p. 1.

20. *Castle of Perseverance,* ll. 6–9, p. 3, in Eccles, ed., *Macro Plays.*

21. See Kahrl, *Collections VIII,* pp. 70–74, for the entries relating to Long Sutton; p. xi for a map of the towns mentioned in the Long Sutton accounts.

22. See particularly J.W. Robinson, "The Art of the York Realist," *Modern Philology,* 60 (1962–63): 241–51, reprinted in *Medieval English Drama: Essays Critical and Contextual,* ed. Jerome Taylor and Alan H. Nelson (Chicago: Univ. of Chicago Press, 1972), pp. 230–44.

23. A.C. Cawley, in his edition of *The Wakefield Pageants in the Towneley Cycle*

(Manchester: Manchester Univ. Press, 1958), pp. xii–xiii, discusses the evidence for so describing the Towneley manuscript.

24. For a facsimile of a single page, with transcript, see C.E. Wright, *English Vernacular Hands from the Twelfth to the Fifteenth Centuries* (Oxford: Clarendon Press, 1960), pp. 22–23. For a full facsimile of the manuscript, see *The N-Town Plays: A Facsimile of British Library MS Cotton Vespasian D. viii,* with an introduction by Peter Meredith and Stanley J. Kahrl (Univ. of Leeds School of English: Scolar, 1977). This facsimile is the fourth in the Leeds Medieval Drama Series. Others include *The Chester Mystery Cycle, The Towneley Cycle,* and *The Digby Plays.*

25. For a more complete discussion of this point, see *N-Town Plays,* intro. Meredith and Kahrl, pp. xiii–xv.

26. For a discussion of the changes, see ibid., pp. xiv–xv and xxii–xxv.

27. For a complete description of the manuscript, see Norman Davis, ed. *Non-Cycle Plays and Fragments,* EETS, supp. text 1 (London: Oxford Univ. Press, 1970), pp. lviii–lxiii.

28. Ibid., p. lxi.

29. Rosemary Woolf, in *The English Mystery Plays* (Berkeley: Univ. of California Press, 1972) appendix A, pp. 327–35, discusses two other semidramatic pieces, the Shrewsbury Fragments and the Bodley plays of the Burial and Resurrection, which also seem to have been intended primarily for meditation.

30. For a concise, readable description of the contents of the four major cycle manuscripts, as well as a balanced discussion of the relations between the four texts, see Woolf, *English Mystery Plays,* chap. 13, "The Four Cycles," pp. 303–11.

31. For an extended discussion of the relations between these two cycles, see Hardin Craig, *English Religious Drama of the Middle Ages* (Oxford: Clarendon Press, 1955), pp. 199–238; also Woolf, *English Mystery Plays,* pp. 310–11. The texts cited are *The Towneley Plays,* ed. George England and Alfred W. Pollard, EETS, e.s. 71 (London: Oxford Univ. Press, 1897), p. 65; and *The York Plays,* ed. Lucy Toulmin Smith (Oxford: Clarendon Press, 1885), pp. 69–70.

32. Davis, *Non-Cycle Plays,* pp. xiv–xxii, includes a full discussion of the textual taditions of which this fragment is a part.

33. Smith, *York,* p. 122; Davis, *Non-Cycle Plays,* p. 2.

34. R.W. Ingram, "To Find the Players and All That Longeth Therto: Notes on the Production of Medieval Drama in Coventry," in *The Elizabethan Theatre,* vol. 5, G.R. Hibbard (Hamden, Conn.: Archon, 1975), pp. 17–44. The discussion of Crow's activities occurs on pp. 25–29. The various entries referred to in the article have since been published as part of REED, *Coventry.*

35. REED, *Coventry,* p. 123, lists the Candlemas payments.

36. Ingram, "To Find the Players," p. 26.

37. Ingram (ibid., p. 27) lists this payment as being made in 1557. However, in REED *Coventry,* this entry does not appear under 1557, but instead in a list entitled "Undated Drapers' Accounts," appendix 2, among the payments written on f. 38 dated 1568. The discrepancy is not really explained in the introduction to Ingram's appendix. 1557 must be the date given the entry by Sharp, but it is no longer a date that Ingram, the editor of the records, feels comfortable with.

38. Ingram, "To Find the Players," p. 27; REED, *Coventry*, p. 225.

39. REED, *Convetry*, p. lxii, n. 11.

40. Nicholas Orme, *English Schools in the Middle Ages* (London: Methuen, 1973), p. 204.

41. The list appears in ibid., on pp. 293–325. Also extremely valuable is chap. 7, "The Schools from 1400–1530," pp. 194–223.

42. Kahrl, *Collections VIII*, p. 55.

43. For a more complete discussion of these events, see Kahrl, *Collections VIII*, pp. xviii–xxi. The relevant entries appear on pp. 42–50.

44. Orme, *English Schools in the Middle Ages*, p. 195.

45. A.P. Rossiter, *English Drama from Early Times to the Elizabethans* (London: Hutchinson, 1950), p. 71.

46. *Ludus Coventriae*, ed. Block, ll. 61–63, p. 227.

47. Ibid, II 773–74, p. 257.

48. *The Play Called Corpus Christi* (Stanford: Stanford Univ. Press, 1966), ch. 5, pp. 101–23.

49. See, in this regard, A.C. Cawley, "Medieval Drama and Didacticism," in *The Drama of Medieval Europe: Proceedings of the Colloquium Held at the University of Leeds, 10–13 September 1974* (Leeds: Graduate Center of the University, 1975), pp. 3–12, and the discussion following, pp. 13–21.

50. Robinson, "Art of the York Realist."

51. Meg Twycross, "Books for the Unlearned," in James Redmond, *Themes in Drama* (Cambridge: Cambridge Univ. Press, forthcoming).

52. Terence Hodkinson, *English Medieval Alabasters* (London: Her Majesty's Stationery Office, 1976), [p. 2].

53. For a model study using such material, see Gail McMurray Gibson, "Bury St. Emunds, Lydgate, and the *N-Town Cycle*," *Speculum* 56 (1981): 56–90. Similar studies defining the connections between the plays performed in Norfolk, Suffolk, and Essex are being undertaken by such scholars as Donald Baker, John Coldewey, and Richard Beadle. As the work of the Records of Early English Drama becomes more widely known, it is hoped that many more scholars will be attracted to this field of study.

Romance

Edmund Reiss

$\mathcal{A}$lthough the romance has been
seen as the major secular genre from the time of Chrétien de Troyes in the
late twelfth century to at least that of Sir Thomas Malory three hundred
years later, the English romances represent, paradoxically, the body of
literature most puzzling to medievalists. For all the work done on them,
Lillian Hornstein's 1971 list of what we do not know is still pertinent.
Lacking an exact methodology for defining, delimiting, and differentiat-
ing them, we are not sure of their number, authors, dates of composition,
audiences, or methods of publication, much less their literary traditions,
principles, and techniques: "Although the romances have never been
considered difficult to understand, no one has been able to tell us exactly
what they are."[1] Even though the "abyss of ignorance" gaping before us
may not be so deep as it was when Hornstein wrote, in 1980 Derek
Pearsall is still puzzled as to "how a form so apparently amorphous and so
resistant to definition can create so powerful an impression of
homogeneity," and "why poems that are so bad according to almost
every criterion of literary value should have held such a central position in
the literary culture of their own period."[2]

Inasmuch as the 115 extant works traditionally classified as Middle
English romances range from "armor-plated fairy tales to multi-volume
histories," our first impression of this body of literature is not unex-
pectedly one of chaos.[3] And in the search to find order here, scholars have
attempted various systems of classification: according to the "legends"
they reflect; the subjects and themes they express; the folk motifs, archetypal patterns, and narrative structures they reveal; even their verse
forms, lengths, and literary merit.[4] Moreover, the romances have been
compared and contrasted with other narrative forms, such as epic and
chanson de geste, exemplum and saint's life, chronicle, folk tale, and ballad,

as well as with what were termed in medieval England *storie, spelle, geste,* and *tragedie.*[5] Rewarding as some of these studies have been, we may well have done all we can with such distinctions; and rather than continue to insist on clear-cut and rigid systems of differentiation, we might better note how the romance tends to encompass and synthesize otherwise discrete forms.[6]

In fact, differentiation may even be foreign to the medieval understanding of romance, for when the term meant something other than "the French book," it apparently could be applied to virtually every kind of narrative, including works which were essentially allegorical (the *Romance of the Rose*), historical (Barbour's *Bruce*), monitory (the *Mirror of Lewed Men*), and devotional *(Meditations on the Life and Passion of Christ).*[7] But for all the sense medieval authors and audiences may have had of what a romance is, this has not carried over to modern times. As "one of the most comprehensive of literary forms," romance in medieval England has been said to refer to anything we might today call "a good story," and has been seen having "no homogeneous essence which would make possible a brief and valid description of the genre."[8] Thus, some critics have sought to replace the term, have preferred to talk about romance as a mode instead of a genre, or, seeking a meaningful definition, have rejected at least half of the commonly designated Middle English romances as "not romances in any meaningful sense."[9]

We should realize that some romances are epic and historical (the Alliterative *Morte Arthure, King Alexander,* the *Destruction of Troy,* the *Siege of Jerusalem*), others are exemplary *(Amis and Amiloun, King Robert of Sicily),* and still others are saints' lives (the Eustace-Constance group), folk tales, and ballads *(Sir Cleges, The Marriage of Sir Gawain).* Rather than seek to remove these from the canon of romances, we should instead recognize that romance is a purposeful mix of these and other forms. Combining otherwise separate forms, the romance is at once heroic, historical, erotic, and religious. And as such the Middle English romance is similar to both that composed on the continent in the twelfth century and that produced in late antiquity.

Although they are often scorned either as a poor relation of their more elegant continental cousins or dismissed as a later curiosity having little in common with the great French and German romances, the English romances, though perhaps more "popular" than their continental forebears, may be meaningfully grouped with them.[10] Just as Chaucer and the *Gawain*-Poet are hardly representative of the fourteenth-century English accomplishment, so Chrétien de Troyes and Marie de France, Gottfried von Strassburg and Wolfram von Eschenbach are not typical of the twelfth-century romance. While recognizing the important role of the romance in the renaissance of the twelfth century, we should also see that the later English romances reveal a range of subject matter and a diversity of metrical forms unequaled in any early body of romances. And although the heroes of a few English works may be less than noble— Gamelyn, Rauf Coilyear—and the works themselves may include various minstrel tags, we should not conclude that they were produced by wandering minstrels in village taverns and market places for an audience limited to uneducated burghers and peasants.[11]

The homely nature of much English romance has made it seem necessary to distinguish the "popular" from the "courtly," and the dominant English "romance of adventure" from the French "society romance" and "ancestral romance."[12] Still, virtually all of the extant English romances are about knights and ladies. Beggars are knights in disguise (Horn), kitchen boys are Fair Unknowns destined to take their proper place in society (Havelok), and the smith's apprentice turns out to be a knight undergoing penance (Isumbras). Moreover, the definitions of this romance, notwithstanding their number and their differences in emphasis and form, suggest "by almost common consent" that it concerns aristocratic figures and involves love.[13] For all of our uncertainties about the Middle English romance, we also seem to have "a fairly tidy sense" of it as "a narrative poem dealing with the adventures of a chivalric hero."[14]

At the same time, the heroes of romance, like those of late medieval biblical drama, represented familiar figures drawn from traditional material. The heroes of romance were the well-known figures of antiquity (Alexander, the heroes of Troy) and of the idealized near-past (Arthur, Charlemagne), or they were heroes modeled on these figures. Sometimes they were historical, like the crusaders Richard the Lion Hearted and Godfrey of Bouillon; sometimes they were the ancestors of great families, like Bevis of Hampton; and sometimes they were local heroes, like Havelok. But whether historical or manufactured from folk traditions and literary conventions, they were designed to appear both familiar and larger than life. Even when, as with Guy of Warwick, they gave the impression of being actual historical personages, the important thing was that they appealed to the romance audience.

Just as the audience of these romances did not consist of the common people alone, so it was not composed solely of courtiers. Even though some romances—certainly Chaucer's and probably the *Gawain*-Poet's— were doubtless created for court audiences, these would have included a range of listeners from gentry to servants. A successful romance would have had to appeal to many different kinds of people, including both "the learned and the lewed." While the literature which was popular with such an audience may well have been that which demanded "the minimum of previous verbal experience and special education" from its members,[15] we should not assume that it necessarily had to be inferior, any more than "elite" literature had to be superior. It might be the product of conventions without being conventional in the pejorative sense of the word, or seem familiar without being a copy. In fact, the romance would seem to build on the expectations derived from the traditions and conventions its audience already was aware of.

At the court of Richard II, for instance, the audience was most likely familiar with the tale of Constance and with the tale of the Knight and the Loathly Lady before Chaucer told his tales of the Man of Law and Wife of Bath. Although the Knight's Tale (from Boccaccio) was doubtless new to this audience, the traditional legend of Theseus (already included by Chaucer in his *Legend of Good Women)* and the conventions of courtly love were certainly familiar enough for its members to see how Chaucer manipulated romance material here in combining it with Boethian philosophy. Similarly, this audience could see how in the "original" Squire's Tale, Chaucer was purposely mishandling the machinery of tale-telling. Sir Thopas is certainly not Chaucer's only ironic use of romance material, and one might even make the case that in all of his romances Chaucer intentionally refers back to traditions and conventions which he then garbles.[16]

What we should realize in reading Chaucer's recasting of romance is that he often relies on his audience's familiarity with the material he presents, not only the conventional formulaic tags that fill Sir Thopas, but the episodes themselves, and certainly the subjects of the romances, such as those he alludes to in passing:

> Men speken of romances of prys,
> Of Horn child and of Ypotys,
> > Of Beves and sir Gy,
> Of sir Lybeux and Pleyndamour.[17]

There was obviously no need for Chaucer to identify these figures or remind his audience of their stories. And even though Chaucer himself may have been influenced in his list by the contents of the famous Auchinleck manuscript, he knew he could count on his audience's knowing or at least making sense of these figures.[18] In fact, Horn, Bevis of Hampton, Guy of Warwick, and Libeaus Desconus (or the Fair Unknown) are four of the most popular subjects of the English romance. And although Ypotys and Pleyndamour have never been identified as the names of actual romance heroes, recognition was probably not a problem for Chaucer's audience. Without going into the matter in detail here, we may note that Ypotys may well be a variant form of *hippotes,* the Greek word for knight, and exists, even in fourteenth-century England, as a generic term for knight, as it does in the version of the Prose *Tristan* called *Ho Presbys Hippotes* [The Old Knight]. Similarly, Pleyndamour, another figure in the Prose *Tristan,* may be an allegorical expression for the knight as man "full of love," the trait that distinguishes the heroes of romance from those of epic. The list in Sir Thopas, containing names of actual heroes and generic and allegorical names, could be effective only if Chaucer's courtly audience was already familiar with both the popular heroes and the conventions of romance.

Since allusion would seem to be a possible way of measuring popularity, we might look at the other lists of romance heroes found in Middle English literature to get a sense of the romances that were popular. The early romance *Richard Coer de Lyon* (ca. 1300) includes, along with the well-known heroes of antiquity and the cycles associated with Arthur and Charlemagne, such figures as Bevis, Guy, Octavian, Partonope, and Ipomedon. One hundred years later, in another list in the Laud *Troy-Book* (ca. 1400), we find, again along with the classical, Arthurian, and Carolingian figures, Bevis, Guy, and Octavian, and now Havelok, Horn, and Richard. Two other lists of heroes, from fourteenth-century works that are not romances, offer further additions to our collection of popular romances. At the beginning of the biblical *Cursor mundi,* where the author distinguishes his work from romances (and offers the earliest instance of the term *romance* in English), he cites, along with figures from the Arthur and Charlemagne narratives, Isumbras and Amadace; and in the *Parliament of the Three Ages* a comparable list includes Amadace, Ipomedon, Generides, and Eglamour of Artois.[19]

Regardless of the prosodic requirements and the place of the formulaic in these lists, it would seem that the heroes they cite may be regarded as common property of authors and audiences alike throughout at least the fourteenth century. And even though several of the figures are from romances little known or little valued by readers today, they were obviously significant to late medieval English audiences.

Another way of assessing popularity is to note the number of manuscripts of the extant romances. More than two dozen of these romances exist in three or more medieval manuscripts. With the exception of the classical *King Alexander* and *Seege of Troy,* and the biblical *Siege of Jerusalem* (also known as *Titus and Vespasian),* these popular romances concern medieval heroes. A few are Arthurian—*Arthour and Merlin,* the

Awntyrs of Arthur, and *Libeaus Desconus*—but the great bulk are noncyclical: *King Horn, Bevis of Hampton, Guy of Warwick, Gamelyn, Richard Coer de Lyon, Sir Isumbras, Sir Eglamour of Artois, Octavian,* the *King of Tars, Sir Triamour, Sir Degaré,* the *Earl of Toulouse, Floris and Blancheflur, Amis and Amiloun, Sir Orfeo, King Robert of Sicily, Generides, Partonope of Blois,* and *Ipomedon.* Given the fact that about fifty—or almost half—of the extant Middle English romances have come down to us in only one manuscript, it is remarkable to find ten medieval manuscripts of *Robert of Sicily;* nine of *Isumbras;* seven of *Bevis* and *Richard;* six of *Libeaus, Eglamour, Degaré,* and *Partonope;* and five of *Guy.*[20]

Reinforcing the manuscript evidence of popularity is the frequency of early printings. Although William Caxton neglected the English verse romances, his successors, Wynkyn de Worde, Richard Pynson, and William Copland, published in the late fifteenth and early sixteenth centuries slightly modernized verse versions of *Bevis, Guy, Richard, Isumbras, Eglamour, Triamour, Degaré,* and *Generides,* as well as a prose version of *Ipomedon.*[21]

Although few of these romances would be on any modern reader's list of the best medieval English romances, on the basis of their popularity between the fourteenth and sixteenth centuries they cannot be merely ignored or dismissed out of hand. To reject *Isumbras* as simply "bad," as having "a tone of flat mediocrity," or *Degaré* and *Libeaus* as "unremarkable even in their failures," or *Robert of Sicily* as "crude, sprawling and morally unimpressive," or the *King of Tars* as "thoroughly pedestrian," is hardly to deal with their significance as popular and representative romances.[22] Even though many of these romances may not be in accord with modern tastes, they indicate the nature and the accomplishment of the form more than do such works as *Sir Gawain and the Green Knight* and the alliterative *Morte Arthure,* which exist in only one manuscript. These works are unique, like *Don Quixote, Tristram Shandy, Moby Dick,* and Joyce's *Ulysses;* for all of their merits they hardly typify the achievement of the narrative literature of their times.

Interestingly, earlier versions in French are extant for about a dozen of these popular romances, including *Horn, Bevis, Guy,* and *Libeaus* (cited by Chaucer), as well as *Octavian, Isumbras, Floris, Amis,* and *Ipomedon.* Although it has been thought that the English romances were intended for an audience which did not know French,[23] some of these romances were most likely designed to appeal to listeners familiar not only with French romance in general but with the French originals of the English romances they were hearing. At the same time, it should be noted that multiple versions in English exist of several romances, including *Bevis,*

Guy, Arthour and Merlin, the *Seege of Troy, Octavian, Generides, Partonope,* and *Ipomedon.* And the variant versions of others are sufficiently distinct to be classified as separate poems. These include four versions of the Horn story and the Launfal story, three versions of the *Siege of Jerusalem,* two romances about Gawain and the Carl of Carlisle, and two about Gawain and Dame Ragnell.[24] These different versions not only offer further proof of the popularity of certain romances, but they also indicate that the authors of romance may have been concerned with playing their individual treatment against a standard or familiar version of a story which, no matter whether it was in French or in English, they could count on their audience to know.

To say this is to suggest that popular as these romances are, they should be regarded as literary creations produced not by wandering minstrels but by professional authors sitting at desks, as it were. And indeed, for all their indications of oral performance, the romances also reveal a concern with the poem as written composition. At the beginning of *Sir Gawain and the Green Knight,* for instance, the poet writes that if his audience will listen to his "laye," he will tell it as he heard it: "As hit is stad and stoken / In stori stif and stronge, / With lel letteres loken, / In londe so hatz been longe."[25] That is, he will reflect its existence as it is set down and fixed ("stad and stoken") in history, as it is fastened together as a written work ("with lel letteres loken"), and as it has remained for a long while. This passage refers less to the way the narrative will be told than to the nature of that which is being told. It is, on the one hand, something oral and auditory and thereby ephemeral, and, on the other hand, something tangible, even monumental. Similarly in the prologue to the *Destruction of Troy* the poet laments the old worthy stories which have passed out of mind. In telling of Troy, he is not only writing of the past but revealing it "by lokyng of letturs þat lefte were of olde."[26] It would seem that both of these romances are to be regarded simultaneously as something to be listened to for a little while and something permanent and authoritative. And as such they may indicate the way we should view romance in general.

Without denying the existence of what Northrop Frye (adapting Schiller) has termed "naive romance," that is, folk tales and *Märchen,*[27] we should recognize that most if not all of the romances which have come down to us from the Middle Ages are self-conscious literary productions. Regardless of how these pieces—or rather their progenitors—may have been in an oral state, in manuscript they reveal more erudition and craftsmanship than the modern reader, misled by a superficial under-standing of Sir Thopas, is prepared to find. For all of their conventional

oral formulas, they are designed to do more than simply pander to the
fantasies of their audience.[28] While offering more "pleasing entertainment" than most complaints, sermons, catechisms, and monitory pieces,
these romances are basically didactic. Virtually all of them in effect "urge
religious behavior, the availability of redemption, the necessity for repentance, and the bliss of eternity."[29]

The didactic or religious element is more than a matter of including
such verbal tags as "so Crist me blesse," or swearing by saints, or beginning and ending with a prayer—"Jesus, þat is of heuene king,/ʒeue vs
alle His suete blessing"—or having characters take religious orders. In
King Horn, when Godhild leaves court to become a religious recluse, her
holiness is given particular significance because of the pagans' prohibi-
tion of Christianity: "Þer heo seruede Gode /Aʒenes þe paynes forbode /
Þer he seruede Criste / Þat no payn hit ne wiste." Her action thus
reinforces the Christian dimension of this romance, in which the hero
not only regains his kingdom and revenges himself on those who have
persecuted him and killed his father, but also works to do God's will. At
the beginning of the romance, when the Saracens meet King Murray,
they tell him of their intention to kill all Christians: "Þi lond folk we
schulle slon, / And alle þat Crist luueþ vpon." When the boy Horn kills
the Saracen pirates, and later a Saracen giant, he is doing God's work. In
each instance his action is more than one of personal revenge: it is to
defeat the enemies of God.[30]

Such details are hardly limited to the Horn story. In fact, they fill the
most popular romances and make clear their religious dimension. *Bevis,
Guy, Isumbras, Eglamour, Octavian, Triamour, Libeaus,* and *Richard,* for
instance, all show the hero fighting Saracens, giants, or dragons.
Moreover, conversion is important not only in the Charlemagne romances but also in *Isumbras,* where at the end an angel leads the hero, his
wife, and their three sons in killing more than thirty thousand pagans
who have refused conversion; in *Bevis,* where the hero agrees to marry a
Saracen girl if she will become a Christian; and in the *King of Tars,* where
the happy ending is the result of conversion. Similarly, miracles fill the
romances. They are not only the basis for the ending of the *King of Tars,*
but also the impetus to action in *Richard,* and the solution in *Amis and
Amiloun* and *Robert of Sicily.*

Rather than seek to differentiate the romance from the exemplum or
the saint's life by saying, for instance, that didacticism is not overt in
romance or not its primary intention, we might more accurately note that
the didactic and the religious are the warp and woof of romance, and in
fact had been from the beginnings of the genre in late antiquity. Such

Hellenistic Greek works as the *Ethiopica* of Heliodorus and the *Ephesian Tale* of Xenophon, as well as the Latin *Golden Ass* of Apuleius, are finally and essentially *apologiae* for the cults of Artemis-Isis. In like manner, romance and religion are inextricably joined in the Old Testament Book of Tobit—included by Jerome in his Vulgate—and in such New Testament apocrypha as the Acts of Paul and Thecla, the Acts of Andrew, and the Acts of Thomas, as well as the *Recognitions* attributed to the early Church Father, Clement.[31] In the Middle Ages religious teachings continue to be part of the actual fabric of romance, and not just in such obvious instances as the narratives of the Holy Grail or the works that make up the Eustace-Constance group.

Moreover, writers of religious and secular compositions were frequently one and the same. Not only did such courtly *romanciers* of the twelfth century as Wace and Marie de France write saints' lives and visions of the other world, but an eleventh-century German monk wrote the Latin romance *Ruodlieb;* the fourteenth-century author of the overtly didactic *Pearl, Purity,* and *Patience* also (most likely) composed *Sir Gawain and the Green Knight;* and the fifteenth-century monk John Lydgate wrote a *Troy-Book,* a *Siege of Thebes,* and a version of *Guy of Warwick.*[32]

The mixing, if not the amalgamation, of romance and religious material may also be seen in the various medieval manuscript collections. For instance, in the Auchinleck manuscript (ca. 1340), representing one of the earliest and largest compilations of Middle English verse, eighteen romances are joined by eight saints' lives, two pious tales, and one visit to the other world, as well as a dozen or so other pieces, most of which are nonnarrative and overtly didactic.[33] Although it might be argued that the romances here provide an *entrée* to the religious works, or a *relève* from them, it may be more accurate to say that they represent variant or oblique expressions of the sentiments presented directly and explicitly in the religious writings. In some cases the manuscripts themselves may be other than mere anthologies. Some may represent compilations of writings purposely chosen and organized in accord with a specific artistic and thematic intention. Comparable to a work like the *Canterbury Tales,* these compilations may mix genres and modes, or like the Winchester manuscript of Malory's Arthur-saga and the Harley manuscript of Marie's *lais,* they may offer separate works that are actually parts of a larger work. One may be most tempted to make a case for the unity of the collection found in Cotton Nero A x, the writings of the *Gawain*-Poet. For all their differences, the allegorical dream vision *Pearl,* the homilies *Purity* and *Patience,* and the romance *Sir Gawain and the Green Knight* would seem to be unified in terms of artistic method and theme; and as the last of the four works, *Gawain* not only occupies a key place in the manuscript, but it needs to be assessed in the context provided by the overtly religious pieces.

The romance may very well be "secular scripture," as Frye calls it, in the sense that its hero is man, not God, and that its myth is displaced "in a human direction."[34] But medieval romance—which, Frye admits, presents "different structural problems" from the works he prefers to take up—may be more meaningfully viewed as "the secular counterpart to the piety of Cîteaux. Of both, love is the theme."[35] Love certainly fills the medieval romance, and perhaps even more than chivalric adventures is its proper subject and even its essence. The standard plot of Greek romance—a pair of lovers separated from each other and traveling about the world in adversity until they are finally and happily reunited—is likewise a standard plot of English romance.[36] Although the "courtly" love celebrated by most romances is hardly Christian charity, this love between the sexes may call up the Christian ideal. In the twelfth century, the love between Tristan and Iseut may be an expression of the ideal love found in the biblical account of the friendship between David and Jonathan. And Chrétien's account of Lancelot's ineffectual attempt to rescue Guenevere may, for all the comedy, provide a parallel to Christ's love for mankind.

Love is also the main distinguishing factor between the hero of epic and the hero of romance, who is more (or other) than the man of arms, or warrior. He is essentially the man of love, but at the same time it is incumbent on him to love wisely and well: love must be a virtue in him and not a vice. From as early as the twelfth century the problem of the hero of romance was to learn to be simultaneously the man of love and the warrior. This was the dilemma of Chrétien's Erec, who, when he married, left off doing chivalric deeds; and it was the problem of his Yvain, who stayed in the world of chivalric adventure and forgot his love. It is also an essential ingredient in the Middle English romances.

The happiness offered by romances would seem to be of this world, and, indeed, the hero's regaining what he has lost and being reunited with his love is a standard feature of the most popular English romances. Still, more important than the happy ending itself is the struggle of the hero before this ending comes about. While the happy ending insures the comic nature of romance, the comedy is actually of a Dantesque sort, in that the hero generally has to go through a purgatory of loneliness and pain before he is able to reach happiness.[37] Sometimes, as in the case of *Isumbras* and *Robert of Sicily*, where the hero is humbled by God because of his pride, his repentance and struggle for redemption are clearly positive acts being cited for the edification of the audience. But in other works where the hero is exiled and humiliated, and made to atone for his sins for many years and in various ways, the suffering may seem undeserved and his journey back not so clearly an exemplum. But in both kinds of romances the adventures are far different from those that show the knight riding out and conquering whatever foe he meets. Rather than be an expression of his prowess, the journey of the outcast is more properly regarded as a pilgrimage, a testing and re-forming of the inner man. It is like the quest of the Holy Grail, which, as the knights who search for the Grail come to realize, is no ordinary quest. Just as one achieves the Grail not by feats of arms but by a demonstration of inner worth, so one achieves what one has lost through being re-formed. What begins as a journey of atonement becomes the vehicle for effecting the transformation and, indeed, the rebirth of the hero. Whereas it is necessary for the hero to demonstrate fortitude and perseverance, on his pilgrimage he is often in the hands of forces beyond his understanding, much less his control.

Sometimes the testing of the hero is marked by his being disguised as a pilgrim (Horn, Bevis), while at other times he becomes an actual pilgrim. Isumbras, after losing all of his wealth, bears a cross on his shoulders and goes "to seke God wher he was quykke and dede." When tempted, he refuses to renounce his religion or give up his wife. These, however, are merely preliminary tests and, even after losing his wife and children, Isumbras does not despair. Instead he prays to God for direction: "For all amysse have I gone." His exile and humiliation continue, and after seven years as an apprentice to a blacksmith, he is able through God's grace to defeat a heathen king. Isumbras rejects the honors offered him, and then for seven more years he becomes a pilgrim in the Holy Land. After an angel tells him that God has forgiven him, he continues to do God's work, even after regaining his rank, wife, and children.[38]

The alienation of the hero is more permanent in the second part of *Guy of Warwick*, which begins with the hero's awareness and acknowledgment of his sin of pride. Although God has given him great honors, Guy realizes that he has done nothing for God but instead has wrought war and woe. To atone for his sins, he intends to become a pilgrim: "To bote min sinnes ichil wende / Barfot to mi liües ende." He plans to leave his wife and home and journey to the Holy Land. It is as a poor pilgrim that he henceforth fights God's enemies, but he continues to renounce earthly honors and remains a religious recluse until at his death he joins his wife for a brief moment.[39]

Such humbling and perseverance as Isumbras's and Guy's may be seen as the basis for the pilgrimages of other romances. Horn, though bereft of everything and in exile, acts in accord with God's will and fights the pagans, restores churches, and brings back Christian worship. Finally, he is guided by prophetic dreams in the task of regaining his lands and his love. Through his adversity and acts of atonement, Horn has apparently been re-formed, and at the end he and his lady live and love properly. As the Harley version puts it, "in trewe loue hue lyueden ay, / ant wel hue loueden godes lay."[40] In like manner, Launfal, after being poor and desolate, finally finds happiness through his otherworldly love. And even Gamelyn, before he can take his proper place as lord, must be an outcast in the greenwood where, as the proper exponent of "Seynte Charité," he punishes the corrupt clergy.[41] Orfeo and Partonope of Blois, after losing their loves and wandering mad and like beasts in the woods, are finally able to regain what they have lost. For at least these two heroes, the loss of love is equivalent to the loss of self.

The search for identity, the attempt to find one's self, may be what romance is actually most about in its various accounts of adventure and of the reunion of lovers. Many of the heroes, not only Libeaus Desconus, are Fair Unknowns seeking recognition; and their several disguises, as in *Horn, Bevis, Guy,* and *Orfeo,* function primarily as vehicles for discovery. Moreover, it seems beyond coincidence that so many of the heroes of romance are children. In fact, all of the earliest Middle English romances—that is, those before 1300—are about children: *King Horn, Floris and Blauncheflur, Arthour and Merlin, Havelok, Sir Tristrem, Amis and Amiloun, Guy,* and *Bevis.*[42] Even though they may be described as "essentially stories about growing up to adulthood, both literally and symbolically,"[43] these and comparable romances are more than mere *Bildungsromanen,* concerned with the development of a character. Rather, they reveal the establishment of identity which may come about through finding one's other half, as in *Floris and Blauncheflur* and *Amis and Amiloun,* or through finding and reuniting one's parents, as in *Octavian, Triamour,* and *Degaré.* And the marriages that conclude so many romances *(Horn, Gamelyn, Floris, Eglamour, Generides)* are less a sign of growing up than evidence of fulfillment, as though through this sacrament in which human union is consecrated, man orders his passions and sets right his world.

This reaffirmation of order may be seen as the result of pilgrimage and, in effect, its justification. Although Guy of Warwick would prefer to leave the world forever—like the knight-hermits in Wolfram's *Parzival* and Galahad and Perceval in the *Queste del Saint Graal*—such action is not in accord with the nature of romance, which prefers a return to the world. And in the case of Guy, the return is suggested in the sequel, showing the adventures of his son, Reinbron. Typically, the hero makes his return from whatever depths he has been in and tests the world. This test is usually of his lady's fidelity *(Horn, Isumbras, Ipomedon)* though it may also be of his steward's loyalty *(Orfeo, Generides)*. By taking over his realm from the steward, who has been his surrogate, the hero shows that he has indeed found his identity. The private re-forming of the hero is finally given a public existence. So in *Robert of Sicily,* when given back his identity by the angel, the king feels he must make his story known to all.

In fact, it is the confrontation with the supernatural that serves as both the impetus to and the way of re-form. While at times taking the form of the overtly miraculous—as it does in *Richard Coer de Lyon* and the *King of Tars,* as well as *Amis* and *Robert*—the supernatural does not have to be explicitly Christian. Magic hunts set the tone for the adventures in *Generides* and *Partonope;* the underworld journey in *Orfeo* and the other-worldly love in *Launfal* offer a basis for the final happiness; and the breaking of the enchantment in *Libeaus* provides its climax.

Romance, to be sure, is a proper setting for the marvelous. As a realm between the everyday world and the other world, it partakes of both but is part of neither. It is like the never-never land of dream visions where virtually anything can happen, and where everything that does happen has a *significatio* demanding recognition. With its "charm'd magic casements, opening on the foam / Of perilous seas, in faery lands forlorn," medieval romance uses its shadows and mysteries to offer a bright world of possibility that, like the transformed light and sound of the churches, contrasts with the limitations and dullness of ordinary life. And like the romance of antiquity, which may have owed much to the pervasive Neoplatonism of the time,[44] medieval romance offers glimpses of the reality that is beyond actuality. Though making little distinction between visions and waking dreams, it insists on man's recognizing that these glimpses may assist him in his own pilgrimage, or journey of re-forming.

A work that shows dramatically the confrontation with the supernatu-ral—as well as the essential relationship between religion and romance—is the *Awntyrs of Arthur,* one of the earliest of the English Gawain romances. The work is in two parts. In the first, while Arthur and his court are hunting, the ghost of Guenevere's mother appears during a storm to the queen and Gawain. After offering the general lesson of how the mighty fall and how death comes to all, the ghost warns against pride and prophesies the downfall of Arthur and the Round Table. In the second part, while the court is dining, a lady brings in Sir Galeron, who challenges Arthur for taking his lands and giving them to Gawain. Gawain fights Galeron, and when he is about to defeat him, Galeron's lady asks Guenevere to stop the fight. She in turn has Arthur make the combatants put up their swords. The work ends happily with Galeron being given his lands and a place at the Round Table, and with Guenevere arranging for masses to be said for her mother.

The two parts of the *Awntyrs* are traditionally described as unrelated, even as two poems artifically joined together and as fragments of a larger work.[45] But although modern readers have had trouble understanding the structure of this poem, medieval scribes and audiences apparently did not, for the work exists in virtually the same form in four manuscripts. Instead of trying to separate the parts, we might do better to see how they work together. Not only are they of almost equal length, but at the end of the second part a stanza is included to reinforce the connection between them. Moreover, the ghost's words to Guenevere and Gawain provide a context for the action of part two. To the queen's query of the way to bliss, the ghost stresses the importance of the Works of Mercy— "Mekenesse and mercy, þes arn þe moost, / And haue pité on þe poer, þat pleses Heuenking"—and to Gawain's question about knights' seeking fame and wealth through prowess even in lands belonging to others, where they have no right to be, the ghost warns against covetousness.[46] It is the understanding of these words that is, in effect, tested in the second part, where Guenevere shows mercy, and Gawain and Arthur act to give justice. Moreover, the queen's act of having masses said to speed the release of the tormented spirit is a final act of charity. What is demonstrated is that the characters have learned from the vision given them and have passed their test. They have fled pride and the concern with temporalia, and even though their actions will not finally save Arthur's realm, their own future beyond this world has been helped by their actions on this day.

Moreover, through its tour de force of alliteration, the poem suggests a relationship between the hideous ghost of part one and the splendidly attired lady and knight who come to court in part two. Not only does their brilliance counter the grotesquerie of the ghost, the three figures provide the whip and rein, as it were, for the salvation of Guenevere and Gawain. Without the first part the mercy of part two would appear gratuitous; without part two the warning of the first part would be conventional didacticism.

Although the *Awntyrs of Arthur* might be criticized as essentially a composite of traditional knightly adventures and religious teachings, this is what romance by and large is. While such works as *Generides, Parto-*

nope, and *Ipomedon* have been classified as "artificial composites," and others like *Isumbras* and *Eglamour* as "variants" of the Eustace-Constance legend, all romance would seem to be purposely derivative and encompassing.[47] But beyond noting that several romances employ comparable ingredients, we might wonder whether anything meaningful can be said about the different ways in which these ingredients function, especially when they may seem to be similar if not identical.

In the last part of *Sir Orfeo,* after the king has successfully brought back his wife from the underworld, he tests the loyalty of his steward. This episode should not be scorned as extraneous or gratuitous; though not a part of the classical myth, it is an essential ingredient in the romance. In comparison, the romance *Generides* begins with the story of King Aufreus, whose wife is unfaithful with his steward. After being deposed, Aufreus, with the help of a fairylike lover, regains his land and position. Not only are the names Aufreus and Orfeo (Orpheus) similar, but so are the two stories. The account of Aufreus concerns a wife and an otherworldly being—who, as their names (Serenydes and Sereyne) indicate, may be two aspects of the same figure—and a false steward. The story of Orfeo concerns a wife who becomes an otherworldly being, and a faithful steward. While one story may seem to be the mirror image of the other, both show a king who, after losing his wife and kingdom, is able through supernatural help to win the day.

Given such similarities in two romances without any other apparent connection, we might wonder whether the otherworldly element dominant in the Orfeo story may have influenced the account of Aufreus and his fairylike lover, or whether the false steward of the Aufreus story may have been inserted into the rendition of the classical myth, or even whether there may have been a common Orfeo-Aufreus hero, whose story is recast in the two romances. Regardless of our conclusions, we may understand that just as some romances (*Sir Thopas, Richard,* the Laud *Troy-Book*) could allude to romances and their heroes, so other romances might include these as part of their own narrative. In their recasting of familiar material, such composite romances might, instead of concealing their borrowing, actually rely on audience recognition, so that their achievement could be all the more appreciated.

We may also see how two quite different kinds of romances—one regarded as sophisticated, the other as popular—use a similar detail. In the elegant and artful *Sir Gawain and the Green Knight,* while the hero rests at Bercilak's castle dallying with his host's wife, Bercilak goes out on three separate hunts, for deer, boar, and fox, which at the end of each day he presents to his guest. The episode, which has been much discussed in terms of the special significance it gives to the testing of Gawain at home, is clearly at the heart of the poem. A comparable episode exists in the little-valued *Sir Eglamour of Artois,* even though the parallel has never been recognized. To win his lady, the hero in this romance must perform three tasks for her father. He must fetch a great deer, seek out a terrible boar, and slay a mighty dragon. These detailed adventures, occupying more than two-fifths of the work, are clearly at its heart. On the first quest Eglamour easily kills the deer as well as the giant who owns the herd and cuts off both their heads. On the second quest he journeys to Sidon, where he fights the boar for more than three days. Finally when he is almost exhausted, he kills the animal as well as the giant who is its master, and again cuts off their heads. The King of Sidon's daughter wishes to marry him, but, when he says he cannot, offers him instead a magic ring which will preserve him from death. On the third quest, Eglamour journeys to fight the Dragon of Rome. Although he finally prevails and cuts off the dragon's head, the dragon gives him a wound in his own head. Although everyone thinks he will die, the daughter of the Emperor of Rome tends his wounds for a year and he recovers.[48]

The progression of the three hunts in *Eglamour* is very much like that in *Gawain.* Even though the third hunt is for a dragon rather than a fox, both animals are traditional symbols of the devil. In *Eglamour* the dragon is in fact referred to as the fiend, and the fire which comes from its mouth is likened to hell fire. Moreover, both creatures are foul: in *Eglamour* the stench from the "fowle" dragon causes people to swoon, and in *Gawain* the fox skin is cursed as worthy of the devil: "þis foule fox felle—þe fende haf þe godez!"[49] It is on the third quest that Eglamour receives a wound in the head, and it is because of his lapse in honesty after the third hunt that Gawain receives a nick in the neck from his supernatural foe.

Without discussing here additional relationships between these two hunts,[50] we may still comment on the role of the hunts of deer, boar, and dragon-fox in the two romances, both of which have been dated in the mid-fourteenth century and placed in the North Midlands. Although one might tend to see the episode in *Gawain* as a sophisticated rendering of the folk motif expressed more baldly in *Eglamour,* the two versions may represent equally literary treatments of commonplace motifs. It is not that one set of hunts is qualitatively better than the other, and we should not assume that the *Gawain*-Poet has transformed what is in *Eglamour.* Rather, the two hunts—one performed by the lady's lord (husband), the other commanded by the lady's lord (father)—are, for all their differences, designed both to test the hero and to give symbolic and thematic significance to the story at hand.

Ritualistic as the hunts are, they are also the basis for comedy. There is hardly a need nowadays to point out the humor in *Gawain,* which, like Chaucer's romances, has been increasingly celebrated for its play, its irony, and its "anti-romance" elements.[51] Similarly, humor is found throughout *Eglamour.* Most obviously, this is the humor of incongruity, as when the first giant, realizing that someone is trying to steal his deer, swears "by hym þat werede þe crown of thorne," and when the second giant, seeing the head of the boar on a spear, laments "Allas, my gud bare! ert þou dede?" and addresses the dead creature as "my littill spotted hoglyn."[52] Similar incongruity may be found when Eglamour, unlikely suitor of the daughter of the earl he serves, takes to his bed and, sick with love, prays to Christ, who died on the Cross for him, to grant that he may have his lady as his wife: "To blysse þan ware I broghte."[53] The humorous excess here leads to the religious dimension of the romance.

Just as in *Isumbras* and *Robert of Sicily,* the attitude of the hero would seem to provide the basis for what happens to him. His success in the quests that follow seems to result from his prayer and to have divine sanction. But at the same time, Eglamour, apparently unwilling to wait for his "blysse," acts rashly and consummates his love before marriage. Although the sin is not explicit—as it is in *Amis and Amiloun,* where a voice from heaven says that because of his deception the hero must be punished—after this Eglamour is wounded by the dragon. Needing a year to recover, he cannot return to claim his bride who, having given birth to a child, is sent into exile. On the verge of having his prayer granted in full, Eglamour loses everything, and when on his return home he finds what has happened, he himself becomes an exile. No longer seeking to work his own will, he becomes a pilgrim to the Holy Land, where he remains for fifteen years fighting "agaynes þam þat did wrange." It is after atoning for his sin that Eglamour, still "cled in care" and not knowing what he is doing, is finally permitted to find and win his lady. This happy ending is not the result of the knight's conscious efforts, and it is a "blysse" that is a sign of that to come. The sentiment of the closing lines may have special significance: "Now Ihesu brynge vs to his blysse / Pat lastis wythowttyn ende!"[54]

Just as ancient romance may have been composed to illustrate the problems found in collections of rhetorical *controversiae,*[55] so medieval romance, including such popular works as *Eglamour of Artois,* is very much concerned with presenting incongruities and dilemmas. Often these are in the form of dramatic situations: a character does not deserve what happens to him, a son unknowingly fights his father or marries his mother, a hero is called upon to break an oath to preserve his life or his love, a father must lose his child to save his friend. While expressing moral and ethical issues, and thus providing intellectual interest, these situations are also an occasion for playfulness. Alongside the rough humor of much medieval romance—Gamelyn beating the corrupt clergy; Clement, the butcher in *Octavian,* outwitting the Saracens; Richard dining on a boiled Saracen's head instead of the pork he has requested—is the more subtle humor of possibility: how Gawain would give Bercilak his winnings if indeed he enjoyed the lady's favors. And this is often comparable to the humor found in fabliau.

Although romance and fabliau have generally been considered opposites, and twenty-five years ago scholars could confidently identify romance with "the courtly tradition" and fabliau with "the bourgeois tradition," we now know that neither form is the exclusive property of any segment of society,[56] and the two forms themselves may not be so different after all. Whereas the romance is idealizing, rhetorical, and ostensibly serious, and the fabliau is gross, plain, and unmistakably comic, such differences may be more superficial than real, more the result of manner and language than of matter and theme. Not only are both forms ultimately cheerful, with some sort of happy ending, they may be considered *contes à rire,* purposely creating laughter. While the laughter may be quite different, the comic impulse is much the same.

The earliest Hellenistic romances are erotic and humorous: Longus's *Daphnis and Chloe* concerns two young lovers who cannot figure out how to make love, and Xenophon's *Ephesian Tale* is full of attempts on the virtue of heroine and hero alike. In their open bawdiness works like Apuleius's *Golden Ass* and Petronius's *Satyricon* may seem closer to fabliau than to romance. Similarly, the deceptions and bawdy humor that fill such twelfth-century romances as Béroul's *Tristan,* Chrétien's *Lancelot,* and Marie's *Equitan* are the stuff that fabliau is made of. The two forms often go hand in hand. Chaucer can insert the fabliau-like scene at Deiphebus's house in his romance of *Troilus,* and his juxtaposition of romance and fabliau in the *Canterbury Tales* (Knight's Tale followed by Miller's Tale) is less to contrast the two forms than to bring out essential relationships between them.

For all of its apparent realism, the fabliau offers no more verisimilitude than the romance. Both are dominated by the spirit of make-believe, and both are properly regarded as fantasy literature.[57] We suspend our sense of disbelief in both and take intellectual pleasure in the unraveling of complexities and the solving of apparent dilemmas. We may even take pleasure in the abortion of our erotic expectations: the seduction of Gawain by Bercilak's wife takes a different form from what we anticipate,

the innocence of the children Floris and Blauncheflur is preserved, and
when Amis sleeps with Amiloun's wife, he puts a sword between them.
The approach of romance is, like its language, more oblique and indirect
than that of fabliau. But marked throughout by the artificial and the
incredible, neither is to be taken at face value, and the pleasures of both
are more intellectual than emotional.

Because the lessons of romance are the standard ones of Christianity,
these may function more as givens to be built on than as actual concerns
of either author or audience, who may be interested more in the play of
possibilities and incongruities than in actual solutions, or in some instances more in the intricacies of verbal artistry than in the effectiveness
of a moral. As the epitome of "the mythos of summer,"[58] romance is
essentially trivial, and for all of its didacticism, no one was likely to turn to
it—any more than to the fabliau—for spiritual guidance. What one may
have valued most in romance was the play of the unexpected against the
expected. While on one level this may be merely a matter of plot, on
another level it is the play of the individual expression against the
standard, the traditional, and the familiar. It may be that this interchange
gave medieval romance its vital character, and that the desire to participate in the interchange kept the form alive for so long.

N O T E S

1. Lillian Hornstein, "Middle English Romances," in *Recent Middle English
Scholarship and Criticism: Survey and Desiderata,* ed. J. Burke Severs (Pittsburgh:
Duquesne Univ. Press, 1971), p. 64.
2. Derek Pearsall, "Understanding Middle English Romance," *Review* 2
(1980): 105.
3. See Kathryn Hume, "The Formal Nature of Middle English Romance,"
Philological Quarterly 53 (1974): 158. These are the anonymous romances described in J. Burke Severs, ed., *A Manual of the Writings in Middle English
1050–1500* (New Haven: Connecticut Academy of Arts and Sciences, 1967),
vol. 1.
4. In Severs' *Manual,* as well as in John Edwin Wells' earlier *Manual of the
Writings in Middle English, 1050–1400* (1916), the romances are organized
according to whether the legends are English, Arthurian, Carolingian, etc. In
Velma Bourgeois Richmond, *The Popularity of Middle English Romance* (Bowling
Green: Bowling Green Univ. Popular Press, 1975), they are organized according
to fate, the supernatural, friendship, and love. For folk motifs, see Gerald
Bordman, *Motif-Index of the English Metrical Romances,* FF Communications,
190 (Helsinki: Academia Scientiarum Fennica, 1963); for archetypal patterns,

see Kathryn Hume, "Romance: A Perdurable Pattern," *College English* 36 (1974): 129–46; for narrative patterns, Susan Wittig, *Stylistic and Narrative Structures in the Middle English Romance* (Austin: Univ. of Texas Press, 1978); for verse form see especially J.P. Oakden, *Alliterative Poetry in Middle English* (Manchester: Manchester Univ. Press, 1935), esp. 2:38–51; and A. McI. Trounce, "The English Tail-Rhyme Romances," *Medium Aevum* 1 (1932): 871 ff.; for length, see Dieter Mehl, *The Middle English Romances of the Thirteenth and Fourteenth Centuries* (London: Routledge & Kegan Paul, 1968); for merit, see George Kane, "The Middle English Metrical Romances," *Middle English Literature* (London: Methuen, 1951), pp. 1–103. See also Derek Pearsall's attempt at a "historical morphology" in "The Development of Middle English Romance," *Mediaeval Studies* 27 (1965): 91–116.

5. Of the more recent studies, for epic see D.M. Hill, "Romance as Epic," *English Studies* 44 (1963): 95–107; and Morton W. Bloomfield, "Episodic Motivation and Marvels in Epic and Romance," *Essays and Explorations* (Cambridge: Harvard Univ. Press, 1970), pp. 97–128. For exemplum see Hanspeter Schelp, *Exemplarische Romanzen in Mittelenglische*, Palaestra, 246 (Göttingen: Vandenhoeck and Ruprecht, 1967); and Mehl, *Middle English Romances*, pp. 17–20. For chronicle see Pamela Gradon, *Form and Style in Early English Literature* (London: Methuen, 1971), pp. 270–72; Mehl, *Middle English Romances*, pp. 20–22. For folk tale and ballad see Dorothy Everett, "A Characterization of the English Romances," *Essays on Middle English Literature* (Oxford: Clarendon Press, 1955), pp. 16–22; and Bruce Rosenberg, "The Morphology of the Middle English Metrical Romance," *Journal of Popular Culture*, 1 (1967): 63–77. For *storie*, etc., see Paul Strohm, *"Storie, Spelle, Geste, Romaunce, Tragedie:* Generic Distinctions in the Middle English Troy Narratives," *Speculum* 46 (1971): 348–59.

6. This is also what Mehl suggests, *Middle English Romances*, p. 20.

7. See Paul Strohm, "The Origin and Meaning of Middle English *Romaunce*," *Genre*, 10 (1977), esp. p. 7; and Reinald Hoops, *Der Begriff 'Romance,' in der mittelenglishchen und frühneuenglischen Literatur*, Anglistische Forschungen, 68 (Heidelberg: Carl Winter, 1929).

8. See Maldwyn Mills, ed., *Six Middle English Romances* (London: Dent, 1973), p. vii; Mehl, *Middle English Romances*, p. 17; Donald B. Sands, ed., *Middle English Verse Romances* (New York: Holt, Rinehart and Winston, 1966), p. 6. For us today, writes Hume, this romance seems to be a "spectrum of interrelating forms" ("Formal Nature of Middle English Romance," pp. 158–59).

9. Dieter Mehl has preferred *Versnovelle;* see his "Die kürzeren mittelenglischen 'Romanzen' und die Gattungsfrage," *Deutsche Vierteljahrsschrift für Literaturwissenschaft und Geistesgeschichte*, 38 (1964): 524 ff. Northrop Frye presents romance in general as a mode in his *Anatomy of Criticism: Four Essays* (Princeton: Princeton Univ. Press, 1957), pp. 33 ff.; Pamela Gradon focuses on the medieval romance as a mode, *Form and Style*, pp. 212 ff. See the recent attempt to reclassify romances, John Finlayson, "Definitions of Middle English Romance," *Chaucer Review*, 15 (1980): esp. p. 178.

10. See the views cited in Richmond, *Popularity of Middle English Romance,* pp. 200–201, n. 9. It is unfortunate that Eugène Vinaver in his *Rise of Romance* (Oxford: Oxford Univ. Press, 1971) speaks only of Malory's work among the English romances, and that D.H. Green includes as his representatives of English romance only *Sir Gawain and the Green Knight* and Chaucer's *Troilus;* see his *Irony in the Medieval Romance* (Cambridge: Cambridge Univ. Press, 1979). Of the recent studies of medieval romance, only John Stevens's *Medieval Romance: Themes and Approaches* (London: Hutchinson, 1973) has attempted to discuss a range of English as well as continental romances.

11. See, e.g., Mehl, *Middle English Romances,* pp. 7–13.

12. See Finlayson, "Definitions of Middle English Romance," p. 56; also Sarah F. Barrow, *The Medieval Society Romances* (New York: Columbia Univ. Press, 1924); and M. Dominica Legge, "The 'Ancestral' Romance," *Anglo-Norman Literature and Its Background* (Oxford: Clarendon Press, 1963), pp. 139–75.

13. See Finlayson, "Definitions of Middle English Romance," p. 45; also the definitions in, e.g., Everett, "Characterization of the English Romances," p. 3; Helene Newstead, "Romances: General," in Severs's *Manual,* 1:11; and A.V.C. Schmidt and Nicolas Jacobs, ed. *Medieval English Romances* (New York: Holmes & Meier, 1980), 1:1.

14. Strohm, *"Storie, Spelle, Geste,"* p. 354. Even Northrop Frye views medieval romance as expressing "the ascendancy of a horse-riding aristocracy"; see *The Secular Scripture: A Study of the Structure of Romance* (Cambridge: Harvard Univ. Press, 1976), p. 57.

15. Frye, *Secular Scripture,* p. 26.

16. See Edmund Reiss, "Medieval Irony," *Journal of the History of Ideas,* 42 (1981): 223 ff.

17. Sir Thopas, B* 2087–90, in *The Works of Geoffrey Chaucer,* ed. F.N. Robinson, 2d ed. (Boston: Houghton Mifflin, 1957).

18. See Laura Hibbard Loomis, "Chaucer and the Auchinleck MS: Sir Thopas and Guy of Warwick," *Essays and Studies in Honor of Carleton Brown* (New York: New York Univ. Press, 1940), pp. 111–28.

19. *Richard Coer de Lyon,* ll. 6725–34; see also the earlier list in *Der mittelenglische Versroman über Richard Löwenherz,* ed. Karl Brunner, Wiener Beiträge zur Englischen Philologie, 42 (Vienna: Braumüller, 1913), ll. 7–20; Laud *Troy-Book,* ed. J.E. Wülfing, EETS, o.s. 121 (London: Kegan Paul, Trench, Trübner, 1902), ll. 11–26; *Cursor Mundi,* ed. Richard Morris, EETS, o.s. 57 (London: Trübner, 1874), ll. 1–20; *Parliament,* ed. M.Y. Offord, EETS, 246 (London: Oxford Univ. Press, 1959), ll. 614–29. The Amadace cited in these works is apparently different from the hero of the English *Sir Amadace.*

20. The twenty-five manuscripts of *Gamelyn,* all in manuscripts of the *Canterbury Tales,* and the twenty manuscripts of the three different versions of the *Siege of Jerusalem* would seem to represent special cases.

21. See Ronald S. Crane, *The Vogue of Medieval Chivalric Romance during the English Renaissance* (Menasha, Wis.: Banta, 1919), pp. 4–6.

22. Such are the evaluations of George Kane, "Middle English Metrical Romances," pp. 13–14, 19.

23. See, e.g., Finlayson, "Definitions of Middle English Romance," p. 51.

24. This list might easily be extended. For instance, the six manuscripts of *Libeaus* are so divergent that they might well represent different versions; and the Charlemagne romances known as the *Ferumbras* group and *Otinel* group, as well as the several lives of Alexander, could be counted as separate versions.

25. *Sir Gawain and the Green Knight*, ed. J.R.R. Tolkien and E.V. Gordon, 2d ed., rev. Norman Davis (Oxford: Clarendon Press, 1967), ll. 33–36.

26. *The 'Geste Hystoriale' of the Destruction of Troy*, ed. G.A. Panton and D. Donaldson, EETS, o.s. 39 (London: Trübner, 1869), esp. l. 26.

27. Frye, *Secular Scripture*, p. 3.

28. See Mehl, *Middle English Romances*, pp. 7–13; Stevens, *Medieval Romance*, p. 110.

29. Richmond, *Popularity of Middle English Romance*, p. 20.

30. *King Horn*, ed. Joseph Hall (Oxford: Clarendon Press, 1901), ll. 555, 665, 1529–30, 75–78, 43–44.

31. See Moses Hadas, trans., *Three Greek Romances* (Indianapolis: Bobbs-Merrill, 1953), pp. ix–x.

32. See Albert C. Baugh, "The Authorship of the Middle English Romances," *Annual Bulletin of the Modern Humanities Research Association*, 22 (1950): 13–28; also Baugh, "The Middle English Romance: Some Questions of Creation, Presentation, and Preservation," *Speculum*, 42 (1967), esp. p. 4; and Hume, "Formal Nature," p. 177.

33. See Mehl, "A Note of Some Manuscripts of Romances," in *Middle English Romances*, pp. 257–62, also pp. 10–12, 17–18; Karl Brunner, "Die Überlieferung der mittelenglischen Versromanzen," *Anglia*, 76 (1958): 64–73; Laura Hibbard Loomis, "The Auchinleck Manuscript and a Possible London Bookshop of 1330–1340," *PMLA*, 57 (1942): 595–627.

34. Frye, *Secular Scripture*, passim; also *Anatomy of Criticism*, pp. 136–37.

35. Frye, *Secular Scripture*, p. 4; R.W. Southern, *The Making of the Middle Ages* (New Haven: Yale Univ. Press, 1953), chap. 4: "From Epic to Romance," esp. p. 243.

36. Ben Edwin Perry, *The Ancient Romances: A Literary-Historical Account of Their Origins* (Berkeley: Univ. of California Press, 1967), p. 28.

37. Schmidt and Jacobs, *Medieval English Romances*, 1:6.

38. *Sir Isumbras*, in *Six Middle English Romances*, ed. Mills, ll. 134, 384.

39. *Guy of Warwick*, ed. Julius Zupitza, EETS, e.s. 49 (London: Trübner, 1887), pt. 2, stanza 22, ll. 10–11; see also stanzas 26, 29.

40. *King Horn* (Harley), ed. J. Rawson Lumby, rev. G.H. McKnight, EETS, o.s. 14 (London: Kegan Paul, Trench, Trübner, 1901), ll. 1641–42.

41. *Gamelyn*, in *Middle English Metrical Romances*, ed. W.H. French and C.B. Hale (New York: Prentice-Hall, 1930), ll. 451, 513.

42. See Newstead's list in Severs's *Manual*, 1:13.

43. Derek Brewer, "The Nature of Romance," *Poetica*, 9 (1978): 37.

44. Bruno Lavagnini, *Le origini del romanzo greco* (Pisa: Mariotti, 1921); Perry, *Ancient Romances,* p. 33.

45. See Newstead's analysis in Sever's *Manual,* 1:61; also Ralph Hanna III, ed. *The Awntyrs off Arthure at the Terne Wathelyn* (Manchester: Manchester Univ. Press, 1974), p. 18; and John Speirs, *Medieval English Poetry: The Non-Chaucerian Tradition* (London: Faber & Faber, 1957), pp. 252 ff.

46. Hanna, *Awntyrs,* ll. 250–51, 261–64.

47. See the classifications in Severs's *Manual,* 1: 147, 120.

48. *Sir Gawain and the Green Knight,* ll. 1126–1997; *Sir Eglamour of Artois,* ed. Frances E. Richardson, EETS, 256 (London: Oxford Univ. Press, 1965), ll. 232–798.

49. *Eglamour,* ll. 700, 741, 738, (Cotton) 796–98; *Gawain,* l. 1944.

50. These, including the role of the beheadings and the ladies, are discussed in a forthcoming article.

51. See, e.g., Sacvan Bercovitch, "Romance and Anti-Romance in *Sir Gawain and the Green Knight,*" *Philological Quarterly* 44 (1965): 30–37; and Green, *Irony,* pp. 352 ff.

52. *Eglamour* (Lincoln), ll. 292, 545, 547.

53. Ibid., l. 108. This ironic reading, found in the Thornton manuscript, is apparently toned down in the other versions of the poem.

54. *Eglamour* (Lincoln), ll. 1020, 1221, 1376–77.

55. See Perry, *Ancient Romances,* p. 19.

56. See the distinction between the courtly and the bourgeois in Charles Muscatine, *Chaucer and the French Tradition* (Berkeley: Univ. of California Press, 1957), pp. 1–97; see the valuable work by Per Nykrog, *Les Fabliaux: Etude d'histoire littéraire et de stylistique médiévale* (Copenhagen: Munksgaard, 1957).

57. See the perceptive remarks by Brewer, "Nature of Romance," p. 16; also Stevens, *Medieval Romance,* p. 68.

58. This is Frye's term, *Anatomy of Criticism,* pp. 186 ff.

The International Medieval Popular Comic Tale in England

Derek Brewer

I

Comic tales presumably exist in plenty in any society at any period. In medieval England a caution was issued against such tales in 1292, but a few were included even among the exempla compiled to be used in sermons.[1] There are however very few such tales written in English (as compared with other vernaculars) before 1400. Though comic tales, fables, and fabliaux were undoubtedly cuously lacking in the vernacular compared with, for example, the literature of France and Germany. The first example of a written comic tale in English is *Dame Sirith*. It recounts, in tail-rhyme verse, the seduction of a young wife by a young clerk. He invokes the aid of an old woman, who makes the eyes of her bitch stream by feeding her with pepper and mustard. The old woman then tells the young wife that the bitch is the old woman's daughter, magically transformed to a bitch because she resisted the advances of a young clerk, and now weeps with regret. The young wife tells the old woman to hurry away and find the clerk, whom she then enthusiastically receives. The narrative is closely related to the dialogue called *Interludium de clerico et puella* and is elsewhere recorded in brief in Latin. It is in fact a widespread folk tale of ultimately Indian origin, Aarne-Thompson Type 1515.

Also in the thirteenth century appears the poem *The Fox and the Wolf,* telling how the Fox tricks the Wolf into rescuing him from a well by coming down in another bucket on the promise of arriving in Paradise. This too is a very well-known story (Type 32).[2] It appears in collections of Latin prose beast-fables, which were well liked in England. Stories about animals, and especially those centered on the fox, constitute almost

131

a class in themselves, but granted the special nature of the actors, which determines much of the action (as catching hens, etc.), they are sufficiently anthropomorphic to bear out the generalizations that may be made about other comic tales.

It is customary to regard as a comic tale the short poem "A Peniworth of Witte," recorded in the Auchinleck MS which was written about 1345. The poem thus probably dates from the early fourteenth century. A later version in a fifteenth-century Cambridge MS entitled "How a Merchande dyd hys Wyfe Betray" is more condensed.[3] The French and German versions are said to be amusing; in the English version the story runs as follows. A merchant neglects his wife and lavishes gifts on his mistress. On departure abroad he promises his wife nothing but what she will pay for. She gives him a penny to buy some sense. A wise man sells him the advice to appear before each of the women with a tale of woe. The mistress rejects him; the wife cherishes him, and he is grateful. Admirable as is the sentiment there is little that is comic in this version, probably just because the sentiment is so admirable.

Rather more essentially comic, though still modified by English solemnity, is the comic romance *Sir Cleges,*[4] written in tail-rhyme stanzas toward the end of the fourteenth century, perhaps, as McKnight suggests, as a minstrel's Christmas story. Two manuscripts of the late fifteenth century survive. The story tells how the knight Cleges falls into poverty because of his liberality. His wife comforts him, and after he and his wife and children have been to church on Christmas Day, he prays in a garden and miraculously finds ripe cherries. These his wife advises him to present to the king. The porter, the usher, the steward in hall each demand a third of his reward. When he eventually gets to the king, who is delighted with the gift, he asks for twelve blows, which he deals out with great zest to the servants. When it is explained, the lords laugh so that they cannot sit, and the king rewards Sir Cleges suitably. Both the pious and the comic elements are very widely known, the latter being A-T Type 1610. In the seventeenth century, as McKnight shows, the tale became attached to historical persons, and it also appears in collections of moral exempla, such as the *Gesta Romanorum,* which though primarily moralistic and religious includes some other comic tales and appears to have originated in England even in its Latin form.[5]

Collections of stories appeared from the twelfth century onward in Europe, and though they were often designed as sermon material they contained some comic tales. An example of such collections which appeared in English in the late fourteenth century is *The Seven Sages of Rome.*[6] The collection is ancient and orginates in the East. It became immensely popular in Europe, rather less so in Britain, where there are nine manuscripts, not all complete, comprising several versions, all probably composed in the second half of the fourteenth century. There are some fifteen stories in all, some by the Emperor's wife in favor of women, others by the sages showing that one should not trust women. A typical example tells of a man who has an unfaithful wife (A-T Type 1377). He refuses to let her in when she returns late in the night, but keeps her out in the cold. She threatens to commit suicide and drops a stone in the well. Hearing the splash he dashes out, whereupon she nips into the house and locks him out. The story is told in the *Decameron*, 7.4. It is genuinely popular.

By the end of the fourteenth century a considerable number of collections of stories had been made in Europe, without an overriding didactic or religious aim. The outstanding examples are the *Decameron* and the *Canterbury Tales*. Each of these comprises a number of comic tales, for which indeed they are now mostly famous. Notwithstanding their secularity it is worth remarking that, as with *The Seven Sages of Rome*, comic tales are mingled with others of a quite different kind, pious, edifying, in praise of women, of love, of goodness in all its forms. It is necessary to isolate the comic tale for practical purposes of analysis and discussion, but we misunderstand them if we consider them only in isolation, even though, in the form of jest-books, the sixteenth and later centuries did so gather some comic tales together.

Increasing literacy in the fifteenth and sixteenth centuries led to the recording of a number of comic tales, though they may survive only in sixteenth-century versions. W.C. Hazlitt's *Early Popular Poetry*, 4 vols., 1864, and David Laing's *Early Popular Poetry of Scotland and the Northern Border*, revised by W.C. Hazlitt, 2 vols., 1895, though now out of date as editions, are as collections still unreplaced, and usefully collect a number of texts, though not all are comic. An example of one of the comic tales is *The Frere and the Boye*, first printed by Wynkyn de Worde, which in its present form probably dates from the fifteenth century. It is a widely spread tale, A-T Type 592, full of characteristic folk-tale motifs. A boy ill-treated by his stepmother is sent by his father, to protect him, to look after the cows in the fields. An old man to whom the boy gives his dinner rewards him with a magic pipe, a bow which shoots arrows that cannot miss, and the faculty of making his stepmother "blow" whenever he wishes. On his return he gets his own back on his stepmother by causing her acutely to embarrass herself by letting off wind in company. Next day she sends a friar to the fields to discipline the boy. By playing the pipe the boy forces the friar to dance among brambles until he is naked and lacerated, and on their return the whole company in the house is forced to dance. The stepmother and friar have the boy up before the "official" in court. He too is forced to dance, as is the whole community, to their embarrassment, shame, and exhaustion. There are other such stories, like Adam Cobsam's *The Wright's Chaste Wife,* of familiar type, and *The Cokwold's Dance.*

The Cokwold's Dance, which in the sole surviving manuscript is probably of the early sixteenth century, tells in verse an ancient story. It is a version of the fidelity test practiced in King Arthur's court by the gift either of a mantle that will fit only a chaste wife, or of a horn from which only a chaste wife can drink without spilling. In *The Cokwold's Dance* men must drink from a bugle horn, and a cuckold is bound to spill the drink. King Arthur himself spills the drink, but "he has no gall," though the queen is ashamed. The other cuckolds dress in scarlet and dance. The narrative line is not so strong in this as in earlier, more properly Arthurian versions.

Another tale of a different yet familiar type is *The King and the Barker,* which tells how a tanner met but did not recognize the king, to his confusion; but he is given a handsome reward. The king incognito is a familiar feature (in the form of the Sultan) in the *Arabian Nights,* but this kind of tale seems more characteristic of the sixteenth than of earlier centuries in England, however ancient its roots. The theme appears in some of the Robin Hood ballads.

The early printers Wynkyn de Worde and William Copland printed a certain amount of unsophisticated popular literature, including a number of romances, and did not forget "Mery Iestes" such as the one just quoted, the *Frere and the Boy, The Wyfe in Morrelles Skin, and How the Plouman lerned his Paternoster.*

The full title of the only imprint of *A Merry Ieste of a Shrewde and curst Wyfe lapped in Morrelles skin,* which was perhaps printed as late as 1570, indicates its general quality. It is an analogue of *The Taming of the Shrew,* but the husband is rougher than Petruchio. He beats his shrewish wife with birch rods until she bleeds, then wraps her in the salted skin of his old horse Morell, slaughtered for the purpose. The method works very well. A reference to the Mass suggests a pre-Reformation origin for this version, but it is a widespread tale, A-T Type 901, and occurs in an earlier French fabliau. The realism of the account of the marriage celebrations of prosperous farmers, notwithstanding some exaggerated sums of gold, is notable.

The mention of Shakespeare recalls the medieval drama. Needless to say, the miracle plays have many folk-tale elements. For example, the story of Mak and the stolen lamb in the *Second Shepherd's Play* of the Wakefield Cycle is Type 1525M.

A final sixteenth-century example will conclude this brief survey of popular medieval comic tales, which aims only to give an idea of them and does not include parodic pieces such as *The Turnament of Totenham*. The example is *A Hundred Mery Talys*, 1526, which is the first book of its kind printed in English and has come to be called a Jest Book. As its title suggests, it contains stories, and it is more than a collection of jests, quips, and repartees, though they are included. The narratives, of which a selection appears in *Medieval Comic Tales*, are well formed of their kind, polished by many tellings.

One story in itself illustrates both how widespread and how long-lasting these tales may be. It is entitled "Of the mylner that stale the nuttes of the tayler that stale a sheep." A miller with a passion for nuts steals a bag and sits in his white coat, cracking the nuts in the porch of the church. His friend, a tailor who is off to steal a sheep, has agreed to meet him in the church to compare their booty. The sexton comes to church to ring the evening curfew bell, sees the miller, thinks him a ghost, and runs home in fear to tell a cripple in his house what he has seen. The cripple scolds him, and says if he could get there he would exorcise the ghost, so the sexton carries him to the church on his shoulders. The miller sees him coming, thinks he is the tailor with a stolen sheep on his shoulders, and comes to meet him, calling out "Is he fat? Is he fat?" The sexton, terrified at the apparition, shouts "Fat or lean, take him there for me!" throws down the cripple, and rushes off to the parson, who puts on his white surplice in order to come and exorcise the ghost. The parson meets the tailor, who thinks that the parson in his surplice is his friend the miller in his white coat, and calls out "By God, I have him, I have him!" meaning the sheep. But this is too much for the priest, who thinks the tailor is the devil carrying away the spirit of a man recently buried (the owner of the nuts), and the priest too takes to his heels. Some other absurd misunderstandings and mishaps of the same kind follow, with all the actors in the farce ending up equally and mistakenly terrified of the others. The essence of this story is a tale known for several centuries from Finland to India, in which the cripple is usually the parson himself (Type 1791).

The unknown collector of *A Hundred Mery Talys* perhaps found this story in *An Alphabet of Tales*, an English fifteenth-century translation of the Latin *Alphabetum narrationum* by the Frenchman Etienne de Besançon, who locates the tale "in a toun in Normandy." If so, he elaborated it in an original but traditional fashion. The story next appears in English, as far as I know, in shortened form in a mid-eighteenth-century chapbook, *A New Riddle Book or a Whetstone for Dull Wits,* printed in Derby. It reappears as an oral narrative collected in the mid-nineteenth century in the Western Highlands of Scotland, with an ox substituted for the sheep. Ever since the invention of literacy, folk tales have moved in and out of the oral and written traditions.[8]

II

The emphasis in this essay has been on the English popular comic tale, but as has already been implicitly demonstrated these tales are part of the web of European storytelling. There is a large number of Latin collections, beginning with the early twelfth-century *Disciplina Clericalis* by Pedro Alfonso, which draws on many ancient sources. The vernaculars follow. In the thirteenth century appear the roughly 150 French fabliaux, now the subject of an extensive secondary literature. They constitute the most striking collection of medieval comic tales and raise some very interesting questions about what we mean by *popular,* a term to which we shall return. That they are folk tales has been insufficiently emphasized, but they flourished only briefly, fading out in the fourteenth century.

In the thirteenth century there also appear the German *Schwänke,* with Der Stricker an outstanding author. In German the tradition remained strong. Hans Sachs is notable as a German author of comic tales in verse in the sixteenth century. In Spanish there are a number of comic tales, both as independent anecdotes and as episodes in such works as the fourteenth-century *Libro de Buen Amor* by Juan Riz. In Italian there are comic tales in several collections of the fourteenth century, as for instance that by Sacchetti, but the supreme examples are found in Boccaccio's *Decameron,* though by no means all the tales told there are comic. (*Medieval Comic Tales* selects a number of tales from the various languages mentioned.) All such tales exist in many versions with many analogues both close and remote. It is rarely useful to seek the source of any individual version, though paradoxically sources are in one sense extremely important in such traditional literature, for repetition, if with variation, is of its essence. Sources may be oral and multiple, or written and again multiple. The retelling of known tales, repetition with variation, is the *modus vivendi* of traditional literature; the difference from neoclassical and subsequent literature, which claims originality and uniqueness, needs to be recognized.

All the standard medieval comic tales must have been known in England. Sometimes such knowledge can be proved by their presence in

English manuscripts that are written in French or Latin. Why there should be so few examples in the local vernacular compared with the other West European vernaculars is an interesting problem. Since the outstanding exception is Chaucer, the answer we are pushed toward is that though the stories must have been widely known, the impulse to record them depends on a high level of literary sophistication. Bédier claimed that the French fabliaux were "middle class." Nykrog claims they are courtly. Muscatine attempts to arbitrate the question.[9]

It may well be that the dilemma is a false one. There is ample evidence of the interpenetration of court and city, of the courtly with the mercantile and legal, in late fourteenth-century London.[10] To see an opposition between court and aristocracy on the one hand and city and trade on the other is to simplify a complex relationship. The two elements are distinguishable, but were closely, even organically intertwined in London, Paris, Florence, Naples, Cologne, etc. Chaucer and Boccaccio drew their strength from both court and city and found support from each. Inevitably the records derive from the literate classes, and equally inevitably the literate classes were the upper classes in the fourteenth century. But all classes were "the folk." The reason why the level of comic tales seems to come down the social scale in England in the sixteenth century, not in terms of subject matter or realistic treatment, but in knowledge, vision, and wealth of style, is mainly because literacy was more widespread down the social scale. On the other hand one must remember that Chaucer calls his popular comic tales "churls' tales," and though he tells them as a courtier to courtiers and gentry, he attributes them to the lower classes.

III

This raises the question of what we mean by popular. From the seventeenth century there was a class distinction in English literature which allocated only to the illiterate "folk" the possession of what we now symptomatically call the folk tale. That folk tale which was most alive in literary terms, to wit, the "fairy tale," became downgraded to children's literature. No doubt comic dirty stories circulated among adults of all classes, as they always do, but they came to be regarded, along with much unsophisticated literature, as "low"—a word applied equally to social class and to literary tone and subject matter.[11] Such an attitude is not unknown in medieval English literature. The condemnation by clerics of the literature of entertainment, romances, and other poems, not only in the Oxford injunctions of 1292, but in the beginnings of *Cursor Mundi* and *Handlyng Synne,* and in various passages of *Piers*

Plowman, are somewhat similar in attitude. Closest of all is Chaucer's own reference to his bawdy tales as "churls' tales" and his representation of his "gentils" as disapproving of "ribaudye."[12] Yet Chaucer is as always deeply ambivalent. After all it is he, among all medieval English authors, who tells the bawdiest, and the most, comic tales. We know moreover that his audience was by no means made up of churls, but of highly educated courtiers, gentry, lawyers, and substantial merchants, and included ladies as well as men. Boccaccio's *Decameron* also includes many bawdy stories, told, according to his fiction, to an upper-class audience of young gentlemen and refined young ladies.

Some comic tales, though not the bawdiest, were included in collections intended for the use of preachers in their sermons. The literary evidence inevitably tends to give us implicit or explicit evidence that writers of comic tales, however bawdy or realistic, were highly educated, whether lay or clerical. Their audiences were lay and upper-class, for certain. Although the congregations which heard sermons may occasionally have included some illiterate artisans or peasants, it is well to remember that medieval Christianity, perhaps all Christianity, had a bias toward the better educated upper classes. Even medieval saints came from socially superior classes.[13] Thus the evidence would appear to be that in the fourteenth century comic tales were thought to be "vulgar," "common," "low" (the very words are redolent of class-distinction), but were particularly enjoyed by the more emancipated, secularized, literate, lay upper classes, both men and women.

The question might then be, did the illiterate lower classes enjoy them? The difficulty of obtaining evidence, short of a time-machine, may be partly overcome by looking at the phenomenon of oral delivery and examining the methods used by investigators in the nineteenth and twentieth centuries who traced the stories. Oral narration does not require literacy, though there is no doubt that it calls for high skills of an associated kind. Modern folk-tale collectors, of whom K.H. Jackson may stand as an example, and anthropologists leave no room to suppose that illiteracy *must* imply a poor or degraded state of culture, or that the storyteller lacks any high art. A genuinely illiterate culture, which has not had the cream skimmed off it by literacy, may be as rich and complex as any that is literate, and it will be less divided. Pockets of illiterate, unified culture have survived even in Europe, though mainly on its margins, east and west, until almost the present day. They show that there must have been more extended, similar societies throughout Europe in the Middle Ages, which might equally claim an elaborate oral culture. Oral tradition, and oral communication of stories, is the basis of the Aarne-Thompson listing in *The Types of the Folktale*. Tales which have not been recorded from oral delivery at some stage are not included there. Since every tale discussed in this essay has been shown to belong to one of the types of folk tale, that is convincing evidence that the genre belongs in the general oral popular tradition, even if it can be shown in a particular instance to have a written source.

Moreover, while literacy in English carried no social prestige, and even Chaucer at times seems to apologize for his English, as well as complaining about its scarcity of rhyme (*Complaint of Venus*, 1. 80), Chaucer and many medieval writers of romances and other poems at least pretend to evoke the conditions of oral delivery: conventions which a reciter could easily turn into the oral reality which undoubtedly prevailed in many European countries in the twelfth, thirteenth, and much of the fourteenth centuries. Oral delivery may coexist with literacy, and literacy is often influenced by the conventions of oral delivery. Oral delivery shows that these tales were popular with the illiterate, and their survival in manuscript shows that they were popular with the literate. In short, they were, as we should expect, popular with all classes, even if some pretended to or really did despise them.

Chaucer's comic tales are all examples of types of the popular international comic tale. They have no known written sources, and no convincing argument has been put forward for Chaucer's knowledge of the *Decameron*, though *The Canterbury Tales* shares several folk-tale types with the *Decameron*. Chaucer's tales have many analogues.[14] The likelihood is that Chaucer knew several versions of these stories, possibly both written and oral, and that he then improved them by his own supreme genius—for his versions are always far richer than the analogues, even Boccaccio's. The Miller's Tale conforms to Type 1361, and The Reeve's Tale to Type 1363—somewhat closely allied, as may be seen from the closeness of the numbers. The Friar's Tale is Type 1186, and The Summoner's Tale perhaps 1176, since it is about that subject so exquisitely funny to medieval men and women, the breaking of wind. (The well-established literary theme of the Satirical Inheritance does not seem to occur in folk tale.) The Shipman's Tale is Type 1420C, and The Merchant's Tale Type 1423. The Nun's Priest's Tale is Type 6, though it has a long literary heritage.[15] The popular, traditional nature of Chaucer's subject matter and interests is very clear. There are more comic tales than any other kind in *The Canterbury Tales*, though their bulk is less. It should be added that the treatment of this traditional material is very highly wrought and in some ways antipopular. The Miller's Tale and The Reeve's Tale are both patronizing toward village people, and there is an element of intellectuality in all the stories which contributes to the greatness of the poems and which cannot be called exactly popular. But the main point here is the popular, traditional nature of the subject matter and much of its treatment.

The nature of acutal oral delivery or its imitation molds all traditional narrative in prose or verse. Many of the consequential characteristics are common to serious as well as comic tales and are to be found even in the Gospels.[16] They need little elaboration here. The kernel of the story is traditional, not invented; the action is primary, the characters insofar as they are individualized are secondary. Though the internal structure must be repeated, the storyteller may vary within quite broad limits the events, the characters, the descriptions, the very attitude he implies toward the story. A particular version may contain several layers, as it were, of plot and event, not always easily compatible with each other. The audience normally either knows or can easily guess the general shape and outcome of the story. Although each teller is an individual, and many audiences differ from each other, so that each telling is its own unique work of art and has different details, there are some aspects of the story outside the teller's control, as outside the teller's invention, which derive from earlier tellings, or which make the story *that* story and no other, so that each traditional narrative has some degree of social representativeness. Any version, or group of versions, is an expression of the interests of a whole historical society, not in any mystical way, as *das Volk dichtet,* but simply as an accumulation, as well as a set of implicit rejections, from many tellers and hearers over a long period. A folk tale has therefore some impersonality, a quality larger than any individual teller. In this respect the folk tale tends toward myth, preserving long-tested insights and attitudes. Each version of a folk tale is a verbal realization of a given cluster of elements which the teller partly selects from, partly must accept, and which he must then make the best of, with vivid narration, interesting characterization, clear description, and personal comment, according to his own ability. It is here, in the selection and even addition of narrative elements, and in their verbal realization, that the great traditional poet, a Chaucer or a Shakespeare, comes into his own. We must call their works "popular" in the true sense, deriving from and speaking to all classes in their own community. Everybody is part of "the folk" as far as traditional literature is concerned, from courtier to peasant, countryman to city-dweller, intellectual to illiterate, men and women. The supreme example of the popular author is Shakespeare, even more than Chaucer, and it is notable that both Shakespeare and Chaucer are hospitable to "merry tales" and jest-book material.

This comic material does not in itself constitute the full range of popular literature by any means. The idealistic and the pious have equally their place. But here it is desirable briefly to characterize the kind of material that is offered by "merry tales" and to speculate on its deeper effects.

One point may be made by emphasizing the kind of story the comic medieval tale *never* tells—that major type of folk tale which, though now downgraded for children, survives most vigorously in the form of the so-called fairy tale. Such a tale tells of a youth or girl who undergoes adventures which lead to marriage and acceptance in the world of adults. The structure of such tales and the complex web of family relationships which they depend upon, and which lasts with variations through many centuries, I have discussed in my *Symbolic Stories*. The Aarne-Thompson classification somewhat obscures the importance of this type of folk tale, which includes many of the types numbered 300 to 1000, with the archetypal story of Cinderella as Type 510—a story which has many hundred versions. This type of story deals symbolically with the most fundamental problems of personal relationships, identity, and maturation. Although it has plenty of room for touches or even episodes that are comic, it is not in itself material for the comic in the modern sense. The "fairy tale" type of "ordinary" folk tale is very closely connected with the medieval romance in structure and intrinsic concerns, and has many of the same characteristics.[7] Fairy tale and romance define, largely by contrast, the popular comic tale, which itself is hard to define.

The popular medieval comic tale is much more miscellaneous in subject matter than is romance, but it seems safe to say, first, that even if the ostensible characters are animals, or the events patently ridiculous, the material deals with the everyday world. The Aarne-Thompson so-called "Stupid Ogre" stories (types 1000–1199), for example, are often trickster stories about everyday transactions in a peasant or rural society, concerned with buying and selling, doing or avoiding hard work, repairing the house, marital discord, etc., with no mention of an ogre at all. Even many "religious" folk tales are jokes of a similar nature, reflecting ordinary concerns or ordinary attitudes to life. For example, a widespread folk tale (Type 791) tells how Christ and Peter on earth spend the night in lodgings, sleeping in the same bed. When the drunken host comes home, he beats Peter, who in consequence changes place with Christ. The drunken host returns to beat the other lodger, and Peter catches it again. The setting and the sense of rough-and-tumble are perfectly commonplace. The humor is at the injustice of life, and perhaps at the selfish simplicity of Peter. Though there are religious overtones there is nothing pious or transcendental about the story. It is set in an utterly everyday world.

By contrast, the action itself is schematic and in a sense fantastic. Its elements are ordinary: the structure is a heightening of the ordinary; it is incredibly, indeed ridiculously neat, systematic, and thus fantastic—as it were, too good to be true—the very hyperbole of event, as popular style is so often hyperbolic while yet using familiar, proverbial elements. The conjunction of realistic setting and amazingly schematic reversals or accidents, so beautifully neat, is essential to the comedy.

Many, perhaps most, comic stories are about folly, which is mocked. Popular humor is derisive rather than satirical. Folly may either be self-generated, so to speak, as with Peter in the present instance, or caused and exploited by a quick-witted trickster. Since everyday life is the normal subject matter it is natural that married couples form the characters of a very large number of comic stories. Some of these stories are about simple silliness on the part of husband or wife, but this is often combined with adulterous intrigues. A large proportion of comic tales about marriage seem to be at the expense of the woman, and even those which show the woman successfully committing adultery are inclined to condemn women for behavior which is condoned in men.

A number of medieval comic tales are jokes about corpses. The most famous one is the Matron of Ephesus (Type 1510), originating in classical times and too well known to need repeating here. Another very widespread tale is that of the Three Hunchbacks, based on the difficulty of getting rid of embarrassing corpses (Type 1536B; cf. *Medieval Comic Tales*, pp. 4, 74). This theme may be combined with sexual deceit since sex and death, to which we are all subject, have the widest possible human interest.

The attitude in these stories is the traditional one, summed up in Sir Philip Sidney's comment in *The Apology for Poetry* that "we laugh at cripples." In other words, there is a strict limitation of sympathy, and the notion that laughter is kindly is impossible to maintain for these tales. The dominant attitude is that unsympathetic derision which marks all humor up to at least the eighteenth century, and which may be validated even today by asking, who likes to be laughed at? Only the conscious jester, who divides his absurd persona from his "real" self, wants to be laughed at. The tradition that clowns in real life are melancholy is not without basis; in our own persons we recognize that laughter is essentially derisive. Derision must be separated from the literary forms of satire, irony, burlesque, and parody. All these may use derision, but they are mixed with other attitudes—moralistic, didactic, or aesthetic—which may bring in more systematic elements. Derision is in itself a relatively simple matter, arising from a repulsion which dominates a perhaps unconscious sympathy. It has, however, been neglected in modern conceptions of the comic, which have therefore overemphasized both the subversiveness and the gentleness of comic tales.

V

The general view of medieval comic tales has for a long time been, in the words of McKnight (who goes back to Pater), that they "owed their origin in great to a spirit of revolt against the rigidity of the ideals of chivalry and of religion and against the stiffness and formality of prevailing literary conventions."[18] Such an essentially Romantic view of literature, which conceives of the serious poet as the superior Outsider, the unrecognized legislator of mankind, yet rebellious to society, tends to see comedy also as subversive of established values, though in a different way. Freud and, in a different way, M. Bakhtin are outstanding and influential exponents of this view.[19] More recently it has been reiterated by the distinguished social anthropologist Mary Douglas. She considers that all jokes have a "subversive effect on the dominant structure of ideas." "The joke is an image of the relaxation of conscious control in favour of the unconscious." "It is frivolous in that it produces no real alternative, only an exhilarating sense of freedom from form in general." "It is an image of the levelling of hierarchy, the triumph of intimacy over formality, of unofficial values over official ones."[20] This stimulating essay, based on African material, raises many interesting questions. The indulgence offered to the "unofficial culture" is clearly present. The outstanding example in English of this medieval tradition of comedy, as of other medieval traditions, is to be found in Falstaff. He is often nowadays taken, in a sense, quite seriously and thus subversively, as in his view of honor (*I Henry IV* 5:1.). Yet we do well to remember the end of him when his former boon companion coldly remarks, "I know thee not, old man" (*II Henry IV* 5.5.46).

Can the medieval popular comic tale be regarded as subversive, or does the frame of convention, which to achieve humor it must break, in fact constrain it fully?

The medieval popular comic tale breaches decorum by treating of indecorous subjects, e.g., breaking of wind, and breaches morality by treating in an indulgent or nonmoralistic way drunkenness, theft, fornication, adultery. It mocks certain kinds of persons in authority, or who claim authority, such as minor ecclesiastical officials or parish priests, occasionally knights, especially when such persons abuse their authority for personal advantage. In many cases those who commit breaches of decorum or morality escape with little or no punishment, and there is general sympathy with the young, or in some cases even the old if downtrodden by petty tyrants. The very contemplation of sinful or at any rate self-indulgent acts that most of us with natural feelings would like in fantasy to commit is a refreshing escape from the tedious constrictions of responsibility, respect for others, self-sacrifice, entailed by conventional morality.

But this is not quite all the story. Little allowance has been made for the great variety of points of view to be found in such narratives. Furthermore, despite the variety, there are certain frequent factors that are not subversive. There is a prevailing comedy of bossy wives, for example, who are taken down a peg or two. Perhaps only Chaucer really allows for sympathy with the domineering wife, in the person of the Wife of Bath, in the long "confession" that constitutes her Prologue. Chaucer is unusually complex. In the popular tale generally no figure of major authority—a king or a bishop—is mocked, only the minor usurper of authority (wife, summoner), or that minor figure of authority, the husband who is a weakling or a cuckold.

All humor is ambivalent, depending upon a close conjunction of attraction and repulsion, of sympathy and dislike, which may coexist in varying proportions. Here it is well to recall the characteristic derisiveness of popular literature. The amount of sympathy extended to the "unofficial" is strictly limited. The Romantic view which turns Cervantes' Don Quixote or Chaucer's January, both of them thoroughly silly old men, into tragic figures, is not without some slight truth based on inevitable sympathy with those whom society or the course of events draws into ridicule; but to take such sympathy very far is grossly anachronistic. The generally harsh lack of sympathy in medieval popular comic tales for the innocent victims of bad luck, for elderly cuckolds, for outraged parents, for unmarried pregnant girls, cannot be denied. And similarly, their acceptance of the norms of society, of hierarchy, of conventional standards, of common sense, is equally striking. It is those who are in some way outside the norms, or who abuse them, who are mercilessly mocked.[21]

The social norms which are implicitly evoked by medieval popular comic tales are, however, it is important to note, not entirely those of the dominant official ecclesiastical culture. This official ecclesiastical culture had so nearly complete a monopoly of the literacy which provides most of our evidence for medieval culture that we are in danger of believing its own claims to be total. It was not, could not, be so, and medieval popular comic tales are precious evidence of a vigorous *secular* culture whose norms were not ecclesiastical, or not entirely so. The tales give us only part of the secular culture. They have little to say about fighting and virtually nothing about love. But they give us a good view of the stable, middling, everyday, neither too courtly nor too poor, neither too young nor too old, center of society.

That center may be imaged as young middle-aged, married, moderately prosperous, confident, aware of temptation, not too shocked by yielding to it, aware of alternatives. Its members know that life does go on, with knocks and cuts and bruises, but also with fun and feasts and a little comfort, with many injustices and some satisfying revenges. The simplest image to represent it is the amused contemplation of the seduction of more or less willing girls by smart-alec young men. It is natural; it is wrong; it should not happen; it does go on; and possibly tragic outcomes are ignored. On the whole, sympathy is with the young men. The general point of view is not purely masculine, for married women enjoyed these jokes, but it is pervaded with a worldly masculinity.

We may recall Kenneth Jackson's discussion of storytelling in Western Ireland in the first half of the twentieth century. When a known storyteller arrived in a district, as the news got round there gathered an audience mainly of grown-up men, with the prattle and distraction of children excluded. Yet women were present and some of the great story-tellers were women, like Peig Sayers, whom Jackson celebrates.[22] In grown-up secular society women are fortunately rarely far away. *The Canterbury Tales* and the *Decameron,* to go no further, amply witness the possibility of easy sociability between the sexes. And it should again be recalled that not all the tales told are comic, and the comic tales are only an element in a larger complex pattern. In this pattern women play a more significant though not more important part than in the comic tales. For comedy to have been subversive women would have to have been shown as successfully and not absurdly dominant. But even the Wife of Bath was eventually beaten by her fifth husband. The medieval popular comic tale is not subversive: it reinforces, even in jest, the dominant, secular this-worldly culture of which it is so important and entertaining a witness.

NOTES

1. For the caution see G.H. McKnight, ed., *Middle English Humorous Tales in Verse* (Boston: D.C. Heath, 1913), p. xiv. McKnight's introduction is still a very valuable survey, with many references.

2. For *Dame Sirith,* besides ibid., and for the *Interludium* and *The Fox and the Wolf,* see J.A.W. Bennett and G.V. Smithers, ed., *Early Middle English Verse and Prose* (Oxford: Clarendon Press, 1966). Aarne-Thompson types refer to A. Aarne, *The Types of the Folktale,* trans. and ed. Stith Thompson (1928; rpt. New York: B. Frankling, 1971). *Dame Sirith* is translated in *Medieval Comic Tales* by P. Rickard, et al. (Cambridge: D.S. Brewer, 1972).

3. *The Auchinleck Manuscript* (facsimile), introd. D. Pearsall and I.C. Cunningham (London: Scolar Press, 1977). "A Peniworth of Witte" is item 28, ed. E. Kölbing, *Englische Studien,* 7 (1884): 113–17. "How a Merchande dyd hys Wyfe Betray" is edited by W.C. Hazlitt, in *Early Popular Poetry of England,* 4 vols. (London: John Russel Smith, 1864–1866).

4. *Sir Cleges,* in McKnight, *Humorous Tales,* pp. 38–80.

5. *Gesta Romanorum,* EETS, e.s. 33 (1879; rpt. London: Oxford Univ. Press, 1962).

6. *The Seven Sages of Rome,* ed. K. Brunner, EETS, o.s. 191 (London: Oxford Univ. Press, 1933). Also in the Auchinleck MS.

7. *Medieval Comic Tales.* Further references on p. 153. See also S.J. Kahrl, "The Medieval Origins of the Sixteenth-Century English Jest-Books," *Studies in the Renaissance,* 13 (1966): 166–83.

8. Further references in Aarne-Thompson, *Types of the Folktale.* For the general proposition see K.H. Jackson, *The International Popular Tale and Early Welsh Tradition* (Cardiff: Univ. of Wales Press, 1961). The episode is also listed in S. Thompson, *Motif-Index of Folk-Literature,* 6 vols. (Bloomington: Indiana Univ. Press, 1955–1958), 5:510.

9. J. Bédier, *Les Fabliaux,* Bibl. de l'école des hautes études, fasc. 98 (Paris: Emile Bouillon, 1893); P. Nykrog, *Les Fabliaux: Etude d'histoire littéraire et de stylistique médiévale* (1975; new ed. Geneva: Droz, 1973). C. Muscatine, "The Social Background of the Old French Fabliaux," *Genre,* 9 (1976): 1–20; idem, "Courtly Literature and Vulgar Language," *Court and Poet,* ed. Glyn S. Burgess, ARCA, 5 (Liverpool: Francis Cairns, 1981).

10. S.L. Thrupp, *The Merchant Class of Medieval London, 1300–1500* (Chicago: Univ. of Chicago Press, 1948); Derek Brewer, *Chaucer and His World* (London: Eyre-Methuen, 1978).

11. Derek Brewer, ed. and introd., *Chaucer: The Critical Heritage,* 2 vols. (London: Routledge and Kegan Paul, 1978), 1:8–15.

12. *The Canterbury Tales,* frag. 1, 1. 3169; frag. 6, 1. 324.

13. A. Murray, *Reason and Society in the Middle Ages* (Oxford: Clarendon Press, 1978).

14. *The Literary Context of Chaucer's Fabliaux,* texts and trans. by L.D. Benson and T.M. Andersson (Indianapolis: Bobbs-Merrill, 1971). Derek Brewer, "The Fabliaux," in *Companion to Chaucer Studies,* ed. Beryl Rowland, rev. ed. (New York: Oxford Univ. Press, 1979), pp. 296–325; Derek Brewer, "Structures and Character-Types of Chaucer's Popular Comic Tales," in *Estudios sobre los* Generos Literarios, vol. 1, ed. J. Coy and J. de Hoz (Salamanca: Univ. of Salamanca, 1975).

15. Reprinted in Derek Brewer, *Chaucer: The Poet as Storyteller* (London: Macmillan, 1984).

16. Derek Brewer, *Symbolic Stories* (Cambridge: D.S. Brewer; Totowa, N.J.: Rowman and Littlefield, 1980), pp. 1–14 and references.

17. Derek Brewer, "The Nature of Romance," *Poetica*, 9 (1978): 9–48; idem, "Medieval Literature, Folk Tale and Traditional Literature," *Dutch Quarterly Review*, 11 (1981): 3–16.

18. McKnight, *Humorous Tales*, p. 25.

19. S. Freud, *Jokes and Their Relation to the Unconscious*, trans. James Strachey, rev. ed. Angela Richards (Harmondsworth, N.Y.: Penguin, 1976); M. Bakhtin, *Rabelais and His World*, trans. Helene Iswolsky (Cambridge, Mass.: MIT Press, 1968).

20. Mary Douglas, "Jokes," in *Implicit Meanings: Essays in Anthropology* (London: Routledge and Kegan Paul, 1975), pp. 90–114, especially pp. 95–98.

21. Derek Brewer, afterword to *Medieval Comic Tales*.

22. Jackson, *International Popular Tale*, pp. 52 ff., cites both the earlier scholar Delargy and his own experience.

Chaucer and Erasmus on the Pilgrimage to Canterbury: An Iconographical Speculation

John V. Fleming

In a recent essay on Chaucer and the visual arts of his time I ventured the suggestion that his poetry might in certain instances be illuminated by the study of the popular arts of the fourteenth century, as it has already been much illuminated by the study of the more imposing and magnificent artifacts of the "high culture."[1] I propose now to put that suggestion to a concrete test, after a fashion, by examining certain references in the *Canterbury Tales* from the point of view of one neglected body of popular iconography, that of pilgrims' badges. The iconographic aspects of my essay will be both tentative and speculative, to be sure, and they will form only a part of a larger argument; yet I hope they may suggest a certain potential in the study of popular iconography for literary texts that may be anything but "popular" in nature.

In the year of grace 1370, the Lord Pope having declared a jubilee at the shrine of St. Thomas the Martyr, large crowds thronged Canterbury with the first early spring days, and continued in numbers unabated through the unusually sharp frosts of late December, around the saint's very day itself.[2] The pilgrims came from all parts of Europe, as we know from the archaeological remains of leaden ampules and badges scattered from Scandinavia to the Black Sea, but the saint's own countrymen were of course especially numerous. We reckon that thousands of Londoners will have made the journey, including much if not most of the burgher class, and Geoffrey Chaucer was probably among them. He surely *should* have been, if only for the tidy purposes of historical and poetical justice; for it was to be Chaucer's destiny to immortalize for generations of

English-speakers yet unborn, in verses more durable than the brazen monuments hacked to bits by the inquisitors of Henry VIII, the glittering memory of the holy blissful martyr's shrine. No reader of his poem will willingly believe that he could have constructed his fictive journey to Canterbury as he did, had he not tested the model first against the more humdrum empirical reality; but we shall never know with certainty.

In the case of another and a greater literary pilgrim the uncertainty disappears. About a century and a half later, in the second decade of the sixteenth century, Desiderius Erasmus of Rotterdam made the pilgrimage. The precise year was 1514. Erasmus, nearly fifty years old and beyond question the most famous man of letters in Christendom, visited the shrine of Becket in company no less august than that of the great John Colet, the Dean of Paul's. Erasmus probably did not travel along the London road from Southwerk, as Chaucer did, if not in fact then in fiction; rather he came from the North, from the fen country of East Anglia and the Marian shrine of Our Lady of Walsingham, after the stained pavement of Canterbury church the holiest piece of ground in all of England. Erasmus, indeed, was a rather fervent pilgrim. Two years before he had visited Walsingham and there saluted the blessed Virgin in a most original way, laying upon her altar not the wonted poultry or coin of the realm, but a poem written in classical Greek, a language read in those parts by very few beyond the holy Mother herself. His literary memorial of the second pilgrimage was, if possible, more problematical still. What he wrote this time was dangerously readable, a dialogue called "Peregrinatio religionis ergo" or "A Pilgrimage for the Sake of Religion," and it was immediately successful as one of the most stinging satires in the *Colloquia.*[3]

The speakers in the dialogue are Menedemus and Ogygius. The latter, clearly Erasmus himself speaking in a voice of contrived naiveté, recounts his experiences on a recent pilgrimage to Walsingham and Canterbury. A third character, Gratianus, plays an important role in the dialogue though he does not speak in his own voice. Gratianus probably represents John Colet, and his attitude toward the fraud and superstition of the Canterbury saint-trade contrasts starkly with the deadpan of Ogygius, who reports his speech in all its explicit censoriousness. The "Peregrinatio religionis ergo" is a wickedly funny debunking of the cult of relics, the principal feature of Becket's shrine, and it was so understood by Erasmus's friends and enemies alike. To begin with the latter, the English Dominicans attempted—and apparently with some success, to judge from the aggrieved remonstrances of the author—to have the book banned from English shops and stalls. His friends were just as keen to be sure that the book was available, and available in the King's English; and by the time it appeared, in the heady days of the Lutheran revolt, it was inevitably viewed as a powerful blast of the Protestant trumpet. In his preface, the work's first English translator wrote that "the noble and famouse clerke Desiderius Erasmus hath set forthe to the quycke ymage, before mennys eyes, the supersticyouse worshipe and false honor gyuyn to bones, heddes, iawes, armes, stockes, stones, shyrtes, smokes, cotes, cappes, hattes, shoes, mytres, slyppers, saddels, rynges, bedes, gyrdles, bolles, belles, bokes, gloues, ropes, taperes, candelles, bootes, spoores with many other soche dampanable allusyones to the duuylle to use them as goddes contrary to the immaculate scripture of gode."[4]

Such a judgment, to be sure, leaves certain questions concerning Erasmus and his motives unanswered, such as why he went on the pilgrimage in the first place, or why having gone once he went a second time, or why he tells us in a letter without visible traces of irony that he wrote Greek verses to our Lady *ex voto,* in fulfillment of a religious vow; but as a characterization of the dialogue's contents it is highly accurate. The "Peregrinatio religionis ergo" is a scathing attack on the superstitions of pilgrimage in general and upon those of the shrine of Becket at Canterbury in particular. Erasmus seems perfectly to capture the revulsion of the reform-minded churchmen in the English universities who enthusiastically backed King Henry's spiritual policies (if not always his domestic arrangements) and who would shut down the shrine forever even before Desiderius Erasmus was cold in his grave.

Thus it is that we have two accounts of the Canterbury pilgrimage which, though certainly grounded in fact of a sort, are no less certainly fictions. In each of them the empirical historical author has been effaced by a fictive *alter ego* of naive intelligence, a man whose apparently genial tolerance enables the morally problematical elements in each work. Concerning the relationship between these two narratives I have a bold if improbable theory, and it is that Desiderius Erasmus, a man who so far as we know left behind him not a single monosyllable of vernacular writing, has cast his Latin colloquy in the mold of the vernacular poem of an Englishman two generations dead at the time of his own birth. I state the theory thus baldly and irresponsibly not because it is the subject of this essay or even the essay's premise. I introduce Erasmus not as Chaucer's echo but as something more like his foil; for what interests me most about the two fictional pilgrim-narrators in their attitude toward the Canterbury shrine is the comparative simplicity of the Renaissance when set alongside the comparative complexity of the Middle Ages.

A demonstration of the point may begin with a brief history of

Chaucerian scholarship. Although Chaucer studies in the last century reveal an astonishing variety, a number of the most vigorous and fruitful critical approaches to Chaucer's poetry are still relatively young, and even as I write, colleagues in many lands are busy trying to pour the old wine of premodern literature into the new bottles of postmodernist critical theory. A good deal of the wine has of course been spilled in the process but, thanks to Chaucer's genius, enough is good as a feast. For purposes of my essay the critical movement that most concerns me is what I will call the New Historicism, which, though it is nearly as old as the positively ancient New Criticism, can be called new in distinction to the paleohistoricism of Skeat, Manly, Lowes, Tatlock, Kittredge, and most of the founding fathers and mothers of modern Chaucer studies.

Many of these scholars assumed as a matter of course that Chaucer was, within his immediate historical context, a religious dissenter if not a religious skeptic, a man whose religious views and sensibilities looked forward to the moderate Anglicanism of happier centuries. This inference seemed clear from the geniality and secular engagement of the verse, as well as from the profound theme of ecclesiastical satire in the *Canterbury Tales*. The ending of the *Troilus* and the ending of the *Tales* were tasteless but necessary obeisances to an oppressive priestcraft, and to the power of a public religious atmosphere that even a genial genius could not entirely escape. This view was not unchallenged but it was not effectively challenged until the early 1950s, with the appearance of two publications connected with the Johns Hopkins University. In 1952 D.W. Robertson published in *ELH*, the Hopkins' journal, a lengthy and revolutionary reading of *Troilus and Criseyde* called "Chaucerian Tragedy." Three years later Ralph Baldwin published, in Copenhagen, his book, in origin a Hopkins dissertation, entitled *The Unity of the "Canterbury Tales."* Each of these works attracted considerable notice; and in particular Robertson's essay, which proved to attract the early alarums of the controversy that would swirl around his *Preface to Chaucer*, stimulated immediate response and elaboration. What both scholars had done, in rather different ways, was to insist on the centrality of important fourteenth-century Christian ideas to the understanding of and critical evaluation of Chaucer's two major poems. They posited a Chaucer whose authorial stance was one of Augustinian Christianity—learned, dogmatic, Bible-centered, and deeply spiritual at the core. Though both "Chaucerian Tragey" and Baldwin's *Unity of the "Canterbury Tales"* have been overtaken by revisions and elaborations, the critical tendencies they represented and the critical controversy they invited have had the indisputable effect of valorizing the pursuit of sophisticated religious ideas in Chaucer, who is now widely though not universally regarded as a conservative Catholic Christian of his time.

Similar tendencies are discernible in the criticism devoted to the great Continental figures from whom Chaucer learned so much, particularly Jean de Meun in France and Boccaccio in Italy. I myself have of course been caught up in this general way of approaching texts, and I have done my best to defend the Christian orthodoxy of Jean de Meun in particular; yet at the same time I have come to believe that the whole question of religious attitude in Chaucer's poetry is perhaps in need of a subtler examination than it has so far had. I have no intention of declaring apostasy from the New Historicism, but I do want to take a second look at one of the issues fruitfully raised in the 1950s, and that is the issue of the Canterbury pilgrimage itself. The essential claim of Baldwin's *Unity of the "Canterbury Tales"*—a claim further expounded by numerous other critics—was that the spiritual metaphor of pilgrimage was the great unifying theme of Chaucer's poem, and that we should find in the disjunctions of the pilgrimage—spiritual aspirations sadly contradicted by carnal realities—an ambiguous emblem of the human condition. For Baldwin, Chaucer's good Parson held the key to understanding the truly religious dimension to the poem; for far from being the dull and gauche tag-along of earlier critics, he now became a kind of privileged traveler, the one pilgrim able to move from the mundane to the transcendent plane. This view seems to me so nearly right that it is perhaps ungenerous to attack it. But I find that it does not really explain one extraordinary fact about the *Canterbury Tales,* which is this: in framing his great fiction in the historical pilgrimage to the shrine of St. Thomas at Canterbury, Chaucer was framing it in the institution that was the single most conspicuous target of religious dissenters of his day, and an institution which thinking Christians could defend only with the keenest embarrassment.

The term *Lollard,* a Netherlandish word, first appears around 1300 and then weaves its mysterious way through the religious lexicon of the fourteenth-century vernaculars. It has a wide application as a satirical term, especially in antimendicant texts, but it generally means one who makes a hypocritical show of religious observance. By Chaucer's day, however, the range of its connotations had narrowed, and it generally meant a member of a more or less formally identifiable dissenting sect, a follower of John Wycliffe. But this specificity is only comparative, and it is probably most useful to think of "Lollardry" as incorporating a number of common dissenting attitudes rather than any kind of corporate entity. Most of our archival evidence concerning Lollardry in England comes from the fifteenth century, from the juridical proceedings following the enactment of *De haeretico comburendo* in 1401, but we can suppose that Lollard doctrines of the 1420s were different from those of the 1390s chiefly in their spread from an elite to a popular following. The Lollards were much exercised over eucharistic definition, but the most popular plank in their program, if I can call it that, was their vehement, sustained, and growing attack on pilgrimages and the shrines, images, and relics of the saints associated with them. Of the English pilgrimages the Canterbury pilgrimage was preeminent, and of the English shrines that of Becket was most execrated by the Lollards—and others. The English historian J.F. Davis has devoted a richly documented article to the attacks on the shrine from the time of Archbishop Courtenay in the early 1380s to that of Henry VIII, who utterly destroyed it in 1538.[5]

So far as Chaucer is concerned this evidence is in and of itself ambiguous, for just as religious dissenters attacked the pilgrimage, religious conservatives defended it. We find one Canterbury friar as late as 1535 calling those who refuse to give alms at the shrine Judases, and declaring that it is far more meritorious to give a penny to St. Thomas than a noble to the poor, "for one is spiritual and the other corporal."[6] Chaucer's choice of the Canterbury pilgrimage for his setting can hardly be entirely innocent, given the controversy that swirled around it, but his motives could be either those of the "heretic" or of the ultramontanist.

I conclude that they are nearer those of the former than of the latter, and, if this intuition is correct, it must necessarily qualify the nature of the poem's religiosity. Of the several overt and covert references to the shrine of Becket in Chaucer's poem, I find none that is free of a dissenter's scorn, however innocent the text appears on the first reading. Let me try to support this claim by reference to one of both kinds of allusions. The saint and his shrine are first and most famously evoked in the opening lines of the General Prologue:

> And specially from every shires ende
> Of Engelond to Caunterbury they wende,
> The hooly blisful martir for to seke,
> That hem hath holpen whan that they were seeke. (ll. 15–18)

This seems entirely positive until we enquire how it was exactly that the saint helped sick people, for it turns out that the miraculous cures were effected as much by ingestion as by intercession. Shortly after Thomas's murder, in the heady enthusiasm of the foundation of his cult, a certain London priest, William by name, initiated the novel and somewhat alarming devotion of drinking sips of the holy blissful martyr's blood, which had poured out in measurable quantities onto the stone floor of Canterbury cathedral. "Never had such a thing as drinking a martyr's blood been done before," writes Dr. Rock, subdued by the wonder of it all; "never has it been done since."[7] This remarkable piety might have seemed limited by finite resources, but there was in a double sense a solution to the problem of a supply of archiepiscopal blood that fell far short of popular pilgrim demand—to wit, "Canterbury Water," a sanctified tincture composed of well water and, one supposes, ever more minute traces of Thomas's blood and brains sponged up from the floor. The Canterbury Water was the best-selling snake-oil of the late fourteenth century; and it was packaged in the characteristic ampule of the Canterbury pilgrimage, a molded metal bottle about three inches high and two inches wide, surrounded by a decorative metal ribbon bearing an inscription. One side of the bottle showed a three-quarters, head-on view of the archbishop in full regalia; the obverse was a casting of some other wonder of the shrine. The legend around the metal band was *optimus egrorum medicus fit Thoma bonorum* ("Thomas is the best doctor for good folk"). It is probable that Canterbury Water was sold in different proofs, so to speak, with the de luxe and more expensive medicine enriched by minute quantities of gold. There is no avoiding Chaucer's irony when he says of the doctor

> For gold in phisik is a cordial;
> Therefore he lovede gold in special.   (ll. 443–444)

It is a couplet redolent of what we might call "medical dissent." I think the couplet

> The hooly blissful martir for to seke
> That hem hath holpen whan that they were seeke   (ll. 17–18)

is perhaps quietly pregnant with what we can legitimately call "religious dissent."

My second textual example is more covert and oblique, and whether we can see it or not will depend upon whether we ourselves can in historical imagination travel to Canterbury as pilgrims. We are aided in this imaginative journey by a good many literary and visual sources, and in particular by a rich body of surviving pilgrims' badges which depict the shrine's most conspicuous sights.[8] Just as there can today be few visitors to Paris who have not already encountered the Eiffel Tower in the form of an ashtray or a paperweight, there can have been few medieval pilgrims to Canterbury who did not already know something of the scene from the leaden brooches and ampules. What would Canterbury pilgrims of fact or fiction actually have done when they reached their destination?

A standard contribution of the wealthier pilgrims to Canterbury—and this group would have included most of Chaucer's ecclesiastics, the franklin, the doctor, and perhaps the knight—would seem to have been forty-two shillings, distributed in individual donations of seven shillings apiece at each of the six major stations of the church.[9] These were the shrine in the chapel of the Trinity behind the chancel, the "sword's point" in the northwest transept, the saint's tomb, the famous image of the Blessed Virgin in the crypt—and two other relics, cryptic on other grounds, the *corona* and the *chlamys*. Each of the stations undoubtedly had its own specific iconographic associations, and each must have been memorialized in its own badge or ampule. Chaucer's pilgrims would certainly have known what to look out for in Canterbury, for they had seen it all before. We have ampules depicting the *feretrum* or shrine, and the burial of the archbishop in his tomb. The miraculous image of the Virgin has of course been lost, but it is probable that it is memorialized, thus far unidentified with confidence, in one or more of the dozens of rather vague Virgins of the pilgrim badges.

The other three stations, more intimate relics of the blessed martyr, likewise had their popular images. Sir Richard de Breton, in his enthusiasm for our secular liberties, struck so fiercely at the unruly priest as to sever the scalp entirely free from his head and, in the process, to shear off the blade of his sword against the stone floor. The fragments of sword and archbishop alike were of course carefully preserved. The *punctus gladii*, a major relic of the cathedral, was also reflected in a popular pilgrims' badge.

The *corona* is more problematical. It surely will have been the severed scalp or its effigy encased in a reliquary. One of the mournful statues on the west front of Wells shows Thomas holding this crown as an attribute, and the motif exists elsewhere in the saint's iconography as well. But the *corona* was not the same thing as the *caput*, another major attraction of the pilgrimage. This would have been the entire skull or its simulacrum, presumably separated from the other remains at the time of the translation of 1220. The *caput Thomae*, kissed by hundreds of thousands of kneeling pilgrims, was a most famous relic, and there are many surviving examples of ampules in the form of stamped heads.

The sixth and final station, the very end of the pilgrimage so to speak, was the *chlamys*. This was the blood-soaked shirt that Thomas was wearing when he was murdered, now hung on a kind of coat-hanger from the church wall. The precise appearance of this relic *in situ* is not known. One of the windows in Canterbury may allude to it, though there the garment looks possibly ecclesiastical. I suspect, however, that Thomas' *chlamys* is what we see on a number of pilgrims' badges usually associated with the pilgrimage of St. Roche—a simple "T-shirt" set against a circular frame.[10] I further suggest that this somewhat strange end of the Canterbury pilgrimage can explain the beginning of Chaucer's.

Chaucer's pilgrimage begins, as every reader knows, at the public house and commercial hotel called the Tabard. An establishment of that name actually existed in Southwerk in Chaucer's time and later, and it is probable that, could we but recover what was common knowledge in the fourteenth century, we would find a typically Chaucerian joke or gibe in this bit of *realia*. There is probably a hint of this in the information that it was a "gentil hostelrye" (l. 718) and that "the chambres and the stables weren wyde / And wel we weren esed atte beste" (ll. 28–29). Here there seems perhaps to be some play with that disjunction of which so much is made elsewhere in the poem between those on the *via* to the heavenly Jerusalem and those who take their ease in Zion. The suspicion gains possible support from Chaucer's second reference to the Tabard:

> In Southwerk at this gentil hostelrye
> That highte the Tabard, faste by the Belle.   (ll. 718–719)

If the Belle, which was a whorehouse in Stowe's day, was the same thing in Chaucer's, it would be a fact not without sentence or solace. A fancy motel in the red-light district does not sound like the first rung on the ladder to heaven. But the question I want to raise is how an elegant public house came to be called "The Shirt"?

One complicating factor in the study of the history of signboards, according to Bryant Lillywhite, who has catalogued 17,000 of them from London, might be called their linguistic fragility. Few other "texts" can be so susceptible to "scribal error" and other kinds of "corruptions." It may not be the case that the Goat and Compasses was once the God Encompasseth Us, but it is almost certain that Saint Peter's Finger was indeed once Saint Peter in Vincula. Whether such mutations, which are extremely numerous and often enough quite droll, are always the result of ignorance is unlikely. In our own day we have seen a fast-food chain rename itself in response to cultural sensitivities, and we cannot doubt that similar things happened in the past, particularly with regard to names with compromising religious attachments. "At the time of the Reformation, signs such as the Cardinals Hat, or Cap, and the Popes Head fell into disfavor for various reasons, and thus in 1554 we find the house between Lombard Street and Cornhill described as 'formerly called le popes-head and now le Bishoppeshead.' "[11]

Against this background two facts gain a particular speculative importance with regard to Chaucer's Tabard. The first is this. The Tabard is a rare name for London public houses. Except for one quite modern tavern (predictably enough called "The Old Tabard") Lillywhite lists only three, and all three, of which the oldest is Chaucer's, are witnessed by late medieval, pre-Reformation documents. The second fact is that the name of the Chaucerian Tabard was indeed changed: it became the Talbot. As Lillywhite remarks, "No convincing explanation has yet appeared to account for Chaucer's 'Tabberd in Southwerk' being changed to the Talbot; on which subject many discrepancies are to be noted."[12] Now a talbot is a breed of hunting dog which seems to appear in England in the second half of the sixteenth century. All earlier appearances of the word in the *OED* are the names of specific dogs, as in Chaucer's catalogue of the animals in pursuit of the colfox in the Nun's Priest's Tale. Lillywhite catalogues some two dozen public houses called the Talbot, mostly from the seventeenth and eighteenth centuries.

Concerning this change of name Chaucerians have for the most part been at the mercy of John Aubrey, writing in the late seventeenth century, who ascribed the change to an ignorant landlord of the previous decade. This is certainly incorrect. Indeed it would seem that the lengthy and generally accurate remarks in Stowe's *Survey,* first published in 1598, described the Tabard sign as Stowe would have known it in his youth, nearly half a century earlier; for Lillywhite records that by 1556–1558 the inn was distinctly being referred to as "the Talbott in Southwarke", and that it is indeed the first of the many London public houses to bear that name. There are numerous additional complexities to the onomastic mystery, but the most plausible interpretation of the evidence is that sometime about the middle of the sixteenth century the Tabard became the Talbot, about the time, that is, that the Pope's Head became the Bishop's Head. My speculation is that there was something distinctly popish about the Tabard and its associations: namely, that the sign of the tabard alluded to the *chlamys* or shirt of Thomas à Becket, the sixth and final toll-booth in the Chaucer pilgrimage. (Its neighbor the Bell, incidentally, almost certainly took its sign from the famous Canterbury bells that were sold to pilgrims in their thousands as miniature souvenirs, and which survive today in the name of a common English garden flower.)[13]

Medieval theology recognized two levels or registers of worship—*latria,* worship to be accorded to God alone, and *dulia,* veneration appropriately directed toward God's creatures out of a pure religious motive. Such creatures might be the saints (or parts thereof piously preserved in monstrances of crystal and latten), statues or paintings of saints, or representations of sacred symbols, particularly of the Cross. The trouble was, of course, that sinful men displayed a distressing tendency to adore with the worship of *latria* mere contingent material creatures that were at the most deserving of pious *dulia*. And this was idolotry. It is precisely in terms of the confusion of *dulia* and *latria* that the powerful Lollard polemic against images, relics, and pilgrimages was framed, a polemic that most historians now recognize as the distinctively English contribution to fourteenth-century religious dissent.

Chaucer certainly was aware of the distinction between *dulia* and *latria,* for in addition to the soberer discussion of idolatry in the Parson's Tale, there is a playful yet profound presence of the theme in the Knight's Tale. When Palamon first sees Emelye from his prison tower, he mistakes her for the goddess Venus—thus parodying, incidentally, the young Aeneas, who mistook Venus for a mortal woman—but Arcite immediately recognizes her for what she is, gorgeous human flesh. This discrimination plays a principal role in their comically otiose argument about who rightly loves her. (We may recall that both men have seen the lady in question precisely once, at a distance that I roughly estimate as seventy-five to a hundred yards, for a period of time which I generously estimate at forty seconds.) Arcite claims that although Palamon saw her first, it is he, Arcite, who deserves her:

> For paramour I loved hire first er thow.
> What wiltow seyen? Thou woost nat yet now
> Wheither she be a womman or goddesse!
> Thyn is affeccioun of hoolynesse,
> And myn is love, as to a creature. (ll. 1155–59)

That is, Arcite accuses Palamon of adoring Emelye with *latria,* "affeccioun of hoolynesse," which is to say of idolizing her. This presents no moral problem for a pagan lover, but it does suggest a mental impairment and probably also a sexual one. A man who adores Emelye as goddess hardly deserves to enjoy her as woman. As so often in the *Canterbury Tales,* explicit parameters of "earnest" and "game" allow maximal ambiguity. "Wheither seistow this in ernest or in pley?" asks Palamon, when Arcite becomes the second man to fall in love with Emily within ten lines.

> "Nay," quod Arcite, "in ernest, by my fey!
> God helpe me so, me list ful yvele pleye." (ll. 1126–28)

The shifting registers of earnest and game, of *latria* and *dulia,* of truth and fable, are of course precisely those that control the poetic image of the pilgrimage itself. We see this most clearly only in the sobering and priviliged conclusion to the whole poem, the Parson's tale, when the Parson knits up all the feast with an earnestness that abandons the tale-telling game and with it the subordinate realm of contingent creation and the fiction of the poets. More than one critic wants us to believe that his performance is deeply and intentionally boring, that through it Chaucer advances covert but powerful claims for the vivacity of fiction as against the dullness of theological truth. I find I cannot accept this view. Even less can I accept that of Harry Bailley, the worst interpreter of Chaucerian text to be born before the year 1800, or the Shipman, a murderous pirate, when they tell us that the Parson is a Lollard. One fact that a historical reading of Chaucer can establish almost conclusively is that if the Parson were a Lollard, wild horses could not have dragged him to the shrine of Becket at Canterbury—let alone the humble mount that we are to imagine does in fact bear him there.

I think, instead, that we might regard the Parson and Geoffrey Chaucer as colleagues in anxiety, each attempting in his own way to maintain, against the importunate empirical moment, the cherished beliefs of a thousand years of Christian community. Neither can face the moment with an assured confidence, but both face it with utter honesty. The Parson's honesty is of the simpler sort, even as he is a simpler sort of man than Geoffrey Chaucer. "Life is a pilgrimage," he says: the destination is the earnest, the journey the game. At that last moment when dancing ends and dancers fail, the claims of poetry will seem so paltry that it would be the merest irrelevance to press them:

> I kan nat geeste "rum, ram, ruf," by lettre,
> Ne, God woot, rym holde I but litel bettre. (ll. 43–44)

Chaucer's honesty is, correspondingly, of the more difficult sort. He must make the Parson eschew alliteration and rhyme alike in a rhyming couplet in which the very word *rym* is made to be a principal part on an ablaut chart—*rum, ram, rym*. This is an honesty unable to cram the square pegs of practical experience into the round holes of theory. The Parson can transport himself from Bobbe-up-and-Doun-Under-the-Blee to "thilke parfit glorious pilgrymage / That highte Jerusalem celestial," on the wings of a metaphor clichéd already in Augustine's youth; but Chaucer does not travel so light. The pilgrimage he shows us through the filtering drama of the *Tales* is the sordid mélange of superstition, quackery, hypocrisy, and carnality represented in its lighter side by the Wife of Bath and in its darker side by the Pardoner: the pilgrimage to the shrine of Becket, the single most prominent focus of religious dissent in England from the time of the jubilee in 1300 until the enthusiastic destruction of the shrine in the sixteenth century.

The Canterbury pilgrim came into a dramatic environment bringing his gifts, not the least of which were the intensity of his faith and his freely given awe. His own dramatic role was, indeed, to be awestruck. The extraordinary *miracula* literature of pilgrimage shrines shows us wooden virgins fierce in their punishment of two crimes, nonchalance and skepticism. On the other hand Our Lady is remarkably merciful to those who, however blackened with capital sins, respect her images: that is the lesson of the Jongleur de Notre-Dame. Credulity, or to put the matter more neutrally, simplicity of belief, was an essential feature of "popular" religious experience in the later Middle Ages. It is this feature, indeed, that is most fixed upon by those inquiring and critical minds—Chaucer's, for instance, or Erasmus's—who found in it an ingredient of satire.

The pilgrims to Canterbury were led to the relics and images of the church as to a series of discrete yet incremental "scenes." The cathedral, with its various levels and visually constrained areas, provided an ideal "stage" for this pilgrimage within a pilgrimage. The physical movement around the building, the solemn transfer from one set of guardian-guides to another, the time-consuming devotions and oblations, must have heightened the sense of dramatic participation. Furthermore, certain aspects of the experience were clearly consciously designed for dramatic effect. At the *feretrum*, or shrine, the pilgrims were invited to kneel before an altar covered with a simple wooden canopy. At a given moment this covering was suddenly removed, probably by a system of ropes and pulleys, revealing the splendor of a profusion of gleaming gold and sparkling gems.[14]

We must call such a practice, I suppose, a gaud, a trick or stunt. It is a gaud that crowds the mind with poetic images poignantly relevant to Chaucer and his poem. The two registers of the plain wood and the glitter are in a sense those of *sentence* and *solace,* of earnest and game, fruit and chaff, the anagogical world and the empirical. The monks of Canterbury could claim with Paul that they kept their treasure in an earthen vessel; but the Lollards and the Henrician inquisitors thought more readily of another scriptural image, the whited sepulchres that masked an infinite corruption. Chaucer's good Parson, again catching a metaphor from the Bible, asks, rhetorically, "If gold rust, what shall iron do?" There was much rusted gold in Canterbury, and on the road to Canterbury. As every reader of Chaucer will know, and as many scholars before me have taken pains to point out, the character within the poem most closely identified with the more unsavory aspects of the saint-trade is the Pardoner, who is a kind of walking or riding reliquary.[15] For our understanding of the theme of pilgrimage in the *Canterbury Tales* the Pardoner is the one absolutely inescapable and inexorable pilgrim; but it will not do to speak of him alone.

One does not have to be a card-carrying structuralist to see a certain operation of the binary principle in the *Canterbury Tales*. Things come in pairs—at least when they are not coming in threes, thirteens, twenty-nines, and so forth. The Knight's Tale and the Miller's Tale are a pair, the latter being something of a blue-collar travesty of the chivalric extravagances of the former. At the same time the Miller's Tale is one of a pair with the Reeve's Tale, told by the Reeve with the explicit motive of "quiting" the Miller. What is true of the tales is truer still of their tellers as described in the General Prologue. Chaucer's pilgrims are like potent magnetic forces which, depending upon the alignment of their poles of force, either powerfully attract or sturdily repel each other. We see both the positive and the negative forces at work in the very first pair, Knight and Squire. They are father and son, yet utterly unlike in their conceptions and accouterments of the chivalric calling. The one entirely benign and unironic pairing of the Prologue threatens to pass us by unobserved, as understated and undeveloped as it is: the pairing of the good Parson and the good Plowman, brothers in the flesh no less than in the quiet spirit of peace. But the reader faces no such risk with what is surely Chaucer's oddest couple, odder even than January and May, and that is the Pardoner and the Summoner. They are not merely a pairing but an actual duet. After describing the Summoner, the narrator turns to the Pardoner, whom he first defines in terms of his relationship with the Summoner:

> With hym ther rood a gentil Pardoner
> Of Rouncivale, his freend and his compeer,
> That streight was comen fro the court of Rome.
> Ful loude he soong "Com hider, love, to me!"
> This Somonour bar to hym a stif burdoun;
> Was nevere trompe of half so greet a soun.   (ll. 669–674)

This image of boisterous two-part harmony seems stable enough until we turn it over, like a half-rotted log in the woods, to discover corruption exquisitely disgusting. For the moment, however, it is enough to take in the fine justice of the pairing (*freend, compeer*) in which the double and indeed the ambivalent poles of the pilgrims' formal motivations merge.

The Summoner, stèrn bailiff of an ecclesiastical court, threatens God's wrath against sinners in excommunication and its larger antitype, eternal damnation. The Pardoner, privileged bank-teller in the treasury of grace, offers forgiveness and *its* larger implication, eternal life. The fear of hell, the hope of heaven—such are the crude but powerful engines which, in theory, account for the medieval phenomenon of pilgrimage. How clearly we see them exemplified in this most hateful pilgrim pair.

We shall best learn why Chaucer sends his pilgrims two by two from consulting the medieval pilgrimage book *par excellence,* the first narrative of the passage to the Promised Land, and that is the Book of Exodus. In this book, wrote Rabanus Marus, all the sacraments of the Christian church were clearly prefigured; and in it, according to Dante, was the ancient and eternally comic plot of every Christian's salvation. Now the leader of the Exodus pilgrimage was Moses, but he did not travel alone. From the time of his earliest commission he has with him his brother, the priest Aaron, a man whose considerable gift of eloquence can compensate for the forensic inadequacy of tongue-tied Moses. Moses and Aaron both carry around what the King James Version calls "rods" and what the Vulgate calls *virgae,* and these rods do quite remarkable things such as turn into snakes that eat up other snakes or strike water from the flinty rock. Whatever a "rod" was, it must have been fairly large and stout, for Moses seems once in the old days to have killed an Egyptian with one. Medieval scriptural scholars were pretty sure these "rods" were what they knew as pilgrims' staves.

With this in mind, let us return to the Summoner and the Pardoner and their duet. "Ful loude he soong 'Com hider, love, to me!" says Chaucer of the Pardoner. "This Somonour bar to hym a stif bourdon." The principal meaning of this last line is that the Summoner accompanied the Pardoner with his deep bass voice. The Pardoner's voice is loud, but also "small" as Chaucer puts it: "A voys he hadde as small as hath a goot." It is surely a counter-tenor. But the principal meaning of the word *bourdon* is not a bass voice but a "big stick," and specifically a pilgrim's staff. No one who has read the ending of the *Roman de la Rose*—a poem demonstrably implicated with Chaucer's descriptions of Pardoner and Summoner alike—will soon forget the studiedly revolting development there of the lover's *bourdon* as phallus, poked into the aperture of the rose's "sanctuary". Thus I fear that the filthy implications of the line, "This Somonour bar to hym a stif bourdon," are absolutely and horribly inescapable. Both Sommoner and Pardoner, who are elsewhere associated with libertine heterosexuality, are here implicated in the unnamable medieval "crime against nature." The polymorphous perversity of the

Pardoner is particularly remarkable given the fact that, if we are to believe the General Prologue, he had no sexual organs at all. But if the musical is the primary, and the sexual the secondary implication of the "stif bourdon," there is certainly yet a third and mythic reverberation to the image in the potent and mysterious "rod" that Moses and Aaron pass between themselves as a kind of mystical baton. The good Parson, the postive image of apostolic life in comparison with whom the Summoner and the Pardoner reveal the morally shadowy opacity of a photographic negative, walks the boundaries of his parish like the fence-lines of a sheep-farm, "and in his hand a staf."

I myself burden my readers with what may seem a rather labored exegesis of a single line not because I want to convince them that the Pardoner and the Summoner are *tout court* perverted images of Moses and Aaron—though I think that is a fairly accurate if critically crude manner of seeing one important textual truth—but because I want to insist on the richly polysemous character of Chaucerian language, which can be fully as complex and captious as anything in Dante Alighieri or James Joyce. Chaucer wants us to think of the Exodus when we encounter the Pardoner and the Summoner; indeed, if we be Bible-readers at all, he *makes* us think of it. The Summoner loves garlic, onions, and leeks in part because the backsliding children of Israel, tiring of their diet of angel food and miraculous water provided by God in the Sinai Desert, longed for the fleshpots of Egypt. "We remember the fish, which we did eat in Egypt for nought; the cucumbers, and the melons, and the leeks and the onions and the garlick; but now our soul is dried away; there is nothing at all: we have nought save this manna to look to" (Num. 11:5–6).[16] When Moses tarried on the mountain of God fetching the Ten Commandments, Aaron wasted little time in accommodating the idolatry of the Israelites. He gathered together the women's golden earrings and melted them into a bovine idol, a golden calf. One can almost see the blush on Chaucer's face as he pursues the idea, but pursue it he does nonetheless. At the end of his tale, inviting his fellow pilgrims to come up and be gulled or gauded, the Pardoner makes a special offer to the women:

> . . . offre nobles or sterlynges
> Or elles silver broches, spoones, rynges.
> Boweth youre heed under this hooly *bulle* (ll. 907–909)

The *Peregrinatio religionis* concludes with a description of what happened on the way back from the shrine at Canterbury along the London road. At a narrow point where, because of the contours of the hills, travelers must perforce pass by, some friars had established their house;

and when they heard the hooves of horses these well-situated mendicants would rush out and sprinkle the returning pilgrims with an asperges of holy water, and beg for alms. When Gratianus and Ogygius passed by, they were presented with a filthy old slipper, claimed to be that of Saint Thomas, that they might kiss it and then make their offering. At this Gratianus became wroth: "What (saythe he) mean these bestes, that wold haue vs kysse ye shoes of euery good man? Why doo they not lyke wyse gyue vs to kysse the spottle, & other fylthe & dyrt of the body?"[17] But Ogygius, though he later admitted that Gratianus had a point, gave the old beggars a piece of money.

The success of religious fraud, as impenitently evil as it may be, depends upon a strangely satisfying symbiosis of shill and mark. It does not take the learning or the piety of a John Colet to see through false relics, for even a Harry Bailley will not be duped on terms other than his own. The Pardoner invites the pilgrims to worship the bull, but none is inclined to do so, not even the publican "most enveluped in synne."

> . . . it shal nat be, so theech!
> Thou woldes make me kisse thyn olde breech
> And swere it were a relyk of a seint,
> Though it were with thy fundement depaint.   (ll. 947–950)

It is Harry Bailley's finest hour, and, one might say, a triumph of the popular mind over the educated sensibility. For what of the pilgrim Chaucer, who has called the Pardoner "gentil," and described him as a nonpareil of showmanship and eloquence? This pilgrim is silent, as he almost always is when we most need to hear from him; but he seems to offer the coin of poetic approbation, the salute of one artist to another. We have perhaps not often thought of the pilgrim Pardoner and the pilgrim poet as one of the natural pairings of the *Canterbury Tales,* but there may be reason to do so. The good Parson, when his privileged moment comes, does not reject pardoners, pardons, pilgrimages, shrines, or images—but he does reject the fictions of the poet's art. He rejects, that is, not the Pardoner's gauds, but Chaucer's, not the orchestrated fictions of the stations of Becket's relics, but the orchestrated fictions of the *Canterbury Tales:* "Thow gettest fable noon ytoold fro me." What those of us "that herkne this litel tretys or rede" are to make of this remains wonderfully unclear; but we begin to see that Chaucer's poem is an endlessly uncomfortable one. Among the signs we must seek in the interpretive quest, some undoubtedly come from the learned traditions of Chaucer's wide-ranging literary education. But I suggest that others are of a humbler sort, cheaply stamped lead and pewter medallions scraped from the mud of the Thames.

NOTES

1. John V. Fleming, "Chaucer and the Visual Arts of His Time," in *New Perspectives in Chaucer Criticism*, ed. Donald M. Rose (Norman: Pilgrim Books, 1981), p. 128. My present essay is a somewhat revised version of my Shannon-Clark Lecture in English delivered at Washington and Lee University on 6 October 1983. I wish to record here my lively gratitude to the faculty of the Department of English at that university for the honor of the invitation.
2. See Raymonde Foreville, *Le Jubilé de Saint Thomas Becket* (Paris: Ecole Pratique des Hautes Etudes, 1958), pp. 14–15.
3. There is an elaborately annotated translation of this colloquy by John Gough Nichols, *Pilgrimages to Saint Mary of Walsingham and Saint Thomas of Canterbury by Desiderius Erasmus* (London: Westminster, 1849), rich in background materials. For Chaucerian applications, see the excellent article of Daniel Knapp, "The Relyk of a Seint: A Gloss on Chaucer's Pilgrimage," *ELH* 39 (1972): 1–26, to which I am happy to record a general indebtedness.
4. *The Earliest English Translations of Erasmus' Colloquia*, ed. Henry de Vocht (Louvain: Uystpruyst, 1928), pp. 104–5.
5. J.F. Davis, "Lollards, Reformers and St. Thomas of Canterbury," *University of Birmingham Historical Journal* 9 (1963): pp. 1–15.
6. Ibid., p. 15.
7. Daniel Rock, *The Church of Our Fathers*, edd. G.W. Hart and W.H. Frere (London: Murray, 1905), 3:349.
8. On this general topic see two excellent articles by Brian Spencer, "Medieval Pilgrim Badges," *Rotterdam Papers*, ed. J.G.N. Renaud (Rotterdam: *Rotterdam Papers*, 1968), pp. 137–53; and "King Henry of Windsor and the London Pilgrim," in *Collectanea Londiniensia: Studies Presented to Ralph Merrifield*, ed. Joanna Bird, Hugh Chapman, and John Clark (London: *Collectanea Londiniensia*, 1978), pp. 235–64. For further bibliography and illustrations see Kurt Köster, "Pilgerzeichen-Studien," in *Bibliotheca Docet: Festgabe für Carl Wehmer* (Amsterdam: *Erasmus*, 1963), pp. 77–100. A large number of the Canterbury badges are collected in the plate facing p. 113 in Cecil Brent, "Pilgrims' Signs," *Archaeologia Cantiana* 13 (1880).
9. My account of the stations of the shrine is indebted to the stunning researches of the Rev. W.A. Scott Robertson, "The Crypt of Canterbury Cathedral (II)," *Archaeologia Cantiana* 13 (1880): 500–551.
10. For published examples of this type of medal see Kurt Köster, "Religiöse Medaillen und Wallfahrts-Devotionalien in der flämischen Buchmalerei des 15. und frühen 16. Jahrhunderts," in *Buch and Welt: Festschrift für Gustav Hofmann zum 65. Geburtstag dargebracht* (Wiesbaden: Otto Harrassowitz, 1965), pp. 459–504; and Spencer, "Medieval Pilgrim Badges," plate 1 (p. 148).
11. Bryant Lillywhite, *London Signs* (London: George Allen and Unwin, 1972), pp. 40–41.
12. Ibid., p. 546.
13. See the plate in Brent's "Pilgrims' Signs."

14. I parphrase from the golden pages of Dean A.P. Stanley, *Historical Memorials of Canterbury,* 1st American ed. (New York: A.D.F. Randolph, 1888), pp. 258 ff.

15. See, especially, Melvin Storm, "The Pardoner's Invitation: Questor's Bag or Becket's Shrine?," *PMLA* 97 (1982): 810–18 and cited bibliography.

16. See R.E. Kaske, "The Summoner's Garleek, Oynons, and eek Lekes," *MLN* 74 (1959): 481–84.

17. *Earliest English Translations of Erasmus' Colloquia,* p. 188.

The Middle English *Planctus Mariae* and the Rhetoric of Pathos

George R. Keiser

Pathos abounds in later medieval English literature, demanding of its audience both an unqualified acceptance of the idea that what is said is what is meant and an unqualified emotional response to what is said. The usual response of the modern reader to such demands is embarrassment. Nowhere is that more apparent than in Chaucer criticism. Four of the twenty-four tales told by the Canterbury pilgrims—those of the Man of Law, the Prioress, the Clerk, and the Physician—are in the pathetic mode, and several others make significant use of that mode. Yet there is great reluctance among modern readers to believe that Chaucer found pathos a legitimate mode of expression and that it posed interesting artistic challenges for him. Instead, they prefer to believe that Chaucer's pathetic tales are either a lapse from a truly Chaucerian—that is, an ironic—standard, or they see the tales as parodic responses to an inferior, popular taste.[1]

Such attitudes are beginning to give way in the face of what we are learning about lay piety, for which pathos was an essential mode of expression, and the literary consequences of that piety. As long ago as 1942 C.A.J. Armstrong, in a study of Cicely of York, recognized that the brilliant synthesis of late medieval thought and culture by Johan Huizinga, which has long dominated studies of the religious art and literature of that age, was far less than satisfactory: "An emphasis altogether too great has been laid upon the alleged disharmony in the spirit of the waning middle ages. The picture of a society in ossified magnificence alternating with melancholy resignation between the feverish enjoyment of an outworn world and the lurid and terrifying contemplation of the next, ignores the very considerable degree of unity which

167

existed in the mind of that age."[2] Armstrong, it must be admitted, focused on lay piety as an aspect of the life of aristocratic women in the latter half of the fifteenth century. In the years since his study we have learned that lay piety is important in much wider social circles and over a longer period of time than Armstrong had in mind, and we are coming to realize that it shaped, to a very great extent, the entire understanding of life and art in the age. Indeed, Heiko Obermann has recently observed that fourteenth-century religious thought "can no longer be described only in terms of philosophy and academic theology, as we have been inclined to do. Lay thought and lay piety now begin to occupy the center of the stage."[3]

In literary criticism the fruits of this attempt to understand later medieval piety include some extremely valuable studies of Middle English devotional literature, among the best of which are the sustained examinations of the religious lyric by Rosemary Woolf and Douglas Gray and of the poetry of the Passion by J.A.W. Bennett.[4] Additionally, there have been several important explorations of the shaping influence of popular devotionalism on vernacular drama and, specifically, of the use of the pathetic mode in achieving the didactic purposes of the Passion plays.[5] Even in Chaucer studies evidence of a more positive attitude can be seen in explorations of the relation between popular piety and Chaucer's poetic and ethical vision, both in analyses of individual works and in more comprehensive views of Chaucerian pathos.[6]

This present paper is an attempt to contribute to the growing understanding of popular piety by examining a form of devotional literature that enjoyed a long and perhaps even a wide popularity in later medieval England, the *planctus Mariae*. The *planctus,* or lament of the Virgin for the suffering and death of her Son, is most often a free-standing lyric poem, but it can also be found imbedded in a dramatization or a narrative of the Passion. Alternately, it can be a prose or verse narrative of the Passion told by the Virgin herself. This lament, describing the Virgin's Compassion, may be spoken as a monologue, or it may be part of a dialogue with Jesus, the Cross, or St. Bernard; it may be spoken as the Virgin stands at the foot of the Cross, as she holds the corpse of her Son, or as she looks back upon the events of the Passion from a later time. In these descriptions of the Virgin's Compassion, we hear an account of a spiritual suffering corresponding to the physical sufferings of Jesus. Pathos is the dominant mode, and necessarily so, for the purpose of the work was to inspire a meditator to share in the sorrows of Mary and thereby to achieve a pathetic union with both Mary and her Son.

For the writer of the *planctus* the artistic challenge, then, was to delineate the sorrows of the Virgin in such a deeply affecting way that her "grief is both an incentive to the meditator's and also a measure of what his should be."[7] Not surprisingly, these writers relied upon rhetorical adornment, especially the apostrophe and graphic description, to evoke an affective response in the meditator. Without wishing to diminish the immense importance of those forms of adornment, I hope to show that a more fundamental aspect of the rhetoric of the *planctus* was the use of an antithetical style and structure which had been established as conventions of the form long before it reached medieval England.

The nature of this antithetical style and structure and the way in which the writers of the *planctus* used it to create pathos will be the concerns of this study. In the first part I shall look at three specific antitheses which are found, in varying combinations, in the English *planctus*. All of the *planctus* make use of at least two of these antitheses; several make use of all three. In the second part of the paper I shall look closely at one *planctus*, a prose work of the late fifteenth century. This work, like all the others of its kind, is exceedingly conventional, yet it is also of more than usual interest, as I hope to show. Finally, in a brief conclusion I shall explore some implications that this study of pathos in the *planctus Mariae* has for the study of other Middle English writings, particularly those of Chaucer.

I

While the line of transmission is still far from clear, we can be reasonably confident that the ultimate source of the English *planctus*, and its French and Latin antecedents,[8] was the Byzantine Marian lament, which had a learned tradition going back at least to the early sixth century and a popular tradition probably going back to antiquity. In a study of these Byzantine laments Margaret Alexiou has shown that they are part of a continuity of Greek ritual lament extending from antiquity to the present and that they "absorbed certain features of the ancient laments for gods and heroes."[9] Among the most important of these features is an antithetical style which, Alexiou demonstrates, is "a fundamental and integral part of the structure and thought of the lament"—so integral, in fact, that "in the best of the ancient and Byzantine literary laments, it is not external to, but dependent upon, the structure and thought."[10] This stylistic legacy from the ancient world, reinforced by other traditions, was, as I shall show, seized upon and put to good use by the authors of the English *planctus*.

For the authors of the *planctus*, presumably clerics with some knowledge of Scripture and the Latin rhetorical tradition, antithetical style would have been a familiar and congenial form of expression. Antithetical parallelism appears frequently in Old Testament Wisdom literature, in Lamentations, and in the speeches of Jesus; as a result, it is a not uncommon feature of the liturgy, the best example of its use there being the *Improperia,* or Good Friday reproaches. Furthermore, many of the rhetorical treatises known to these authors explained and illustrated antithesis as a figure of speech and a figure of thought, maintaining the distinction observed in the *Rhetorica ad Herennium:* "The first consists in a rapid opposition of words; in the other opposing thoughts ought to meet in a comparison."[11] Though no rhetorical treatise prescribes the use of antithesis for emotional effect, the *Rhetorica ad Herennium,* enumerating techniques for appealing to pity, prescribes one that almost demands antithetical style, "comparing the prosperity we once enjoyed with our present adversity."[12] Geoffrey of Vinsauf must have had such a prescription in mind when he produced this witty complaint in which a worn-out tablecloth bewails its misfortune: "I was once the pride of the table, while my youth was in its first flower and my face knew no blemish. But since I am old, and my visage is marred, I do not wish to appear. I withdraw from you, table; farewell!"[13]

Misfortune of any kind, and especially an untimely death, invites a contrast between present sorrows and past joys, and the contrast is inevitably poignant:

> Now with his love, now in his colde grave
> Allone, withouten any compaignye.[14]

Thus, an artist or writer wishing to describe the Compassion inevitably focused on the antithetical contrast between the Virgin's present sorrows and her joys at the Nativity and in the Childhood of Jesus. The *pietà* in sculpture and painting, with its image of the Virgin holding the dead body of Jesus, is all the more moving because of its implied allusion to the ubiquitous image of the Madonna and Child.[15] Similarly, the *planctus Mariae* incites the pity of the meditator by alluding to the earlier joys of the Nativity and Childhood, sometimes in several different ways within the same work.

One of the most common of these allusions is to the prophecy of Simeon in Luke 2:35. G.C. Taylor, in a survey of motifs in Middle English *planctus Mariae,* found that nine of the twenty-five he examined contained references to the dramatic and ominous prophecy that intrudes upon the celebratory account of the presentation of Jesus and that was long believed to foretell the Compassion of the Virgin: "He seyde .o. woman innocent / Thy herte with woo schal persyde be / My sones passion then he ment" (VI. 12).[16]

More clearly evocative of the contrast between earlier joys and present sorrows is the allusion to the idea that Mary experienced none of the usual pains of childbirth when she bore Jesus. Thus, in *Meditations on the Supper of Our Lord* Mary tells us, "Y feled no sorow yn hys beryng, / Nedys þan mote yn hys deyyng" (XII.815–16). It would appear that a much less explicit allusion to the same idea is the point of these lines from the earliest of English *planctus,* imbedded in the thirteenth-century *Assumption of Our Lady:* "Hu mai ihc al þis soreȝe iseo? / Ne cuþe ihc neure of soreȝe noȝt' " (II.3–4).

References to Mary's nursing the child Jesus are still another common way to invoke the contrast with past joys. In the Lambeth "Filius regis mortuus est" Mary recalls, "My sone þat y was woont to fede . . . And sones haue y no mo to souke my brest" (X.A. 17, 22). Similarly, in the Digby "Burial of Christ" Mary takes the body of Jesus with these words: "Yit suffere me to hold yow a while in my lap, / Which sum-tym gafe yow mylk of my pap!" (XXIII.752–53). Another fifteenth-century *planctus* (XVIII) uses "Þat chylde is ded þat soke my brest" as its refrain in the first nine stanzas, giving way eventually to "He rose agayn þat soke my brest" in the tenth and "The childe is risen þat soke my brest" in three further stanzas.

In the longer and more fully developed laments, especially those of the fifteenth century, the contrast is evoked in numerous other ways. There are, for example, apostrophes to Gabriel, as in the Lambeth "Filius regis": "A! gabriel, þou clepidist me ful of grace. / Nay! ful of sorowe þou now me seest" (X.A.45–46). One fifteenth-century work that is of particular interest—among other reasons, for the fact that it assumes the meditator to be a laywoman—evokes the contrast in a series of some-times charming reproaches, resembling those of Christ on the Cross in the Good Friday *Improperia:* "Your childur ȝe dawnse vpon your kne / With laȝyng, kyssyng, and mery chere; / Be-holde my childe, be-holde now me" (I.A.5–7). As the last line indicates, the Virgin speaks while holding the body of Jesus. Apparently this poem and others like it were intended for use while the meditator had before her a painting or sculpture of the *pietà,* in which is implied the contrast developed in the poem.

Elsewhere the Virgin also alludes to the Nativity and Childhood of Jesus in reproaches, usually set forth in antithetical style, to death:

> O deeþ, deeþ, þou doost me wrong!
> Mi babe þou sleest, þat neuer was wielde;
> Come, sle þe modir! whi tariest þou so longe?   (X.A.52–54)

or to the cross:

> Wiþ my brestes, my brid I fed;
> Cros! þou ȝeuest him Eysel and Galle   (IX.66–67)

or to the other instruments of the Passion:

> O ȝe creaturis vnkynde! þou iren, þou steel,
> Þou scharp þorn!
> How durst ȝe slee ȝoure best frend,
> Þe holiest child þat euere was born?   (X.A.85–88)

The fact that the first and third of the three preceding quotations are taken from the same work illustrates the proliferation and elaboration of such allusions in the fifteenth-century *planctus*.

It is tempting to speculate on reasons, beyond the general tendency toward copiousness among late medieval poets, for the abundance of these allusions to the Nativity and Childhood of Jesus. Looking at the *planctus Mariae* in conjunction with a substantial number of romances in which unjustly banished mothers lose their children to marauding lions, bears, or griffons, we may readily conclude that the theme of the bereaved mother had an enduring appeal. To suggest that men would not be susceptible to this appeal would be an oversimplification. Medieval men certainly knew the experience of grief, if we may judge from the laments spoken by men in romances—that of Arthur over Gawain in the Alliterative *Morte Arthure* being the best example.[17] Still, it seems reasonable to suppose that the insistence in the *planctus* on the childlike innocence of Christ would have had a particularly immediate appeal to women, many of whom would have experienced the loss of a child and even more of whom would have had to comfort a relative or friend upon such a loss. Of another explanation we can be more confident. That is, the constant reminders that the dead Christ was as innocent as the newborn infant at the Nativity would surely have kept before the meditator the absolute injustice of his death and, thus, the inestimable generosity of his sacrifice in the event. The effect would have been to intensify the pathos.

"Inseparable from the contrast between past and present" in ancient Greek laments, M. Alexiou observes, "was the contrast between mourner and dead."[18] A similar contrast between the Virgin and Jesus occurs in the Middle English *planctus Mariae,* expressing an intense feeling of separation and isolation, as in the following passages from "Filius regis mortuus est":

my fadur, my broþer, my spouse he was,
myne helpe, myne socour and all my chere.
nowe without broþer and spowse y moste hens pas,
fadurles & modurles y am lafte here,
as a woman forsake þat no goode has.
. . . .
ded is my dere childe, alasse!
nowe y may walke in þis falce worlde
as a wrecchyd wyȝte þat wantyth grace.   (X.C. 52–56, 122–24)

Hoccleve's "Compleynte of the Virgin before the Cros" returns again
and again to this contrast:

Now thee fro me, withdrawith bittir deeth
And makith a wrongful disseuerance.
. . . .
I needes mourne moot / & fare amis;
It seemeth þat thow makist departynge
Twixt thee & me for ay / withoute endynge.   (V.A. 78–79, 173–75)

Later in the same poem Hoccleve elaborates the contrast in a clever, if
perhaps strained, image:

Wel may men clepe and calle me "Mara"!
From hennes forward, so may men me calle.
How sholde I lenger clept be "Maria,"
Syn "I," which is Ihesus, is fro me fall
This day / al my swetnesse is in-to gall
Torned, syn þat "I," which was the beautee
Of my name / this day bynome is me.   (V.A.183–89)

Yet other means were found by authors of English *planctus* to drama-
tize and intensify the feelings of separation felt by Mary. There are, for
example, references to the height of the Cross which keeps Mary from
kissing Jesus or to the Jews' refusal to permit Mary to approach the Cross,
motifs found combined in the following passage from the Vernon "Disputation between Mary and the Cross":

Cros! þou holdest him so heigh on heiȝþ,
   Mi fruites feet I mai not kis.
Mi mouþ I pulte, my sweore I streiȝt
   To cusse his feet soþ þing hit is.
Þe Iewes from þe cros me keiȝt;
   On me þei made heore mowes amis.   (IX.90–95)

Where the burial of Jesus is described, Mary is made to beg that his body
be left with her, rather than being placed in the tomb:

Hit is my sone I loue so muche,
ffor Godes loue, burie him nouȝt!   (XX.B.667–68)

or that she may join him in the tomb:

> When he was lyvynge, to leve I desirid:
> Now sithen he is ded, all my Ioye is expirid;
> There-for lay the moder / in grave with the child! (XXIII.807–9).

As in the preceding quotation, the dread of separation is often combined with a wish that the Virgin might share in the physical sufferings of
her son and join him in death: "Taket doun on rode my derworþi child, /
Or prek me on rode with my derling" (III.3–4). However unseemly this
wish may appear to the modern reader, it has its origins in ancient
laments and, more important, it serves the meditative and didactic purposes of the *planctus*.[19] The portrayal of the Virgin yearning to share in
her son's sufferings establishes her as the example for the meditator, who
is to join her in her sorrows and her desire to share in the sufferings of her
son—in short, to achieve a pathetic union with them. Further, by having
the Virgin describe life without Jesus as one of emptiness and despair, the
planctus points the way both to the pathetic union and to what lies
beyond it, the life of virtue and love inspired by that union and the
ultimate hope of salvation.

The discussion of the Virgin's extreme feelings of isolation makes this
an appropriate moment to turn briefly to an important modern critical
statement on pathos as a mode, that of Northrop Frye's in *Anatomy of
Criticism*, a statement that has been applied without qualification to
medieval pathos in some earlier studies of the subject. There can be no
doubt that the Virgin's isolation makes her fit the paradigm for the
central figure of pathos, as set forth by Frye: "often a woman or a child
(or both, as in the death-scenes of Little Eva and Little Nell) . . . isolated
by a weakness which appeals to our sympathy because it is on our own
level of experience." It also seems appropriate to apply to the Virgin's
plight Frye's larger view of pathos as "low mimetic or domestic tragedy."
However, we must keep in mind that in the *planctus* the tragedy proves to
be more apparent than real when seen from the perspective of the
Resurrection, which is imposed at the end of many *planctus* and assumed
at the end of most, if not all, others. It is in light of that qualification that
we must consider Frye's observations that in low mimetic tragedy "pity
and fear are neither purged nor absorbed into pleasures, but are com-
municated externally, as sensations" and that pathos, thus, "has a close
relation to the sensational reflex of tears."[20] When viewed from the
perspective of the Resurrection, "the sensational reflex of tears" for
which the *planctus* strives is not an end in itself. The tears, if they are
meaningful, cleanse and soften the heart, preparing the meditator both

for a union with Jesus and for the virtuous life that was presumed to follow as a consequence of that union and to lead to the ultimate union made possible by the Resurrection.

Still further qualification of Frye's view of pathos is necessary when we consider, on the one hand, the efforts of the medieval authors to endow the Virgin with as much eloquence as their abilities permitted and, on the other, Frye's observation that pathos "is increased by the inarticulateness of the victim" and that "highly articulate pathos is apt to become a factitious appeal to self-pity, or tear-jerking." Despite a strong temptation to agree with Frye, the modern reader must recognize that the *planctus* are the product of an aesthetic very different from that implied in his analysis. Their authors subscribed to a rhetorical poetic, believing that poetry is "the art of clothing the already discovered truth in fitting language"[21] for the purpose of moving the audience to an acceptance of that truth. If the rhetorical *copia* seems excessive at times in the *planctus,* it is necessary to keep that belief in mind and to recognize as well that in an age of sumptuary excess, the idea of clothing the words of the Virgin in the best rhetorical finery must have seemed wholly appropriate and decorous to the authors of the *planctus.* The audience for whom they wrote was, owing to the increased literacy among the middle and upper classes and to the pious devotionalism widespread among these classes, large and enthusiastic, as well as given to sumptuary excess.[22] The opportunity to compose works of such seriousness in one's own tongue and for such an enthusiastic audience must have been a heady experience for these authors, who, clearly determined to make the most of their rhetorical skills, were striving to approach the merits and achieve the purposes of such devotional masterpieces as the pseudo-Bonaventuran *Meditationes* or Saint Bridget's *Revelations.*

Accustomed as we are to associating rhetoric with insincerity, we may have some difficulty seeing that for the medieval writer, making the most of one's rhetorical skills was an assured way to evoke pathos in the meditator. In an interesting attempt to argue that Chaucerian pathos depends upon rhetoric, T.H. Bestul has culled from rhetorical treatises known to the Middle Ages evidence of an intention to evoke an emotional response, and he concluded that there are "enough specifics to be of immediate practical use to an author, especially one of genius—such as Chaucer—who might realize the aesthetic potential of these rudiments." Almost as an afterthought, Bestul also suggests that the use of rhetoric to evoke pathos may be "generally related to the medieval doctrine that the emotions had potential for goodness, and perhaps to scholastic theories on the emotional apprehension of moral beauty."[23] Much work remains to be done before we understand fully how medieval authors perceived the affective function of rhetoric in moving an audience toward goodness. However, even at this early point we can be confident that long before Chaucer composed his pathetic tales, writers of devotional literature—Richard Rolle being the most obvious English example[24]—made ample use of rhetorical figures for the purpose of moving a meditator to pathos and, consequently, to virtuous living. The authors of the *planctus* were simply following that tradition. Overwhelmed by the often strained eloquence of the *planctus,* the modern reader can easily lose sight of the larger, didactic purposes of the adornment.

One final point from Frye's observations on pathos is pertinent to the *planctus* and brings us to the last set of antitheses to be discussed here: "The exploiting of fear in the low mimetic is also sensational, and is a kind of pathos in reverse. The terrible figure in this tradition . . . is normally a ruthless figure strongly contrasted with some kind of delicate virtue, generally a helpless victim in his power." The terrible figure in the *planctus* is, sad to say, the Jew, who is regularly seen in an antagonistic and antithetical relation to Mary or Jesus or both. For those of us living in the century of Auschwitz the treatment of the Jew in the *planctus* and indeed in all of late medieval literature is unspeakably horrifying and repugnant. Yet however much we may deplore it, we must also try to understand it, both for what we may learn about medieval literature and for what we may learn about ourselves.

Some recent studies of English cycle plays make important contributions to that understanding. Stephen Spector argues that "the abasement of the Jew in the drama . . . seems to have been essentially pedagogical" and that the Jew is merely a personification of a wrongheaded attitude. The Jew of the mystery cycles, Spector argues, is "made to reject Jesus because of blind devotion to the Old Law, fierce self-interest, and an adherence to the natural and reasonable that is so rigid as to be unnatural and irrational."[25] Though his conclusions have much to recommend them, Spector overstates the intellectual quality of the plays and seems to overlook the affective response to the Jews' torture of Jesus, which all the authors of the Passion plays clearly intended to evoke. To strike a more satisfactory balance, we must consider the work of two other critics who, complementing Spector's work, stress the affective quality of the Passion plays. Clifford Davidson has shown that the actions of the torturers are an essential element in the realism in the York plays, which is directed toward evoking an affective response in the audience.[26] Similarly, T.J. Jambeck has demonstrated how the Towneley Crucifixion play makes unique use of the torturers to evoke an affective response essential to its didactic purpose. Christ's *O vos omnes* appeal from the Cross, Jambeck observes, "inextricably identifies the playgoers with those *tortores* who historically crucified Jesus" and compels "a shocked recognition that the gamesome cruelty of the *tortores* is a tacit confirmation of the onlookers' own moral deformity."[27]

None of the *planctus* under discussion goes so far as to insist upon such an identification. However, all those that treat the Jews, or the unspecified torturers whom we may assume to be Jews, represent them as a negative ideal, an antithesis of Jesus and Mary and, thus, an antithesis of what the meditator should strive to be. Without fail the *planctus* uses an affective response to realize that didactic purpose. We can see this best by looking at the Vernon "Disputation between Mary and the Cross," which contains the most protracted and also the most interesting treatment of the Jews in any Middle English *planctus*. In the following passage, spoken by Mary, the "Disputation" establishes the antithesis:

> Þe feolle Iewes, wiþ false oþe,
> Iewes ston-hard in sinnes merk,
>   Beoten a lomb wiþ-outen loþe,
> Softer þen watur vndur serk,
>   Meode or Milk [i-]medled boþe.
> Þe Iewes weoren harde stones:
>   Softur þen watur or eny licour,
> Or dew3 þat liþ on þe lilie flour
> Was cristes bodie, in blod colour:
> Þe Iewes wolden ha broken his bones.   (IX.221–30)

Essential to the affective expression of the antithesis is the description of the Jews as "ston-hard" and "harde stones" and the contrasting association of Jesus with softness—"a lomb," and various liquids, including "blod." As J.D. Burnley has pointed out, the use of "hard-heartedness" to describe those unable to sympathize with others, such as the tyrant, the churl, and the homicide, reflects the medieval understanding of "the process of perception as the gathering of sense data followed by its resolution into images which were, so to speak, projected on to some receptive faculty of the human organism, or less concretely, of the soul."[28] Use of such traditional analogies as that of wax receiving the impression of a signet ring to explain the projection of impressions on the receptive faculty, whether the foremost cell of the brain (as in medical science) or the heart (as in the Stoic tradition), lies behind poeticized images of hard-heartedness. As a result the images in these lines from the "Disputation" would have evoked both an intellectual response and,

reinforcing that, an affective response from the contemporary meditator.
Wherever they appear in the Middle English *planctus Mariae*, the Jews
are a symbol of hard-heartedness and a lack of *pite:*

> Þe Iewes sei3 me ful sori,
> Þer as I stod in þe plas:
> ffor þat I made sereweful cri,
> Þei beede me schome and harde gras.   (XX.B.365–368)

> Wy haue 3e no reuthe on my child?
> Haue reuthe on me ful of murni[n]g.   (III.1–2)

> Alle oþere creaturis ben peteuose;
> Þe sunne, þe cloudis, for his dolour,
> Schewith her moornynge; but 3e viciose,
> 3oure lau3inge dooþ him dishonour.   (X.A.125–28)

Thus, the Jews are the antithesis of the mutual *pite* shared by Mary and
Jesus and in which the meditator is exhorted to join:

> Wepe with me, both man and wyfe,
> My childe is youres & lovys yow wele.
> If your childe had lost his life
> 3e wolde wepe at euery mele.   (I.A.65–68)

> Thyne herte so indurat is þat þu cane not wepe
> ffor my sonnes deth ne for my lamentacyoun?   (XVII.15–16)

What may be implicit in these statements—that is, that those who fail to
respond with *pite* are as hard-hearted as the Jews—becomes very nearly
explicit in these lines from the Digby "Burial":

> Who can not wepe, com lern at mee!—
> To see so meke a lambe her slayn;
>   Slayn of men that no mercy hadd;
> Had they no mercy, I reporte me see;
> To se this bludy body, is not your hart sadd?
> Sad & sorowfull, haue ye no pitee,
> Pite & compassion to se this crueltee?
> Crueltee, vnkindnese! O men most vnkind!
> Ye that can not wepe, com lern at mee!   (XXIII.708–16)

Another interesting variation on the theme appears in the Vernon "Disputation." There the decorum prevents Mary from addressing any pleas
directly to the audience. Instead she tells us, supposedly using their own
words, of the affective response of three Jews to the Crucifixion. That
response—"Þo weop I water, and teeres leete, / To care I was enclyned,"
says the second (IX.316–17)—is expected of the meditator too.

The emotional intensity generated by the antitheses involving the "wikkid" and "cruel" and "harde" Jews, on the one hand, and the sorrowful Mother and her "swete son," on the other, must have been very great indeed. From the eleventh century onward social, economic, and intellectual forces encouraged development of anti-Jewish and, eventually, anti-Semitic attitudes.[29] At the same time the overwhelming interest in the humanity of Jesus created an almost insatiable appetite for artistic and literary works based on New Testament Apocrypha, which had the authority of tradition.[30] Some writings of the Apocrypha, such as the *Gesta Pilati* and the *Transitus,* are explicitly anti-Jewish; others, especially those preoccupied with proving the virginity of Mary and defending her from charges of adultery,[31] must have seemed implicitly so to readers of the later Middle Ages. The *Transitus,* which tells of Jewish attempts to defile Mary's body after her death, invites a belief in an antagonism between Mary and the Jews that is a common theme in later Middle English Marian literature: "Gywes hatieþ our Leuedy muche & hure swete sone also," we are told in the *South English Legendary;* "I am Mary þat thow and all þi nacyon despysyþe, and sayne I bare neuer Goddys sonne of my body" Mary tells a Jew in *Mirk's Festial.*[32] Modern studies of the Prioress's Tale have made us conscious of the significance of the theme in the Miracles of the Virgin, but less attention has been given to its significance in such other works as the *Cursor mundi,* the Life of Saint Anne, accounts of the Assumption in dramatic and nondramatic verse, and even itineraries of the Holy Land. Given the currency of the belief in such an antagonism, we can be surprised only at the fact that fewer than half the extant *planctus* make any significant use of the antitheses involving Jews.

II

From the preceding discussion of the *planctus* as a form, I should now like to turn to a close examination of one particular *planctus,* a fifteenth-century prose work entitled "Lamentacioun of Oure Lady" by its editor, Carl Horstmann.[33] This work is of interest for several reasons, not the least of which is that it is a prose piece and, as a result, somewhat unusual. Like almost all other Middle English *planctus Mariae,* "Lamentacion" is undeniably conventional to an extreme; however, it is also undeniably a modest artistic success. As well as achieving a successful interweaving of the three antitheses discussed above, "Lamentacioun" has a thoroughly consistent point of view, and shows a remarkable, at times almost compelling, use of affective detail. Moreover, it is written in a well-managed and idiomatic prose style.

The success of "Lamentacion" can be illustrated by the following passage:

> And anone Pylatys assentyd to hem: & firse þei bete him with scourgys & þanne cloþede him in purpure, & afterward toke him to þe Jewes to spille on þe croys. And þan þei brought oute be-fore þe eyne of þe wrecchyd moder ihesu, my swete sone, corounede with a coroune of þornes vpone his hed, & his eyne al paal & his face al rede of blode & þe her of his hed hangyng ouer his eyne al be-bled, and beryng a croys vpone his bak þat he schuld on dye, and a corde abowte his nek, as a comun thef put be-twene to theuys. And whan I say þis cruel syght, þanne faylyd I al my strenkþe. (456.42–50)

The corresponding passage from another prose *planctus,* written perhaps a half-century earlier than "Lamentacioun" and preserved in Pepys Library MS 2498 (pp. 449–59), provides an instructive comparison:

> And onon token þe wicked men my swete son & ledden hym in-to a chaumbre & maden hym al naked an after-ward bounden hym vn-to a piler & beten hym so strongelich wiþ scourges knotted þat he resembled from þe hede vn-to þe hele as a man þat were flayn. And whan hij hadden so beten hym þat hij ne miȝtten no lengere duren onon hij vnbounden hym & al naked ledden hym out of þat chaumbre. And atte out-comynge bitwene me & iohn my cosyn we mette hym al blody. & j bigan forto crie & wiþ my cryyng myne herte failed me. & j fel to þe erthe as ded. (p. 453)

The latter passage gives a conventional account of the scourging, such as can be found in any Passion narrative. The emphasis is on its force and brutality, with the effects described only in cliché and hyperbole ("from þe hede vn-to þe hele as a man þat were flayn"). Nothing in the passage, except for "my swete son," makes us conscious of the Virgin's presence until we reach the end and hear of her crying and swooning. By contrast, "Lamentacioun" provides only a summary account of the scourging, which Mary did not witness. Immediately we move to what Mary did witness and, assured that we are seeing Jesus through "þe eyene of þe wrecchyd moder," we hear the effects of the scourging described in well-chosen, affective detail. Thus we understand precisely why Mary responded as she did.

In view of its artistry, it is not surprising that "Lamentacion" had a wide circulation in the London area. It is preserved in three devotional manuscripts, two associated with the abbey at Westminster—Bodley 596(A) and Cotton Cleopatra D.7—and a third associated with Norfolk (Cambridge Univ. Library Ii.4.9).[34] In addition, it was known to the early sixteenth-century London scribe of Huntington Library MS HM 144, who interpolated a portion of it into the Pepys prose *planctus* when he copied the latter work. The London connections suggest that "Lamentacion" probably had its origins there and also indicate how it came to the attention of Wynkyn de Worde, who printed it, with a woodcut of the *pietá* on the front, probably in 1509 or 1510.[35]

"Lamentacion" opens, apparently echoing Lamentations 1:1 ("Quomodo sedit sola civitas plena populo"), with "I, mary, ihesus moder" speaking of how she "sat in Jerusalem In the holy feest of estern a-lone In my hous, for the moche multitude of peple þat cam to the Cete I closed my dores and sat a-lone as I was woned to doo" (454.1–3). As this description continues, it emphasizes Mary's isolation, extending the antithetical contrast between Mary "a-lone" and "the moche multitude" with further references to "a grete noyse of peple In þe cete crying as wode peple" (454.8–9) and "þe rennyng of the peple to-geders" (454.10–11). All the while Mary is meditating upon "my swete sone ihesu" (454.4) and "hopying þat the eue be-fore ester he wolde come to me" (454.6). Finally, the intrusive noise of the crowd creates such anxiety that Mary exclaims, "wold god I were with my sone ihesu! A, who shal telle me any tydyngis of my swete sone ihesu?" (454.11–455.1). The meditator, aware of how the events now set in motion will culminate, recognizes the irony that the "tydyngis," when they come, will merely intensify Mary's isolation.

The isolation of Mary from Jesus continues as a theme of major importance in the rest of the work. In developing that theme, "Lamentacion" makes further use of the mob, which insists upon the death of Jesus and prevents Mary from coming near him on the *via dolorosa:* "& for moche pepyl I myght not come ny him, I cryed to him & he myght not here me for þe pepyl þat folowed him" (456.52–54). When Mary does reach Jesus, she speaks in terms recalling the antithesis of mourner and dead: "What thenkyst þou to do with þi moder to lete me þus alone & in dispeyre? thenkyst þou forsake me þus?" (457.6–7). Similarly, when she sees him on the Cross, she asks, "Why wolt þou leue me þus alone? whedir schal I go, my swete sone ihesu?" (457.34–35). Finally, the antithesis is made explicit when Mary holds the body of Jesus: "A, my swete sone ihesu! I, þi wrecchid moder, wende neuer to haue seyn þis of þe, noþer þise sorowes haue suffred for þe, but I wende for to haue had many ioyes & neuer a departyd fro þe" (458.27–29).

At the beginning of the work Mary's wish for "tydyngis" is answered by Magdalen, who reports that "ȝour swete sone & my reuerende mayster . . . is now take and with cordes now ybounde and wikkedly & cruelly of þe iewes betyn & drawyne" (455.14, 18–19). As she receives these tidings the Virgin, recalling the prophecy of Simeon and thus the Nativity and Childhood, describes herself as "ysmete with þe swerde of sorow" (455.11; cf. 455.20). With a sense of structure that is at times overbearing, "Lamentacion" has Mary use this image again and again, culminating in this elaboration after the death of Jesus: "And aboute þe houre of none þer come cruel knyʒtys & stode before my sone, & one of hem with a spere openyd his syde and clefe his hert on-two, & þat sorowe cleft myn hert on-two" (457.52–458.1).

After delivering her tidings Magdalen, without notice or explanation, disappears from the scene, leaving Mary alone again to bewail her sorrows. Verisimilitude and narrative are sacrificed for further development of Mary's intense feelings of isolation by, it would appear, another allusion to Lamentations. The image of the weeping Jerusalem in Lamentations 1:2 ("plorans ploravit in nocte et lacrimae eius in maxillis eius / non est qui consoletur eam ex omnibus caris eius") is probably meant to be recalled in Mary's account of her own misery: "It was In þe bygynny(n)g of þe nyght, & þe derknesse come about me, þat I weste neuer whedir I went; and mannys help had I none, but as I lay al þat nyght vpone þe erthe wepyng and crying, þat heuen myght be fyllyd þer-with, and al my hous I wette with weping of myn eyen" (455.22–26).

This account of Mary's extreme grief, remarkable for its occurrence in anticipation of the events of the Passion, is elaborated with a conventional series of apostrophes to God the Father, to Gabriel, and to Mary herself. Only one of these requires some notice: "Beholde now, gabriel: for þe Joye þat þou behete me, now haue I payne, and for þe gladnesse now haue I sorow, and (for) þe moderhede I am bereuede of my childe, and for þe grace I haue schame, and for þe lyf I haue deth, and for the blissyng þat þou behete me now is come curs vpone me" (455.32–36). The sense of the passage recalls Lamentations 1:7 ("recordata est Hierusalem dierum adflictionis suae et praevaricationis / omnium desiderabilium suorum quae habuerat a diebus antiquis") and perhaps 4:1 ff. ("Quomodo obscuratum est aurum mutatus est color optimus" etc.), and the antithetical style may echo Isaiah 3:24 ("et erit pro suavi odore fetor / et pro zona funiculus / et pro crispanti crine calvitium / et pro fascia pectorali cilicium").

Balancing these apostrophes near the beginning of "Lamentacion"— and attesting to the sense of structure on which I have already commented—are a complementary series near the end. There Mary again speaks in antithetical figures to express the conventional contrast between her present sorrows and joys promised at the Annunciation: " 'Blyssyd be þe fruyte of þi wombe,' & byholde, now my sone, þat is þe

fruyte of my wombe, is here wykkedly I-sleyn & now lythe here in
toumbe fulle of woundys" (458.54–56).

Not surprisingly, the author of "Lamentacion," steeped in the conventions of the *planctus Mariae,* extends the antithesis between Mary and the
"peple" with the conventional contrast between "þe wikked iewes"
(456.35; 457. 17, 19, 23, 29) and their cruelty (455.19; 457. 20, 53), on
the one hand, and "my swete sone ihesu" (455.16; 456.34; 457. 14, 25,
31), "þat lotheles lambe" (456.34; 457.23), on the other. The hard-
heartedness of the Jews is made manifest in contrast to Mary's tender-
heartedness at several points. For example, when Pilate offers to set free
Jesus "oþer baraban þat is mansleer" (456.24), Mary is elated: "I lift vp
my hert as though I had be arered fro deth to lyue" (456.25). When the
people do not choose Jesus, "I was smete with þe swerde of sorowe and as
a dede woman I fel vpone þe erthe" (456.29–30). Clearly, as the contrasts between "lift" and "fel" and "deth" and "lyue" indicate, for the
author of "Lamentacion" antithetical style and structure are the fundamental rhetorical devices for evoking pathos.

Earlier I noted that the Middle English *planctus Mariae* frequently ends
with the perspective of the Resurrection imposed upon the events of the
Passion, an imposition that, I would maintain, is another aspect of
antithetical structure. The fact and purpose of this imposition can be
understood by looking at "Lamentacion," where, as in almost all other
English *planctus,* the pathos inspired by Mary's Compassion is not an end
in itself, but a means to realize didactic and moral purposes. What Mary
comes to learn from her experience, and what the meditator by sharing in
her experiences learns too, is that pain and penitence provide the way to
joy and salvation. Following a tradition in English poetry that goes back
at least to "Stond wel, moder, ounder rode" (VII), the lesson is taught by
Jesus; "for in my deyinge I shal sle deth & with þe victorie of my passioun
I schal aryse þe thrid day" (457.45–46). Unquestionably, "Lamentacion" and most other *planctus* are overburdened with weeping, wailing,
and despair. Thus it is easy to lose sight of the fact that the concluding
vision is one of joy: "And whanne we saugh him aryse fro deth to lyue,
þanne were we fulfylled with more ioye þanne we were raþer with
sorowe, I-blyssyd my swete sone ihesu" (459.17–19).

In imposing this vision of joy the authors of the *planctus* were observ-
ing a convention of Passion literature, to which Sister M.F. Madigan and
J.A.W. Bennett have called attention. Examining the *Passio domini* theme
in Richard Rolle's writings, Sr. Madigan observed that "far from revealing a morbid sentimentality in the author, or eliciting such in his read-

ers," the graphic description of Jesus's sufferings "leads to the 'delyght and savour of heauen,' since for Rolle the Crucified is never 'atwyned' from the 'Kyng of myȝt.' "[36] Casting a wider net, Bennett pointed out that for Rolle, Ludolf of Saxony, Walter Hilton, and Margery Kempe, "the lessons of the Cross are to be applied not only in penitential prayer but in daily practice." Bennett's conclusion concerning the nature of the devotional attitudes in Middle English Passion poetry applies as well to "Lamentacion" and all *planctus Mariae:* "The Easter Liturgy, familiar in the Middle Ages to every child, lies behind every poem here considered."[37]

III

Of Griselda and Custance, Charles Muscatine has written, "characters of this class owe much in turn to Chaucer's vision of the sorrowing Mary," but he backed away from discussing Chaucer's debt because "the very sacredness of the pathetic subject-matter exempts it from criticism or even from ventilation."[38] If I have, as I hope, proved the discretion of the latter contention mistaken, I should now like to offer some support for the former contention.

Chaucer's three pathetic heroines—Griselda in the Clerk's Tale, Custance in the Man of Law's Tale and Virginia in the Physician's Tale—are, like the Virgin in the *planctus,* women of extreme virtue whose sufferings are intensified by their isolation. Custance, the most isolated of the three, is sent from Rome "to strange nacioun / Fro freendes that so tendrely hire kepte" (B.268–69). Twice she is set adrift, once alone and once with her little child, on "salte see." When accused of murdering Hermengyld, "she hath no wight to whom to make hir mone" (656). Her isolation seems more intense and pitiable because the Sowdanesse, the slayer of Hermengyld, and Alla's mother, owing to their associations with the fiend (365–71, 582–88, 782–84), are so aggressively evil, whereas Custance is utterly passive, committing herself to the care of God and his Mother. The antithetical contrast is reinforced with affective diction reminiscent of that found in the *planctus.* While Custance is "ful of benignytee" (446), the Sowdanesse is "welle of vices" (323) and Alla's mother "ful of tirannye" (696). Custance is "wrecched" (274, 285, 918), "woful" (316, 522, 978), "innocent" (618, 682), and "wery" (514, 596). By contrast, like the Jews in the *planctus,* the enemies of Custance and their actions are "wikked" (404, 816, 958), "cursed" (432, 433, 697, 821, 891), "feendly" (751, 783), and "false" (619, 687).

Of particular interest is the use of such diction in the words spoken by

Custance at the shore (826–63) when she compares her "litel child" and the Virgin's child and, further, draws a contrast (ironic to the informed audience, of course) between the child and "thyn harde fader" (857) and "housbonde routheless" (863). P.M. Kean has observed, "In writing this prayer of Constance, Chaucer clearly has in mind the popular devotional form of the *planctus.*"[39] And so he probably did, though what he wrote was also determined by the conventions of accused-queen stories.

Virginia too is in a seemingly unequal contest with a "false juge" (C. 154, 158, 161; see also 164), into whose heart "the feend . . . ran" (130). The only recourse for the "mayde" and "deere doghter" is to accept death at the hands of her father, "with fadres pitee stikynge thurgh his herte" (211).

Griselda's plight is different because the Clerk's Tale is so much more complex than those of the Man of Law or Physician. Yet the isolation of Griselda, made to seem more intense by the use of antithetical diction, fits the same pattern that we have seen in the other tales. To illustrate, we need only look at the scenes with the (apparently) "cruel" (E.539), "suspect" (541, 542), "ugly sergeant" (673), where Griselda remains the very image of meekness (538, 548, 566) and patience (495, 623, 644, 670, 677, 688).

The pathetic tale that provides the strongest evidence of Chaucer's knowledge of the *planctus Mariae* is that of the Prioress, where the pathos is evoked by an antithetical structure remarkably similar to that of the *planctus.* R.O. Payne, examining the use of *circumlocutio, epithetum,* and *determinatio* in the tale, concluded that "the tendency to black-and-white contrasts . . . is characteristic of the whole machinery of elaboration in the poem."[40] Of the embellishments examined by Payne, the most relevant are the descriptions of the Jews and their murder of the boy as "cursed" (B.1760, 1764, 1768, 1789, 1875) and the contrasting descriptions of the boy and things and persons associated with him as "innocent," "litel," and "yonge."

The antithetical structure in the tale begins with the opening stanzas where we hear, first, of the "Jewerye" (1679) and, then, of the "litel scole" (1685), the "smale children" (1691), and the "litel clergeon" (1693). Perhaps the most significant element in the antithetical structure occurs in the following lines, where the imagery recalls the contrast, commonly found in the *planctus,* between the proud, obstinate, hardhearted Jews and the humble, tender-hearted Mary and her "swete sone."

> The swetnesse hath his herte perced so
> Of Cristes mooder that, to hire to preye,
> He kan nat stynte of syngyng by the weye.

Oure firste foo, the serpent Sathanas,
That hath in Jues herte his waspes nest,
Up swal, and seide, "O Hebrayk peple, allas!"   (1745–50)

Immediately following the death of the *clergeon* are two contrasting apostrophes, the first addressing "O cursed folk of Herodes al newe" (1764), the second, "O martir, sowded to virginitee" (1769). Finally, we find the antithetical structure implicit in the placement of the stanza describing the "torment and . . . shameful deeth" (1818) of the Jews between two stanzas describing the funeral of the *clergeon*.

In retelling this popular story Chaucer very likely intended to bring to mind the Compassion of the Virgin. The widowed mother, "with moodres pitee in hir brest enclosed" (1783), crying "ever on Cristes mooder meeke and kynde" (1787) as she searches for her child, recalls, as John Hirsh has noted,[41] Mary's anxiety when the child Jesus remained behind at the temple, and it may also recall the account, found in some *planctus*, of her search for Jesus on Good Friday morning. The "mooder swownynge by the beere" (1815), who must be led away, recalls the Virgin's behavior at the burial of Jesus. Other elements in the tale make clear that the audience is to recall the Passion. Along with the allusions to the Holy Innocents, whose deaths prefigured the death of Jesus, the tale ends with a prayer to "yonge Hugh of Lyncoln" (1874), who was believed to have died in a Jewish ritual parodying the Crucifixion.

Yet the tale, like the *planctus* and other Passion literature, does view the Passion from the perspective of the Resurrection. The boy-martyr, after all, is raised from the pit, singing "Alma redemptoris," a song of praise to the mediatrix, "this welle of mercy, Cristes mooder sweete" (1846). As promised in the Prioress's Prologue, the tale is told "in laude . . . Of thee [i.e., Jesus] and of the white lylye flour / Which that the bar" (1650–52). The tale is, in short, a celebration of the victory of the Passion, which was made possible through Mary. Thus Morton Bloomfield's observation on the Man of Law's Tale applies here as well: "We cry in the conviction that ultimately the tears will be washed away from all faces and that we shall enter into our final home."[42]

Perhaps the most interesting aspect of the Prioress's Tale, in view of our study of the *planctus,* is that Chaucer has recast it to make it an expression of a sensibility shaped by popular devotionalism—that is, the sensibility of one accustomed to responding with pathos to the *planctus,* the miracles of the Virgin, saints' lives, and other pious literature preserved in such volumes as the Vernon MS. As yet we know less than we might wish about the pathetic sensibility of the later Middle Ages, but what we do know suggests that Chaucer has captured it with remarkable precision and genius in the portrait of the Prioress and in her tale. That genius is especially clear if we look at one detail from the Prioress's portrait, her tender-hearted feelings for mice and dogs, which have been seen as evidence of thwarted maternal feelings or of grossly misdirected charity. Such interpretations must be, at least, qualified when we consider some words of Margery Kempe, who, like the Prioress, was deeply absorbed in Marian piety and whose visions of the Passion suggest more than passing acquaintance with the *planctus Mariae:* "& sumtyme, whan sche saw þe Crucyfyx, er yf sche sey a man had a wownde er a best wheþyr it wer, er ȝyf a man bett a childe be-for hir er smet an hors er an-oþer best wyth a whippe, ȝyf sche myth sen it er heryn it, hir thowt sche saw owyr Lord be betyn er wowndyd lyk as sche saw in þe man er in þe best."[43] It seems reasonable to conclude that for both the Prioress and Margery their excessive concern for animals and children has a clear relation to their meditations on the Passion and Compassion. The feelings of pathos for the sufferings of Mary and Jesus were meant to lead to compassion and charity for the sufferings of all. Extending that compassion to include all suffering creatures, especially those of diminutive size, would be natural enough in one whose head was full of juxtaposed and overlapping images of the Madonna with the Child Jesus in her arms, and of the torn, crucified body of the "swete sone" in the arms of the sorrowing Mother.[44] As Chaucer obviously recognized, for such a sensibility mice and dogs might evoke more tears than a mob of anonymous, murderous Jews.

A P P E N D I X

Following is a list of the Middle English *planctus Mariae* consulted for this study; the list does not purport to be exhaustive of works, versions, or editions. For each item I have provided the number given in Carleton Brown and R.H. Robbins, *The Index of Middle English Verse* (New York: Columbia Univ. Press, 1943); and R.H. Robbins and J.L. Cutler, *Supplement to the Index of Middle English Verse* (Lexington: Univ. of Kentucky Press, 1965)—cited as *IMEV*. Additionally, I have provided, where it exists, the number given the work in G.C. Taylor, "The English 'Planctus Mariae' " *Modern Philology* 4 (1907): 605–37, cited as "Taylor."

Non-Dramatic Verse

I. A. "An Appeal to all Mothers," in *Religious Lyrics of the XVth Century,* ed. Carleton Brown (Oxford: Clarendon Press, 1939), pp. 13–16, item 7 *(IMEV* 2619; Taylor X); B. "Klage der Mutter Jesu zu anderen Müttern," in R. Cords, "Fünf me. Gedichte aus den Hss. Rawlinson Poetry 36 und Rawlinson C.86," *Archiv für das Studium der neueren Sprachen und Literaturen* 135 (1916): 300–302 *(IMEV* 1447).

II. "Assumption of Our Lady": A. in Taylor, p. 3; see also *King Horn,* ed. G.H. McKnight, rev. ed., EETS, o.s. 14 (London: Kegan Paul, 1901), pp. 111–36 *(IMEV* 2165; Taylor I); B. in *Cursor mundi,* part 4, ed. R. Morris, EETS, o.s. 66 (London: Trübner, 1877), p. 1150; and part 5, ed. R. Morris, EETS, o.s. 68 (London: Trübner, 1878), p. 1602 *(IMEV* 3976; Taylor I).

III. "The Blessed Virgin's Appeal to the Jews," in *Religious Lyrics of the XIVth Century,* ed. Carleton Brown (Oxford: Clarendon Press, 1952), p. 81, item 60 *(IMEV* 4159).

IV. "The Blessed Virgin to her Son on the Cross," in Brown, *XIVth Century,* p. 228, item 128 *(IMEV* 14).

V. A. "The Compleynte of the Virgin before the Cross," in *Hoccleve's Works: The Minor Poems,* ed. F.J. Furnivall and I. Gollancz, rev. J. Mitchell and A.I. Doyle, EETS, e.s. 61 & 72 (1892 & 1925; rev. rpt. in one vol., London: Oxford Univ. Press, 1970), pp. 1–8; B. "A lamentacioun of the grene tree, complaynyng of the losyng of hire appill," in *Hoccleve's Works: The Regement of Princes,* EETS, e.s. 72 (London: Kegan Paul, 1897), pp. xxxvii–xlv. *(IMEV* 2428; Taylor XI).

VI. "De arte lacrimandi," ed. R.M. Garrett, *Anglia* 32 (1909): 269–94 *(IMEV* 2347).

VII. "Dialogue between Our Lady and Jesus on the Cross," in *English Lyrics of the XIIIth Century,* ed. Carleton Brown (1932; rpt. Oxford: Clarendon Press, 1950), pp. 87–91, item 49 *(IMEV* 3211; Taylor III).

VIII. "A Dialogue of the Virgin and Child," in *The Early English Carols,* ed. R.L. Greene, 2d ed. (Oxford: Clarendon Press, 1977), pp. 104–5, item 156 *(IMEV* 2530).

IX. "Disputation between Mary and the Cross," in *The Minor Poems of the Vernon MS,* part 2, ed. F.J. Furnivall, EETS, o.s. 117 (1901; Millwood, N.Y.: Kraus, 1975), pp. 612–26, item LII *(IMEV* 2718; Taylor VI).

X. "Filius regis mortuus est": A. (MS Lambeth 853) *Political, Religious, and Love Poems,* ed. F.J. Furnivall, rev. ed., EETS, o.s. 15 (1903; rpt. London: Oxford Univ. Press, 1965), pp. 233–37; B. (MS Harley 3954) ibid., pp. 238–42; C. (MSS Douce 78 and Rawlinson C.86) in Brown, *XVth Century,* pp. 8–13, item 6 *(IMEV* 404; Taylor VIII–IX).

XI. "Lamentacio dolorosa," in Brown, *XIVth Century,* pp. 82, item 63 *(IMEV* 3245).

XII. *Meditations on the Supper of our Lord,* ed. J.M. Cowper, EETS, o.s. 60 (1875; rpt. Millwood, N.Y.: Kraus, 1975), pp. 25–35 *(IMEV* 248; Taylor IV).

XIII. "Of Our Lady and Her Son," in Greene, *Carols,* p. 110, item 164 *(IMEV* 377.5).

XIV. A–E. "Of the Passion" ("Gaudeamus synge we"), in Greene, *Carols,* pp. 105–7, item 157A–E *(IMEV* 1219, 2111, 2036; Taylor XIII–XIV).

XV. A–B. "Of the Passion" (" 'O, my harte is woo,' Mary she sayd so"), in Greene, *Carols,* pp. 109–10, item 163a–b *(IMEV* 4023; Taylor XVIII).

XVI. "Of the Passion" ("To see the maydyn wepe her Sonnes passion"), in Greene, *Carols,* p. 109, item 162 *(IMEV* 548; Taylor XIX).

XVII. "O Thou, with Heart of Stone," in Brown, *XVth Century,* pp. 16–17, item 8 *(IMEV* 3692).

XVIII. "Our Lady's Imprecation," in Brown, *XVth Century,* 18–22, item 10 *(IMEV* 1899; Taylor XII).

XIX. "Quis dabit meo capiti fontem lacrimarum?" in *The Minor Poems of John Lydgate,* ed. H.N. MacCracken, EETS, e.s. 107 (1911; rpt. London: Oxford Univ. Press, 1962), pp. 324–329 *(IMEV* 4099).

XX. A. "St. Mary's Lamentation to St. Bernard on the Passion of Christ," in *Yorkshire Writers,* ed. C. Horstman (London: Swan Sonnenschein, 1896), 2:274–82 *(IMEV* 771; Taylor V); B. "Þe Lamentacioun þat was bytwene vre lady and seynt Bernard," in *The Minor Poems of the Vernon MS,* part 1, ed. Carl Horstmann, EETS, o.s. 98 (1892; Millwood, N.Y.: Kraus, 1975), pp. 297–328, item XXXVI *(IMEV* 1869; Taylor V); C. "The Sorrows of Mary," in *Cursor mundi,* part 5, ed. R. Morris, EETS, o.s. 68 (London: Trübner, 1878), pp. 1368–1413 *(IMEV* 3208; Taylor II).

XXI. "The Sorrowing Mary" ("Mary moder, cum and se"), in Greene, *Carols,* p. 107, item 158 *(IMEV* 3575; Taylor XV).

XXII. "Who Cannot Weep, Come Learn at Me," in Brown, *XVth Century,* pp. 17–18, item 7; see also Greene, *Carols,* pp. 108–9, item 161 *(IMEV* 4189; Taylor XVII).

Dramatic Verse

XXIII. "The Burial of Christ," in *The Digby Mysteries,* ed. F.J. Furnivall, New Shakespere Society, ser. 7, no. 1 (London: Trübner, 1882), pp. 171–200; and *The Digby Plays,* ed. F.J. Furnivall, EETS, e.s. 70 (1896; rpt. London: Oxford Univ. Press, 1930), pp. 171–200 *(IMEV* 95; Taylor XXV).

XXIV. *The Chester Mystery Cycle,* ed. R.M. Lumiansky and David Mills, EETS, s.s. 3 (London: Oxford Univ. Press, 1974), pp. 314–17 *(IMEV* 716; Taylor XXIII).

XXV. *Ludus Coventriae,* ed. K.S. Block, EETS, e.s. 120 (London: Oxford Univ. Press, 1922), pp. 267–69, 298, 305, 311–12, 320–22 *(IMEV* 2321; Taylor XXIV).

XXVI. *The Towneley Plays,* ed. George England, EETS, e.s. 71 (1897; rpt. Oxford Univ. Press, 1925), pp. 253–54, 267–72, 363–66 *(IMEV* 715; Taylor XXII).

XXVII. *The York Mystery Plays,* ed. L.T. Smith (1885; rpt. New York: Russell, 1963), pp. 342–43, 363–67, 461–62 *(IMEV* 1273; Taylor XXI).

Prose

XXVIII. "The Complaint of Our Lady": see J.F. Drennan, *"The Complaint of Our Lady* and *Gospel of Nicodemus* of MS Pepys 2498," *Manuscripta* 24 (1980): 164–170, for information concerning this unpublished work.

XXIX. "Lamentacion of Oure Lady," ed. C. Horstmann, *Archiv für das Studium der neueren Sprachen und Litteraturen* 79 (1887): 454–59.

NOTES

1. Charles Muscatine asserts that "while the pathetic contributes to the variety of the *Tales,* it is not an important axis of his style" and suggests that pathetic subject matter "allows Chaucer to write some of his least successful verses": *"The Canterbury Tales:* Style of the Man and Style of the Work," in *Chaucer and*

Chaucerians, ed. D.S. Brewer (University: Univ. of Alabama Press, 1966), p. 107. For the other attitude, that Chaucer parodies the pathetic, see H.P. Weissman, "Late Gothic Pathos in the *Man of Law's Tale*," *Journal of Medieval and Renaissance Studies* 9 (1979): 133–53.

2. C.A.J. Armstrong, "The Piety of Cicely, Duchess of York: A Study in Late Medieval Culture," in *For Hilaire Belloc,* ed. D. Woodruff (New York: Sheed & Ward, 1942), pp. 69–70.

3. Heiko Obermann, Fourteenth-Century Religious Thought: A Premature Profile," *Speculum* 53 (1978): 93.

4. Rosemary Woolf, *The English Religious Lyric in the Middle Ages* (Oxford: Clarendon Press, 1968); Douglas Gray, *Themes and Images in the Medieval English Religious Lyric* (London: Routledge & Kegan Paul, 1972); J.A.W. Bennett, *Poetry of the Passion* (Oxford: Clarendon Press, 1982).

5. E.C. Dunn, "Popular Devotion in the Vernacular Drama of Medieval England," *M&H,* n.s. 4 (1973): 55–68; T.J. Jambeck, "The Dramatic Implications of Anselmian Affective Piety in the Towneley Play of the Crucifixion," *AnM* 16 (1975): 110–27.

6. J.C. Hirsh, "Reopening the *Prioress's Tale*," *Chaucer Review* 10 (1975–1976): 30–45; C.P. Collette, "Sense and Sensibility in the *Prioress's Tale*," *Chaucer Review* 15 (1980–1981): 138–50; Michael Stugrin, "Ricardian Poetics and Late Medieval Cultural Pluriformity: The Significance of Pathos in the *Canterbury Tales*," *Chaucer Review* 15 (1980–1981): 155–67; J.D. Burnley, *Chaucer's Language and the Philosophers' Tradition* (Totowa, N.J.: Rowman and Littlefield, 1979).

7. Woolf, *English Religious Lyric,* p. 241.

8. Woolf, ibid., p. 247, provides a brief survey and bibliography of these antecedents, including those in Anglo-Norman, which have received little attention. Also of importance are two studies by Sandro Sticca: "The Literary Genesis of the Planctus Mariae," *Classica et Medievalia* 27 (1966): 296–309; and "The Literary Genesis of the Latin Passion Play and the *Planctus Mariae:* A New Christocentric and Marian Theology," in *The Medieval Drama,* ed. Sandro Sticca (Albany: SUNY Press, 1972), pp. 39–68.

9. Margaret Alexiou, *The Ritual Lament in Greek Tradition* (Cambridge: Cambridge Univ. Press, 1974), p. 69.

10. Ibid., pp. 150, 159.

11. *Ad C. Herennium,* ed. and trans. Harry Caplan (1954; rpt. Cambridge, Mass.: Harvard Univ. Press, 1964), p. 377. See also *The Parisiana Poetria of John of Garland,* ed. and trans. Traugott Lawlor (New Haven: Yale Univ. Press, 1974), pp. 115, 131.

12. Ibid., p. 151.

13. *Poetria Nova of Geoffrey of Vinsauf,* trans. M.F. Nims (Toronto: Pontifical Institute of Medieval Studies, 1967), p. 34.

14. The Knight's Tale, ll. 2778–79. This and all Chaucer quotations are taken from *The Works of Geoffrey Chaucer,* ed. F.N. Robinson, 2d ed. (Boston: Houghton Mifflin, 1957).

15. Gertrud Schiller, *Iconography of Christian Art,* trans. J. Seligman (Greenwich, Conn.: New York Graphic Society, 1972), 2.180.

16. Citations in parentheses in this part of the paper refer to works listed in the Appendix. Roman numerals refer to the work, capital letters (where used) to versions, and Arabic numerals to lines.

17. For examples see V.B. Richmond, *Laments for the Dead in Medieval Narrative* (Pittsburgh: Duquesne Univ. Press, 1966), pp. 132–87.

18. Alexiou, *Ritual Lament,* p. 171.

19. Alexiou, ibid., p. 178, points out that one of the forms of unfulfilled wish in Greek ritual laments was "that the enemy of the dead might suffer the same fate. The last wish is in fact a curse." Such a curse is not unknown in the *planctus;* see, for example, X.A.123–24; XXIII.648–53.

20. Quotations from Frye in this and the next several paragraphs are taken from *Anatomy of Criticism* (1957; rpt. Princeton: Princeton Univ. Press, 1973), pp. 38–39.

21. R.O. Payne, *The Key of Remembrance* (1963; rpt. Westport, Conn.: Greenwood Press, 1973), p. 57.

22. The sumptuary excesses of the age pervaded all areas of life, as is evident from descriptions of the private chapels of the gentry and nobility; see, for example, Armstrong, "Piety of Cicely," p. 86. Not surprisingly, then, the Virgin was often seen as a lady of elegance and courtly breeding; see H.L. Frank, "Chaucer's Prioress and the Blessed Virgin," *Chaucer Review* 13 (1978–1979):346–62.

23. T.H. Bestul, "The *Man of Law's Tale* and the Rhetorical Foundations of Chaucerian Pathos," *Chaucer Review* 9 (1974–1975): 220, 224.

24. See M.F. Madigan, I.B.V.M., *The Passio Domini Theme in the Works of Richard Rolle* (Salzburg: Institut für englische Sprache und Literatur, 1978), pp. 32–38. For an important study touching on the relation of rhetoric and affect, see A.J. Minnis, "Literary Theory in Discussions of *Formae Tractandi* by Medieval Theologians," *New Literary History* 11 (1979–1980): 133–45.

25. Stephen Spector, "Anti-Semitism and the English Mystery Plays," *Comparative Drama* 13 (1979–1980): 9, 13.

26. See Clifford Davidson, "The Realism of the York Realist and the York Passion," *Speculum* 50 (1975): 275–76; and idem, "Northern Spirituality and the Late Medieval Drama in York," in *The Spirituality of Western Christendom,* ed. E.R. Elder (Kalamazoo, Mich.: Cistercian Publications, 1976), pp. 134–36.

27. Jambeck, "Dramatic Implications," pp. 122, 127.

28. Burnley, *Chaucer's Language,* p. 103. It seems reasonable to suppose that the image of the sword piercing the Virgin's heart would have been enriched by association with this idea.

29. In a recent book on medieval anti-Judaism, with a full bibliography, Jeremy Cohen discusses the contribution of the mendicants to the development of an anti-Jewish ideology and looks briefly at the expression of this ideology in mendicant poetry; see *The Friars and the Jews* (Ithaca: Cornell Univ. Press, 1982).

30. See Emile Mâle, *The Gothic Image* (1913; rpt. New York: Harper, 1958), pp. 202–66.

31. For the early history of the charge that Jesus was the illegitimate child of a Roman soldier, see R.E. Brown, S.S., *The Birth of the Messiah* (Garden City, N.Y.: Doubleday, 1977), pp. 534–42. For the response to the charge of illegitimacy in the Apocrypha, see Edgar Hennecke, *New Testament Apocrypha,* ed. Wilhelm Schneemelcher, English translation ed. R. McL. Wilson (Philadelphia: Westminister Press, 1963, 1:363–417.

32. *The South English Legendary,* vol. 1, ed. C. D'Evelyn and A.J. Mill, EETS, o.s. 235 (London: Oxford Univ. Press, 1956), p. 237; *Mirk's Festial,* ed. T. Erbe, EETS, e.s. 96 (London: Kegan Paul, 1905), p. 249. For a useful discussion of the antagonism between Mary and the Jews, see R.W. Frank, "Miracles of the Virgin, Medieval Anti-Semitism, and the 'Prioress's Tale,' " in *The Wisdom of Poetry,* ed. L.D. Benson and S. Wenzel (Kalamazoo, Mich.: Medieval Institute Publications, 1982), pp. 177–88.

33. "Lamentacioun" is item XXIX in the Appendix; citations in the text refer to page and line numbers in Horstmann's edition. The Pepys prose *planctus,* mentioned below, is item XXVIII in the Appendix.

34. A.I. Doyle, "A Survey of the Origins and Circulation of Theological Writings in English in the 14th, 15th, and early 16th Centuries" (Ph.D. diss., Cambridge University, 1953), 2:222–23. After this essay had gone to press, Doyle called my attention to the existence of a text of "Lamentacioun" in Westminster Diocesan Archives MS H.38, ff. 127b–132. For details see N.R. Ker, *Medieval Manuscripts in British Libraries,* vol. 1: *London* (Oxford: Clarendon Press, 1969), pp. 419–21.

35. Woolf, *English Religious Lyric,* p. 361, n. 3, wrongly reports that STC 17535 is another edition of "Lamentacion."

36. Madigan, *Passo Domini Theme,* p. 100.

37. Bennett, *Poetry of the Passion,* p. 60.

38. Charles Muscatine, *Chaucer and the French Tradition* (1957; rpt. Berkeley: Univ. of California Press, 1969), p. 193; idem, *"The Canterbury Tales,"* p. 107. See also R.W. Frank, *Chaucer and the Legend of Good Women* (Cambridge, Mass.: Harvard Univ. Press, 1972), pp. 94–96.

39. P.M. Kean, *Chaucer and the Making of English Poetry* (Boston: Routledge & Kegan Paul, 1972), 2:193.

40. Payne, *Key of Remembrance,* pp. 168–69.

41. Hirsh, "Reopening the *Prioress's Tale,*" p. 39.

42. Morton Bloomfield, "The Man of Law's Tale: A Tragedy of Victimization and a Christian Comedy," *PLMA* 87 (1972): 388.

43. *The Book of Margery Kempe,* ed. S.B. Meech and H.E. Allen, EETS, o.s. 212 (London: Oxford Univ. Press, 1940), p. 69, ll. 1–7.

44. Margery tells of how she was driven to tears "whan sche sey women in Rome beryn children in her armys, yf sche myth wetyn þat þei wer ony men children" (86.25–27) and when, "as sche cam be a powr womanys hows, þe powr woman . . . had a lytel manchylde sowkyng on hir brest" (94.8–12).

Some Versions of Apocalypse: Learned and Popular Eschatology in *Piers Plowman*

Robert Adams

That Langland is an apocalyptic thinker is certainly no fresh insight; general acknowledgment of the point dates back at least to Morton Bloomfield's *"Piers Plowman" as a Fourteenth-Century Apocalypse* (1961). However, the exact nature of Langland's prophetic expectations has never been satisfactorily explained, nor have the apparent incongruities in tone between the various prophecies been adequately accounted for. Scholars have been at a loss to explain, even in the broadest terms, how it is that various passages from *Piers Plowman,* equally apocalyptic, seem mutually incompatible. Many of these passages reveal a thoroughly traditional, learned, pessimistic hue; but certain others appear to draw on a combination of popular Sibylline legends and intellectually faddish Joachimism in order to offer promises of a millennium.

Resolving this apparent antinomy in the poem's theology will require a lengthy examination of many particulars, in the course of which a chief danger is that the reader may gradually lose his bearings and despair of the goal. At the risk, then, of forfeiting the advantage of surprise and, perhaps, of seeming to force the poem's facts into the confines of a ready-made theory, I will begin with a brief discussion of two key terms, "learned" and "popular," and a glimpse of the central hypothesis about Langland's thought in which they figure. The first term, "learned," will hereafter be reserved to describe the relatively uniform and spiritualized eschatology of the Latin exegetical tradition while the second, "popular," will denote a potpourri of orthodox and heterodox eschatological motifs, some of which are popular in the fullest sense (i.e., they seem to have circulated orally and are widespread in vernacular materials) whereas others are popular only in that they are stylish in certain educated circles and readily assimilable into the amorphous mass of Everyman's hopes and fears about the End. The hallmarks of this "popular" eschatology are that it is syncretistic, that it is highly unstable (constantly readapting its expectations to vicissitudes in the public world), that its tone tends toward fantasy and escapism, and that its content is, paradoxically, very "this-worldly" because of its obsession with the politics of Last World Emperors, Angelic Popes, and earthly kingdoms of the saints.

This use of terms is not intended to deny that many elements of Augustinian (or "learned") eschatology penetrated the popular mind through catechesis as well as through vernacular literature. Nor does it seek to obscure that some of the ultimate sources of what is here being termed "popular" eschatology would qualify, in a different context, as "learned" (e.g., the writings of Joachim of Fiore or those of Peter John Olivi). Finally, there is no wish to suggest that "popular" and "learned" eschatologies, so defined, are absolutely discrete, for there are some interesting and unexpected points of contact, as we shall see. Rather, these contrasting terms should be understood as a heuristic device for highlighting the polarities of this issue as Langland perceived it: an unequal struggle being waged in the hearts and imaginations of his contemporaries between an otherworldly and moralistic vision of human destiny endorsed by many generations of learned exegetes and a volatile melange of popular vaticinations that threatened to poison spirituality at its roots by redirecting mankind's energies from the task of personal *ascesis* to a sterile curiosity about current events.

In harmony with the traditional eschatology of Augustine, which envisions little room for historical progress beyond Christ's Incarnation and for which the remainder of the sixth age of the world is mainly a penitential interlude,[1] many of Langland's prophecies take the form of direful pleas for personal amendment, lest the time of grace expire and find us unprepared. For example, the episode of Hunger in Passus 6 has seemed purely social satire of a well-known sort till Langland injects a startlingly pessimistic and traditional apocalyptic perspective at the end of the passus:

> Ac I warne you werkmen, wynneþ whil ye mowe
> For hunger hiderward hasteþ hym faste.
> He shal awake þoru3 water wastours to chaste;
> Er fyue yer be fulfilled swich famyn shal aryse.
> Thoru3 flood and foule wedres fruytes shul faille,
> And so seiþ Saturne and sente yow to warne.

Whan ye se þe mone amys and two monkes heddes,
And a mayde haue þe maistrie, and multiplie by ei3te,
Thanne shal deeþ wiþdrawe and derþ be Iustice. . . .   (6.321–29)[2]

The same intention is revealed earlier when the poet interrupts his ironic description of Meed's triumphal progress to issue this sobering reminder:

Salomon þe sage a sermon he made
For to amenden Maires and men þat kepen þe lawes,
And took hym þis teme þat I telle þynke:
Ignis deuorabit tabernacula eorum qui libenter accipiunt munera &c.
Amonge þise lettrede lordes þis latyn amounteþ
That fir shal falle & forbrenne at þe laste
The hous and þe hom of hem þat desireþ
Yiftes or yeresyeues bycause of hire Offices.   (3.93–100; italics mine)

Such ominous forecasts are not, however, the exclusive property of Langland as narrative voice. In an anticlerical tirade, Will the Dreamer warns hypocritical priests about the imminence of Judgment in order to remind them of the penitential purpose of present time:

Ac I wene it worþ of manye [clerks] as was in Noes tyme
Tho he shoop þat ship of shides and bordes:
Was neuere wrighte saued þat wro3te þeron, ne ooþer werkman ellis,
· ·
God lene it fare no3t so bi folk þat þe feiþ techeþ
· ·
At domesday þe deluuye worþ of deþ and fir at ones;
Forþi I counseille yow clerkes, of holy kirke þe wri3tes,
Wercheþ ye as ye sen ywrite, lest ye worþe no3t þerInne.
    (10.405–7, 411, 417–19)

Likewise, Reason's sermon to the folk in Passus 5 is broadly apocalyptic in this traditional sense, for his plea for moral conversion is based on an appeal to contemporary disasters (pestilence, the southwest wind on Saturday, etc.) as punishments for sin and signs of God's impending Final Judgment. The basically pessimistic, penitential function of present time in Augustinian eschatology is most forcefully illustrated during the interview between Will and Reason in Passus 11 of the B-version. When Will complains to Reason about his neglect of mankind, a neglect manifested in the lack of measure in human behavior, the reply he receives is not only illuminating but heated and, for Will, embarrassingly personal:

And Reson arated me and seide, "recche þee neuere
Why I suffre or no3t suffre; þiself hast no3t to doone.
Amende þow [it], if þow my3t, for my tyme is to abide.
Suffraunce is a souerayn vertue, and a swift vengeaunce.

Who suffreþ moore þan god?" quod he; "no gome, as I leeue.
He myȝte amende in a Minute while al þat mysstandeþ,
Ac he suffreþ for som mannes goode, and so is oure bettre.
. . . .

Forþi I rede," quod reson, "þow rule þi tonge bettre,
And er þow lakke my lif loke þyn be to preise." (11.376–82,
387–88)

The scriptural source for this warning (2 Peter 3:9–12) makes abundantly plain the eschatological thinking behind Reason's injunction to penance: "The Lord delayeth not his promise, as some imagine, but dealeth patiently for your sake, not willing that any should perish, but that all should return to penance. But the day of the Lord shall come as a thief, in which the heavens shall pass away with great violence and the elements shall be melted. . . . Seeing then that all these things are to be dissolved, what manner of people ought you to be in holy conversation and godliness?"

If the preceding examples were not enough to brand Langland an unexceptional traditionalist in his eschatology, at one point (12.9) he even follows Augustine in dehistoricizing apocalyptic by shifting its reference from a single, final public event (the Second Advent) to a recurrent private moment (the death of the individual Christian).[3]

And yet, throughout *Piers Plowman* one senses a very un-Augustinian urgency, an intense conviction that Judgment may break in on us not only, as Augustine would say, at any time (since God is always judging the world)[4] but that, in fact, Final Judgment is liable to overtake us in a matter of a few months or years. Where Augustine would insist that Christians have always lived, by definition, in the Last Times (the era of grace), the picture Langland presents us with in Passus 19 and 20 is of a world on the very brink of the Last Tribulation — at the mercy of the Great Antichrist.

Langland's pessimism, too, sometimes seems bleaker than what the detached, scholarly tradition of Augustine would warrant. One of the most commonly repeated passages from the discussion of eschatology in Book 20 of *The City of God* is that in which Augustine avers that, even after his loosing at the end of time, Satan will not be able to lead the Church astray.[5] An influential, thirteenth-century commentator on Apocalypse notes that the reason the Evil One will not be able to enter the camp of the saints or prevail against them is *the unity of their will*.[6] While readers have always sensed irony in Langland's choosing the name Unity Holy Church for his subverted fortress of Christendom, the depth and bitterness of that irony stand out afresh when compared to these more conventional expectations for the End.

Admittedly, such aberrances from traditional Augustinianism as these are relatively minor, perhaps mere matters of temperament, and present no insuperable problem in historical interpretation. But what are we to make of the several clearly millennial prophecies scattered through the poem? While less numerous than the type described above, these predictions make up for their infrequency by length, detail, strategic placement, and emotional impact. It is hard to ignore the proto-utopian note sounded when, for example, Conscience tells us, in Passus 3, that Reason will reign and govern realms, that one Christian king will rule over all, that Meed will be forever deposed, that swords will be beaten into plowshares, and that Jews and Saracens will convert (284–330). A similar hope for the future seems to be expressed by Clergy in Passus 10 when he predicts a coming king who will reform existing religious orders to apostolic purity, provide friars with a means to forgo their insidious begging, and even overcome Antichrist (322–25). Anima's prediction of a future reform through confiscation of ecclesiastical wealth (15.551 ff.) can also be understood within this context.

If all, or even a majority, of Langland's apocalyptic utterances sounded like these, we might salvage an understanding of the poet's philosophy by supposing him to be a popularizing radical—someone like John of Rupescissa—reacting against the sterile, antiprogressive formulations of Augustinian exegesis.[7] But adopting that solution would equally require us to explain the presence of so much traditional material.

Seeking to escape the horns of this dilemma, several modern scholars have suggested the influence of Joachim of Fiore on Langland.[8] Professor Bloomfield, especially, in advancing this thesis, locates the fascination of many late medieval thinkers with Joachim in the hypnotic power of his obscure exegetical system. With its reactionary form and revolutionary content, this system appealed simultaneously to learned and popular sources, to conservative and progressive climates of opinion, and to pessimistic and optimistic temperaments.[9] The doublesidedness of his innovative eschatology is readily apparent in a simplified summary of his major tenets: (1) the secret Antichrist is coming soon, bringing a terrible persecution for the Church; (2) *but* he will be overcome by a *novus dux*[10] who will initiate a period of unprecedented spiritual illumination and peace; (3) *but* this marvelous age will be cut short by Satan's loosing and the appearance of the open Antichrist; (4) *but* Christ's final deliverance of the saints will follow shortly![11] Can a series of paradoxical affirmations such as this be at the root of Langland's discordant prophecies? Perhaps. Certainly those who have investigated the possibility of such connections have performed a valuable service in highlighting some important features of the poem that had long been neglected. However, the preponderance of historical, theological, and textual evidence makes it now seem unlikely that the author of *Piers Plowman* was in any important sense a disciple of Joachim or of any of the various popularizers who oversimplified and distorted his ideas in the ensuing century and a half.

The unlikelihood of this influence is not owing to any paucity of evidence for the circulation of these materials in fourteenth-century England. Bloomfield has shown that passing references to the works of Joachim and his imitators abound and that at least some of these works were widely known in educated circles.[12] There can be little doubt that a man of Langland's background and interests would have had a general idea of Joachim's teachings and significance. At least one episode in *Piers* (on which Professor Bloomfield places great emphasis), the Tree of Charity, may indicate a fairly detailed and accurate understanding of authentic Joachite doctrine.[13]

Nevertheless, we now appreciate more fully than we once did that vague chiliastic prophecies may derive from a broader and older tradition than that begun by Joachim, and from more learned and authoritative sources than the various Sibylline prophecies.[14] If, then, we narrow our definition of Joachite thought to such characteristic aspects as the imminent third *status* (to be ushered in by the Angelic Pope[15] and the two orders of spiritual men), the elaborate genealogical symbolism with its numerological garb, and the exegetical method animated by a search for detailed, predictable Church/Synagogue parallels, we discover that the figures who preempted this tradition within little more than a generation of Joachim's death and cross-fertilized it with their own potentially millenarian world view were—almost without exception—Langland's bitterest enemies, the Franciscans.[16] Alexander of Bremen († 1271), Gerard of Borgo San Donnino († 1276), Bonaventura († 1274), Peter John Olivi († 1298), Arnold of Villanova († 1311), Ubertino de Casale († ca. 1329–1341), Angelo Clareno († 1337), John of Rupescissa († 1362), even Telesforus of Cosenza († after 1378):[17] they cover a span of more than a century and range from cautious academics to wild-eyed fanatics, but they comprise the various streams of Joachite and Joachimist thought[18] and they were all associated with the Minors—most of them with the rigorists.

In spite of the fact that he would have sympathized with these men in their fervor for true poverty, Langland was fundamentally at odds with them over such matters as the nature of poverty and the right to beg.[19] Furthermore, as a disciple of William of St. Amour and Richard Fitzralph, and himself apparently a conservative secular in lower orders, Langland was intensely hostile to the whole elitist, progressivist Franciscan ideology shared by Spirituals and Conventuals alike. Hence, there is a sizeable *a priori* improbability in the idea that he would draw his own inspiration from a source so enthusiastically tapped by those whom he depicts as the foragers of Antichrist.[20]

The preceding assessment, based on inferences drawn from Langland's obvious partisanship in the late medieval poverty debate, is buttressed by an examination of the narrative structure of *Piers Plowman* and those of the poem's theological opinions which may reasonably be attributed to the author. To begin with, the poem is designed in such a way as to manifest an emphatically Christocentric perspective on history (climaxing in Passus 18) which is simply incongruous with Joachim's trinitarian philosophy.[21] Where Joachim imagines salvation history as gradually moving toward a final fruition in the contemplative illumination of the third *status,* Langland envisions it as turning a sharp, unprecedented corner in the heroic jousting of God's Son for the apples of Piers. Christ's Harrowing of Hell is the only event in *Piers Plowman* that offers any hope for the complete eradication of evil from the human heart. Unlike the hope of the Joachites, which is in the future, it is a hope in something that has already happened, something that can begin to redeem Will at any moment he chooses to allow it. One used to encounter attempts to argue that Dowel (i.e., Passus 8–15), Dobet (Passus 16–18), and Dobest (Passus 19–20) are presided over, successively, by Father, Son, and Holy Spirit; but these efforts burlesqued the subtleties of Joachim's theology quite as much as they distorted the design of Langland's poem.

Beyond this basic structural incompatibility in their respective visions of history, the author of *Piers Plowman* virtually ignores many of Joachim's most famous themes. For example, although Langland admires those with a sincere monastic vocation and describes the joy of the cloister almost wistfully, he reserves no special role of prominence either for monasticism or the contemplative life. Clergy's prophecy suggests that the orders will be restored to their original observance, not elevated to some new stage of spiritual knowledge; on the other hand, the Abbot of Abingdon "and all of his issue" are cryptically promised "a knock from a king and an incurable wound." It may be possible to view Piers in his stewardship of the Barn of Unity as a type of the Angelic Pope, but there is no explicit mention of this figure nor of the two famous orders of spiritual men.[22] There is no reference, at least near the end of *Piers,* to a coming age of temporal happiness. Likewise, the plural antichrist tradition with the special Joachite emphasis on a double Last Antichrist *(mysticus* and *apertus)* is, so far as I can see, nowhere in evidence in the last two passus of *Piers.*

Readers may certainly differ over how to interpret what we are told at the Tree of Charity regarding the cooperation of Father, Son, and Spirit in man's salvation, but I will rest the case for Langland's independence of Joachite trinitarian philosophy on another passage—the intercessory prayer of Repentance following the Confession of the Sins. *Lex orandi, lex credendi:* nowhere can one see more intimately than in prayer the essence of one's religious beliefs. Even allowing for the fictional nature of the prayer in question, the principle appears to hold true. Here we can, in a sense, perhaps catch the author unawares since a scholastically satisfying discussion of trinitarian theology is not at all the purpose of these lines:

> *O felix culpa, o necessarium peccatum Ade &c.*
> For þoruȝ þat synne þi sone sent was to erþe
> And bicam man of a maide mankynde to saue,
> And madest þiself wiþ þi sone vs synfulle yliche:
> *Faciamus hominem ad ymaginem et similitudinem nostram;*
> *Et alibi, Qui manet in caritate in deo manet & deus in eo.*
> And siþþe wiþ þi selue sone in oure sute deidest
> On good fryday for mannes sake at ful tyme of þe daye. . . .
>
> (5.483–88)

The grammar of the prayer makes clear that this part of it, at least, is addressed to the Father. Yet, so far as I know, no one has ever noticed that this impassioned resumé of *Heilsgeschichte* involves its author in something near to the classical heresy of modalism or Sabellianism. Concerning this passage, Professor Bennett has noted Langland's insistence on the Divine Impassibility and "that the Father did not, as the Monarchians had asserted, suffer with the Son."[23] However, the fact remains that these lines, if read according to the most obvious construction, imply a serious confusion of the work of the Father with that of the Son, an error usually associated with Sabellius' inadequate differentiation of the persons of the Trinity.[24] Even if we construe the grammar of the statement so that "wit" (ll. 486–87) signifies "by means of," the tendency is merely camouflaged; it reappears somewhat later in the same prayer when, without warning or overt change of address, the Son becomes the object of Repentance's meditation:

> þiself ne þi sone no sorwe in deeþ feledest,
> But in oure secte was þe sorwe *and þi sone it ladde:*
> *Captiuam duxit captiuitatem.*

The sonne for sorwe þerof lees siȝt for a tyme.
Aboute mydday, whan moost liȝt is and meel tyme of Seintes,
Feddest wiþ þi fresshe blood oure forefadres in derknesse:
. . . .
The þridde day þerafter *þow yedest in oure sute;*
A synful Marie þe seiȝ er seynte Marie þi dame . . . .
(489–93; 496–97; italics mine)

With the same casual fluidity, Repentance drifts toward addressing the Father and Son together at the close of his prayer:

> *Verbum caro factum est & habitauit in nobis.*
> And by so muche it semeþ þe sikerer we mowe
> Bidde and biseche, if it be þi wille,
> That art oure fader and oure broþer.   (500–503)

One could easily make too much of this passage, and it would obviously be foolish to label Langland (or Repentance!) heretical on the basis of an oversight or misleading nuance in this spontaneous intercession.[25] Still, it is a valuable piece of evidence for the question of Langland's Joachimism since it illustrates that in an unguarded moment he tends toward the modalism of common piety rather than the much rarer opposite extreme of tritheism, toward which Joachim's speculations gravitate.[26] Indeed, the famous excised diagram from the *Liber figurarum* (preserved only in the Dresden MS of that work) reveals that Sabellianism was an especial *bête noir* for Joachim—probably because it amounted to an inversion of his own understanding of the Godhead.[27]

Another small detail of Langland's theology that has gone unnoticed hitherto, his repeated insistence on the motif of Christ's binding of Satan (Apoc. 20:2–3), is equally relevant to the issue of Joachite influence in *Piers*. Though Joachim never explicitly identifies the millennium of Apocalypse 20:1–6 with his so-called third *status* or sabbath age, the assumption that they are interchangeable lies behind his carefully worded comments on the twentieth chapter. The Calabrian admits that the thousand years *per se* may be merely a round number (as Augustine had insisted) used by John to symbolize the entirety of the Christian era,[28] but repeatedly he assumes that the account of the saints reigning with Christ in this chapter refers to some future sabbath. This desire to have it both ways is evident in his resumé of Augustine's description of primitive Christian chiliasts:

> As Augustine says in his *City of God*, certain persons thought on account of this passage that the thousand years were to be deferred to the time of the seventh age in which Christ should reign after the resurrection with the saints, the first six thousand years from the world's beginning having been completed. To these ideas they added certain other things altogether contrary to the Christian faith. As for their opinion, in part it appears acceptable and in part unacceptable, since one aspect of their belief was

true and another empty and inane. For that opinion of theirs whereby they supposed the time to come following the battle previously mentioned [that with the beast and false prophet] would be the seventh age or sabbath was true—indeed not so much an opinion as it is unshakeable knowledge. However, their assertion that this seventh age would be a seventh period of one thousand years remains totally false.[29]

Joachim is likewise ambivalent about the matter of Satan's binding, and for much the same reason. To dispute Augustine's view (that the angel of Apocalypse 20:1 is Christ, Who bound Satan at the moment of His Resurrection) would not only give the appearance of setting his face against a firmly entrenched position but also might seem to derogate from the completeness of Christ's saving work. Therefore, at several points Joachim chooses to gloss over the radical difference between his own approach and Augustine's by manipulating the "already / not yet" dynamic of traditional Christian apocalyptic so as to embrace both alternatives simultaneously, while emphasizing the "not yet" at the expense of the "already." Thus he implies that, in its fullest sense, the binding of the Devil is something that will only happen in the future, not the past: "in part the dragon was imprisoned from that time when Christ conquered him on the day of His death; however, insofar as all of his heads are concerned, he will be confined from that day or hour when the beast and false prophet are thrown into the fiery lake. . . . The seventh age in which that Great Sabbath will occur began in part from the time of that sabbath when the Lord rested in the sepulchre. In its fullness it begins from the time of the fall of the beast and the false prophet."[30] In this same discussion Joachim proceeds to identify the binding angel not with Christ but with the Holy Spirit, that person of the Godhead destined to preside over the mysterious third *status*;[31] this is a very revealing substitution that speaks more loudly of Joachim's deepest convictions concerning the Trinity and the millennium than do all the careful qualifications mentioned above.

On the contrary, Langland exhibits no hesitation in affirming his belief in the completeness and finality of Christ's work. The Samaritan, who first alludes to the subject of Satan's binding in his dialogue with Will in Passus 17, agrees with Augustine and the older commentary tradition— the Devil is to be bound at the time of the Resurrection and his imprisonment will last for the entire period of the Church's history:

> He was vnhardy, þat harlot, and hidde hym *in Inferno*
> Ac er þis day þre daies I dar vndertaken
> That he worþ fettred, þat feloun, faste wiþ Cheynes,
> And neuere eft greue gome þat gooþ þis ilke gate:
> *O mors ero mors tua &c.* (111–14)

Faith also announces, in his prophecy of Christ's saving deeds (18.31–35), that Lucifer shall be bound in the course of the Harrowing. Lest one discount these two brief passages as instances of inconsequential exegetical tidbits that somehow managed to find their way into Langland's theological ragout, it should be noted that the climax of Christ's dramatic debate with the Devil is the actual description of Lucifer's imprisonment:

> "Thus by lawe," quod oure lord, "lede I wole fro hennes
> Tho ledes [þat me louede], and leued in my comynge;
> And for þi lesynge, lucifer, þat þow leighe til Eue
> Thow shalt abyen it bittre!" and bond hym wiþ cheynes.
>
> (18.400–403)

Therefore, in the case of this minor theological motif which can sometimes be used as a sort of litmus test for eschatological deviations, our results prove interesting precisely on account of their unexceptional quality. There is not the slightest hint here of any flirtation with Joachimism or any other heterodox understanding of the millennium, learned or popular.

If, then, the Joachimist explanation must be discarded, where may we look for a satisfactory account of Langland's eschatology? I believe that the first place we should look is at the end of his poem, for it is in Passus 19 and 20 of *Piers Plowman,* and nowhere else, that Langland's prophecies of the End take on reality.[32] After we have evaluated the meaning of the End as he depicts it in these passus, we may still find ourselves at a loss to explain some of the elements in the earlier prophecies, but surely this is the only means of interpretation that offers any promise of solving our problem. Langland himself would have been quick to point out to us that prophecies are to be judged by ensuing events and not the other way around. A commonplace of learned exegesis known to all educated people of Langland's day was that the mysteries and prophecies of the Old Testament are unveiled and interpreted by the events of the New that complete them. This same principle, of course, can apply in a quasi-biblical narrative such as *Piers,* where both prophecies and fulfillment are fictional.[33] So perhaps a major cause of our previous difficulty with this aspect of Langland's poem is that, recognizing its engagement with popular aspirations, we have begun by taking all the details of the millennial visions in the first half of the work literally, at face value, and then sought in vain to reconcile to these the rather pessimistic-sounding events of the last passus. Let us see if reversing this procedure is more satisfactory.

The logical place to begin is with Langland's Antichrist, who appears at the opening of Will's last dream:

> I fil aslepe
> And mette ful merueillously þat in mannes forme
> Antecrist cam þanne, and al þe crop of truþe
> Torned it tid vp so doun and ouertilte þe roote,
> And made fals sprynge and sprede and spede mennes nedes.
> In ech a contree þer he cam he kutte awey truþe
> And gerte gile growe þere as he a god weere.
> Freres folwede þat fend for he gaf hem copes,
> And Religiouse reuerenced hym and rongen hir belles,
> And al þe Couent cam to welcome a tyraunt. (20.53–60)

This passage and the entire campaign that ends with the breach of Unity have been described as though they were early examples of what Spenser does with his Pageant of the Deadly Sins, treated as though they were simply moral allegories beneath their apocalyptic garb.[34] But no amount of selective quoting and no forced identification of Antichrist with Pride (his standard bearer) can escape the poet's own words: "Antichrist came then in man's form." Such an explicit avowal seems intended to underscore the point that no vague social forces, no mere bad man, indeed nothing less than the great "son of perdition" himself is here intended.

Those who find in the earlier millenarian prophecies a central theme of *Piers* have sought to defuse the urgency and pessimism of this concluding episode by circumventing the ordinary inference that this figure is *the* Antichrist of the Last Time. After all, if this is *the* Antichrist, then all that remains is Christ's Second Advent and the Judgment—and no millennium or third *status!* The logic of this conclusion is not inevitable, since if it were assumed that Langland's outlook was that of a primitive chiliast, the thousand years of Christ's earthly rule might be expected to follow the defeat of Antichrist, just as it does in Apocalypse 20. However, it has in fact always been assumed by those who see him as a millennialist that Langland wrote under the combined influence of Joachite and Sibylline prophecies. And in these versions (though they differ among themselves, with most of the former preserving Joachim's distinctive double Antichrist) the time of this-worldly happiness clearly precedes the final Antichrist and Second Advent. Therefore (effectually begging the question), we are told that the tribulations of Passus 20 cannot be the final ones.

Nevertheless, as I have shown at length in an earlier article, there is ample evidence to support the inference that Langland's Antichrist is, in fact, the final Antichrist of traditional Augustinian eschatology.[35] Moreover, these findings have recently been reinforced by the similar conclusions that Richard Emmerson elaborates concerning *Piers* in his *Antichrist in the Middle Ages*.[36] The two most significant bits of evidence on this issue turn out to be scriptural allusions that readers have hitherto overlooked. In the first case, the scene between Will and Need derives from a text in Job (41:13) describing the great Leviathan that has been associated in the learned tradition with Antichrist's advent ever since it was first scrutinized by Gregory the Great in the *Moralia in Iob*.[37] In the second instance, a whole series of episodes (beginning in Passus 19 with the brewer's revolt against Conscience and concluding in Passus 20 with the appearance of Need) is designed to allude to a four-stage paradigm of Church history based on Psalms 90:5–6. This paradigm, a true commonplace of the later Middle Ages, originated in Augustine's *Enarrationes in Psalmos* and was elaborated in such influential sources as St. Bernard's *In Cantica Canticorum*.[38] The pattern's usefulness and the source of its appeal arose from its claim to trace the course of the Church through various forms of adversity to the End: from violent pagan opposition in the earliest times (the brewer's open revolt), to the sedition of heretics (the specious plausibilities of the vicar), to the hypocrisy of false brethren (the rapaciousness of the lord and the king), to Antichrist himself (the encounter with Need, the "noonday demon"). When, therefore, weight of these allusions is added to that of the narrator's description of Antichrist cited previously, it seems safe to conclude that, insofar as it figures in the last passus of *Piers,* Langland's eschatology is essentially traditional.

However, we still must deal with the earlier millennial prophecies. I have already intimated my belief that these may be reconciled to the framework of the rest of the poem and that Langland was not a chiliast— at least in the usual sense of the word. Nevertheless, the investigation itself must be divided into discrete stages in order to keep clearly before our minds where we are and what we are seeking. We must begin by asking which major segments of the poem seem truly millennial and which have merely been misunderstood or taken out of context. Next, we must determine whether the aforementioned genuine prophecies, with their populist hopes for this-worldly happiness, may be interpreted fairly so as to cohere with the "pessimism"[39] of Passus 19 and 20. Finally, on the supposition that these prophecies may not be so straightforward nor their terms so literally intended as they first seem, we must ask why Langland would offer us such enigmatic forecasts that appear to encourage a reading which he ultimately does not endorse.

One passage sometimes misunderstood to have millennial overtones is Reason's vow in passus 4 after he has been approached with a request to pardon Wrong:

Reed me no3t . . . no ruþe to haue
Til lordes and ladies louen alle truþe
And haten alle harlotrie to heren or to mouþen it;
Til pernelles purfil be put in hire hucche,
And childrene cherissynge be chastised wiþ yerdes,
And harlottes holynesse be holden for an heþyng;
Til clerkene coueitise be to cloþe þe pouere and fede,
. . . .
And til prechours prechynge be preued on hemselue;
Til þe kynges counseil be þe commune profit.   (113–19, 122–23)

In concluding, Reason advises the king to rule his realm by a simple maxim of justice: *Nullum malum impunitum; nullum bonum irremuneratum.*

In spite of the uncompromising tone of this conclusion, the repeated promisory pattern of Reason's vow—"till" followed by incredibly beneficent behavior in various social estates—has been intoxicating to some readers. However, as if to emphasize the improbability that Reason will ever have to meet the terms of his own vow and show mercy, Langland moves immediately to the proverbial "smoke-filled room" where down-to-earth politicians seek to assimilate and denature the idealistic advice they have just received:

Clerkes þat were Confessours coupled hem togideres
Al to construe þis clause for þe kynges profit,
Ac no3t for confort of þe commune ne for þe kynges soule.
For I sei3 Mede in þe moot halle on men of lawe wynke
And þei lau3ynge lope to hire and lefte Reson manye.   (149–53)

In genre, Reason's prophecy parodies its own form by couching obvious truths about life in the language of conditional soothsaying so as to emphasize ironically their unconditional permanence. A famous example of the same type is the Fool's mock prophecy in Act 3, scene 2 of *King Lear*.[40] With the case at hand, the painful truth toward which Reason's ironic forecast points is that most people will never amend. In such circumstances it is and always will be unreasonable to expect mercy— which is just what Reason says.

In Passus 13 the light of a utopian dawn glimmers again briefly when Conscience, seeking to patch up his quarrel with Clergy, conjures for his comrade the vision of a glorious future for the two of them, provided they both keep on good terms with Patience:

If Pacience be oure partyng felawe and pryue with vs boþe
Ther nys wo in þis world þat we ne sholde amende;
And conformen kynges to pees; and alle kynnes londes,

Sarsens and Surre, and so forþ alle þe Iewes,
Turne into þe trewe feiþ and intil oon bileue.   (206–10)

Clergy, whose learning considerably surpasses ours, is not at all puzzled
by this obscure promise and agrees to remain behind doing his duty, "Til
Pacience haue preued þee and parfit þee maked" (214). Apparently,
then, Clergy understands the prophecy of Conscience to depend for its
fulfillment on the latter's having achieved perfection through patient
suffering. But Conscience is just embarking on his final penitential
pilgrimage in the poem's concluding lines. Also, the prophecy appears to
be conditional on the reunion of Conscience and Clergy—an event that
never takes place. Indeed, the failure of these two figures to find each
other once more constitutes a major cause of the demise of Unity.[41] For
Langland the two great enemies of mankind are ignorance and moral
indifference; it is clear that wiping them out would eliminate the main
impediments to the conversion of the world, but it seems equally clear
that this is not about to happen in a world where Clergy's role has been
usurped by characters like sire *Penetrans domos*. Conscience's prophecy,
therefore, is simply the expression of a devout wish—one that should
command our hope but not our faith.

Perhaps the greatest danger of confusion lies in Anima's prediction
that ecclesiastical endowments may be confiscated on account of the long
history of their abuse by the prelacy. Anima actually goes so far as to issue
a plea to secular lords to carry out such a policy (15.564). This certainly
reminds one of Clergy's famous prophecy in Passus 10 of a future
savior-king (reminiscent of the Last Emperor of popular Sibylline
legends) who will reform the religious orders and, it is implied, redistri-
bute their wealth. Here lies the danger: Clergy's pronouncement has all
the earmarks of a genuine millennial prophecy, but because its subject
resembles, in its populist appeal, the topic of Anima's forecast, the latter
has sometimes seemed to assimilate apocalyptic overtones that are, in
reality, lacking in the text. Since both statements partake of some of the
cultivated ambiguity common to prophecy, one may force them into the
same mold and choose to interpret Clergy's vision through the less
mysterious context of Anima's remarks. However, the effect of doing this
would be to create greater contradictions in the poem than those we are
seeking to resolve—not to mention that it would coarsen some fine
distinctions that the poet insists on preserving and rather vulgarize his
outlook. To use Anima's forecast as our touchstone for Langland's
eschatology would be to turn him into little more than a Tudor apologist
before his time.

A close examination of Anima's speech will yield three crucial facts that militate against identifying it with Clergy's prophecy. First, there is no mention at all of an apocalyptic savior whose arrival will serve as a cue for the dramatic events predicted. The lords Anima is appealing to clearly are titled English noblemen and nothing more. Secondly, the planned confiscation, though a radical measure, is envisioned as attainable within the normal political process ("If knyghthod and kynde wit and þe commune and conscience / Togideres loue leelly")—a significant reform that will help restore clerical integrity, but hardly the type of unlimited triumph of righteousness depicted in the prophecies of Passus 3 and Passus 10. The final fact is one that applies with equal force to the parting interview of Conscience and Clergy in Passus 13 and to Reason's vow in Passus 4: all of these predictions are cast in the subjunctive mood; each one is hedged about by important qualifications and conditions. On the other hand, the promises of Conscience in Passus 3 and of Clergy in Passus 10 are rendered in absolute, unconditional terms. A deliverer is coming. The forces of Cain will be overcome, ushering in a time of perfect harmony. Jews and Saracens will convert. Where Anima is predicting, and lobbying for, a worthy end, Clergy is prophesying, simply, the End.

However commonplace it may sound, the best explanation for these very different treatments of ecclesiastical disendowment is that Langland was capable of looking at the same subject from more than one perspective. Over and again *Piers Plowman* manifests its author's deep concern for the social damage caused by the hypocrisy of predatory friars, the laziness of peasant wasters, the ignorance and selfishness of clerics—both secular and regular. He would like to see such abuses eliminated and repeatedly urges specific measures to achieve a greater degree of social justice on a purely human scale. Friars should not accept contributions from those they know to be unrepentant. Those who are able-bodied but refuse to labor should be fed a minimal diet till they reform. If bishops will not use the Church's wealth for the sake of Christ's poor, it should be taken out of their control. Many discussions of these matters in *Piers* seem almost devoid of otherworldliness. Yet Langland's social and theological conservatism are such that when he grasps for comprehensive solutions to these problems, he invariably turns to apocalypse.[42] Only supernatural or preternatural intervention can totally reverse the hellbent course of human society. I suspect that Langland would be surprised to see the advice of Anima equated with the prophecy of Clergy. In truth, they are complementary: those who abuse Church wealth ought to have it taken from them now, by force if necessary; but they can be certain, at least, that it will be taken from them in the End.

So far as I can see, then, only Conscience's prophecy in Passus 3 and

Clergy's in Passus 10 preserve their millennial aura on close inspection; but when these two passages are carefully scrutinized in the light of commentary traditions and Langland's own narrative strategy, the nature of that remaining aura may seem quite unlike the simple, popular utopianism it suggests to the untutored eye. So our next task is to explain how reality in these cases differs from first impressions.

The most plausible conclusion that issues from a careful reading of these two prophecies within the framework that we have established is this: notwithstanding appearances, the savior-king whose coming is predicted in both passages is not the Last World Emperor of Sibylline legend but Christ Himself.[43] A few of the hints are so palpable that one could scarcely avoid noticing them. The forecast that includes a pun on baron/burn/barn at 3.321 ("Al shal be but oon court, and oon burn be Iustice"), which was first discussed by Professor Donaldson over thirty years ago and which apparently alludes to the Christ Child, is one example that comes to mind.[44] Far more important, however, is the customary typology associated with the story of Saul's replacement by David in 1 Kings 15 and 16. It is to this story that Conscience draws our attention in order to predict the future analogically.

Permeating the entire narrative of Saul's elevation to the throne and later rejection in favor of David is an intense concern for the corrupting influence of greed and bribery—in a word, Meed—the very factor that Langland blames for political misfeasance in his own day. 1 Kings 8:3–5 ascribes the people's request for a king to their distaste for the avarice of Samuel's sons, who did not follow their father's example but allowed their judgment to be turned aside by bribery. In the same chapter Samuel attempts to dissuade the people from crowning a king by describing the materialism and grasping tyranny they could expect from such a one. Of course this prediction is ignored, but it proves true in 1 Kings 15 (the passage to which Conscience alludes) when Saul disobeys God's explicit orders concerning the Amalekites. The reason for his behavior is not made clear in the Old Testament itself, but Langland appears to trace it back to Samuel's forecast of greed in 1 Kings 8. In sum, he agrees with Nicholas of Lyra, who identifies Saul's motive in sparing Agag as cupidity rather than sentimentality or misplaced mercy.[45] Small wonder that Conscience cuts short (280–83) his explication of the moral of this exemplum! The avarice of kings, and their consequent deposition, was not a subject to be contemplated with equanimity in some quarters. Nevertheless, the story to which Conscience is alluding culminates with the deposition of Saul, and on the basis of this parallel Conscience launches into his long prophecy of a new order of perfect justice analogous to the reign of David:

> I, Conscience, knowe þis for kynde wit me tauȝte
> That Reson shal regne and Reaumes gouerne,
> And riȝt as Agag hadde happe shul somme.
> Samuel shal sleen hym and Saul shal be blamed
> And David shal be diademed and daunten hem alle,
> And oon cristene kyng kepen vs echone.   (3.284–89)

None of the versions of Sibylline prophecy with which I am familiar has the Last World Emperor coming to the throne by means of the kind of coup that Conscience seems to predict.[46] But the learned commentary tradition concerning Saul and David fits well here: it is unanimous in understanding the narrative of 1 Kings 15–16 as foreshadowing the replacement of the Synagogue by the Church and of earthly kings by Christ the King. With characteristic brevity, Bede summarizes the significance of David's assumption of kingship: "David, annointed as king in place of Saul, signifies the changing of the kingdom of the Jews, which was ruled by Law, into the kingdom of Christ's Church."[47] The great exegete goes on to stress the uniqueness, the "singularity," of Christ's rule. In a comment on 1 Kings 16:5 ("And he [Samuel] sanctified Jesse and his sons . . ."), Bede says, "He sanctified all, but David alone he annointed with the oil of chrism; for there are many members of the Church, but the Head is one. John baptized many, but the dove descended on one."[48]

Rabanus Maurus concurs in this explanation of the passage, but his assessment can also help us to construe other details in the prophecy of Conscience:

> This David is annointed as a future king, announcing by that annointing Christ. For Christ is so called on account of the annointing chrism. The seven older sons of Jesse having been rejected, the youngest in age is chosen for the kingship. Thus the Jewish priesthood and the kingly office of the elder people who served by keeping the Sabbath according to the Law were rejected. By contrast, our Lord Christ, the head of the younger people, occupies a perpetual priesthood and is annointed as a king whose reign has no end and whom all peoples, tongues, and nations will serve.[49]

The universal and exclusive power attributed by Conscience to this mysterious future ruler are easy to explain on the assumption that he is referring to Christ the King as Rabanus describes Him. More importantly, this commentary tradition also illuminates one of the more misleading features of the prophecy, the promise that we will be ruled by "oon cristene kyng." Can this be an appropriate phrase for Christ Himself? If the commentaries are believed, He may, in truth, be the only one for whom the title is suitable. The phrase itself is almost certainly derived from the messianic prophecy of Ezechiel 37.22, 24: "one King shall be King over them all. . . . And my servant David shall be King over them." Standard sources such as the *Glossa ordinaria* identify this "one King" as Christ.[50] Furthermore, one of the most emphatic aspects of the whole tradition being tapped by Rabanus is that the identification here of David with Christ stems precisely from his having been annointed with chrism. "For Christ is a name derived from the annointing chrism."[51] Hence, although the line is deliberately deceptive and encourages us to read it as "one Christian king," i.e., an earthly warrior-savior, its implicit meaning, suggested by a pun on the well known etymology of "cristene," is "the One cristened King," the One Whom David prefigured when annointed with the oil of chrism.

Yet another commentary, that of Ruper of Deutz, may provide a clue for the origins of Langland's ironic pun on baron/burn/barn in line 321. This seeming reference to the Christ Child as eschatological ruler grows quite naturally out of the story of Saul's replacement by David, who, Rupert stresses, was a mere boy when chosen king:

> This one [David], who was just a boy, could not have anything of this sort [proud ambition] in his heart while Saul was still alive and reigning, that Samuel should say to him what he previously had said to Saul: "I will tell thee all that is in thy heart [1 Kings 9:19]." For there were no princes favoring and acclaiming him but older brothers envious and angry at the boy. . . . He did not immediately sit down on a throne wielding a scepter, distinguished in purple and illustrious with a diadem or golden crown, but rather, needy and fugitive, he wandered. . . .
>
> Who, I say, of all kings, except for the Lord alone and His Son Jesus Christ, God and Man, went forth and ruled in such a way? For that Boy [Christ], now exalted and raised up, did not exalt or elevate Himself, to Whom the Jews said, "Whom dost thou make thyself?" He answered, "If I glorify myself, my glory is nothing [John 8:53–54]."[52]

This identification of Conscience's royal savior with Christ is further strengthened by his allusion at a later point in his prophecy to Isaiah 2:4 ("they shall turn their swords into ploughshares, and their spears into sickles: nation shall not lift up sword against nation, neither shall they be exercised anymore to war") and its promise of a future time of perfect tranquility. Conscience remarks that the peace of that time will be so complete that

> Iewes shul wene in hire wit, and wexen glade,
> That Moyses or Messie be come into myddelerþe.   (302–3)

How are we to take this ambiguous prognosis? Will such Jews be correct in their interpretation of these marvelous events, or will they be deluded once more? Certainly the fact that their conversion to the Faith is predicted in a later line (327) intimates the truth of their perception. Nicholas of Lyra, whose knowledge of rabbinical exegesis was exceptional in a fourteenth-century commentator, may help to elucidate this reference, for he explains that both Jews and Christians understand Isaiah 2 as referring to the time of the Messiah's Coming: "Nevertheless, they do so in contrary fashion, for Christians say this scripture was fulfilled in the coming of Jesus the Nazarene, whom they confess to be the Christ promised in the Law and the Prophets. The Jews, on the other hand, say that the same text is to be fulfilled in the time of the Messiah whom they expect, since they deny that Jesus the Nazarene was the Christ."[53] Although Nicholas devotes most of his attention to defending the awkward traditional notion (worked out by such uncompromising enemies of chiliasm as St. Jerome) that this passage in Isaiah is simply a prediction of the *spiritual* peace brought by Christ's First Advent (which obviously is not how Conscience—or Langland—understands it), he eventually comes around to admitting that parts of the prophecy are understood by Christians no less than Jews as having a future, eschatological reference. For example, in discussing Isaiah 2:5 ("O house of Jacob, come ye: and let us walk in the light of the Lord"), he notes that "the conversion of the Jews is placed [in this text] after the conversion of the Gentiles, since they will, *near the end of the world,* receive the faith of Christ as a group [italics mine]."[54]

A similarly cautious reservation is voiced by Thomas Aquinas, who quotes the traditional evasions concerning the literal promises of Isaiah 2 but then goes on to admit that this text is better referred "to the peace achieved by Christ, *which will be completed in the future* [italics mine]."[55] He also understands vs. 5 as referring to the conversion of the Jews and quotes John 10:16, where Christ declares that there will be "one flock and one shepherd." Even readers of *Piers Plowman* unacquainted with technical exegesis would have been able to comprehend Conscience's allusion to a time when "nation shall not lift up sword against nation," for this scripture occurs prominently in the liturgy of Advent, the season whose theme not only commemorates Christ's First Coming but anticipates His Second.[56] Apparently, then, this puzzling segment of Passus 3 amounts to a prediction of the return of Christ, Who will be recognized by His own people as Messiah for the first time when He comes as King and Judge of the world.

The accuracy of this reading is vouched for by the ease with which it may be harmonized with the results of a close examination of the predictions of Clergy in Passus 10. As with the earlier forecast, the key to Clergy's perplexing statements is not to be sought in seductively literal imagery and promises, such as that extended by lines 328–30, of an imminent golden age for friars.[57] Instead, the prophecy is once more unlocked by its scriptural allusions. The first of these ("Barons wiþ Erles [will] beten hem þoruȝ *Beatus virres* techyng") is to Psalm 111:1, the Latin version of which begins with the phrase, *Beatus vir*. Clergy has been attacking those who are his special concern, the religious, for their materialism, worldliness, and lack of pity for the poor. Thus, as he envisions a time when they will be punished for their cold indifference by a savior-king and his feudal retainers, it seems only natural that they should be whipped by their tormentors with the rule of Psalm 111, for the heart of this scripture is that salvation is achieved especially by works of mercy.[58] The author of *Piers* seems to have been strongly attracted to the teachings of *Beatus vir* since he uses both vs. 5 ("Acceptable is the man that sheweth mercy and lendeth") and vs. 9 ("He hath distributed, he hath given to the poor") as norms at other points in the poem where he is lamenting the disappearance of neighborly charity.[59]

Though we know the grounds for the punishment of the religious ("Of þe pouere haue þei no pite, and þat is hir pure charite"), the nature and time of their punishment are still to be clarified, having been left obscure by Clergy's actual words. The answer to both questions is indicated in the last verse of Psalm 111: "The wicked shall see [the righteous exalted], and shall be angry; he shall gnash with his teeth and pine away: the desire of the wicked shall perish." Commentaries on this text do no more than render explicit what any medieval person, lay or cleric, lewd or learned, would have understood it to imply:

> Here is shown that the opposite reward will be rendered to the unmerciful. That is, pain and sorrow—which can be expounded thus concerning the present life: "the sinner shall see and be angry" since the wicked observing the prosperity of the just is disturbed, and not only within his soul but even in external signs. Therefore it follows: "he shall gnash his teeth and pine away" . . . for sinners desire to remain in temporal prosperity, which deserts them in death and sometimes quite suddenly. Furthermore, this may be expounded in another way with reference to the future life in which the ungodly will be tormented not only by self-inflicted pains but also by the glory of the righteous. Although they cannot know this glory particularly and intuitively, nevertheless, abstractly and generally they know it since in a certain general way they thirst to be in maximum delight, which adds to their misery.[60]

The somber tone that prevails in later commentaries on this psalm (such

as the fourteenth-century one quoted above) probably results from the
influence of Augustine's stern observations in the *Enarrationes*. Augustine discusses the rewards of the *beatus vir* and the *peccator* of this psalm in
terms of Christ's parable of Judgment in Matthew 25, which concludes
with the words that are the ultimate scriptural source for Piers's pardon:
"these shall go into everlasting punishment; but the just into life
everlasting."[61]

If, therefore, Clergy's prophecy is threatening merciless monks and
friars with the penalties described by Psalm 111—Judgment and Hell—
the identity of their mysterious tormentors becomes easier to ascertain.
Though they may aptly be associated with the literal feudal hierarchy to
whom Anima addresses his appeal, an equally suitable answer is that the
barons and earls of this prophecy may be the reaping angels who, with
their demonic counterparts, figure so prominently in the Judgment Day
motif of the medieval visual arts. Of course nothing in the sparse description of them demands this seemingly arbitrary identification, but it
involves a viewpoint that Langland shows familiarity with elsewhere;
also, the larger context, which seems to identify their royal leader with
Christ, facilitates such a reading. That the angels comprise a hierarchy
analogous to the feudal one was, all recognize, a commonplace; but in
defense of my invoking that commonplace here, let it be noted that
Langland gives every indication of a strong attachment to it in Passus 1,
where Holy Church explains the angels to Will in terms of ten orders of
knighthood (105 ff.). The fall of Lucifer's "meynee" is specifically described as a breach of feudal loyalty. Also, it is worth recalling that we
have just seen, from Conscience's pun on baron/barn in 3.321, Langland's fondness for exploiting the vocabulary of feudalism in ironic or
ambiguous ways.

As for the king in Clergy's prophecy, the evidence for his being Christ
begins with the same phrase that gave birth to the present discussion:
beatus vir. This is not only the *incipit* of Psalm 111 but also of Psalm 1.
Most medieval commentators follow Augustine in identifying the "blessed man" of the latter psalm, who "hath not walked in the counsel of the
ungodly, nor stood in the way of sinners, nor sat in the chair of pestilence," with Christ Himself because of His uniquely sinless life.[62] So in a
more general sense we may understand that the evil religious mentioned
by Clergy will be scourged with the teachings of Christ—which, naturally, emphasize the charity to neighbors enjoined by Psalm 111.

The taunt that will be hurled in the faces of the worldly religious by
their enemies—*Hij in curribus & hij in equis ipsi obligati sunt &c.*—
supplies another clue to the identity of Clergy's savior-king, for this is a

direct quotation from Psalm 19, a prayer for David on the approach of battle: "Some trust in chariots, and some in horses: but we will call upon the name of the Lord our God." Once again, the standard exegesis of this psalm is established by Augustine, who interprets the work as addressed to Christ the King.[63] Hugh of St. Cher, an influential thirteenth-century commentator who stands in this tradition, explains the plea that concludes this psalm ("O Lord, save the king") to mean "we will be saved through the deliverance of Christ the King."[64]

The taunt itself, derived from vs. 8 of the psalm in question, focuses our attention on the pride and avarice of the corrupt regular, who is now "A prikere on a palfrey fro place to Manere, / An heep of houndes at his ers as he a lord were" (313–14). In analyzing vs. 8, Hugh points out that the pronoun "hij" used here is not being used "demonstratively but partitively, as in Matt. 25: 'these will go into everlasting punishment; those, however, into eternal life.' "[65] Somewhat later in his discussion of the destiny of those who "trust in chariots and horses," Hugh removes any doubt that his allusion to Matthew 25:46 was merely for its convenience in explicating a point of grammar. Their punishment is Hell itself: "those who want to ascend chariots and horses are bound to descend like Lucifer, who said, 'I will ascend into heaven. . . .' And the Lord said to him, 'Nevertheless, thou shalt be brought down to hell [Is. 14:13–15]. . . .' "[66]

Finally, after having fleshed out his prophecy with several references to scriptural texts, Clergy concludes the whole matter by offering another scripture as warrant for the truth of his predictions:

> That þis worþ sooþ, seke ye þat ofte ouerse þe bible:
> *Quomodo cessauit exactor, quieuit tributum? contriuit dominus baculum impiorum, et virgam dominancium cedencium plaga insanabili.*   (333)

It seems quite natural that Langland should have associated this passage from the Isaiah 14 prophecy about the King of Babylon's demise ("How is the oppressor come to nothing, the tribute hath ceased?") with the preceding passage from Psalm 19. Evidently the same shared pattern of movement in these two chapters (one of overweaning ascent followed by ignominious decline) suggested the comparison between them to Hugh of St. Cher in the discussion quoted above. More importantly, however, both the text of Isaiah 14.4–6 and the traditional exegesis of the entire chapter can be shown to support the reading that we have been proposing for these two major prophecies of *Piers Plowman.*

The text itself is made up of a riddling, ironic question followed by a straightforward answer. Langland quotes both. The essence of the question is, "How has our oppression come to an end?" Of course, Clergy's prophecy has been promising just such an end to the exploitation of the poor by the proud and powerful religious orders. The answer within the scriptural text itself is unambiguous, the kind of statement that commentaries could amplify but not alter significantly: "The Lord hath broken the staff of the wicked, the rod of the rulers, That struck the people in wrath with an incurable wound." This is the King whose deliverance Clergy has sought to foretell. Moreover, the commentators are unanimous in seeing behind the reference to a fallen wicked ruler of Babylon an allusion to Lucifer himself, especially since he becomes the overt subject of the prophecy later in the same chapter. But the consequence of equating all wicked rulers with their diabolic head is that the commentators are forced to give special emphasis to the uniquely divine source of our deliverance. Remigius of Auxerre († 908) well summarizes this line of thought:

> It should be understood that these things which follow [i.e., Isa. 14:4 ff.] can be referred not only to Nabuchodonosor but also to the devil, from the perspective of the elect on the Day of Judgment. . . . An "exactor" is he who exacts tribute from people. And the devil is an exactor since he wishes us to serve him and demands the servitude of sin. *Since therefore not by human power but by the Lord the tribute will cease when the exactor is killed,* the prophet reveals [this fact] with the following words in the voice of the people of Israel or the elect: "The Lord hath broken, etc. . . ."[67]

As with the predictions of Isaiah 2, the prophecy of Isaiah 14 is considered by typical medieval exegetes to have a double focus. In a certain sense the work of deposing the exactor and breaking his rod has already been achieved by Christ's Incarnation (though Will's vision of this has not yet occurred). The language of the prophecy itself, which uses past-tense verbs, intimates this much. Still, to some extent the time of the complete deliverance from our servitude remains in the future, as Hervé of Bourgdieu († ca. 1150) is quick to stress:

> In fact, the "oppressor" has not yet completely come to nothing nor has the "tribute" ceased, since while we live here the devil tries to incite us to sin and we cannot completely avoid sin. . . . But after this mortal has put on immortality, the "oppressor" will have come to nothing and the "tribute" will have ceased since the devil will never again persuade anyone that he should sin nor will anyone sin. Therefore, it is appropriate that the elect in the Kingdom will then exult triumphantly. . . . For there will be true liberty. For then this will be completed which is added: "The Lord hath broken the staff of the wicked."[68]

In the lines immediately following his citation of Isaiah 14, Langland appears to endorse Hervé's assessment of the text's unfulfilled status, referring to a time of future tribulation that will be culminated by the coming of the long hoped-for deliverer:

> Ac er þat kyng come Caym shal awake,
> Ac dowel shal dyngen hym adoun and destruye his
> myȝte.   (10.334–35)

If we interpret these lines within the framework of Augustinian eschatology seemingly accepted by Langland elsewhere, the natural reading would apply them to the slaying of Antichrist by the Lord at His Second Advent. In fact, Hervé of Bourgdieu understands Isaiah 14 to contain just such a reference to the Enemy of God and his strife with the Almighty at the end of time. He identifies the "smoke that shall come down from the north" (vs. 31), whom none shall escape, as Antichrist, sent by the Devil with "dark doctrinal errors that will blind the eyes of human hearts."[69] The "messengers of the nations" (vs. 32) to whom an answer must be given are interpreted by Hervé as Antichrist's emissaries to the besieged camp of the saints.[70] Isaiah's answer to their threats, however, requires no gloss: "the Lord hath founded Sion, and the poor of his people shall hope in him." This message echoes the thematic refrain of Isaiah 2 ("the Lord alone shall be exalted in that day"), and both texts—no less than 1 Kings 16 and Psalm 19—speak eloquently about the true identity of Langland's Savior-King.

Two objections may be interposed at this point. On the one hand, it is arguable that the scriptural allusions on which I have placed such weight may equally well be interpreted outside their customary boundaries so as to bear an altogether different message. For example, Isaiah 2:2–4 is one of the more famous proof texts appealed to by Joachim and his popularizers because of its vivid portrait of an earthly sabbath of the kind that they expected to end human history.[71] While I have indicated my belief that Langland was not a Joachite millenarian, his use of this text in a boldly prophetic sense embarrassing to conservative commentators might suggest otherwise. Similarly, it might be urged that the symbolism of such well-known characters of biblical legend as Saul and David could define itself independently of the exegetical tradition on account of their survival in the public mind. After all, at least one fourteenth-century pseudo-prophet, the anonymous author of *John of Bridlington*, employs David in his soothsaying as a purely secular political symbol with no typological dimension whatsoever.[72]

Where this argument is based on the possibility of a different interpretation of the scriptures in question, a second may be based on the contention that the scriptural allusions are peripheral and must not be allowed to obscure or distort the details of the prophecies themselves.[73]

Were we to pursue this second course, we might well ask questions of a more general kind, such as, "Doesn't the interpretation given in these pages, though internally consistent, set Langland's ostensible message rather at odds with his imagery?" For much of the imagery, with its suggestions of a golden age, surely stimulates ordinary readers to suppose that they are being promised an earthly millennium; whereas, if the learned commentary tradition is taken as normative, what we are being promised is simply Christ's Second Advent and the end of the world. Or again, "It was admitted earlier that the two prophecies in question preserve their millennial aura under close inspection, but isn't that aura precisely what is eclipsed by reading the details of the prophecies through the lens of scriptural allusions?" In fact, someone adopting this viewpoint might wish to broach the very question I indicated would be our last to answer in this study: What possible motive could Langland have for luring us to embrace a populist, utopian dream which he himself does not finally believe in?

Neither of the objections outlined above seems persuasive to me, but where the second demands extended discussion, the first may be disposed of briefly. If, for the sake of argument, we wish to explicate Isaiah 2 outside the received tradition of Western exegesis, we must first locate an alternative tradition available to Langland and then determine whether it will supply a satisfactory context for the rest of *Piers Plowman*. We have already seen that a Joachite context, though satisfactory to explain this small segment of Passus 3, appears incompatible with the poem's overall design and the author's ecclesiastical, theological, and social biases. Unfortunately, so far as I am aware, no other potential context exists (in fourteenth-century thought) for interpreting the prophecy of Isaiah 2.

Likewise, the point about Saul and David is sound in theory but of little value in application. Joachim discusses their story from 1 Kings 15 in his *Tractatus super quatuor Evangelia*, but his use of it betrays no eschatological dimension: for him it is merely an illustration of the importance of obedience to God's behests.[74] Certainly no one who has read *John of Bridlington* would be in any danger of confusing its author with the author of *Piers Plowman*. The fact that his forecasts are almost devoid of any but the narrowest kind of nationalistic political interest— David, for him, is the King of England; Saul, the King of France—marks him as a man quite different from Langland and not at all plausible as a source or parallel for the prophecies of Conscience and Clergy.[75]

Ultimately, however, the weakness of the first objection has little to do with the relative plenitude or scarcity of alternative interpretations. Even their comparative credibility is not the real issue. Rather, the proper question is this: Why should we search beyond the established exegetical tradition when it provides a suitably consistent reading of these scriptural allusions and when episodes throughout *Piers* repeatedly demonstrate how accustomed its author was to employing standard commentaries for all types of related purposes?

It is the second objection that truly penetrates to the heart of our puzzlement with Langland's eschatology. For the sake of consistency we have read these two prophecies in the light of the modified Augustinianism that elsewhere typifies Langland's thinking about the End. But if we confine ourselves to this perspective, how can we account for all those vaguely golden pictures of temporal harmony and perfection (e.g., no more shall Meed be master on earth; priests will hunt with *Placebo;* no sergeants of law will wear silk hoods; there will be one court and one judge, Truth; there will be no more war; Saracens and Jews will convert; friars will find a key to Church endowments to supply their needs) that form the fictional context for the scriptural allusions in these prophecies? The answer, I believe, is threefold: historical, stylistic, and thematic.

The historical answer may be stated simply enough: what we have been trained to look upon as mutually exclusive options, Augustinian pessimism and renascent chiliasm, were not regarded in quite the same way by Langland and his contemporaries. Thanks to the work of Robert Lerner, we now can recognize that the eschatology of nearly all late medieval thinkers, including Langland, is mingled with a subtle optimism that was virtually nonexistent prior to the twelfth century.[76] In addition, it is becoming clear that Joachim of Fiore was not the originator of this trend (as even his foremost modern student tended to imply little more than a decade ago);[77] rather, he was simply the most unusual and influential proponent of eschatological optimism. While Joachim's sophisticated philosophy of history and innovative exegesis are truly unique, his belief in a final period of earthly peace (if divorced from his dispensational theory) is not the eccentricity we have always thought it to be but instead is orthodoxy itself.

There is even evidence that belief in a final flowering of the Church was attractive to some who were fiercely hostile to the Joachite theology. Thus Guido de Terrena († 1342), the Catalan theologian who was an outspoken critic of Joachim's philosophy of history, stoutly defended the idea that the Jews would convert in an idyllic period following Antichrist's death.[78] That there would, in fact, be such an idyllic period had been inadvertently suggested by Jerome, amplified by Bede, and popularized by the *Glossa ordinaria.*[79] Hence, when Henry of Langenstein

(† 1397), the well-known scientist and theologian, violently repudiates Joachim and his fantastic disciple, Telesforus of Consenza, he still manages to salvage the notion of a last, brief era of earthly peace. Henry insists that, for all he can see, the Church has been in continuous decline for a long time, the world is in its senescence, and nothing shows any promise of changing before the End. Nevertheless, Henry concludes, "after the tribulation brought by Antichrist the Church will spread greatly among all peoples and nations and will be perfected in faith, hope, charity, and in all virtue and sanctity."[80]

Is Langland, therefore, or anyone else in his age innocent of chiliasm? Perhaps it may seem by now that we have completely retreated from our original position on that score. Such is not the case, however. An awareness of the danger of chiliasm led theological conservatives of Langland's stripe to insist on the brevity of this final time of earthly tranquility;[81] also, they tended to see it, in the spirit of Bede, as just a natural foyer through which mankind would pass into its eternal home. Unlike Joachim, such thinkers did not imagine this period to be the outcome of a gradual organic process (however divinized) but the unprecedented result of final supernatural intervention.

Curiously, because of their very insistence on the supernatural origins of "the refreshment of the saints" (as it was called), some conservative theologians tended to blur this interval so as to make it scarcely distinguishable from the Second Coming itself. For if only Christ's power can bring the Tribulation to an end and inaugurate the symbolic forty-five days of peace (the brief extent that Jerome had assigned), then in some sense He must already be present before His open Advent.[82] This outlook may help to explain why in Langland's prophecies the time of the King's arrival seems ambiguous in relation to the sequence of the marvelous events foretold.

With the benefit of hindsight we may easily recognize the extent to which these hybrid opinions were nourished more by meager hopes feeding on despair than by sound exegesis, but the men who held them certainly did not regard themselves as chiliasts! Some of the anger of a Henry of Langenstein may, for example, derive from frustration at seeing the consoling promise of Daniel 12:12 (a blessing pronounced for those who persevere beyond the death of Antichrist) twisted into foolish dreams of mundane glory by real chiliasts such as Telesforus.

All of this suggests that Langland would have considered nothing in the elements of his two major prophecies to be either heretical or inherently incompatible with the vision of the rest of his poem. In the

End there will be only the darkness of the pit and the light of Truth's tower. But in the beginning of the End, at least, the dawn will fall on the field of middle-earth. Cain is coming, but Dowel shall conquer him and destroy his might, causing such love and peace to arise among nations that the Jews will believe their Messiah has arrived.

Some might deem that this historical background by itself constitutes a satisfactory solution to the apparent tension between imagery and scriptural allusion in the prophecies of *Piers Plowman*. On the contrary, however, the events within the poem immediately following Clergy's prophecy indicate that some of the tension is real, intended, not merely the product of our ignorance. When Will concludes, with superficial plausibility, that the wondrous events of Clergy's prophecy must refer to the deeds of some earthly monarch and his feudal nobility—"Thanne is dowel and dobet . . . *dominus* and knyȝthode?" (10.336)—he is straightway informed of his error by Scripture, who speaks here *for the first time in the poem*. What this encounter reveals is that Langland *expects* many of his readers to interpret the prophecies of Conscience and Clergy, as Will does, within the framework of Sibylline folklore or later mixtures of that folklore with a popularized Joachite theology—the sort of product marketed by John of Rupescissa. I think we may go so far as to say that Langland loads his prophecies with appealingly ambiguous metaphors for the very purpose of *provoking* the kind of erroneous response that Will makes here. The sudden intrusion of Scripture at this point, and her insistence that Will has misapplied the terms of the prophecy, is Langland's way of commenting on the absence of any foundation for popular chiliasm, either in the Bible or the Fathers. The focus of the entire discussion is altered when Scripture says, concerning kingship, knighthood, and the material power that they command, that they "Helpeþ noȝt to heueneward." What Will has construed carnally, she understands spiritually.

Over twenty years ago Professor Bloomfield pointed out part of what I have been trying to describe: a development throughout *Piers* wherein an apparently mundane saviour-king is highlighted at several points in the first half of the work, only to be replaced in the end by the King of Kings, whose Harrowing of Hell forever transforms the poem's fictional world.[83] Though Bloomfield saw these two royal figures as complementary, I believe that they are, in reality, competing significations of the same image, both potentially present from the beginning. The value of Bloomfield's description, for me, is that it amounts to a history of Will's (and a typical reader's) experience in arriving at a final understanding of that image. As with Langland's many other unstable, multivalent metaphors,[84] this one allows us to choose the tenor we prefer, the kind of savior we would like; in doing so, however, we not only define what this aspect of the poem will signify to us but also what we will signify. Langland proceeds on the assumption that we will never fully appreciate the spiritual depth of truths that we have heard all our lives until we are enticed into betraying our superficiality by repeated misreadings of his enigmas. Though he takes it to extraordinary lengths, this predilection for rhetorical deception is rooted in a commonplace of medieval aesthetics, the assumption that only what is obtained through strenuous mental exertion will be long remembered or highly valued.[85]

But what about Langland's specific purpose in this case? I think that his use of potentially chiliastic imagery in the prophecies of Conscience and Clergy is intended to fix our attention on a central theme of *Piers Plowman,* the difference between true and false kingship and, by implication, kingdoms. This theme is written across the face of the whole poem; part of the experience of reading it should be to make us progressively more aware of where our own citizenship lies, whether in Unity, to which Will's pilgrimage finally brings him, or whether in the field of folk itself, the only home that many will ever know (cf. 1.7–9).

From our previous analysis of Langland's scriptural allusions (1 Kings 15–16, Psalm 19, Isaiah 2, and Isaiah 14), it is clear that they especially cohere around this theme of true versus false kingship. The most obvious example is Isaiah 14, the passage to which Clergy makes his final appeal. As everyone knows, this chapter predicts the damnation of an earthly ruler for presuming to seize the throne of Heaven. Israel will be delivered from the rod of this tyrant-imposter by the power of her true King (cf. Is. 14:32). In a similar vein, commentators on Psalm 19 imply that those who trust in chariots and horses desire an earthly rather than a heavenly deliverance.[86] Augustine relates this text to the motive of the Jews in crucifying Christ—their fear of losing their earthly kingdom to the Romans caused them to sacrifice their true King.[87]

One has only to survey commentaries on these passages and notice the number of cross-references to realize their coherence in medieval eyes. An exegete of Psalm 19:8 will allude to Isaiah 14.[88] A writer on Isaiah 14 will refer to the heavenly reward reserved for the *beatus vir* of Psalm 111.[89] Almost every commentator on Isaiah 2:8 (a verse, following the prophecy of peace, which attributes the rejection of the Jews to their amassing horses and chariots) explains this text by comparing it to Psalm 19:8. Because of their shared subject matter, the patterns of exposition for Isaiah 2 and Isaiah 14 often parallel each other closely. In fact, of the texts we have been examining, only 1 Kings 15–16 seems outside this system of overlapping references.

Yet this last passage is far from being an anomaly. Besides the general aptness of its symbolic contrast between Saul and David,[90] 1 Kings 15–16 is closely related to the theme of the other scriptures invoked in the two royal prophecies. The key consists in recognizing that this pair of chapters supplies the tragic end of a story begun in 1 Kings 8, where the Israelites first implore Samuel to give them a monarch. As was noted earlier, Samuel admonishes them to consider the kind of greedy, tyrannical behavior they will be sanctioning, should he fulfill their rash request. There follows a catalogue of predicted abuses—all of them typical of oriental potentates—whose first entry reads: "He will take your sons, and put them in his chariots, and will make them his horsemen, and his running footmen to run before his chariots" (vs. 11). The king whom Samuel is predicting (who turns out to be the disobedient Saul of 1 Kings 15) is plainly one who will put his trust in the "chariots and horses" scorned by the author of Psalm 19—the same "chariots and horses" to which partial blame is assigned in Isaiah 2 for the rejection of Israel at the coming of the Messiah.

In its turn, moreover, this prophecy of Samuel echoes an earlier prophecy of Moses, in which the great deliverer of the children of Israel foresees a time when the people will desire a king such as the nations have. After stipulating that no foreigner may be chosen for this office, Moses enumerates the rules such a future monarch must follow in governing God's people. The first of these provides that "when he is made king, he shall not multiply horses to himself, nor lead back the people into Egypt, being lifted up with the number of his horsemen" (Deut. 17:16).

Medieval commentators nearly always refer to this text in Deuteronomy, and frequently to its counterpart in 1 Kings 8, when glossing other passages that treat horses and chariots in an unfavorable light. For example, in commenting on Isaiah 2:8 ("their land is filled with horses and their chariots are innumerable"), Albert the Great first alludes to Psalm 19:8 and then refers to Moses' command in Deuteronomy 17:16. As he continues to comment on the rest of verse eight ("Their land is full of idols"), he naturally thinks of Saul's disobedience in 1 Kings 15![91] Likewise, Hervé of Bourgdieu, in discussing the same passage from Isaiah 2, points out that the law forbade the kings of Israel to multiply their chariots and horses. But because Deuteronomy 17 and 1 Kings 8 exist in his memory as parts of a single scriptural nexus, Hervé mistakenly cites the latter text as his authority.[92] Both commentators agree in tracing this theme to its ultimate source in the destruction of Pharaoh's horses and chariots (Ex. 14:23–28). And with Pharoah we have simply reached a cousin of Saul or the King of Babylon—all of them types of the prototypical tyrant, the Lucifer of Psalm 14.

Here someone may wish to call a halt and remind us that, however nicely the aforementioned texts from Exodus 14, Deuteronomy 17, and 1 Kings 8 appear to mix with the rest, their evidential value is nil since Langland never actually cites them. The general principle on which this *caveat* is based is undeniably sound; but in developing an interpretation of a given passage of *Piers Plowman* it may be of small worth. Such a rule is manifestly obtuse when applied to Need, whose identity is defined by texts from Job and Proverbs to which no explicit reference is made! Certainly Langland's repeated subtleties in the use of scriptural allusions indicates the folly of trying to dictate in advance, by means of an extrinsic rule of modern literary criticism, what he may or may not be allowed to do with them. If we neglect total scriptural contexts in order to satisfy an overly fastidious concept of the textual limits of *Piers,* we run the risk of following the example of Meed, who, on reading *omnia probate,* was so well pleased that she failed to pursue the verse to its conclusion. In any event, it is not my desire, nor is it necessary, to allege these three scriptures as evidence that Langland intends to develop the theme of true versus false kingship. The texts that he does cite establish that fact. Rather, because Exodus 14, Deuteronomy 17, and 1 Kings 8 form a thematic core around which traditional commentaries see the other texts as coalescing, a brief glance at some of this material may bring Langland's understanding of the theme into sharper focus.

The verses from Deuteronomy and 1 Kings not only reflect interestingly on the prophecies of Conscience and Clergy but also on other facets of the poem. For these scriptures are perhaps the two most detailed in all of the Old Testament concerning the nature and extent of royal authority—a question of some importance in both the opening and concluding scenes of *Piers.* In the Prologue a king has a highly ambiguous authority conferred on him; in Passus 19 one who appears to be the same figure asserts a doubtful authority to tax his subjects or confiscate their property without restriction. Langland seems to be of two minds concerning this authority. On the one hand, his use of the parable of the mice indicates an Augustinian view of the political order: rulers exist as a providential punishment for sin. Hence, even when arbitrary they are not to be resisted. But on the other hand, because such rulers are chosen by the popular voice (Prol. 145), their careers tend to mirror that of Saul.

However good their intentions initially, they end by forgetting the *iura regis christi* (Prol. 133) and confusing the good of their realm with their own selfish aims (19.466–76).

As we might expect, this same ambivalent perspective on monarchy characterizes 1 Kings 8 and, to a lesser extent, Deuteronomy 17. In the latter case, Moses appears to sanction the choosing of a king, which, nevertheless, he depicts as an idea inspired by gentile customs. Though he sets forth rules that presuppose the legitimacy of choosing a king, the rules themselves appear to anticipate that the people will, inevitably, choose badly. In a similar vein, the Lord is described in 1 Kings 8 as *permitting* the election of an earthly monarch for Israel but as doing so *in order to punish* the presumption of the people: "And the Lord said to Samuel: Hearken to the voice of the people in all that they say to thee. *For they have not rejected thee, but me, that I should not reign over them*" (vs. 7; italics mine). Like the author of 1 Kings 8, Langland has theocratic inclinations. He is so acutely conscious of the eternal kingship of Christ that he tends to see all temporal claims to sovereignty (however necessary for good order) as potential affronts to the divine. Thus the options offered by the angel and the goliard to the king in the Prologue[93] are the only options that Langland will countenance for an earthly monarch: either a merciful vice-regent of Christ or a merciless lieutenant of Antichrist.

As a confused wanderer in search of a royal deliverer, Will finds his choices likewise circumscribed. The two alternatives—an earthly or a heavenly king—are presented most starkly at the end of Clergy's prophecy in Passus 10; but they remain the only ones available as late as Passus 20, when Will finally turns his back on Need and joins with a few fools in rejecting the reign of Antichrist, the last ruler mentioned in *Piers Plowman*. Relatively few passages in the poem directly confront this choice of kings, but each decision Will makes in his spiritual pilgrimage moves him, in spite of his frantic efforts to locate safe middle ground, ever closer to one of only two realms, the Castle of Care or the Tower of Truth. He would like to know *about* Dowel but does not really wish to make His aquaintance. When Will is first goaded into a recognition of this division within himself by Scripture's taunt *("multi multa sciunt, et seipsos nesciunt")*, the experience precipitates him into the land of longing, where he swears fealty to Fortune. Later, when he momentarily reverts to this same posture of sterile curiosity, Anima shocks him into renewed self-knowledge by labeling him one of "Pride's knights"—for, apart from the true King, there is only Leviathan, who is "king over all the children of pride." Even after Will has given up his flirtation with the Prince of

Darkness, he must yield allegiance to Truth Himself rather than to one truth at the expense of another. He cannot have Abraham without Moses (as he has always desired) but must instead become a squire to the master of both, the Samaritan.

At certain points in *Piers* where the question of the true deliverer's identity is not at issue, it is replaced by an equally probing one concerning the proper means of deliverance. Thus the treatment of the Samaritan as a knight on his way to a joust revives the imagery of militant salvation from the earlier prophecies and keeps this option alive in our imaginations well into Passus 18. Despite hints of the inadequacy of this ideal in intervening episodes (e.g., the motto of Patience: *Patientes vincunt*),[94] it is not until we reach Langland's actual account of the Crucifixion that we recognize how far we have accommodated our understanding of the Kingship of Christ to specious martial imagery. We expect an allegorical tournament, something like Huon de Meri's (fl. 1234),[95] but we have been the victims of a pun. Christ is the just, and He achieves perfect justice through His sacrifical death; only Longeus does any jousting.[96]

The ironic outcome to this episode forces us to ask, in conclusion, whether Langland's theology is truly, as one scholar has termed it, a theology of "glory."[97] That is what we might expect of a work focused on the theme of Christ's impending return. In actuality, however, only one extended passage employs triumphal, regal imagery for a completely straightforward purpose, the description of Christ's progress through Hell during the Harrowing. Significantly, this is an event that takes place in a spiritual realm beyond the scope of all but inspired human vision. Yet when Will awakens and goes to Easter Mass immediately afterwards, he sees a Piers who

> was peynted al blody
> And com in wiþ a cros bifore þe comune peple,
> And riзt lik in alle lymes to oure lord Iesu.   (19.6–8)

Asked by Will to explain this figure's composite identity, Conscience responds by noting the possibility of any person's having several roles or titles. As Conscience gradually relates Christ to the roles of knight, king, and conqueror, it becomes clear that one of his concerns is to account for the appearance of weakness that has troubled Will when his exalted vision of Christ the King has been succeeded by one of the bleeding Savior:

> Ac for alle þise preciouse presentз [of the Magi] oure lord prynce Iesus
> Was neiþer kyng ne conquerour til he comsed wexe
> In þe manere of a man and þat by muchel sleighte,

> As it becomeþ a conquerour to konne manye sleightes,
> And manye wiles and wit þat wole ben a ledere.
> And so did Iesu in hise dayes, whoso dorste telle it.
> Som tyme he suffrede, and som tyme he hidde hym,
> And som tyme he fauȝt faste and flieȝ ouþer while,
> And som tyme he gaf good and grauntede heele boþe.
> Lif and lyme as hym liste he wroȝte.
> As kynde is of a Conquerour, so comsede Iseu
> Til he hadde alle hem þat he for bledde.   (19.96–107)

That Conscience ultimately intends to identify Christ with the David of his earlier prophecy is revealed when he proceeds to trace for Will the Savior's course from being *"filius Marie"* to being acclaimed as *"Fili david, Iesus"*:

> For david was doghtiest of dedes in his tyme;
> The burdes þo songe, *Saul interfecit mille et david decem milia.*
> Forþi þe contree þer Iesu cam called hym *fili david,*
> And nempned hym of Nazareth; and no man so worþi
> To be kaiser or kyng of þe kyngdom of Iuda. . . .   (134–38)

As Professor Thomas Hill has recently pointed out, even the preceding summary of Christ's earthly ministry, with its emphasis on His vulnerability, generally parallels Old Testament accounts of the early career of David, whose many reverses and unpromising background made him a very unlikely king but a most fitting type for the humble Lamb of God.[98]

Thus Will has his entire conception of Christ's Kingship deepened by the realization that, like David, Christ must endure countless hardships between His annointing and His final, triumphant coronation—which is not yet. As Will sees Him during Mass, he is still being offered to the Father for the sins of the world. As the Bridegroom, He suffers in the continuing tribulations of the Bride. Yet this very suffering makes Him the conqueror that He will be on His return. The lesson is the same one learned by the Adam of *Paradise Lost,* whose creator had also once dreamed the millennial dream:

> Henceforth I learn, that to obey is best,
> And love with fear the only God, to walk
> As in his presence, ever to observe
> His providence, and on him sole depend,
> Merciful over all his works, with good
> Still overcoming evil, and by small
> Accomplishing great things, by things deem'd weak
> Subverting worldly strong, and worldly wise
> By simply meek; that suffering for Truth's sake
> Is fortitude to highest victory. . . .   (12.561–70)

If Langland's theology is a theology of glory, the last two passus show it to be a theology of glory postponed. The poem does not conclude with a divine progress but with a human pilgrimage. Far from being popular escapism, Langland's message is animated by the imperative of the future, but it addresses the suffering of the present.

NOTES

1. In a recent essay, Peter Brown avers that "There are no verbs of historical movement in the *City of God*, no sense of progress to aims that may be achieved in history." See "Political Society," in *Augustine: A Collection of Critical Essays*, ed. R.A. Markus (Garden City, N.Y.: Doubleday, 1972), p. 322.

2. All citations, unless otherwise stated, are to passus and line of the B-version of *Piers Plowman* as edited by George Kane and E. Talbot Donaldson (London: Athlone Press, 1975).

3. See, for example, Augustine's letter to Hesychius: "In whatever state his own last day finds each one, in that state the last day of the world will overtake him" *Letters*, trans. Sister Wilifred Parsons (Washington, D.C.: Catholic Univ. Press, 1951–56), 4:358–59. Cf. *PL*, 33.899–925. Wilhelm Kamlah's discussion of this feature in the eschatology of such influential later commentators as Bruno of Segni and Rupert of Deutz establishes its by then thoroughly conventional nature. See his *Apokalypse und Geschichtstheologie: Die mittelalterliche Auslegung der Apokalypse vor Joachim von Fiore* (Berlin, 1935), p. 128, n. 27.

4. Augustine, *The City of God*, trans. Henry Bettenson (Baltimore: Penguin, 1972), pp. 895–96 (20.1).

5. Ibid., pp. 910–13 (20.8).

6. Hugh of St. Cher, *Opera omnia in universum Vetus et Novum Testamentum* (Venice, 1754), vol. 7, fol. 422r. According to Beryl Smalley, "John Russell, O.F.M.," *Recherches de théologie ancienne et médiévale*, 23 (1956): 305, the attribution of this Apocalypse commentary to Hugh is doubtful.

7. In his *Liber secretorum eventum*, John explicitly rejects Augustine's view of the millennium (fol. 25r) and indicates that Joachim comes closer to the truth (fol. 27v). See Jeanne Bignami-Odier, *Etudes sur Jean de Roquetaillade* (Paris: J. Vrin, 1952), p. 125. For a brief summary of his career and thought, see E.F. Jacob, "John of Roquetaillade," *Bulletin of the John Rylands Library* 39 (1956–1957): 75–96.

8. Excluding Bloomfield, the most prominent of those who have advanced this thesis cautiously are Robert Frank, *"Piers Plowman" and the Scheme of Salvation* (New Haven: Yale Univ. Press, 1957), pp. 17–18; and R.E. Kaske, "The Speech of 'Book' in *Piers Plowman,"* *Anglia* 77 (1959): 117–44.

9. Morton Bloomfield, *"Piers Plowman" as a Fourteenth-Century Apocalypse* (New Brunswick, N.J.: Rutgers Univ. Press, [1961]), p. 63.

10. For one of Joachim's most important references to this key figure, see the *Concordia Novi ac Veteris Testamenti* (1519; rpt. Frankfurt: Minerva, 1964), fol. 56r: "In ecclesia incipiet generatio 42ᵃ, anno vel hora qua Deus melius novit. In qua videlicet generatione peracta prius tribulatione generali et purgato diligenter tritico ab universis zizaniis, ascendet quasi dux novus de Babylone, universalis scilicet pontifex nove Hierusalem, hoc est sancte matris ecclesie."

11. This pattern is evident, for example, in the commentary surrounding the Seven-Headed Dragon of the *Liber figurarum:* "Ille qui designatus est in capite septimo veniet occultus, sicut Iohannes Baptista qui nesciebatur esse Helyas. Ille qui designatus est in cauda veniet manifestus, sicut venturus est Helyas. . . . Nam pro eo quod Christus Iesus venit occultus, etiam ipse Sathanas operabitur occulte opera sua, signa scilicet et prodigia et mendatia ad seducendum si fieri possit etiam electos. Et quia in fine seculi Christus Iesus venturus est manifestus ad iuditium, etiam ipse diabolus exibit in fine mundi et apparebit manifestus in diebus Gog." Immediately preceding this passage, it is explained that the third *status* will occur between the hidden and open advents of Satan. Quoted from Marjorie Reeves and Beatrice Hirsch-Reich, *The Figurae of Joachim of Fiore* (Oxford: Clarendon Press, 1972), p. 151. A lucid summary of this same eschatological program is provided by Henri de Lubac, *Exégèse médiévale* (Paris: Aubier, 1959–64), 2: 1, 545.

12. Bloomfield, *Fourteenth-Century Apocalypse,* pp. 83–97, 157–60.

13. See Bloomfield's *"Piers Plowman* and the Three Grades of Chastity," *Anglia* 76 (1958): 227–53, esp. pp. 246–53. Recent discussions have tended to discount his effort to link the Tree's hierarchy of chastity directly to the three ecclesiastical estates and to Joachim's prophetic reinterpretation of that metaphor: e.g., A. Joan Bowers, "The Tree of Charity in *Piers Plowman,"* *Literary Monographs* 6 (1975): 27; Marjorie Reeves also indicated some years ago her disbelief in the notion that the Tree of Charity is a Joachite tree. See *Figurae*, pp. 312–14.

14. That the originator of belief in an earthly period of peace after Antichrist was actually St. Jerome was first suggested by Wilhelm Bousset, *Der Antichrist in der Überlieferung des Judentums, des Neuens Testaments und der alten Kirche* (Göttingen: Vandenhoeck und Ruprecht, 1895), p. 149. It remained for Bernhard Töpfer to bring the connection of Joachite chiliasm with Jerome's exegesis to the attention of scholars in *Das kommende Reich des Friedens* (Berlin: Akademie Verlag 1964), p. 88. However, Robert Lerner is the only scholar to pursue the matter intensively; see his "Refreshment of the Saints: The Time after Antichrist as a Station for Earthly Progress in Medieval Thought," *Traditio* 32 (1976): 97–144.

15. Marjorie Reeves, *The Influence of Prophecy in the Later Middle Ages* (Oxford: Clarendon Press, 1969), pp. 396–97, insists that "Joachim had never actually formulated a clear concept of an Angelic Pope to be the symbol of the third *status,* though he comes fairly close to it." She attributes the first full statement of the idea to Roger Bacon in his *Opus tertium* (1267–1268). Nevertheless, following the passage cited previously (n. 10 above) concerning the *novus*

dux, Joachim connects this pontifical figure to the angel "ascendentem ab ortu solis" (Apoc. 7:2). It is easy to see how Joachim's disciples were able to infer the nature of the Angelic Pope from this and the Master's other mysterious references to Peter's successor, the "Spiritual Father" of plate 12 in the *Liber figurarum.* As early as the *De prophetia ignota* (1184), Joachim had foreseen a holy pope who would preach to the pagans in the days of Antichrist.

16. Marjorie Reeves, "History and Prophecy in Medieval Thought," *Medievalia et Humanistica,* n.s. 5 (1974), pp. 62–63, opines that the Spiritual Franciscans did not derive their millenarianism from Joachim, especially not from the exegetical system or Trinitarian theory of history. Rather, their sense of the uniqueness of Saint Francis and the promise of the future made possible by his example led them to seek corroboration in Joachim, among others, for what they already wished to believe in—a system of three Advents (one in Saint Francis) that would give their own time heightened significance instead of relegating it to Augustine's view of post-Resurrection history as a long, undifferentiated anticlimax. On the other hand, Professor E. Randolph Daniel, *The Franciscan Concept of Mission in the High Middle Ages* (Lexington, Ky., 1975), pp. 27 ff., sees a basic difference between the Franciscan eschatology (which he labels an eschatology of "renewal") and the Joachite program, which he recognizes as fundamentally progressivist. This distinction, however, is one that Daniel wishes to insist upon only insofar as the origins of the Order are concerned and not so as to exclude later Joachimist influences.

17. On the possibility that "Telesforus of Cosenza" (who predicted the Great Schism in his *De causis, statu, ac fine praesentis schismatis et tribulationum futurarum)* was an actual Franciscan hermit, see E. Donckel, "Studien über die Prophezeiung des Fr. Telesforus von Cosenza," *Archivum Franciscanum Historicum* 26 (1933): 29–104, 282–314 (incl. ed. of text). Also see P. Paschini, *Enciclopedia Italiana,* 33:437–38.

18. On the variety of usage of these terms among scholars, see Marjorie Reeves, "The Originality and Influence of Joachim of Fiore," *Traditio* 36 (1980): 297–98, n. 107. My usual practice follows that of Reeves, but I have attempted to make my meaning clear, on occasions where misunderstanding might arise, by erring on the side of explicitness.

19. On these matters, see my "Nature of Need in *Piers Plowman* XX," *Traditio* 34 (1978): 287–91.

20. The fact that others, for example the anonymous author of the treatise on monasticism cited by Bloomfield *(Fourteenth-Century Apocalypse,* p. 83), could appropriate Joachim's thought does not diminish the force of this argument. It is not impossible for an influence to have operated on Langland—merely unlikely in the light of his known prejudices and the public association between Joachim and Franciscan thought.

21. Even the Abbot's most admiring modern critics, including Reeves and De Lubac, admit that his theology is not Christocentric. But see Reeves's recent effort to defend Joachim from this charge in "Originality and Influence," pp. 289–91.

22. Conversely, the secular savior-king of Sibylline legend who seems to appear in Langland's millennial prophecies is a figure for whom Joachim has no use. See Reeves, "Originality and Influence," p. 287.

23. J.A.W. Bennett, *"Piers Plowman": The Prologue and Passus I–VII* (Oxford: Clarendon Press, 1972), p. 183.

24. See Reinhold Seeberg, *Text-Book of the History of Doctrines,* trans. Charles E. Hay (1905; rpt. Grand Rapids, Mich.: Baker, 1952), 1:168–72. Also Harry A. Wolfson, *The Philosophy of the Church Fathers,* 3rd ed. (Cambridge, Mass.: Harvard Univ. Press, 1970), pp. 583–99.

25. And yet, is it an oversight? The tendency is even more noticeable in C, where Langland replaces the two quotations from Genesis and John with "Ego in patre, et pater in me est" (John 14:10), a text whose assertion of Divine Consubstantiality may easily be construed in a Sabellian sense. Also, a meaningful change later in C's version of the prayer (Pearsall, 7.144–45) makes the entire address more conformable to modalistic theology by emphasizing that the relationships of Father and Son to mankind are *successive* rather than simultaneous.

26. Joachim himself was aware that he was suspected of such tendencies: "Non enim deesse possunt qui cogitent mala in cordibus suis, arbitrantes nos unitatem scindere, quia Trinitatem in misteriis predicamus." See *Expositio in Apocalypsim* (1527; rpt. Frankfurt: Minerva, 1964), fol. 38r; cited by Reeves, *Influence of Prophecy,* p. 31.

27. See Reeves and Hirsch-Reich, *Figurae,* pp. 212–13.

28. *Expositio in Apocalypsim* fol. 211r.

29. Ibid. Unless otherwise noted, all translations are my own.

30. Ibid.

31. Ibid., fol. 211v.

32. A good example is the quick fulfillment of Pride's prophetic boast in 19.344–54 concerning Unity's destruction.

33. On the importance of "the end" as that which defines a work of art in medieval aesthetics, see Robert Jordan, *Chaucer and the Shape of Creation* (Cambridge, Mass.: Harvard Univ. Press, 1967), pp. 104–10, 227–41.

34. E.g., P.M. Kean, "Justice, Kingship and the Good Life in the Second Part of *Piers Plowman,*" in *"Piers Plowman": Critical Approaches,* ed. S.S. Hussey (London: Methuen, 1969), p. 334, n. 36.

35. Adams, "Nature of Need," pp. 273–301.

36. Richard Emmerson, *Antichrist in the Middle Ages* (Seattle: Univ. of Washington Press, 1981), pp. 193–203.

37. Adams, "The Nature of Need," pp. 283–87.

38. Ibid., pp. 298–300.

39. This term is only accurate in a relative sense, with respect to mundane hopes, for *all* medieval Christian eschatologies are optimistic in this basic regard, that they expect the ultimate triumph of Good over Evil.

40. "When every case in law is right; / No squire in debt, nor no poor knight; / When slanders do not live in tongues; / Nor cutpurses come not to throngs; / When usurers tell their gold i'th'field, / And bawds and whores do churches

build; / Then comes the time, who lives to see it, / That going shall be us'd with feet." (ll. 87–94, Riverside Edition)

41. The apocalyptic significance of the disappearance of learning in the Last Days appears in several places, including the Tegernsee *Play of Antichrist,* trans. John Wright (Toronto: Pontifical Institute, 1967), p. 82. I have been unable to locate its final source.

42. David Aers, *Chaucer, Langland, and the Creative Imagination* (London: Routledge and Kegan Paul, 1978), pp. 63–79, also notices this phenomenon; however, Aers' committment to the poet as social reformer causes him to see the apocalyptic elements only as "a romantically revolutionary evasion of complexities" and as constituting "a dramatic failure of the poet's normally powerful grasp of social and historical reality" (p. 67).

43. D.W. Robertson, Jr., and B.F. Huppé, *"Piers Plowman" and Scriptural Tradition* (Princeton: Princeton Univ. Press, 1951) made this identification (p. 125) but seemed altogether unaware of the potential ambiguity.

44. E. Talbot Donaldson, *"Piers Plowman": The C-Text and Its Poet* (New Haven: Yale Univ. Press, 1949), p. 103. Donaldson recognizes that this speech contains "a prophecy of the Second Coming, when all government and governing classes will be superseded by the rule of *on berne*—namely, Christ; and at that time—and not until then—the *comune,* the common people, will find relief." On the other hand, in their edition of the B-version, Kane and Donaldson print the reading of C, *burn;* they do so in spite of the attestation of *baron* by all extant B manuscripts and in spite of Donaldson's apparent recognition some twenty-five years earlier of the *baron/berne* (i.e., *barn*) pun. What C . . has done in this case is, of course, typical of that version: the allusive, enigmatic wordplay of B has been leveled to a neutral *burn*-man. But by their editorial practice, Kane and Donaldson have tried to read that leveling back into B, where the rich ambiguities of *baron/barn* properly resonate. All three words are attested in forms that are homographic, and they are virtual homophones; the *MED* attests to these overlaps as well as to their common semantic roots and the difficulty, in a given context, of knowing which word we are dealing with.

45. For Nicholas' opinion, see his *Postilla super totam Bibliam* (Rome, 1471–1472), vol. 1, fol. 304r.

46. The standard edition of the Tiburtine and Pseudo-Methodian versions of Sibylline oracles is Ernst Sackur, *Sibyllinische Texte und Forschungen* (Halle: Niemeyer, 1898), pp. 3–96 (Pseudo-Methodius) and pp. 117–87 (Tiburtine). For discussions of the history and significance of the oracles, and for bibliography, see Richard Emmerson, *Antichrist in the Middle Ages* (Seattle, 1981), pp. 254–55 and passim. Also Bernard McGinn, *Visions of the End: Apocalyptic Traditions in the Middle Ages* (New York: Columbia Univ. Press, 1979), pp. 43–50, 70–76.

47. *PL,* 91.603B. Unless otherwise noted, all translations from the *PL* are mine.

48. Ibid., col. 605A.

49. Ibid., 109.49C–D.

50. *Textus biblie Cum Glosa ordinaria, Nicolai de lyra postilla, Moralitatibus eiusdem....* (Basle: Johannes Petri et Johannes Frobenus, 1506–1508), vol. 4, fol. 263r.

51. St. Isidore, ibid., 83.399A. This material seems to have originated with Isidore and later spread to many commentators, including Peter Riga, author of the famous versified Bible summary, *Aurora.*

52. Ibid., 167.1095A–C.

53. *Postilla,* vol. 3, fol. 5r.

54. Ibid., fol. 6r.

55. Thomas Aquinas, *Opera omnia,* ed. S.E. Fretté and P. Maré (Paris, 1874–1889), 18:685.

56. Isaiah 2:4 is part of the first matins lesson for Tuesday of the first week in Advent in the Sarum Breviary. Isaiah 14:4 is divided between the fifth matins lesson for Thursday and the first matins lesson for Friday in the fourth week of Advent.

57. In the light of Langland's expressed attitudes toward both the friars and Constantine's endowment of the Church (15.557–67), this forecast appears to veil the poet's wish that the mendicants might, like Chaucer's three treasure-hunters, eagerly drink their fill of poison. See R.E. Kaske's review of Bloomfield's *Fourteenth-Century Apocalypse* in the *Journal of English and Germanic Philology* 62 (1963): 205–6, for further discussion of this reference.

58. For a typical comment on this psalm, see Nicholas of Lyra, *Postilla,* vol. 2, fol. 275r.

59. Passus 5.243 and Passus 15.326–31.

60. Nicholas of Lyra, *Postilla,* vol. 2, fol. 275v.

61. *PL,* 37.1469–70.

62. Ibid., 36.67.

63. Ibid., cols. 164–65.

64. *Opera omnia,* vol. 2, fol. 44r.

65. Ibid.

66. Ibid.

67. *PL,* 116 (under the name of Haymo of Halberstadt), col. 790B; my italics.

68. Ibid., 181.162B–C.

69. Ibid., col. 173B.

70. Ibid.

71. The commentary surrounding the Seven-Headed Dragon in the *Liber figurarum* provides one example of the Joachite understanding of this passage (quoted in Reeves and Hirsch-Reich, *Figurae of Joachim,* p. 151). The same passage is employed in a millennial context in connection with the elevation of Mardocheus at the end of cap. 92 of the *Concordia,* fol. 122v. The author of the pseudo-Joachim commentary on Isaiah also applies this text to the millennial sabbath: *Super Isaiam Prophetam,* (Venice, 1517), fol. 3r.

72. Although he never alludes to the Amalek episode, the author describes (as though he were predicting) an attack on Edward at Calais in 1347 by drawing an analogy to Saul, Samuel, and David. *Political Poems and Songs Relating to English*

History, Composed during the Period from the Accession of Edw. III to That of Ric. III, ed. Thomas Wright (1859; rpt. [n.p.], 1965), 1:166–67. As for Joachim's use of David, Reeves notes *(Influence of Prophecy,* p. 304) that the shepherd-king signified the ideal beneficent ruler to Joachim, but she adds that he "is given a priestly character and the apotheosis is seen in terms of Church rather than State." Also Reeves points out that when David appears in this role, he is compared to Constantine/Sylvester, with no hint of a third great empire. This indicates that Joachim's pattern of twos is operative here. As for David's function within the pattern of threes, de Lubac has noted *(Exégèse médievale,* 2: 1, 481) that he invariably symbolizes in such contexts the second rather than the third age. For example, in the *Liber figurarum,* the great image of *Misterium Ecclesiae* shows Saul as the king of the first age, that of the carnal; David is king of the second era, that of Christians; and Solomon is the peaceful figure who dominates the third age. The *Concordia* (fol. 95v) also supports this view of David's role.

73. John Alford's article, "The Role of the Quotations in *Piers Plowman,*" *Speculum* 52 (1977): 80–99, makes this contention seem very tenuous for *any* part of the poem.

74. *Tractatus super quatuor Evangelia di Gioacchino da Fiore,* ed. E. Buonaiuti (Rome: Tipografia del Senato, 1930), pp. 186–87.

75. *Political Poems and Songs,* 1:167.

76. Lerner, "Refreshment of the Saints," pp. 97–144.

77. Cf. Reeves, *Influence of Prophecy,* p. 48; and Lerner, "Refreshment of the Saints," p. 120. Also cf. Reeves, "Originality and Influence," passim.

78. Lerner, "Refreshment of the Saints," p. 135.

79. Ibid., passim.

80. Quoted in Reeves, *Influence of Prophecy,* p. 427.

81. Conservatives such as Vincent of Beauvais and Hugh of St. Cher leave nothing to chance concerning the brevity of this final time. Both adhere strictly to the formula of forty-five literal days for penance of lapsed Christians. See Lerner, "Refreshment of the Saints," p. 121.

82. Gerhoch of Reichersberg well illustrates this entire viewpoint in his interpretation of 2 Thess. 2:8, a reference to the death of Antichrist ("The Lord Jesus shall kill [him] with the Spirit of His mouth; and shall destroy him with the brightness of His coming"). Since Gerhoch believes that the "refreshment of the saints" will occur *between* the death of Antichrist and Christ's Second Coming, he must account for this text's assertion that Christ Himself will dispatch the Enemy. His solution is to fix on "the brightness of His coming" and read it as literally as possible. This allows him to offer as an analogy the distinction between dawn and sunrise. Before the Son Himself appears, the brightness of His coming will disperse the dullness of Antichrist. Hence brevity is stressed. The time for the "refreshment" becomes a fleeting moment in the continuum of the Last Things—an earthly prelude to the heavenly fugue. *De quarta vigilia noctis,* in *Libelli de lite Imperatorum et Pontificum saec. XI et XII,* ed. H. Boehmer (Hanover: Hahn, 1891–97), 3:513–14.

83. Bloomfield, *Fourteenth-Century Apocalypse,* p. 125.

84. On this aspect of Langland's style, the best discussion is still John Burrow, "The Action of Langland's Second Vision," *Essays in Criticism* 15 (1965): 247–68.

85. The *locus classicus* for this theory is St. Augustine, *On Christian Doctrine*, trans. D.W. Robertson, Jr. (Indianapolis: Bobbs-Merrill, 1958), pp. 37–38 (II.vi.7–8).

86. For instance, see Hugh of St. Cher, *Opera omnia*, vol. 2, fol. 44r. Also cf. Manegold of Lautenbach († 1103), *PL*, 93 (under the name of Bede), col. 586D.

87. *PL*, 36.165.

88. Hugh of St. Cher, *Opera omnia*, vol. 2, fol. 44r.

89. Hervé of Bourgdieu, *Commentaria in Isaiam* in *PL*, 181.162A.

90. On this symbolic contrast, see Rupert of Deutz, *De Trinitate et operibus eius* in ibid., 167. 1061A, 1095C–D.

91. *Postilla super Isaian*, ed. Ferdinand Siepmann in *Opera omnia* (Münster: Aschendorf, 1951–), (Münster: n.p., 1952), 19:40.

92. *PL*, 181.48B.

93. I interpret the goliard's words, as does Donaldson *(C-Text*, pp. 99–100), to mean that he is advocating a form of strict legalism. P.M. Kean's counter-argument, "Love, Law, and *Lewte* in *Piers Plowman*," in *Style and Symbolism in "Piers Plowman*," ed. Robert Blanch (Knoxville: University of Tennessee Press, 1969), pp. 137–40, is unconvincing.

94. Another hint is offered at 15.164–65: " '*Charite is no3t chaumpions fight* ne chaffare as I trowe.' / 'Charite,' quod he, 'ne chaffareþ no3t *ne chalangeþ,* ne crauþ' " (my italics).

95. *Li tornoiemenz Antecrit*, ed. Georg Wimmer (Marburg: Elwert, 1888).

96. On this pun, see Maureen Quilligan, "Langland's Literal Allegory," *Essays in Criticism* 28 (1978): 103–10.

97. Bloomfield, *Fourteenth-Century Apocalypse*, p. 125.

98. Thomas Hill, "Davidic Typology and the Characterization of Christ: *Piers Plowman* B.XIX, 95–103," *Notes and Queries*, n.s. 23 (1976), 291–94.

Chaucer and the Written Language

John H. Fisher

Popular culture in the Middle Ages is thought of as a principally oral phenomenon, but the example of Geoffrey Chaucer indicates that by the fourteenth century, it was fast becoming literate. Chaucer was a civil servant whose professional career entailed the reading and writing of official documents. The letter appointing him Controller of Customs in 1374 specified "idem Galfridus rotulos suos dicta officia tangentes manu sua propria scribat" (the same Geoffrey shall write his rolls touching the said office in his own hand).[1] Since both the hand and the language in which official enrollments were entered were professional accomplishments, the terms of Chaucer's appointment indicate that he had had instruction either privately with a writing master or, more likely, as a student at the Inns of Chancery and Inns of Court. The period between the 1360 record of his military service in France and 1366, when he reappears traveling in Spain, is the longest gap in the Chaucer life-records after their commencement in 1357. Three years in the Inns of Chancery and three in the Inns of Court were the normal period for education in what came to be called "England's third university."[2] Chaucer's education remains a surmise, but his proficiency in the *ars dictaminis* is no surmise. Without it, he could not have pursued his official career.

As employed for government and commerce in Chaucer's time, the *ars dictaminis* was still largely a Latin tradition. Its significant characteristic was that it was a written not a spoken language. This had begun in ancient times. Imperial Latin—what we today call Classical Latin—was a written standard which came down into the Middle Ages and beyond relatively unchanged. The spoken dialects of Latin developed into the romance languages. However, although it was transmitted in writing, the classical ideal of communication remained essentially oral. As James

J. Murphy has observed in *Rhetoric in the Middle Ages*,[3] the Ciceronian ideal of discourse depended upon occasion rather than upon audience: the three varieties of speaking were forensic, deliberative, and occasional. The author of the pseudo-Ciceronian *Rhetorica ad Herennium* added the notion of three levels of style—grand, middle, and plain—but these were still regarded as manners of speaking to the same audience in different situations.[4]

The principal transformation in the medieval *ars dictaminis* was that the receiver of the communication replaced the occasion as the factor which determined the style. The Englishman John of Garland (ca. 1250) has been identified as the rhetorical theorist who transmuted the Ciceronian manners of speaking into styles for writing to three different kinds of audience: the grand style for writing to courtiers (*curiales*), the middle style for writing to citizens (*civiles*), and the plain style for writing to peasants (*rurales*).[5] An important consideration in the *ars dictaminis* became the choice of the salutation, which would at once identify the relationship between the sender and the receiver. It is significant that in the first important treatise on the *ars dictaminis*, Alberic of Monte Cassino (ca. 1087) speaks not of the Ciceronian "orator" and "auditores" but of the "scriptor" and "lector."[6] Hugh of Bologna's *Rationes dictandi prosice* (ca. 1120) lists seventeen (not quite Chaucer's thirty) kinds of salutations, ranging from "a papa ad imperatorem" to "civitas ad civitatem," including "ad patrem," "ad amicum," "ad magistrum" and so forth.[7] The model letters in the formularies which served as textbooks for the *ars dictaminis* exemplify the different styles to be employed to the various addressees of the letters, and thus helped introduce into the writing process the conception of point of view.

The importance of this development to our understanding of Chaucer's art becomes clear when we observe the importance modern criticism has placed upon the development of point of view in Chaucer's writings. "It is not merely that . . . Chaucer tells a story with different layers," says Raymond Preston, "he tells it . . . from different points of view." "With this statement," observes William Crawford, "modern criticism of Chaucer may be said to have had its beginning."[8]

Point of view is intrinsic to the development of written as distinct from spoken communication. Walter Ong, in his prize-winning essay "The Writer's Audience Is Always Fiction" (*PMLA*, January 1975) explores the literary implications of this phenomenon at some length. He is concerned with the difference between the signals in an oral presentation to an audience which is moved by group psychology and the signals in a written presentation to an individual reader who must be addressed in a more personal, more intimate tone. The graphemic signals in written communication as to how the reader is expected to react are different from the paralinguistic signals that accompany speech. Ong argues that role playing—the assumption of a mask—is inevitable in any kind of human communication, both for the sender and for the receiver. The signals which establish the roles in speech and writing are, however, very different. When the late John Gardner appeared before a student audience, his blue jeans, his leather jacket, and the cut of his hair indicated clearly the role he was adopting, and it was immediately understood by the students, who adopted a complementary anti-Establishment role in their reception. In writing there are no blue jeans or leather jackets. There are only the marks on the page. Ong describes the period from Dante to Fielding as one in which both writers and readers were devising and learning to comprehend the signals of written communication. He sees both the persona and the frame story as early devices through which the writer attempted to direct the reaction of the reader—to indicate what mask he should adopt in order to respond appropriately to the mask being adopted by the writer.

This interest in the transformation of narrative technique from oral to written has grown widespread since Northrop Frye in *The Anatomy of Criticism* (1957) distinguished the oral "epos" from written "fiction," and Scoles and Kellogg in *The Nature of Narrative* (1966) pointed up the difference between the voices of the "orator" and the "narrator." In an essay in the distinguished volume published in 1974 in honor of Rossell Hope Robbins's sixtieth birthday, Dieter Mehl traced in detail the effect of the fictional reading audience upon the narrative voice of *Troylus and Criseyde*. Robert Jordan, Piero Boitani, and others have approached Chaucerian narrative as a literary vehicle.[9] What I am suggesting here is that awareness of the masks of writer and reader was reinforced by the social interpretation of style in the *ars dictaminis*.

The courtly and bourgeois styles discerned by Charles Muscatine and Per Nykrog may be recognized as extensions of the styles proposed for letters "ad curialem" and "ad civitatem" in the formularies. In 1984 Jane Fisher, Malcolm Richardson, and I published *An Anthology of Chancery English*, containing 241 of the earliest official documents in Modern English.[10] One hundred and four are the signet letters of Henry V (1417–1422), and the rest are petitions to the King, the Chancellor, and Parliament from a variety of institutions and individuals, and responses to these petitions (1388–1455). The striking fact is that virtually all of these documents, be they instructions, requests, appointments, or contracts are epistolary in form. In all cultures, the letter emerges as the first form of expository writing. The communicative situation of the letter is closest to speech. It is addressed to a single individual, whose identity determines the style of address. The first document we print in our anthology is an exemplar of about 1420 from either the Office of the Signet or the Office of the Privy Seal. It begins: "Trusty and welbeloued, ffor asmuche as in certain matiers . . ." After giving the body of the letter, it continues, "This style of trusty and welbeloued may be direct to oon persone, or to as many to gider as it shal lyke the said Commissioners, and it may serve for all maner men yif nede be except Bisshops. . . . To the Right Dere in god, and Dere in god—euerich of þees styles may serue for Abbottes, Prioures, Denes, Archediacones. And for need for thrifty persones."

Instructions such as these show a concern about the social condition of the recipient of the message that marks written communication, which is not discussed in the classical rhetorical tradition. Other manifestations of social concern also begin to appear in le medieval ecclesiastical literature. The *sermones ad status* take into account the professions of the audience. In the penitential manuals, priests were advised to show the same concern as the physician for the condition of the sinner.[11] This sort of sensitivity helped introduce into written communication the sort of signals for directing the reactions of the reader that have become the preoccupation of modern transactional theories of composition. Although much has been written about the socially conscious salutations, I know of no study of the linguistic markings in letters addressed to different kinds of recipients. A larger study might be made of the written signals in the *ars dictaminis* and the influence of these signals on the styles of poets like Dante, Jean de Meun, Petrarch, Boccaccio, and Chaucer himself, all of whom must have been trained in the dictaminal arts. None of the studies of the emergence of the authorial voice has, so far as I know, taken into account the dictaminal rhetoric of the formularies.

However, this is a topic too broad to develop at this time. What I am concerned to pursue here is the evidence that the fictional audience for Chaucer's poems was as much the reader as the listener. In spite of seminal studies like those by Walter Ong and Dieter Mehl, the tradition that Chaucer created his poems to be read aloud still flourishes. In Beryl Rowland's *Companion to Chaucer Studies,* alongside Robert Jordan's informed summary of the arguments for readership, Albert Baugh could still write: "Everyone knows, but we are inclined to forget, that Chaucer read his poetry aloud to assembled audiences at the court, as indeed we see him doing in the beautiful Corpus Christi College manuscript of the *Troylus.*"[12] And he quotes Bertram Bronson:

It is a current fashion, not to say a fad, to discuss . . . Chaucer's *persona*, meaning the "I" in his poetry. I have little hesitation in saying that nine-tenths of this talk is misguided and palpably mistaken. . . . Lip service is paid from time to time to the knowledge that Chaucer wrote for oral delivery, but this primary fact is continually lost sight of or ignored by those who write on the *persona*, and its implications are seldom fully realized.

Now I do not argue that Chaucer never read his poems aloud. After all, many modern authors from Charles Dickens to Eudora Welty have made great capital from reading aloud works that were manifestly composed for a reading public. But there is more direct evidence that Chaucer was composing for a reading audience than has so far been adduced. Baugh appeals to the illustration in the Corpus manuscript, but the narrator of *Troylus* himself appears to be concerned as much about the reader as the hearer. At the end of the poem he prays:

> And for ther is so gret dyversite
> In Englyssh and yn wrytyng of oure tonge,
> So prey I God that noon myswryte the,
> Ne the mysmetre for defaute of tonge.
> And red wherso thow be, or elles songe,
> That thow be understonde, God I beseche.[13] (*TC* 5.1794)

The reference to "songe" here implies an audience listening to the reader, but earlier in book 5, the poet had appealed specifically to his reader:

> Who koude telle aright or ful discryve
> His wo, his pleynt, his langour, and his peyne?
> Nought al the men that han or ben on lyve.
> Thow, redere, mayst thyself ful wel devyne
> That swych a wo my wit kan nat defyne.
> On ydel for to write it sholde I swynke,
> Whan that my wit is wery it to thenke. (*TC* 5.267)

This passage exemplifies exactly the mask that Father Ong finds characteristic of written communication—the confidential, cozy, one-to-one tone: "thow, redere," and "my wit." Mehl compares it to the "dear reader" stage directions of Fielding and Sterne in the eighteenth-century novel. He traces in detail the devices by which the fictional narrator in *Troylus* creates empathy with the fictional reader with whom we are asked to identify ourselves. The proems are intended directly to influence the reader's reactions; the asides about the character of Criseyde convey in writing reservations that a speaker might be able to convey by tone of voice; the final exhortation, "Go litel bok. . . And kys the steppes where as thow seest pace / Virgile, Ovyde, Omer, Lukan, and Stace" (*TC*,

5.1785) refers to Latin poetry, which by Chaucer's time, was certainly intended to be read individually rather than recited to a group.

Throughout the Middle Ages, Latin literature had enjoyed a readership. One feature of the Renaissance was the emergence of a similar readership for vernacular literature. This readership was not only clerical but popular. A.C. Baugh has shown how many of the French and English romances imagine a reader as well as a listening audience.[14] In *Eger and Grime:*

> Into a window Sir Egar yeede
> Bookes of romans for to reede
> That all the court might hem heare.   (627–29)

In *Yvain:*

> Þe mayden red at þai myght here
> A real romance in þat place.   (3088–89)

Although it was still impossible for the author of the romance to imagine a solitary reader, he envisaged himself as a solitary writer. The author of *Arthour and Merlin* speaks of "þis Nacions of whom y write" (8909), and

> Her after sone in þis write
> Whi he it dede, 3e schul it wite.   (9655–56)

And Baugh cites other examples. But although the romance author imagines himself as a writer composing for a reader, he still imagines the listening group as the ultimate audience. The author of *Arthour and Merlin* begins his romance:

> 3eue heom alle good endyng
> Þat wolon listne þis talkyng   (3–4)

just as the author of *Beves of Hamptoun* begins:

> Lystonythe, lordinges, yf ye will dwell;
> Of a doughty man I wyll yow tell.   (1–2)

This is the style that Chaucer was burlesquing in the Tale of Sir Thopas.

Chaucer's early poems are nearly at the stage of the romances. They show great sensitivity to the oral effect. We recall the "goodly" speech of the Black Knight in *The Book of the Duchess,* who "made hyt nouther towgh ne queynte" *(BD,* 531); and first the "esy voys," then the "facound voys" of Dame Nature in *Parliament of Fowls (PF,* 382, 521); the harsh voice in *House of Fame* that usually woke Geoffrey up, in contrast to the reassuring professional voice of the eagle *(HF,* 565), and the "goodly" voice that asked him near the end of the poem, "Frend, what is thy name? / Artow come hider to han fame?" *(HF,* 1870). However, like the romances discussed by Baugh, Chaucer's early poems are full of references to the writing process. Only in the *Book of the Duchess* is such allusion lacking. In the *Parliament* the poet prays to Cytherea, "Whan I began myn swevene for the write, / So yif me myght to ryme and ek t'endyte" *(PF, 118)*, and Affrican promises, "I shal the shewe mater for to wryte" *(PF, 168)*. An *occupatio* in Book 1 of the *House of Fame* begins, "And nere hyt were to long t'endyte / Be God, I wolde hyt here write" *(HF, 382)*. In Book 2 the eagle accuses Geoffrey, "In thy studye, so thou writest" *(HF, 633)*. In describing the House of Rumor in Book 3 the poet observes, "And loo, thys hous of which I write" *(HF, 1977)*. In the *Legend of Good Women*, Alceste refers to the task she is assigning the dreamer as a book, "And whan this book ys maad, yive it the quene" *(LGW, 496)*. The G prologue adds two more references to his writing (G, 530, 532) and the Legend of Phyllis two more still *(LGW, 2494, 2513)*. Although the early poems do not refer specifically to the reader, the authorial mask is that of a writer, and there are no signals, like those in the romances, to a listening audience.

As Chaucer moved along in his development, the listening audience became the fictional pilgrim audience rather than the imagined real audience of the romances, and the reactions of the fictional audience become part of the drama of the *Canterbury Tales*. However, the pilgrims' reactions are not themselves addressed to a listening audience. Whatever the imagined audience for the tales when they were originally composed, the links between the tales are directed to the solitary reader. In the Miller's headlink, the reader is directed to "Turne over the leef and chese another tale" (1.3177). In the prologue to the Second Nun's Tale, he is appealed to, "Yet preye I yow that reden that I write" (8.78). In the Retraction, the narrator agains appeals "Now preye I to hem alle that herkne this litel tretys or rede" (10.1080), here recalling the practice of oral reading. But such appeals to the reader in the *Canterbury Tales* do not occur within the tales proper.

Even though some of the tales may have been originally composed to be recited, the style and subject matter of others indicates that they were almost certainly composed to be read, most notably the Tale of Melibee and the Parson's Tale. It is interesting to observe how the vocabulary of these more formal, literary productions crops up in the links. For example, in the Miller's headlink, which we think of as a triumph of colloquial ease, there are two technical terms, *protestacioun* ("But first I make a protestacioun," 1.3137) and *apeyren* ("It is a synne and eek a greet folye / To apeyren any man," 1.3147). Both of these are technical terms found also in Chancery documents, *protestacioun* meaning a legal demurral

(Document 221.1), and *apeiryd* meaning to impair legally (an heir's income is not to be "amenusyd ne aperyd," Document 188.21). According to the Tatlock-Kennedy *Concordance, protestacioun* occurs only once more in the *Canterbury Tales,* in the Parson's Tale, 10.59. Two other occurrences are in *Troylus* (2.484, 4.1289), which supports the impression that that piece is more literary than colloquial. The only other occurrence of *protestacioun* is when Egiste speaks to Ypermestre in the final story in the *Legend of Good Women* (2640). *Apeyren* occurs also in Parson's Tale (10.1075) and *Troylus* (2.329), and in the eagle's lecture to Geoffrey in *House of Fame* (2.756—sound floats up to the House of Fame "there hit shulde not apaire").

Conversely, it is interesting to see that the technical terms in the glossary of the Chancery documents occur principally in Chaucerian pieces that are literary in manner and tone. For example, from the letter A, *abet* in the sense of assist occurs only in *Troylus. Affinity* in the sense of blood relationship occurs only in the Parson's Tale and *Boece.* The inflected form *aforne* ("before") occurs only in *Troylus. Aggregge* ("to burden or weigh down") occurs only in the Parson's Tale and Melibee. *Amenuse* ("to reduce in size or value") occurs only in the Parson's Tale, *Boece,* and the *Astrolabe. Amoeve* ("to remove") occurs only in *Boece. Anientissed* ("diminished") occurs only in Melibee. *Arten* ("to compel") occurs only in *Troylus.* And *apert* ("evident or overt") occurs in the Wife of Bath's Tale, the Squire's Tale, and the *House of Fame,* in the legal collocation "pryvee and apert." Only in the Parson's Tale and *Boece* does it occur alone (as in the phrase "a synne of apert folye," 10.649). These and other words shared with the Chancery glossary suggest that there was a vocabulary found chiefly in pieces like *Troylus,* Melibee, the Parson's Tale, *Boece,* and the *Astrolabe* which were intended for reading rather than for recitation.

Presumably all of the links date from the period after Chaucer began to think of the *Canterbury Tales* as a compilation to be read rather than as a collection from which individual pieces could be selected for oral recitation. I have elsewhere presented my argument that the links represent various stages in Chaucer's revision and organization of his fascicles, and Charles Owen in *Pilgrimage and Story-Telling* has developed this argument in even more detail.[15] In addition to the appearance in the links of references to the reader and words from the literary vocabulary, the General Prologue and the links are the passages which contain the sort of authorial commentary that Ong and Mehl would see as establishing rapport between the solitary writer and the solitary reader. The General Prologue is replete with asides like that on the Monk, "And I sayde his opinioun was good" (1.183), and the Merchant, "But, sooth to seyn, I noot how men hym calle" (1.284), of direct judgments like that on the Lawyer, "And yet he semed bisier than he was" (1.322), and on the Physician, "Therefore he lovede gold in special" (1.444). Such ironic glosses are signals of the written style. They serve, in the absence of facial expression, gesture, and tone of voice, to put the reader on guard, to suggest, as I once heard John Crow Ransom remark, that in Chaucer "we can never be sure who's getting the bird."

The author's personal commentary in the *Canterbury Tales* extends only as far as the famous "dear reader" passage that I referred to before:

> And therefore every gentil wight I preye,
> For Goddes love, demeth nat that I seye
> Of yvel entente, but that I moot reherce
> Hir tales alle, be they bettre or werse,
> Or elles falsen som of my mateere.
> And therfore, whoso list it nat yhere,
> Turne over the leef and chese another tale. (1.3171)

Again we perceive the confidential, one-to-one tone, here tempered by exquisite use of the impersonal. The writer is careful not to imply that the reader he addresses is naive and a prude: whoever is, and therefore doesn't want to hear an indelicate story, may turn over the leaf and choose another tale—but you, of course, dear reader, are too sophisticated for that!

When we reach the Reeve's headlink, we find a device other than the reactions of the poet persona for directing the reader's response—that is, the commentary of the Host. As much by negative example as by positive statement, the Host indicates what mask the narrator is assuming for the next tale, and so suggests what mask the reader should assume in response. His exchange with the Reeve modulates from a somber, lyrical complaint about old age, about memory as the stuff of literature, to the feisty fabliau that follows. This technique is elaborated in the subsequent links. The Host's exchange with the Pardoner calls attention to the contrast between the character of the Pardoner and that of his Tale. His exchange with the Canon's Yeoman provides occasion and motivation for the exposé that follows. And so on through the other headlinks. The role of the Host has been discussed so often that we need not rehearse it again.[16]

There is a marked contrast between the editorializing in the links and the apostrophes within the tales themselves, like that in the Man of Law's Tale:

> Imprudent Emperour of Rome, allas,
> Was ther no philosophre in al thy toun?
> Is no tyme bet than oother in swich cas?
> Of viage is ther noon eleccioun,
> Namely to folk of heigh condicioun?   (2.309)

This heightens the pathos but it does not instruct the reader how to react. Similarly, the aside in the Clerk's Tale, "But as for me, I seye that yvele it sit / To assay a wyf whan that it is no nede" (4.460) helps to achieve suspension of disbelief but does not direct the response of the reader. As Mehl observes, the signals in oral composition are strictly one-way. They appeal to the listeners only for their attention and belief.[17] In contrast, the signals in written composition seek to enlist the cooperation of the reader in completing the composition. The signals in the links are particularly effective when the Host's remarks serve to raise doubts as to the correct reception of the tale that follows. "Straw for your gentilesse" (5.695) says the Host to the Franklin, and the reader is thrown into doubt as to the reliability of the Franklin as a narrator and consequently how to react to the genteel behavior he expounds in his Tale. The Host addresses the Nun's Priest "with rude speche and boold":

> Be blithe, though thou ryde upon a jade.
> What thogh thyn hors be bothe foul and lene?
> If he wol serve thee, rekke nat a bene.
> Looke that thyn herte be murie everemo.   (7.2812)

These lines speak from the point of view not of the Host but of the Prioress and raise interesting questions as to how the reader should react to the tale of the lordly Chauntecleer and his subservient wives.

As might be expected, the Wife of Bath's Prologue does not fit the pattern. This is the only link in the *Canterbury Tales* that lacks the monitoring presence of either the persona or the Host and it is the passage in the *Tales* for which we find it most difficult to decide what mask to assume. The older tradition was to regard the Wife as the butt of Chaucer's humor, but more recent critics have found her an exemplary figure, working out the problems of female independence and integrity centuries before these became self-conscious themes in literature.[18] Only the interruption of the Pardoner and the words between the Summoner and Friar at the end offer a gloss on the Wife's diatribe. The Pardoner speaks from the characteristic narrow, male-chauvinist point of view— who would want to marry a woman like that anyway? The Summoner and Friar set the stage for their own quarrel. The right reception for the Wife's prologue and tale remains elusive, but that, of course, is one of our principal delights in Chaucer's poetry.

Nevertheless, the Wife of Bath's Prologue, like the other links, appears to be composed as much with the reader as with the hearer in mind. Certainly Chaucer himself thought so when in the "Envoy to Bukton" he instructed his friend, "The Wyf of Bathe I pray yow that ye rede" ("Bukton," 1.29). In spite of its marvelous colloquial ease, virtually every line in the Wife of Bath's Prologue is a quotation or paraphrase from a literary source. And it is full of terms shared only with the formally literary productions. *Engendrure* it shares only with *Boece; indulgence* only with Melibee; *femele* and *male* only with the Parson's Tale and *Boece; persevere* only with Melibee, Parson's Tale, and *Troylus; practik* only with the *Astrolabe;* and so on.

The complexity of Chaucer's poetry, which has become the hallmark of modern critical interpretation, may be partly the bequest of the traditions of Latin, French, and Italian poetry, but the explicit awareness of the situations of writer and reader were reinforced by the dialectic of the *ars dictaminis*. It is no longer satisfactory for us to think of Chaucer as merely producing a libretto to be performed, although in many cases he may have been doing that, too. His principal achievement is that he was one of the first writers to produce *literature* in English, literature in its etymological sense of Latin *literatura,* that is, written composition directed to the solitary reader.

The connection between Chaucer's style and the Chancery tradition is reinforced by the language of the manuscripts. One of the most interesting articles that has appeared recently is A.I. Doyle's and Malcolm Parkes's study of the scribal hands in manuscripts of the *Confessio Amantis* and *Canterbury Tales*.[19] They find that Thomas Hoccleve, the English poet, was one of the five scribes who copied a Trinity College manuscript of the *Confessio*. Another of the five was the scribe who copied both the Ellesmere and Hengwrt manuscripts of the *Canterbury Tales*. This conjunction is of some importance as an indication of how the Chancery tradition could have influenced literary documents. Hoccleve was for some thirty-five years a clerk in the Privy Seal office, and at the end of his life he compiled a formulary of Latin and French writs employed in the work of his office. He wrote in a typical Chancery hand, as did the other four copiests in Doyle's and Parkes's study. Presumably they would all have been influenced by the Chancery orthography and idiom. One reason that Chaucer's and Gower's poems are so much easier to read than *Gawain* and *Piers Plowman* is that they were perhaps written and have certainly been preserved in this official orthography. In lines 2 and 16 of the Hengwrt manuscript text of the General Prologue (in Paul Ruggier's facsimile) all of the OE velar fricatives (as in *droght* and *nyght)* are spelled *gh*. This may well have still represented the pronunciation to Chaucer, but one of the significant evidences that Chancery standard in the next century began to move away from phonetic towards ideographic spelling is that it preserved this *gh* spelling after it ceased to be pronounced. Another example of nonphonetic spelling in the Hengwrt is *compignye* (1.24). One can see the *ig* spelling in French words slowly disappearing in the fifteenth century, but it is still retained in modern for*eign*, sover*eign*, r*eign*. One reason for preserving it in r*eign* is to distinguish the *reign* of a king from the *rein* of a horse and from the *rain* that falls. This movement of Chancery standard toward distinguishing homophones with different meanings (as in Modern English we *rode* to the lake and *rowed* across) is already at work in Hengwrt, where the rhyme words of lines 17 and 18 are spelled *seke* ("The hooly blisful martir for to seke") and *seeke* ("That hem hath holpen whan that they were seeke"), even though the former word *(seke)* had been spelled with double *e* only four lines earlier ("And palmeres for to seeken straunge strondes").

The spelling of the best Chaucer manuscripts is quite similar to that of Chancery documents—which may simply be another way of saying that the spelling in official documents remained quite varied until after the advent of printing, although a *quantitative* analysis of the sort found in the glossary of our Chancery anthology shows the modern forms usually in the majority. The *drift* towards standardization can be clearly documented.

While the fifteenth-century scribes either modernized Chaucer's spelling or enshrined his archaisms in their emerging standard, they were much less likely to tamper with his grammar. In the first eighteen lines of the Hengwrt there are six *-en* inflections: *maken* (9), *slepen* (10), *longen* (12), *goen* (12), *seeken* (13), *holpen* (18). Such *-en* inflections occur in only 13 of the 104 extant English letters of Henry V (12 percent), in 6 percent of the Privy Seal documents, and 15 percent of the Chancery documents in our anthology. Most of these occurrences are in the period before 1430. The past participle with *y-* prefix *(yronne,* l. 8 of the Hengwrt) is never found in Signet or Chancery documents, and—to go on to other Chaucerian forms not found in this passage—Chancery writing seldom uses the proclitic negative *(nill, nis)*; its adverbial ending is never *-lich;* it never uses the second person singular pronouns *thee* and *thou* but always plural *you* and *ye,* and almost always *their,* although *hem* still occurs more frequently than *them* up through 1455. Clearly the morphology in the Chaucerian manuscripts is from an earlier stratum than the orthography.

The development of a standard that speaks more to the eye than to the ear has a different history in each of the European vernaculars. In each of them, as in Latin, artistic use of the language represents a tension between the rhetorical nuances of the oral and the logical analyses of the written. What makes Chaucer's writing so interesting is that it comes near the beginning of this development. His prose treatises—*Boece, Melibee,* the *Treatise on the Astrolabe,* and possibly the *Equatorie of the Planetis*—represent some of the first attempts in English to write technical exposition of the sort that would be polished in Chancery writs and expository essays throughout the next century. Such productions imply a readership as well as a clerisy. The prose treatises by Chaucer, and the didactic and historical writings of Wycliffe, Trevisa, Usk, and others signal the emergence of a reading public for English of the sort that had existed for a millenium for Latin and for more than a hundred years for French and Italian.

Poetry, of course, was another matter. Presumably Chaucer and other poets continued for a long time to entertain audiences with oral recitations. It is the tension between the oral residue and the literary initiative in their poems that students of style are beginning now to examine most carefully. The subtlety and complexity of thought and expression that mark the poetry of Dante and Petrarch, Jean de Meun and the French court poets, and Chaucer and the *Pearl* and *Piers Plowman* poets represent the extension to nonutilitarian writing—that is, to literature in the modern sense of the term—of the sensitivities and signaling devices that characterize the utilitarian written language of the *ars dictaminis.*

Himself a clerk in the national administration, trained in the written tradition of the *ars dictaminis,* Chaucer was in the mainstream of the development of written expression in English. He capitalized on this fortunate situation to produce some of the earliest literature in English addressed more directly to the eye than to the ear, to the individual reader rather than to a listening audience.

N O T E S

1. *Chaucer Life Records,* ed. M.M. Crow and C.C. Olson (Oxford: Clarendon Press, 1966), p. 148.
2. Philip Anstie Smith, *A History of Education for the English Bar* (London, 1860), pp. 10 ff., discusses the nature and duration of fifteenth-century education in the Inns of Chancery and Inns of Court. Reginald James Fletcher, introduction to *The Pension Book of Gray's Inn* (London, 1910), pp. xiii ff., discusses the similarities and differences between education at the Inns of Court and the universities. R.E. Megarry, *Inns Ancient and Modern: A Topological*

Introduction to the Inns of Court, Inns of Chancery, and Sergeants' Inns (London: Selden Society, 1972), offers an informed, anecdotal account of early legal education.

3. James J. Murphy, *Rhetoric in the Middle Ages* (Berkeley: Univ. of California Press, 1974), p. 9.

4. Ibid., p. 19.

5. Per Nykrog, *Les Fabliaux: Etude d'histoire littéraire et de stylistique médiévale* (Copenhagen: E. Munksgaard, 1957), p. 232; and John M. Steadman, " 'Courtly Love' as a Problem of Style," in *Chaucer und seine Zeit: Symposium für Walter Schirmer*, ed. A. Esch (Tübingen: Niemeyer, 1968), pp. 7 ff, accept John of Garland as the father of the social interpretation of the three styles. Garland's text has been edited by Giovanni Mari, "Poetria magistri Johannis anglici de prosayea metrici et rithmica," *Romanische Forschungen*, 13 (1902): 883–965. Its application to Chaucer has been discussed by J.H. Fisher, "The Three Styles of Fragment I of the Canterbury Tales," *Chaucer Review*, 8 (1973): 119–27.

6. Murphy, *Rhetoric in the Middle Ages*, p. 205.

7. Ibid., p. 217.

8. Raymond Preston, *Chaucer* (New York: Sheed and Ward, 1952), p. 65, as discussed by W.R. Crawford, "New Directions in Chaucer Study," in his *Bibliography of Chaucer 1954–63* (Seattle: Univ. of Washington Press, 1967), p. xxii.

9. Discussion of and references to studies of Chaucer's poems as literary rather than oral productions are found in Robert Jordan's essay, "Chaucerian Narrative" in *A Companion to Chaucer Studies*, ed. Beryl Rowland, rev. ed. (Toronto: Oxford Univ. Press, 1979), pp. 95–117. Of special interest are Dieter Mehl, "The Audience of Chaucer's *Troilus and Criseyde*," in *Chaucer and Medieval Studies in Honour of Rossell Hope Robbins*, ed. Beryl Rowland (London: Allen and Unwin, 1974), pp. 173–89; and Piero Boitani, *English Medieval Narrative in the Thirteenth and Fourteenth Centuries* (Cambridge: Cambridge Univ. Press, 1982), esp. pp. 199 ff.

10. *An Anthology of Chancery English*, ed. John H. Fisher, Malcolm Richardson, Jane L. Fisher (Knoxville: Univ. of Tennessee Press, 1984).

11. On the social sensitivity of the homiletic and penitential traditions see J.H. Fisher, *John Gower* (New York: New York Univ. Press, 1964), pp. 137 ff.

12. A.C. Baugh, "Chaucer the Man," in *Companion to Chaucer Studies*, p. 13. Bertrand Bronson, *In Search of Chaucer* (Toronto: Univ. of Toronto Press, 1960), pp. 25–26, quoted by Baugh.

13. All Chaucer citations are from *The Complete Poetry and Prose of Geoffrey Chaucer*, ed. J.H. Fisher (New York: Holt, 1977).

14. A.C. Baugh, "The Middle English Romances: Some Questions of Creation, Presentation, and Preservation," *Speculum*, 42 (1967), 1–31. The quotations from the romances are from this article.

15. J.H. Fisher, "Chaucer's Last Revision of the Canterbury Tales," *Modern Language Review*, 67 (1972): 241–51. Charles A. Owen, *Pilgrimage and Story-Telling in the "Canterbury Tales"* (Norman: Univ. of Oklahoma Press, 1977.)

16. Among the many treatments of the Host are R.M. Lumiansky, *Of Sondry*

Folk: The Dramatic Principle in the Canterbury Tales (Austin: Univ. of Texas Press, 1955), p. 85 et passim; Barbara Page, "Concerning the Host," *Chaucer Review*, 4 (1970): 1–13; Cynthia C. Richardson, "The Function of the Host in the Canterbury Tales," *Texas Studies in Language and Literature*, 12 (1970): 325–44.

17. Mehl, "Audience of Chaucer's *Troilus and Criseyde*," p. 186.

18. A traditional view of the Wife of Bath is found in Robert A. Pratt, "Jankyn's Book of Wicked Wives: Medieval Antimatrimonial Propaganda in the Universities," *Annuale Mediaevale*, 3 (1962): 5–27. Two recent feminist interpretations are Sheila Delany, "Sexual Economics: Chaucer's Wife of Bath and *The Book of Margery Kemp*," *Minnesota Review*, n.s. 5 (1975), 104–15; and Mary Carruthers, "The Wife of Bath and the Painting of Lions," *PMLA*, 94 (1979): 209–22.

19. A.I. Doyle and M.B. Parkes, "The Production of Copies of the *Canterbury Tales* and the *Confessio amantis* in the Early Fifteenth Century," in *Essays Presented to N.R. Ker*, ed. M.B. Parkes and A.G. Watson (London: Scolar, 1978), pp. 163–212.

The "Tone of Heaven": Bonaventuran Melody and the Easter Psalm in Richard Rolle

William F. Pollard

The influence of St. Bonaventure upon European mysticism in general and upon English mysticism and Richard Rolle in particular has been widely accepted since the pioneer work of Carl Horstman at the end of the nineteenth century.[1] As evidence of their similarity, Margaret Deanesly noted in 1914 the confusion of the Quaracchi editors in printing Rolle's *Incendium amoris* as St. Bonaventure's *De triplici via.*[2] And certainly no two men of their respective periods were more consistently accused of fathering manuscripts they had never seen. In the decades following Bonaventure's death, Franciscan thought was a dominant force throughout England. Although he had declined the Archbishopric of York in 1265—six years after visiting England—the Seraphic Doctor was still very much there in spirit; and that spirit was transmitted to Richard Rolle, the Yorkshireman often called "the English Bonaventure."

This Franciscan influence helps to explain the content and thrust of English and European mysticism, but in the case of Rolle it explains his literary tone as well. In his English commentary on Psalm 39:4, Richard says God sends into the heart a "new sange, that is the melody of the tone of heuen, that nane may synge bot his derlyngs."[3] It is in the hermit's discussion of song or *canor* that his direct debt to Bonaventure and "Bonaventuran" writings may be seen. His *English Psalter* and the lyrics that flow from his mystical treatises explain and demonstrate the "sweet fire of heavenly song"—the *calor, canor,* and *dulcor* so consistently at the center of Rolle's contemplation. Richard's lyric strain is that of St. Francis and St. Bonaventure. All three are God's "derlyngs" and his

252

troubadours; the "tone of heaven" is in their prose as well as in their song. The "joy" of the Poverello is in Richard Rolle's itinerary no less than in Bonaventure's *Itinerarium mentis in Deum*. Rolle's life and work are embodiments of Bonaventure's comment on the *Sentences* that "God disposed the world as if it were a very beautiful poem."[4]

A recent study of the English lyric states flatly: "The Middle English lyric is, essentially, a Franciscan song."[5] To this conclusion, one could easily add that Middle English mystical writings are Franciscan wedding songs. Each meditation, prose or lyric, is an epithalamium celebrating or anticipating the spiritual union of Lover and Beloved. These treatises represent Franciscan redactions of the traditional exegesis of the Song of Songs and the Psalms of David. Typological convention saw the lovers of the Canticles as Christ and the Church and the voice of the Psalms as David prefiguring Christ. While pointing to the rapture of final union, both Old Testament books were seen to foretell the final *jubilatio* after a penitential conformation to the crucified Christ. The Bridegroom on the "bed" of the Cross bends his head to kiss, opens his hands to give, and stretches his arms to embrace. His naked breast awaits the suffering response of his lover to the Passion.[6] Here are the twin foci of Franciscan spirituality: affective piety and ecstatic joy. The funereal gives way to the hymeneal. From meditations on the Cross, the mystic moves to a glimpse of the *Majestas Domini*. Lamentation leads to celebration.

Richard Rolle's "tone of heaven" is, naturally, the harmony of the spheres. Perfect harmony is spiritual—to be heard by the ears of the soul—just as perfect vision is no spectrum of colors but perfect clarity. The end of Rolle's mystical journey is the spiritual apprehension of all color and all harmony in the silent clarity of perfection. In the "sweet fire of love" the soul "cries" or "shouts" in eagerness for the perfection of its Bridegroom. The lover praises God in song, but his song is silence: "For sweit gostly songe truly & ful speciall it is giffyn, with vtward songe acordis not þe qwhilk in kyrkis & elsqwer ar vsyd. It discordis mikyll, for all þat be mans voys vtward is formyd with bodily eris to be hard, bot emonge aungels twnys [tunes] it has a acceptabyll melody & with meruale it is commendyd of þam þat has knawen it."[7] Clearly, Rolle understands the "tone of heaven" as the angelic "sweetness" or "delightful fire" sent from above to transform human meditation into an approximation of celestial harmony or angelic song: "Slike songe [the contemplative's] als is of aungell, so is þe uoys of þis trw lufar, þof it be not so greet or parfyte for freylte of flesch þat 3itt cumbyrs þe soule." Again, Rolle emphasizes that the "tune" or "tone" makes the song, not "þe dity þat is sunge."[8] Throughout his Latin and vernacular works, Rolle identifies true melody with the gift of God's grace; it infuses his lovers, who burn, sing, rejoice, praise, and glow like the fiery seraphim.[9]

This Christian Neoplatonism places Rolle at the end of a millennium of musical theology. As early as the second century, Clement of Alexandria identified Orpheus with David and David with Christ. While Orpheus was possessed by demons, David was able to put them to flight, as when he healed Saul by playing the harp. Clement then sees Christ as a new "Harp" of David—as the "all harmonious instrument of God, melodious and holy, the wisdom that is above this world, the heavenly Word."[10] Christ as Logos was before David, however, and ordered both the macrocosm and the little world of man into harmony. Christ, the heavens, and the mind of man are thus all instruments of praise. As St. Augustine says in the famous sixth book of *De musica:* "Terrestrial things are subject to celestial, and their time circuits join together in harmonious succession for a poem of the universe."[11] At roughly the same time, John Chrysostom was insisting that the Christian sing "without voice" to God, "who can hear our hearts and enter into the silences of our minds."[12] By focusing on the crucified Christ, Richard places these patristic views of harmony at the center of his typically Franciscan synthesis of Bernardine and Victorine affective piety. For the hermit of Hampole, song or *canor* is a more central concern than it is for his fellow English mystics. Musical metaphor and the language of heaven's tone provide a *leitmotif* unifying Rolle's works.

It would be difficult not to see the *Incendium amoris* as a popularization of Franciscan theology and its emphases—an *omnium gatherum* reflective of an exuberant spirit. Its organization is not a linear movement through the stages of contemplation, but an incremental repetition of themes shouted in the prologue. Song is the symbol of the ineffable transcendence of the spirit over the flesh; it is the human response to the "honyly flaume" and might be a cry of simultaneous joy and sorrow (or contrition).[13] As the purgation continues, the shout diminishes and the inner eye is cleansed for the Seraphic Vision God's lovers may glimpse in this life. Contrition, Confession, Satisfaction; Reason, Discretion, Contemplation; Purgation, Illumination, and Union—these sets of three do not line up with *calor, canor,* and *dulcor*. Rolle's terms seem simultaneous and not hierarchical.[14] Taken together, they may illustrate contrition or purgation as God's grace is first experienced by the penitent; or Rolle's three terms may illustrate the penitent's earthly foretaste of celestial harmony—the cry of anguish or the sounds of silence. Perhaps Rolle is inconsistent as well as exuberant, but his trinity reflects the unity and diversity of the Trinitarian Godhead.

One cannot read Richard's *Psalter* (English or Latin), the *Incendium,* his lyrics, or the English epistles without being constantly reminded that for this Yorkshire hermit—as for his predecessor in Umbria—the spiritual journey of Everyman begins with an affective meditation on the life of Christ as the source of that journey. Affective piety, the cult of the Holy Name, exemplarism, and celestial harmony—all come together in meditation on Christ's suffering. Hugh of St. Victor's etymology of *music* is of special consequence in this context: "Music takes its name from the word 'water,' or *aqua* because no euphony, that is, pleasant sound, is possible without moisture."[15] For both Bonaventure and Rolle, the blood of Christ makes supple a hardened heart.[16] No harmony, no spiritual journey, no operation of penance is possible without the tears of contrition shed for Christ's Passion.

The Franciscan emphasis upon the cult of the Name of Jesus and upon a suffering response to the Exemplar's suffering is the flowering of a rich tradition of Christian theology and iconography. This tradition sees Christ's body as the tightly drawn strings of an instrument of torture which becomes, paradoxically, the instrument of salvation. The Cross moves Christ's lovers from the anguish of purgation (a shout of pain and a cry for help) to the joy of union. The words of Christ from the Cross are the words of a second David whose body has become not simply an instrument of praise, but an instrument of celestial harmony. A twelfth-century German psalter gives a visual exegesis of the essential text—see the plate below.

Psalm 56 (Vulgate) was traditionally the Easter Psalm. Historically it speaks of David driving the demons from Saul, but typologically the harp David invokes becomes the crucified Christ. Verse nine is the key: "Exurge, gloria mea; Exurge, psalterium et cithara; Exurgam diluculo." ("Arise, O my glory, arise psaltery and harp: I will arise early.")[17] St. Augustine's exegesis of this text remains the model for all later medieval interpretations. He interprets David's words as an invocation to Christ, his "Glory," to rise after the Passion. But "what," says Augustine, "is the psaltery and what is the harp?" David's poetic redundancy becomes a mystical figure for the two natures of Christ:

> The flesh working things divine is the psaltery: the flesh suffering things human is the harp. Let the psaltery sound, let the blind be enlightened, let the deaf hear, let the paralytics be braced to strength, the lame walk, the sick rise up, the dead rise again; this is the sound of the psaltery. Let there sound also the harp, let Him hunger, thirst, sleep, be held, scourged, derided, crucified, buried. When therefore thou seest in that Flesh certain things to have sounded from above, certain things from the lower part, one flesh hath risen again, and in one flesh we acknowledge both psaltery and harp.

DAVID'S PSALTERY AS A TYPE OF THE CRUCIFIXION

Psalter illumination from Southeast Germany (twelfth
century). Reproduced in Hugo Steger, *David Rex et Propheta*
(Nürnberg: H. Carl, 1961), plate 53a. It is possible to see in
this illumination the kingship of David as foreshadowing the
Majestas Domini (Psalm 150) as well as the ten-stringed harp
as a type of the cross (Psalm 56).

The combined sound of psaltery and harp "fulfills the Gospels" as "both the miracles and the sufferings of the Lord are preached."[18] In his commentary, St. Augustine adroitly displays an expert's knowledge of musical instruments. In speaking of the Psalms as the mouthpiece of the Holy Ghost, St. Basil had said earlier that of all instruments the psaltery has its harmonious rhythms from above; the cithara, sounds from below. Similarly, Isidore of Seville says the psaltery, like the cithara, is in the form of the letter delta but, unlike the cithara, has its wooden soundbox above. "Symphony," according to Isidore, "is the fusion of a modulation of low and high sounds."[19] The implication is that the Incarnation of the Word is also the Incarnation of the Heavenly Symphony.

In the prologue to the *English Psalter,* Rolle calls David's book a "garthen closed" and a "paradyse ful of all appils." It is also Noah's ark bringing "stormy saules . . . in til clere & pesful lyf." The book is called the "psautere" after the Greek, and in English it means "to touche." Rolle goes on to say that the instrument from whence the Book of Psalms derives its name has ten chords giving it its sound from above by the touching of the hand. It speaks of Christ in his Godhood and in his Manhood and "the matere of this boke is crist & his spouse." The Psalms kindle the "fyre of luf" and transmit the "soun & myrth of heuen" (Bramley, pp. 3–5). Thus the message of the prologue is clear: the Psalms aid the penitent by putting him in touch with celestial harmony and by making him an instrument no less than David's harp or the crucified Christ.

As his exegesis of Psalm 56:3 emphasizes, the cry of contrition is the source of Rolle's *jubilatio: "Clamabo ad deum altissimum: deum qui benefecit michi.* I sall cry til god heghest: til god that wele did til me. I sall not be ydell, bot i sall cry with all the myght of my hert til god heghest, forthi me bihoues nede cry. bot i hafe proued his goednes, for he did wele til me, that he herd me criand" (Bramley, p. 202). The mystical journey from sorrow to joy begins at the foot of the Cross as the individual's heart *(cor* or chord) is touched by the New Song of the Passion. The liturgical reading of Psalm 56 as part of the Easter service traditionally focused the attention of the congregation on the harp as a symbol of the Crucifixion. Rolle's commentary on the significant ninth verse combines traditional patristic elements with the special concerns of the mystic:

> *Rise my joy, ryse psautery and the harpe: i sall rise in the daghynge.* That is, isū, that is my ioy, make me to rise in ioy of the sange of thi louynge, in myrth of thi lufynge, and that swa it be, *rise psautery,* that is, gladnes of thoght in life of contemplacioun, and the *harpe,* that is, purgynge of all vices with tholemodnes [patience] in anguys. and swa *i sall rise in the daghynge,* that is in the generall resurreccioun with ioy.

Ihū be thou my ioy, all melody and swetnes,
and lere me forto synge, the sange of thi louynge.
(Bramley, pp. 203–4)

Rolle has maintained the proper relationship between psaltery and harp. Instead of identifying them directly with the divine and human aspects of Christ, however, Rolle identifies the instruments with contemplative thought and with patient suffering. Rather than David's words to the Christ whom he prefigures, God the Father's words to his Son, or Christ's words to his church, Rolle makes his exegesis a love song to Christ. His cry is a lyrical prayer to become an instrument of the "tone of heaven."

In the twelfth century, the Scotsman Richard of St. Victor wrote a *Sermo in die paschae* using the traditional exegesis of cithara and psaltery within the characteristic mystical journey of the Victorine school. The sermon is an appeal to see in Christ's Crucifixion and Resurrection our own double resurrection of spirit now and body later.[20] In seeing the events of Easter as a promise, Richard of St. Victor also sees them as symbolic of the affective nature of the *imitatio Christi*—a dual journey of the penitent. As we participate externally in the Easter service, we should inwardly mortify our sins. The cithara symbolizes this mortification and sounds from below while the psaltery sounds from above and signifies the "exhibition of good works": "He who plays the cithara and does not play the psaltery, or plays the psaltery and does not play the cithara, does not go forward, does not make progress, because neither one without the other gives a pleasant sound."[21] The symphony of Christ's dual nature— the harmony of the Incarnation—provides the model of harmony for the wayfarer who wishes to follow. Good works are simply external signs of the symphonic journey of penance. Good works are man's approxima- tions of Christ's miracles and point to the final miracle of Christ's Resurrection. As Christ rises from the dead, so the pilgrim undergoes a spiritual resurrection in anticipation of the bodily resurrection to come. Richard of St. Victor's homiletic use of Psalm 56 is representative of the context from which Richard of Hampole develops his reading of the text. For both men the harmony of contemplative and purgative tones is the music of spiritual reformation in this life—a reformation anticipating the bodily resurrection of the saints at the Day of Judgment.

In the century separating the monk of St. Victor from the hermit of Hampole, Bonaventure's treatise on the Passion of the Lord, *Vitis mystica (The Mystical Vine)*, describes the *Canticum Novum* in the language of the Song of Songs while centering on the typology of Psalm 56—Christ on the Cross as the New Harp of David: "Seven words, like seven leaves, ever green, came forth from our Vine aloft on the cross. Your Spouse has become a Harp, the wood of the cross being the frame and His body, extended on the wood, representing the chords."[22] Chapters seven through thirteen of the meditation treat the music produced by each of Christ's seven statements—each of the seven chords of the Cross/harp. Every mention of Christ's words focuses the reader's attention on the "sweet" harmony of the New Song: "What Power is in this leaf! How sweetly does this chord resound!"[23] The grafted or hypostatic nature of Christ's voluntarism reaches its consummation in the celestial melody produced in his Passion.

The final half of this treatise on the vine concentrates on Christ as the "plentitude of Grace blazing anew in the *fullness of time* with the flames of burning love."[24] The "fire of love" is the metaphor Bonaventure then employs as he continues his contemplative response to the operation of Love's sweet new song. *Jubilatio* and affective piety, the twin "tones" of St. Francis and the result of the *felix culpa*, are manifest throughout Bonaventure's use of *canor* as the sweet song of penance begun by the New Song of the Cross. As the inheritor of this tradition, Richard Rolle would need to look no further than the *Vitis mystica* or to the images of the *Triplica via* to find his three-in-one: his *calor*, *canor*, and *dulcor*.

The only English reference to the Cross as harp in Rolle's work comes in his exegesis of the Psalms. The final chapters of his *Incendium amoris*, however, break into lyric ecstasy at increasingly frequent intervals. At one point his discussion of the gift of jubilant song is an epithalamium whose initial image is taken from Psalm 56:9. Here is an image of the Passion applied to the Beatific Vision and given the language of the Song of Songs: "O my lufe! O my hony! O my harp! O my sawtre & dayly songe: qwhen sall þow help my heuynes? O my hartis royse, qwen sall þow cum to me & take with þe my spirytt?"[25] Richard Misyn's fifteenth-century translation captures Rolle's awareness of the beatific nature of this melody of love-longing. As the penitent moves toward celestial harmony, he suffers the anguish of separation while contemplating Christ in Majesty. Misyn changes Rolle's "my heart's root" to "my heart's rose." The change might appear quixotic, but Misyn is in line with traditional descriptions of celestial harmony and ecstatic vision. The final four cantos of Dante's *Paradiso*, the rose window behind a gothic altar, and the second half of the *Vitis mystica* all point to the popular application of the rose to the Beatific Vision. In *The Mystical Vine*, moreover, Bonaventure presents Christ as a rose connecting the Passion to the *Visio Dei*: "To illustrate how much He loved us, we must connect the rose of the passion with the rose of love. The rose of love will then display its

260 THE "TONE OF HEAVEN"

crimson flame in the passion, and the rose of the passion will glow with the fire of love.[26] As Christ turns scarlet with the blood of sacrifice, he prefigures the fiery glow of the Final Vision. Misyn's translation of Rolle's *Incendium* connects, in a Bonaventuran fashion, the affective piety of the Crucifixion to the *jubilatio* of the Beatific Vision. Misyn also seems to recognize the appropriateness of this floral image of sweetness and fire to Rolle's hymn to the Model of all heavenly *canor*. The "fire" of love is also the "honeyed-song" *(melos)* of love.

The *Melos amoris* is the most neglected of all Rolle's authentic works. At times it is a maddeningly alliterative tangle of uncertain meaning. It may, in fact, be a youthful experiment in language similar to that of Gerard Manley Hopkins. This Latin intrusion into the Alliterative Revival explodes with energy as words strain to approximate their object—the sweetness or "melody of love." Just as Hopkins' verbal experiments are a poetic "Incarnation of the Word,"[27] so Rolle's verbal gymnastics attempt to transcend the limitations of language dealing with the ineffable. His "sweet song of love" achieves an otherworldly tone. In this difficult text, Rolle mentions the cithara together with the *psalterium* no fewer than eighteen times. As with the *Incendium,* the tone and subject of the references are to the Beatific Vision and to the *celica sinfonica.*

One of the earliest of these references comes at the end of a twenty-three-line summary of Christ's earthly life. Without mentioning the Cross directly, Rolle presents the events at Calvary as the cessation of Christ's song before its resumption at the Resurrection. The earth grows dark and the "instrument" slackens: "The 'Organum' of the angels stiffened among the wicked ones and the 'Psalterium' of the holy ones ceased and grew silent, suffused with blood. Also the 'Cithara' of the simple ones was changed into sadness."[28] Following this vivid image of the broken harp is a "Quid dicam?" describing Christ's bodily suffering as preparatory to the sweet song of Christ in majesty when harp and psalter are again taken up for a *carmen charitatis.* All subsequent references to the twin instruments of Christ's music occur in the context of the contemplative's *Visio Dei* where, "like cithara players," the saints are "carried up into the heavenly *psalterium* and may peacefully play on the organ the neumes of divinity."[29] Rolle's spiritual journey points to the beatific minstrelsy of Psalm 150, but he interprets the injunction to "louys him in psaltry and in harpe" (Bramley, p. 492)—as well as his own sense of *canor*—from the Cross/harp of Psalm 56.

The harmony surrounding this vision and the internal *melodia* of the penitent on his journey to beatific perspective are the contexts for all of Richard's further references to cithara and *psalterium.* Even in his *Medita-*

tions on the Passion, Rolle is quite traditional in his use of the Franciscan imagery of Christ's wounded body as a star-filled heaven, a net, a dove-house, a honeycomb, and a flowery meadow. In his description of the actual Crucifixion, however, Rolle emphasizes the stretching of Christ's body before the hammering of the nails: "Þei drow and streynyd þe streyȝte on brede and on lenkthe, by handys and by feet, and dryve in þe nayles, fyrst in þe ton hand, and drow harde, and after dryve that oþer."[30] This attention to the excessive stretching of Christ's body to fit the span of the Cross was traditional in passion literature. It was certainly the highlight of the Pinners' production of the Crucifixion for the York Mystery Cycle and gave a popular and visual basis for seeing the crucified Christ as a parchment covered with the red ink of the New Law.[31] Continuing his apostrophe to Christ, Rolle ponders the wounds—now gaping widely as a result of the "streynynge"—and describes the body of Christ in terms of the traditional exegesis of Psalm 21: "Þi synwes and þi bonys styrten owte starke, þat þi bonys may be nowmbryd" (Allen, p. 24). Cassidorus's treatment of Psalm 56:9 includes a reference to Psalm 21, "Exurge cithara": "The harp signifies the glorious passion which with stretched sinews and numbered bones [*tensis nervis . . . dinumeratisque ossibus*] sounded forth his bitter suffering as a spiritual song."[32] Rolle's treatment of Psalm 21:18 is an enthusiastic compliment to David's anticipation of Christ's suffering: "The strekynge of his body in the tre myght noght haf ben bettere discryued" (Bramley, p. 80).

At the end of his advice to Margaret Kirkby in *The Form of Living,* Richard extols the life of willful poverty and speaks of the grace which illumines as it directs the penitent to the Celestial Vision: "Þi thoght, þat was ay donward, modeland in þe erth, whils þou was in þe worlde, now be ay upwarde, als fire, sekand þe heghest place in heven, right til þi spows, þare he syttes in hys blys" (Allen, p. 95). As he continues, Rolle reduces the scholastic and patristic treatment of the grace of illumination into a terse summary of the spiraling journey of the penitent from and through the created world to the Creator: "Til hym þou ert turned, when his grace illumyns þi hert, and [it] forsakes all vices, and conformes it til vertues and gude thewes [manners], and til all maner of debonerte and mekenes" (Allen, p. 95). This "clymbande tyll Jhesu-warde" is the song of love and greatly to be preferred over both excessive penance and the cacophony of "seculere sanges." The exemplaristic turning to God in love is a harmonious circle-dance quite unlike the leading of "karols." By implication, the true "karol" is "þe sang of lufe" or the "sang of sanges": "For he þat mykel lufes, hym lyst oft syng of his luf, for joy þat he or scho hase when þai thynk of þat þat þai lufe, namely if þair lover be trew and

lufand." The human lover is one whose thought naturally turns "intil sang and intil melody" (Allen, pp. 96–106). The thought illumines, the song purges, and the melody unites the Lover to the Beloved.

Rolle's exegesis of Psalm 56:9 had stressed the response of Christ's lover as he participates in the Passion through the purgation of the harp and in the Resurrection through the psaltery or the life of contemplation. In his final words to Margaret about contemplation, Rolle divides the mystic's life into a lower and a higher: "*Þe lower party* es meditacion of haly wrytyng, þat es Goddes wordes, and in other gude thoghtes and swete . . . and also in lovyng of God in psalmes and ympnes, or in prayers. *Þe hegher party* of contemplacion es behaldyng and ȝernyng of þe thynges of heven, and joy in þe Haly Gaste, þat men hase oft" (Allen, p. 118). In the *Sermon for Easter*, Richard of St. Victor's use of Psalm 56:9 equates the cithara with sincerity and the psaltery with truth: "Sinceritas partim ad citharam, veritas ad psalterium."[33] Rolle's division of contemplative life into lower and higher parts echoes the traditional discussion of the cithara as sounding *ab inferiori* and the psaltery as sounding *ab superiori*. Acts of sincerity must precede knowledge of truth; purgation must precede illumination. Christ on the Cross is the Exemplar for both "patience in anguish" and "gladness of contemplative thought."

The lyrics of Rolle touch upon the *sinceritas* of the contemplative's affective response to the Passion, but they are more teleologically oriented toward the *veritas* of the Beatific Vision. Patient anguish is preliminary to the hermit's chief interest in the "tone of heaven." As wedding songs, Rolle's lyrics are more concerned with consummation than with initial love-longing. This anagogical concern explains the frequency of images of binding and verbs of coupling in such lyrics as "A Song of Love-Longing to Jesus": "Me langes, lede me to þi lyght, and festen in þe al my thoght" (Allen, p. 41). In "A Song to the Love of Jesus," Rolle identifies the agent of this fastening with Love itself, the personification of God's supreme act of sacrifice: "Lufe es þe swettest thyng þat man in erth hase tane; / Lufe es Goddes derlyng; lufe byndes blode and bane" (Allen, p. 45). An *imitatio Christi* is an act of love binding the penitent to the Cross of Christ. The suffering of this *imitatio* soon leads to joy:

> "Sygh and sob, bath day and nyght, for ane sa fayre of hew.
> Þar es na thyng my hert mai light, bot lufe, þat es ay new.
> Whasa had hym in his syght, or in his hert hym knew,
> His mournyng turned til joy ful bryght, his sang intil glew".
>
> (Allen, p. 46)

In binding sinful man to him, Christ is the true "luf-lace."[34] "The Nature of Love" asks Jesus to "fast in þi lufe me bynd, and gyf me grace to grete" (Allen, p. 50). Again, the sobs of contrition soon give way to eternal *jubilatio:*

> His lufe es lyf of all þat wele lyvand may be.
> Þou sted hym in þi stal, lat hym noght fra þe fle.
> Ful sone he wil þe call (þi setell es made for þe),
> And have þe in his hall, ever his face to se.
>
> (Allen, p. 51)

Christ as a horse with a saddle ("setell") preordained for the lover who stables him in the "stal" of the heart is the vehicle for spiritual journey. This unusual imagery combines the elements of conformation, perseverance, pilgrimage, judgment, and spiritual vision. For Rolle, Christ's Cross is both "setell of lufe" and "þe bede of blysse." In this more traditional vein, he identifies the "setell" with the Cross as the palfrey of the true Knight of Chivalry. The torturers of the Wakefield Crucifixion use the same image as they raise the newly burdened Cross with the hope that Christ "and his palfray / Shall not twyn this nyght."[35] As Christ mounts the Cross, man in his affective response to the Passion "mounts" Christ. The Cross becomes the locus of Christ's suffering and of man's joy:

> Þe settel of lufe es lyft hee, for intil heven it ranne.
> Me thynk in erth it es sle, þat makes men pale and wanne.
> Þe bede of blysse it gase ful nee, I tel þe, as I kanne,
> Þof us thynk þe way be dregh: *luf copuls God and manne.*
>
> (Allen, pp. 43–44)

The Cross is the symbol of the hypostatic union and of man's union with God.

The bed of love and spiritual "coupling" are, of course, standard features in commentaries on the Song of Songs. In the English epistle "Ego dormio" Richard forthrightly identifies himself as a procurer for God: "I wow þe, þat I myght have þe als I walde, noght to me, bot to my Lorde. I will become þat messanger to bryng þe to hys bed, þat hase made þe and boght þe, Criste, þe keyng sonn of heven" (Allen, p. 61). But he cautions the young woman who receives the epistle that "whils þi hert is heldand til lufe any bodely thyng, þou may not perfitely be coupuld with God" (Allen, p. 61). The "Ego dormio" makes clear that all earthly "gamen" is cacophony to those in tune with heaven and the "melody in aungels sang." In the midst of this beatific focus, however, Rolle bursts into a lyric "Meditacio de passione Christi." Here he ponders the mystery of a suffering God:

A wonder it es to se, wha sa understude,
How God of mageste was dyand on þe rude.
Bot suth þan es it sayde, þat lufe ledes the ryng.

(Allen, p. 68)

The allusion to the ring-dance is simultaneously a contrast to the secular "karol" and a symbolic reference to the "tone of heaven" in the eternal presence of God.

In the *Incendium amoris,* Rolle describes Christ's enthusiastic embrace of the Cross with all the energy of the Anglo-Saxon "Dream of the Rood." Unlike the warrior of that poem, Christ is portrayed in this context as the personification of Love and in the language of the Song of Songs, a different *comitatus:* "Criste truly as wer in our lufe longis, qwhils he vs to gett with so greet heet to the cros hyde; bot weil it is sayd in play: 'luf gos before & ledis þe dawns.' "[36] There is probably no connection here with the caroling God of Love in the *Roman de la Rose,* but the metaphor of dance as an image of spiritual ecstasy or "Trunkenheit" is characteristic of much in German mysticism.[37] In a recent study, Wolfgang Riehle parallels Rolle's *Incendium* with Mechthild of Hackeborn's *Liber specialis gratiae* where Christ's Passion and the Last Supper are both ring-dances of love.[38] It is perhaps futile to guess at the problems of influence or transmission between the German and English mystics. Both could have been influenced by the apocryphal Acts of John, where Christ has the disciples form a ring and dance a hymn of praise to the Father.[39] Another possibility is that the common search for metaphors of pilgrimage, ecstasy, and union could explain the popularity of "dance" in European spiritual writings.

Throughout the *Incendium amoris,* Rolle insists on noverbal song as the transformation of prayer and thought and representing the contemplative's approach to the ineffable, and the "Ego dormio" ends as well with song as the essential element of the Final Vision: "And I þi lufe sal syng thorow syght of þi schynyng / In heven withowten endyng" (Allen, p. 72). In *The Form of Living,* Rolle identifies love with penance—the *incendium amoris* is the purgative grace of God. Love is also the grace of perseverance enabling the exile to journey through three degrees of love to the unheard melody of angelic symphony. The "Ego dormio" and *The Form of Living* both speak of these degrees as: "insuperable," when nothing contrary to God's love can overcome it; "inseparable," when the thought never leaves Christ (except in sleep); and "singular," when love's fire turns the soul completely into melody and spiritual song.[40] The *Canticum Novum* might well be called the *Chorea Nova,* begun by Christ's redemptive act and permitting man to participate in the reestablishment of harmony. For Rolle, the three degrees of love are purgative, and the penitential journey is man's response to Christ's melody from the Cross. Joy and sorrow, love and penance are essentially one.

The thrust of Franciscan Exemplarism is that all creation may be read as a sign pointing to its Creator. The redirection of the penitent through the ultimate sign, the Word Incarnate, is a new "ring-dance" of spiritual cleansing and conformation. The fire of love in both Rolle and Bonaventure redirects the pilgrim from the world upward toward the throne of God. The melody of Christ's "harp" directs man back to God in an ongoing penitential spiral of *egressus-regressus*.[41] Man thus comes full circle—from God, through Christ, back to God. The repetition of this spiritual journey through linear time lifts the lover of Christ into a spiral of salvation history—into a "ring-dance" of love—out of the cacophony of the world and into a participation in celestial harmony. The harp and the psaltery of Psalm 56 lead to the harp and the psaltery of Psalm 150, the "Laudate Dominum in sanctis." As Rolle stresses, the intent of this final psalm is "that God be louyd, for he gadrid to gidire his halighis & done away all thaire febilnes. He restored thaim til his ymage, and sett thaim in endles bliss." Rolle's commentary on the third verse adds that God is to be loved "in psautery, that is of all the thyngis of heuen, & in harpe, that is of all thyngis of erth" (Bramley, p. 492). This harmony of heaven and earth, *ab superiori* and *ab inferiori*, is the result of penitential pilgrimage. An incremental repetition of this journey informs Richard's discussion of *canor* no less than Bonaventure's discussion of soteriology, or salvation history. But in the case of the English mystic, *canor*—as the harmony of the spiritual journey—may well explain the organization of his longer prose treatises. They are not linear. *Calor, canor,* and *dulcor* overlap, and one looks in vain for the ordered stages of Bonaventure. Instead, we have with Rolle a symphonic and incremental repetition of *leitmotif.*

Musical metaphor and references to the Neoplatonic and Pythagorean harmony of the spheres are certainly not unique to Richard Rolle among the English mystics. Many analogous references may be found in Margery Kemp, Dame Julian, and Walter Hilton. Two qualities, however, are peculiar to Rolle's mysticism: his consistency of reference to music and his explicit and implicit use of Psalm 56. In the *Revelations,* Julian of Norwich does use the imagery of Psalm 150 in describing a vision of God encircling himself with his "frendes" in "mervelous melody" and in "endeless loue."[42] Of the English mystics, only Walter Hilton uses the harp image, and he speaks not of the Passion but of "the harpe of þe soule," a two-stringed instrument of "meknes" and of "lufe."[43] As with Hilton, the German mystic Mechthild of Magdeburg refers to the soul as "harp" but adds that God is the musician. He plucks the strings of the soul, which he calls "ein lire von minen oren."[44] The language and imagery of Richard Rolle differ from his fellow mystics principally because he was also an exegete. He therefore became the conduit for a rich tradition of typology. His discussion of *canor* is a popularization of that tradition and explains much of his theme and structure.

Of the few pieces of English devotional literature using the typology of Psalm 56, the fourteenth-century *Meditations on the Life and Passion of Christ* is most clearly in the tradition of the hermit of Hampole. Its themes are reminiscent of Richard of St. Victor's Easter sermon and of St. Bonaventure's *Vitis mystica*, and at times it seems to borrow from Richard Rolle.[45] At the beginning, the poet speaks of "Dauides kyn" and asks his reader to praise or weep so "þat it soune as harpe swete." Mary, whose womb had been a second "castel of kyng Dauid" sings a lullaby filled with "ioye and blis" but mixed with "teres."[46] The image of this melody evokes Calvary while celebrating the child in the cradle:

> Nou may þe harpe his stringes slake,
> For it may no myrthes make
> To make oure herte lyking and liȝt,
> As song doth of þe burde briȝt.

(ll. 163–66)

The harp referred to is that of earthly minstrelsy, but it foreshadows the slakening of the "strings" of Christ's body on the Cross. This image of the instrument silenced by Mary's song of the Incarnation provides a thematic link to the silenced instrument of the Passion:

> Now goþ awey þe melodye
> Of harp and of sautrye;
> Þe swete sytole haþ lorn his soun;
> Alle gamon and gle is leid adoun.

(ll.1273–76)

These lines so reminiscent of Rolle's *Melos amoris* are preceded by a couplet identifying Christ's suffering at the hands of Pilate with David and Saul: "Þe kyng Saul boþe felle and kene / Doþ kyng Dauid trey and tene" (ll. 1271–72). The connection of this passage with the traditional exegesis of Psalm 56 is unquestionable. At this point the *stabat mater* theme echoes the dual nature of Mary's earlier lullaby to the child in the manger. As the author collapses time into an approximation of the divine moment, there is a silence anticipating the "ioye and blis" of the Resurrection.

Another English literary example of the Cross/harp typology is *Hand-lyng Synne,* Robert Mannyng of Brunne's translation of William of Waddington's *Manuel des pechiez.*[47] The twenty-seventh exemplum of the Anglo-Norman original tells of a minstrel who was killed for disturbing a bishop. Anxious to mitigate the severity of episcopal authority, Mannyng adds to his translation of this passage an anecdote of Robert Grosseteste, who actually kept a harper next to his bedchamber. When asked "why he helde þe harper so dere," the Bishop of Lincoln answered with a veiled reference to Psalm 56 and Psalm 150:

> Þe vertu of þe harpe, þurgh skylle & ryȝt,
> wyl destroye þe fendes myȝt,
> And to þe croys by gode skylle
> Ys þe harpe lykened weyle.

(ll. 4753–56)

Grosseteste continues to explain that Christ was the melody sent to that tree, but much more joy is with God where he dwells:

> Þe harpe þerof me ofte mones;
> Of þe ioye and of þe blys
> where God hym-self wonys and ys.

(ll. 4762–64)

As with Rolle, the anonymous *Meditations,* and Walter Hilton's *Scale of Perfection,* the Cross connects heaven to earth, melody with melody. Mannyng continues with Grosseteste's quoting of Psalm 150:

> yn harpe, yn thabour, and symphan gle,
> wurschepe God, yn troumpes, and sautre,
> yn cordys, an organes, and bellys ryngyng,
> yn al þese, wurschepe ȝe heuene kyng.

(ll. 4769–72)

In the *Melos amoris* or in his commentary on the psalm, Rolle would understand these lines in the context of the Beatific Vision. Mannyng's *Handlyng Synne* has Grosseteste use the "Laudate Dominum in sanctis" as a justification for earthly minstrelsy when spiritually directed: "ȝyf ȝe do þus, y sey hardly, / ȝe mow here ȝoure mynstralsy" (ll. 4773–74).

Earthly minstrelsy leading to "Pythagorean" harmony is the subject of a fourteenth-century Passion lyric beginning: "I herd an harping on a hille as I lay vndir lynde."[48] The harping is sorrowful, and the singer mysteriously writes four letters on a wall: an X, an M, an I, and a C. Standing for Christ, Mary, John, and the Cross, the letters point to dramatic and vicarious participation of another I in the events of Good Friday. Throughout the poem, the four letters are arranged in various combinations reflecting the drama of the crucifixion. There is no direct mention of the Psalms or of David, but it is intriguing to recall that the Psalmist was traditionally thought to have been inspired to compose the Psalter while sitting under a tree whose wood connects the first Adam to the Cross of the Second. As Roman numerals, the letters could be a sequence of I, X, C, and M. The number one traditionally signifies the unity of God and celestial harmony. Ten is unity and perfection, with reference to the decalogue and the ten spheres. In the context of harp imagery, it is important to remember that the psaltery traditionally had ten strings, making X a numerically significant cipher for Christ.[49] In Hugh of St. Victor's *Exegetica de scripturis,* he speaks of ten as signifying "the rectitude of faith," one hundred as "the amplitude of charity," and one thousand as "the altitude of hope."[50] Harmony and unity, faith, charity, and hope—the handwriting on this wall speaks to the "tone of heaven."

On the continent there are a few scattered literary parallels to Rolle's symphony of the Cross/harp. In the *Epistre d'Othea,* Christine de Pisan offers a moralized allegory of King Midas' judgment that the music of the flute is more pleasant than that of the harp. This false judge is a figure of Pilate who sentenced "the blessid Sone of God to be taken and streyned as an harpe and to be honged on the gebet of the Crosse."[51] In Italy the *Laude* of Jacopone da Todi contain all the *calore,* the *dolzore,* and the *iubilo* of his Yorkshire counterpart without the pictorial image of the exegete:

> O *iubilo del core,*—che fai *cantar d'amore!*
> Quando *iubilo se scalda,*—sì fa l 'uomo *cantare;*
> e la lengua barbaglia—e non sa que parlare,
> dentro non pò celare,—tanto è grande el *dolzore!*[52]

The friar continues to speak in this *lauda* of a love more intense than the pilgrim can bear; it makes him shout and yell, *clamare* and *gridare.* The Cross is the source of this *incendium amoris:* "Non posso portare sì gran calore / che getta la croce" (75, ll. 3–6). The intensity of the heat causes the shout eventually to recede in silence: "lo silenzio ce appare,—chè gli è tolto onne lenguaio" (87, l. 33). Here is the Victorine and Franciscan synthesis most akin in tone to Richard Rolle.

An early fourteenth-century German poem, *Die Erlösung (The redemption),* lacks the tone of Rolle and Jacopone, but it contains a versified exegesis of Psalm 56 in the context of the Harrowing of Hell. The poet makes the traditional identification of the instrument(s) with the two natures of Christ: " 'Stant ûf mîn harpe, / stant ûf mîn psalterium.' Diz dûdet Iêsum Cristum." The *Exurgam diluculo* is, naturally, Christ's promise to rise early in the morning ("Des morgens vrû wil ich erstân").

What follows is an explanation of how the "music" of the Passion and the Resurrection might be compared to the sweet melody of an earthly harp and psaltery. When unspanned ("ungespannen") these instruments are mute ("dum"); and when they are unstruck ("ungeslagen"), they are as silent as a linden leaf which falls from a tree.[53] When tightened, however, the strings of these instruments emit their normal sweetness ("sûzekeit"). The Crucifixion and tormenting of Christ were the "spanning" and "striking" of God's instrument of redemption. This poem is a lecture— not a love song—but it does give evidence that the Easter Psalm made its way directly into the religious lyric on the continent. Still, Rolle is exceptional as a writer of Latin and the vernacular who combines the imagery of this psalm with the affective piety of the Victorines.

This variety of written references to the Cross/harp image points to a more public oral tradition, and at least one extant sermon suggests the Passion be compared to "a harpe of melodye makyng."[54] Jean de Meun, in fact, depends upon the well-known association of cithara and *psalterium* with Christ's flesh and spirit and with the New Song of love. In a comic allusion to the Easter Psalm, the lover of the *Roman de la Rose* values his sexual organs—his two hammers—more than his "citole" or his "harp." Amant's devotion to the cacophony of the Old Song rather than to the melodies of the New emphasizes the disharmony of his sexual orientation.[55]

More contemporary with Rolle, however, are the mystery cycles. If comic allusion to an exegetical image in courtly literature is evidence of its pervasiveness, dramatic hyperbole in the guild plays indicates a less sophisticated but more widespread awareness. For dramatic effect, the guild of Pinners made the most of stretching Christ's body to fit the ill-bored holes of the Cross. As two soldiers in the York *Crucifixion* remark:

> 1 *miles*. Ther cordis have evill encressed his paines,
> Or he wer tille the booringis brought.
> 2 *miles*. Yaa, assoundir are bothe sinuous and veinis
> On ilke a side, so have we soughte.[56]

This same obsession with the stretching of Christ may be found in all the major cycles and clearly reflects the psalm often linked to Psalm 56— Psalm 22 and the "stretched sinews" *(tensis nervis)* and "numbered bones" *(dinumeratisque ossibus)* of the New Harp. These enactments are occasions of dark humor at the point of greatest dramatic (and narrative!) tension. Paradoxically, the lack of direct reference to Psalm 56 and the "humorous" hyperbole of the stretching and nailing are perhaps the best indications of a popular knowledge of this typological commonplace.

The plays contrast the cacophony of the hammers and nails to the harmony of Christ's words from the Cross and the New Song of the Resurrection. In many ways medieval drama itself seems to be a symphony of sounds *ab superiori* and *ab inferiori*—the language of mysticism and the language of the popular romance. As Richard of St. Victor stresses, *veritas* must be joned to *sinceritas*. The harmony of these mystery cycles derives from the union of spiritual journey and temporal narrative.

The literary use of Psalm 56, implicit or explicit, is absent from English literature from the fourteenth century until the seventeenth, when George Herbert uses the psalm as the basis for "Easter":

> Awake, my Lute, and struggle for thy part
>   With all thy art.
> The *Crosse* taught all Wood to resound his Name,
>   Who bore the same.
> His stretched *sinews* taught all strings, what key
> Is best to celebrate this most high Day.[57]

In the years preceding World War I, Ralph Vaughan Williams used Herbert's "Easter" as one of his *Five Mystical Songs*—thus keeping the New Harp of David alive in a musical context of spiritual journey echoing the tone of St. Bonaventure and the Yorkshire hermit.

The music of the Cross in Psalm 56 leads to the music of the heavenly symphony in Psalm 150. And the *calor, canor,* and *dulcor* of Richard Rolle can be accounted for largely through this exegetical convention and the canonical ordering of the Psalms—an ordering reflective of the mystical journey itself. Richard's focus may often be more teleologically oriented than Passion-centered, but it is the melody of the Cross which leads to the "tone of heaven" and explains the popular appeal of the hermit. Only the anonymous English *Meditation on the Life and Passion of Christ* and the *Vitis mystica* of St. Bonaventure can compare with Rolle's tone and specificity of image. Psalm 56 seems to be present throughout Rolle's vernacular and Latin works, giving them emotion, unity, and a structure based on *canor:* the song of spiritual journey and suffering. The penitential spiral begins at the foot of the Cross and leads to the circle of music makers at the throne of God. Thus the symphony of the cithara and *psalterium* unites the sorrow and joy so characteristic of the Franciscan literature. Reflecting also a mendicant emphasis on the "mixed" life of contemplation and good works, Psalm 56 presents the Franciscan Bonaventure and his spiritual counterpart with an ideal text.

NOTES

1. Carl Horstman, ed., *Yorkshire Writers: Richard Rolle of Hampole, an English*

Father of the Church and His Followers, 2 vols. (London: Swan Sonnenschein & Co., 1895–96). See especially the introduction to both volumes.

2. Margaret Deanesly, "The *Incendium Amoris* of Richard Rolle and St. Bonaventura," *English Historical Review*, 29 (Jan. 1914): 98–101.

3. H.R. Bramley, ed., *The Psalter or Psalms of David and Certain Canticles with a Translation and Exposition in English by Richard Rolle of Hampole* (Oxford: Clarendon Press, 1884), p. 146. All quotations from Rolle's *Psalter* are from this edition and will be cited in the text.

4. Bonaventure, *Opera omnia*, ed. F. Fanna and I. Jelier, 10 vols. (Quaracchi, Florence: Coll. S. Bonaventurae, 1883–1902), 2:316: "Divinae autem dispositioni placuit, mundum quasi carmen pulcherrimum quodam decursu temporum venustare" (II *Sent*. d13. a1. q2. ad2).

5. David L. Jeffrey, *The Early English Lyric and Franciscan Spirituality* (Lincoln: Univ. of Nebraska Press, 1975), p. 261.

6. The following reference to Bernard in Bonaventure's *De perfectione vitae ad sorores* is typical of the Cross/bed image. The Quaracchi editors have identified Augustine's *Sermon 32* as the actual source quoted. Quaracchi 8:123: " 'Vide,' inquit Bernardus, 'caput Christi inclinatum ad osculandum, brachia extensa ad amplexandum, manus perfossas ad largiendum, latus apertum ad diligendum, totius corporis extensionem ad se totum impendendum.' "

7. Richard Rolle, *The Fire of Love and the Mending of Life*, trans. Richard Misyn, ed. Ralph Harvey, EETS, o.s. 106 (London: Kegan Paul, Trench, Trübner, 1896), p. 73. One of the chief indications of Rolle's popularity in the late Middle Ages is Richard Misyn's 1435 translation of the *Incendium*. The following Latin text is from Margaret Deanesly's edition of *The Incendium Amoris of Richard Rolle of Hampole*, Univ. of Manchester Historical Series, vol. 26 (Manchester: Manchester Univ. Press, 1915), p. 239: "Istud namque dulce canticum spirituale quidem et speciale ualde, quia specialissimis datum est; cum exterioribus canticis non concordat, que in ecclesiis uel alibi frequentatur. Dissonat autem multum ab omnibus que humana et exteriori uoce formantur, corporalibus auribus audienda; sed inter angelicos concentus armoniam habet acceptabilem admiracioneque commendatum est ab hiis qui cognouerunt." Misyn's English version will be quoted in the text of this study, and Rolle's Latin will be quoted in the notes.

8. *The Fire of Love*, p. 72. cf. "Est enim angelica suauitas quam in animam accipit et eadem oda, etsi non eisdem uerbis laudes Deo resonabitur. Qualis angelorum, talis est iscius concentus, etsi non tantus, nec tam perspicuus, propter carnem corruptibilem que adhuc aggrauat amantem: qui hoc experitur eciam angelica cantica expertus est cum eiusdem speciei: in uia est, et in patria. Sonus enim ad canticum pertinet, non ad carmen quod cantatur" (*Incendium amoris*, p. 237).

9. *Incendium amoris*, pp. 208–9: "Sed conseruat bonitas Dei usque ad tempus statutum, qui dedit illi ut tantum amaret, et ueraciter dicat *Amore langueo*. Uelut seraphym succensus ardet, et amat, canit et iubilat, laudat et estuat."

10. From *The Exhortation to the Greeks* in *Clement of Alexandria*, trans. G.W.

Butterworth, Loeb Classical Library (Cambridge: Harvard Univ. Press, 1953), p. 15.

11. Augustine, *De musica, PL,* 32.1179: "Ita coelestibus terrena subjecta, orbes temporum suorum numerosa successione quasi carmini universitatis associant."

12. John Chrysostom, *Expositio in Psalmum XLI* from the Latin translation in *PG,* 55.159: "Licet etiam sine voce psallere, cum mens intus resonet. Non enim hominibus canimus, sed Deo, qui potest vel corda audire, et in mentis nostrae arcana ingredi."

13. *The Fire of Love,* pp. 2–3. The prologue to the *Incendium amoris* explains the "honeyed flame" metaphorically ("sub metaphora") as God's grace, which both burns and enlightens ("urit et lucet") and comes to the individual according to his particular capacity or "prout carnis fragilitas permittit." This "flame" of grace gives the penitent a burning sense of exile and a sweet vision of heavenly consort singers. The pilgrim will be "captus statim in consorcium canencium laudes creatori" (prologue, p. 146).

14. *Calor* may indeed represent the initiation into the "sweet melody" of mystical contemplation, but the metaphor is not simply an equivalent to the stages of contrition or purgation. The *calor* which begins the mental journey is also present at its consummation. Rolle's overall tone of *jubilatio* has fire and sweet melody coalesce in his discussion of love—*Incendium amoris* and *Melos amoris.*

15. Hugh of St. Victor, *Disdiscalicon,* ed. Charles Buttimer (Washington, D.C.: Catholic Univ. Press, 1939), p. 30: "Musica ab aqua vocabulum sumpsit, eo quod nulla euphonia, id est, bona sonoritas, sine humore fieri possit."

16. The following lines from Bonaventure's *Vitis mystica* are typical of both Bonaventure and Rolle: "O diamond heart [*cor adamantinum*], immerse yourself in the copious blood of our kid and lamb; rest in it in order to become warm; once warm, become softened; once softened, let flow truly a fountain of tears" (Quaracchi 8:181).

17. The biblical quotations throughout this essay are from the Vulgate or from the Rheims-Douay translation.

18. Augustine, *Enarratio in Psalmum LXVI,* trans. by A.C. Cox in *A Select Library of the Nicene and Post-Nicene Fathers,* vol. 8 (New York: Christian Literature Co., 1888), p. 229. Cf. *PL,* 36.672: "Caro ergo divina operans, psalterium est: caro humana patiens, cithara est. Sonet psalterium; illuminentur caeci, audiant surdi, stringantur paralytici, ambulent claudi, surgant aegroti, resurgant mortui: iste est sonus psalterii. Sonet et cithara; esuriat, sitiat, dormiat, teneatur, flagelletur, irrideatur, crucifigatur, sepeliatur. Cum ergo vides in illa carne quaedam sonuisse desuper, quaedam de inferiore parte, una caro resurrexit, et in una carne agnoscimus et psalterium et citharam. Et in ista duo genera factorum impleverunt Evangelium, et praedicatur in gentibus; nam et miracula et passiones Domini praedicantur."

19. Isidore of Seville, *Etymologiarum sive originum,* ed. W.M. Lindsay (Oxford: Clarendon Press, 1911), no pagination: "Symphonia est modulationis

temperamentum ex gravi et acuto concordantibus sonis, sive in voce, sive in flatu, sive in pulsu" (3.20).

20. Richard of St. Victor, *Sermo in die paschae, PL,* 196.1071: The harmony of the penitential journey is "de resurrectione mentium in praesenti, tum de resurrectione corporum quae erit in futuro."

21. Ibid.: "Cithara sonat ab inferiori, et ideo significat vitiorum mortificationem, psalterium vero sonat a superiori, et ideo significat bonorum operum exhibitionem. Qui citharizat et non psallit, vel psallit et non citharizat, non procedit, non proficit, quia neutrum sine altero reddit sonum jucundum, quia psalterium jucundum cum cithara."

22. Bonaventure, *Vitis mystica,* trans. by José de Vinck in *The Works of Bonaventure,* vol. 1 (Patterson, N.J.: St. Anthony Guild Press, 1970), p. 171. Cf. Quaracchi 8:172: "Septem sunt verba, quae quasi septem folia semper virentia vitis nostra, cum in cruce elevata fuit, emisit. Cithara facus est tibi sponsus tuus, scilicet cruce habente formam ligni, corpore vero suo vicem chordarum ligno extensarum."

23. *Vitis mystica.* Cf. Quaracchi 8:173: "O quanti vigoris folium! O quantam resonat dulcedinem chorda ista!"

24. *Vitis mystica.* Cf. Quaracchi 8:187. The New Song is an aubade in which Christ as "Rose of Heaven" *(flos caeli)* unfurls the flames of love in "plenitudine temporis."

25. *The Fire of Love,* p. 78. Cf. "O amor meus! O mel meum! O cithara mea! O psalterium meum et canticum tota die! Quando medeberis merori meo? O radix cordis mei, quando uenies ad me ut assumas tecum suspicientem tibi spiritum meum?" *(Incendium amoris,* p. 245).

26. *Vitis mystica,* trans. de Vinck, 1:191. Cf. Quaracchi 8:182: "Ecce, in expositione huius verbi necessarium habemus rosam passionis rosae caritatis coniungere, ut rosa caritatis in passione rubescat, et rosa passionis igne caritatis ardescat."

27. See the discussion of Hopkins' alliteration and belief in words as "the meeting-place of self, nature, and God in the Word" in J. Hillis Miller, *The Disappearance of God* (Cambridge: Harvard Univ. Press, 1963), pp. 270–359, esp. p. 354.

28. E.J.F. Arnould, ed., *The Melos Amoris of Richard Rolle of Hampole* (Oxford: Basil Blackwell, 1957), p. 91: "Sol celicus occasum habuit obscuratus, Organum angelorum obriguit inter impios et Psalterium sanctorum subticuit cessando, sanguine suffusum, Cithara quoque simplicium mutata erat in merorem." I am grateful to Professor James Shelton of the University of Tennessee Classics Department for guiding me through the *Melos amoris* and for checking other Latin passages as well.

29. Ibid., p. 34: "ut sanctificati supportentur in psalterium celicum et neupmata numinis . . . amicabiliter organizent."

30. Hope Emily Allen, ed., *English Writings of Richard Rolle Hermit of Hampole* (Oxford: Clarendon Press, 1931), p. 24. Excluding the *Psalter,* all quotations from Rolle's English works are from this edition and are cited in the text.

31. See Rosemary Woolf's discussion of Christ's body as a charter or will in *The English Religious Lyric in the Middle Ages* (Oxford: Clarendon Press, 1968), pp. 212–14. See also plate 5 and the discussion of the "Charter of Christ" in Douglas Gray, *Themes and Images in the Medieval English Religious Lyric* (London: Routledge & Kegan Paul, 1972), p. 130.

32. Cassiodorus, *Expositio in Psalmum LVI, PL,* 70.404: *"Cithara* vero gloriosam significat passionem, quae tensis nervis dinumeratisque ossibus, virtutem patientiae intellectuali quodam carmine personabat."

33. *Sermo in die paschae, PL,* 196.1072.

34. The mystical tradition is filled with references to the *unio mystica* as a "love-knot" or *"nodus amicitiae."* Rolle's "Song to the Love of Jesus" develops its imagery within this tradition. Speaking of the penitent's affective response to the bonds binding Christ to the Cross, Rolle speaks of Christ's grace as the force binding man to the Cross in humility for perseverance in the faith: "In luf lacyd he hase my thoght, þat sal I never forgete" (Allen, *English Writings of Rolle*, p. 47). It is worth noting that Gawain ultimately uses Lady Bercilak's "luf-lace" as a means of preserving humility: "And þus, quen pryde schal me pryk for prowes of armes, / Þe loke to þis luf-lace schal leþe my hert"; see *Sir Gawain and the Green Knight,* ed. J.R.R. Tolkien and E.V. Gordon, 2d ed., rev. Norman Davis (Oxford: Clarendon Press, 1967), ll. 2437–38.

35. *The Towneley Plays,* ed. George England, EETS, e.s. 71 (London: Kegan Paul, Trench, Trübner, 1897), p. 264.

36. *The Fire of Love,* p. 102. "Ipse uero Christus quasi nostro amore languet, dum tanto ardore ut nos adquireret ad crucem festinauit: sed uerum dicitur quia amor preit in tripudio, et coream ducit" *(Incendium amoris,* p. 276).

37. See the discussion of the *unio mystica* in Grete Lüers, *Die Sprache der deutschen Mystik des Mittelalters im Werke der Mechthild von Magdeburg* (Darmstadt: Wissenschaftliche Buchgesellschaft, 1966), pp. 65–69, 267–70.

38. *The Middle English Mystics,* trans. Bernard Standring (London: Routledge & Kegan Paul, 1981), p. 49. Riehle juxtaposes the lines of the *Incendium* quoted above (and n. 36) with this passage from the *Liber specialis gratiae* where Christ speaks of the Last Supper: "Recorderis qualem ego speciosus iuvenis post convivium illud choream duxi."

39. "[Christ] bade us therefore make as it were a ring, holding one another's hands, and himself standing in the midst he said: 'Answer Amen unto me.' He began, then, to sing an hymn." In the midst of the hymn which follows, the author describes the "Amen-chorus" as "going about in a ring." From chs. 94–96 of the Acts of John in *The Apocryphal New Testament,* trans. Montague Rhodes James (Oxford: Clarendon Press, 1924), pp. 253–54.

40. See especially ch. 8 in Rolle, *The Form of Living,* in Allen, *English Writings of Rolle,* pp. 104–8.

41. This circular *egressus-regressus* is central to the Bonaventuran-Augustinian pattern of Emanation, Exemplarism, and Return. As a mental journey in linear time, the circle becomes the slow spiral of salvation history at work in the

penitent—the "Tone of Heaven" or *Canticum Novum*—Rolle's third degree of "singular" love.

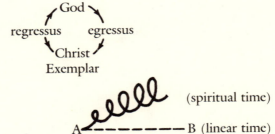

(spiritual time)

A ————————— B (linear time)

42. Sister Anna Maria Reynolds, ed., "A Critical Edition of the *Revelations* of Julian of Norwich (1342c–1416)" (Ph.D. diss., Leeds Univ., 1956), p. 97. From chap. 14 of the long version.

43. S.S. Hussey, ed., "An Edition from the Manuscripts of Book II of Walter Hilton's *Scale of Perfection* (Ph.D. diss., Univ. of London, 1962), p. 73. From ch. 21.

44. P. Gall Morel, ed., *Offenbarungen der Schwester Mechthild von Magdeburg* (Regensburg: Georg J. Manz, 1869), p. 62.

45. The relationship between the anonymous *Meditations* and Richard Rolle has been clear since its first modern edition. See Charlotte D'Evelyn, ed., *Meditations on the Life and Passion of Christ*, EETS, o.s. 158 (London: Oxford Univ. Press, 1921), pp. xxv–xxx.

46. Ibid., pp. 1–6. Future references are cited by line in the text.

47. Frederick J. Furnivall, ed., *Robert of Brunne's "Handlyng Synne,"* EETS, o.s. 119 (London: Kegan Paul, Trench, Trübner, 1901). The following quotations are from this edition.

48. Reproduced in Beatrice Daw Brown, "Religious Lyrics in MS. Don. c. 13," *The Bodleian Quarterly Record* 7 (1932): 2–3. Gray gives attention to this Passion lyric in *Themes and Images*, p. 129.

49. Isidore, *Etymologiarum sive originum*, ed. Lindsay: "Psalterium autem Hebraei decachordon usi sunt propter numerum Decalogi legis" (3.22).

50. Cf. Hugh of St. Victor, *Exegetica de scripturis et scripturibus sacris, PL*, 175.22: "Secundum formam dispositionis, ut denarius, qui in longum tenditur, rectitudinem fidei significat. Centenarius, quia in latum expanditur, amplitudinem charitatis. Millenarius qui in altum levatur, altitudinem spei designat."

51. Curt F. Bühler, ed., *Christine de Pisan's Epistle of Othea*, trans. Stephen Scrope, EETS, o.s. 264 (London: Oxford Univ. Press, 1970), p. 38.

52. Jacopone da Todi, *Le Laude*, ed. Giovanni Ferri, Scrittori d'Italia, no. 69 (Bari: Guiseppe Laterza & Figli, 1915), p. 176.

53. Friedrich Maurer, ed., *Die Erlösung: Eine geistliche Dichtung des 14. Jahrhunderts* (Leipzig: Philipp Reclam, 1934), p. 237: "Die harphe und daz psalter-

ium / sint beide ungespannen dum, / sie sint ungeslagen doup / rehte sam ein lindenloup, daz von dem boume vellet." The imagery of the silent linden leaf evokes the figurative leaves of Bonaventure's *Vitis mystica,* where the newly spanned "tree" is the source of Christ's New Song—"seven leaves, ever green."

54. The Franciscan William Melton gives the following metaphors for the Passion:

> Dolor iste sive passio potest assimilare bene:
> a man of ple and motyng,
> a boke of scripture and wrytyng,
> a harpe of melodye makyng.

See A.G. Little, *Franciscan Papers, Lists, and Documents* (Manchester: Manchester Univ. Press, 1943), p. 248.

55. Jean de Meun, *Le Roman de la Rose,* vol. 3, ed. Félix Lecoy, Les Classiques français du moyen âge (Paris: Libraire Honoré Champion, 1970), p. 142: "Si vos di bien que plus chiers ai / mes .II. martelez et m'escharpe / que ma cithole ne ma harpe." This irreverance of Amant is given a full treatment by John Fleming in *"The Roman de la Rose": A Study in Allegory and Iconography* (Princeton: Princeton Univ. Press, 1969), pp. 239–41.

56. Quoted from David Bevington, ed., *Medieval Drama* (Boston: Houghton Mifflin, 1975), p. 574.

57. George Herbert Palmer, ed., *The English Works of George Herbert,* vol. 2 (Boston: Houghton Mifflin, 1905), p. 153.

The Beguines of Belgium, the Dominican Nuns of Germany, and Margery Kempe

Ute Stargardt

In 1934 a major event in medieval English scholarship occurred with the discovery of a fifteenth-century manuscript now known as *The Book of Margery Kempe*. This unique manuscript describes the physical and spiritual experiences of Margery Kempe, who was born in Lynn in Norfolk about 1373 and who died there sometime after 1438. Late in life she dictated her adventures and mystical revelations to two scribes, neither one of whom has been identified. Although *The Book of Margery Kempe* relates Margery's life from the time of her youth to her old age, the chronology is not strictly observed because, as its proem points out, "Thys boke is not wretyn in ordyr, euery thyng aftyr oþer as it wer don, but lych as þe mater cam to þe creatur in mend whan it schuld be wretyn, for it was so long er it was wretyn þat sche had forgetyn þe tyme & þe ordyr whan thyngys befellyn."[1]

The life revealed on the pages of this manuscript is colorful and exciting. Margery was the daughter of John Burnham, a successful merchant of Lynn. In 1393 she married John Kempe, the son of an equally successful Lynn merchant. Her life as a mystic began after the birth of her first child, when she suffered what appears to have been a severe case of postpartum depression from which she recovered only through the alleged intervention of Christ himself. Her subsequent boisterous demonstrations of faith and devotion made her notorious wherever she went. She visited all the major shrines of Europe and the Holy Land, experiencing physical hardships, mental anguish, and financial reversals. On several occasions she was even in danger of losing her life when she was accused of heresy and Lollardy. She undertook her last journey abroad when she was about sixty years old. Her son Thomas, the only survivor of fourteen children, had lived in Prussia for a number of years and had married a girl from Danzig. When the young couple visited his parents in Lynn, Thomas fell ill and died, and approximately a year and a half later Margery accompanied his widow back to her home town. After her return to Lynn Margery eventually persuaded her second amanuensis, a priest, to revise a draft of her autobiography, which had been written before her departure to Danzig, and to complete her life history under her direction. She is mentioned a few times in various town records of 1439, but the date of her death is not known.

Prior to the discovery of this manuscript, scholars knew of Margery only from a single surviving copy of a pamphlet printed by Wynkyn de Worde in 1501. It contains seven pages of prayers extracted from Margery's autobiography, entitled "A shorte treatyse of contemplacyon taught by our lorde Ihesu cryste, or taken out of the boke of Margerie kempe of Lynn." As Professor Meech observes, the extract presents not a single event of Margery's life, and the only mystical experiences de Worde included are those showing Margery in quiet communion with Christ and the Virgin Mary. Consequently, de Worde's pamphlet gives a totally misleading picture of Margery as a person and as a mystic, which caused scholars to expect the lost original to contain little to distinguish it from other English mystical tracts of the fourteenth and fifteenth centuries. Matters became even more confused through a reprint of de Worde's pamphlet by Henry Pepwell in 1521. To Margery's name Pepwell added the designation "ancresse," so that from then on in works on English religious recluses Margery was always referred to as an "anchoress of King's Lynn in Norfolk."

The reappearance of the long-lost manuscript of *The Book of Margery Kempe* provided many surprises and made a scholarly reappraisal of the "mysticism" of the "anchoress of Lynn in Norfolk" inevitable. Although scholars of English literary history praise Margery's book as a landmark in the development of vernacular literature because it is the first extant biography or autobiography in English, their response to Margery's particular brand of mysticism has been mainly negative. Most studies condemn her behavior, doubt that her temperament was conducive to the development of genuine mystical insights, and therefore question the mystical nature of her religious experiences. Eric Colledge sums up the attitude of the skeptics in dismissing her "ravishings" as fits of hysteria or epilepsy and her "revelations" as subjective, imitative, and excogitated.[2]

One reason for this negative evaluation of Margery as a mystic is no doubt that Margery was almost an exact contemporary of England's most gifted woman mystic, Dame Julian of Norwich. Dame Julian, who was born in 1342 and died after 1416, was an anchoress enclosed in the church of St. Julian in Norwich. In 1373 she suffered a serious illness which ended in a series of "shewings," visions of the Virgin Mary and the passion of Christ. Apparently Dame Julian prepared a brief account of them immediately after her return to health. These visions never reoccurred, but for the rest of her life she pondered their meaning and significance. Finally, twenty years after having recorded them for the first time, she described them once more, including her own meditations concerning them. Unlike Margery's rambling spiritual autobiography, Dame Julian's *Revelations* is a carefully constructed work, complete with cross-references. Because of the quality of the *Revelations'* organization, style, vocabulary, and imagery, Dame Julian has been judged equal to the best prose writers among her predecessors as well as her contemporaries.

A comparison of the content of their work is even more damaging to Margery than Julian's stylistic superiority. In respect to their personalities, for example, Margery's sense of self-importance contrasts unfavorably with Dame Julian's reticence and humility. Margery time and again betrays her conviction that God had set her apart from the rest of humanity and would protect her from those envious people less favored than herself: "Thys is my wyl, dowtyr, þat þow receyue my body euery Sonday, and I schal flowe so mych grace in þe þat alle þe world xal meruelyn þerof. Þow xalt ben etyn & knawyn of þe pepul of þe world as any raton knawyth þe stokfysch. Drede þe nowt, dowtyr, for þow schalt haue þe vyctory of al þin enmys" (p. 17). Julian, on the other hand, always remains a humble soul in search of God's grace: "For sothly it was not schewid me that God lovid me better than the lest soule that is in grace, for I am sekir that there by many that never had schewing ner sight but of the comon techyng of holy Church, that loven God better than I."[3]

But it is the difference in spiritual perception which renders Margery's mysticism inferior to Dame Julian's. As David Knowles says, unlike Dame Julian's revelations, Margery's do not "in any way perceptible to the reader, deepen the writer's spiritual insight or convey any message or programme to her readers. They are, almost entirely, devout conversations or monologues." Margery fails to convey to the reader "any of that sense of mental and emotional and spiritual distinction, and of that exceptional quality of personality of which all readers of Julian's book speedily become aware."[4] Whereas in the opinion of many critics Margery's book describes a woman of little spiritual wisdom and few if any genuine mystical experiences, they recognize in Julian's *Revelations* one of the greatest of the English mystics, who balances the fervor of the continental women mystics with the emotional restraint characteristic of English mysticism, and whose depth of inquiry into the nature of mysticism rivals that of the greatest mystics of her time.[5]

Margery Kempe, on the other hand, as Knowles concludes, "can only improperly and accidentally be classed among the English mystics." The emphasis here is upon "English," for Margery's spiritual experiences, as they are related in *The Book of Margery Kempe,* are much more closely related to those of the continental women mystics of the thirteenth and fourteenth century than to the visions and contemplations of Dame Julian, Walter Hilton, or the unknown author of *The Cloud of Unknowing.* By comparing some of the most notable characteristics of Margery's piety and visions to those of certain feminine mystics who flourished on the continent prior to or at the same time as Margery, I hope to demonstrate how strikingly her religious experiences resemble especially those of the Beguines in Belgium and the Dominican nuns in Germany.

Louise Collis calls Margery an "apprentice saint."[6] As such, Margery had several master saints who introduced her to the mysteries of living the life of a saint, some of whom she acknowledged in her book. She states, for example, that for seven years or more a young priest "red to hir many a good boke of hy contemplacyon & oþer bokys, as þe Bybyl wyth doctorys þer-up-on, Seynt Brydys boke, Hyltons boke, Bone-ventur, Stimulus Amoris, Incendium Amoris, & swech oþer" (p. 143). Among those she had read to her may also have been the abridged English translation of Jaques de Vitry's *Vita b. Mariae Oigniacensis,* which was composed in 1215, two years after Mary's death, for Margery exhibits considerable familiarity with the life history of this Beguine, who almost singlehandedly transformed the local Flemish lay custom of living a religious life outside the convent into one of the most popular religious movements of the thirteenth and fourteenth centuries. When the original English translation was made cannot be ascertained, but a fifteenth-century copy survives in MS Douce 114, which, as an endnote implies, was produced in the area of Nottingham for a Carthusian house in that town: "Iste liber est domus belle Vallis ordinis Cartus. in comitatu Notyngham."[7]

That Margery saw an inspiration in St. Mary is not surprising since Mary, like Margery, was a married woman who despite her lack of purity became one of Christ's chosen brides. While Mary still lived with her husband John and "hadde not openly power of hir owne body, she bare priuely vndir hir smok a fulle sharpe corde with þe whiche she was girdid ful harde" ("Lyf of s. Marye," p. 136). Margery, likewise, successfully concealed her hairshirt from her husband, though she wore it night and day: "Þan sche gat hir an hayr of a kylne swech as men dryen on malt & leyd it in hir kyrtylle as sotyllych & as preuylich as sche mygth þat hir husbond xult not aspye it, ne no mor he dide, & ʒet sche lay be hym euery nygth in his bedde, & weryd þe hayr euery day, & bar chylderyn in þe tyme" (p. 12). After John released Mary from the bonds of matrimony, "þat she myʒhte more frely serue oure lorde," she wore a "hard sakke, þat is callid in open tunge stamyne" next to her body. Her outer garments consisted of "a white wollen cote, & a mauntil of the same coloure, wiþ-outen any skynnes or furrur" ("Lyf of s. Marye," pp. 136, 147).

Margery aspired to the same privileges, but was considerably less successful in obtaining them. Whereas Mary's husband John was very understanding of his wife's spiritual yearnings, released her from her marriage vows, and even went so far as "to gyue alle þat hee hadde for Crystes loue to pore men and to folowe his felowe in holy purpos & holy religyone for euere þe ferre hee was departyd fro hir by carnelle affec-cyone, þe nerre was hee knyyte to hir by loue of sprituel spousehode" ("Lyf of s. Marye," p. 136), Margery's husband John proved reluctant to surrender his conjugal rights. John, in no hurry to abstain from what he clearly did not perceive as a sin, insisted on obedience, "& sche obeyd wyth greet wepyng & sorwyng for þat sche mygth not levyn chast" (p. 12). Margery could break his resistance only after years of threaten-ing him with divine wrath and destruction: "Now, good ser, amend ʒow & aske God mercy, for I teld ʒow ner iij ʒer sythen þat ʒe schuld be slayn sodeynly, & now is þis þe thryd ʒer, & ʒet I hope I schal han my desyr" (p. 23).

As soon as Margery had secured John's promise "as fre mot ʒowr body ben to God as it hath ben to me" (p. 25), she lost no time in proclaiming herself publicly a bride of Christ. Even before John had made his vow of chastity before Philip Repyngdon, the Bishop of Lincoln, to make their separation legal, Margery implored the bishop to grant her certain visible tokens of her new status: "I am comawndyd in my sowle þat ʒe schal ʒyue me þe mantyl & þe ring & clothyn me al in whygth clothys. And yf ʒe clothyn me in erth, owyr Lord Ihesu Cryst xal clothyn ʒow in Heuyn, as I vndyrstond be reuelacyon" (p. 34). But neither the reminder that God himself desired these tokens nor the inducement of being spared purga-tory produced the desired results. The bishop evaded her request to be invested with the insignia of chastity, which in England were apparently reserved solely for widows who had taken a triple vow of celibacy.[8] When all his delaying tactics failed to dissuade Margery from her goal, he

referred her to Thomas Arundel, the Archbishop of Canterbury, claiming to have no authority in the matter since Margery was not a member of
his diocese. To Margery, who, as Hope Emily Allen observes, "takes
white as symbolical of a very comprehensive purity," and whose white
clothing was perhaps "meant to show that she was a maiden in her soul,"[9]
Repyngdon's refusal was a severe blow, and not until she was staying in
Rome during her return from the Holy Land did she actually realize her
desire to be dressed in the white garments of a bride of Christ.[10]

Margery's familiarity with and indebtedness to the spiritual career of
St. Mary of Oigny shows itself beyond question in her discussions
concerning the gift of tears which God so abundantly bestowed upon
her. St. Mary had unfailingly responded to the slightest reminder of
Christ's suffering with a deluge of tears of compassion. During church
services, for example, she frequently cried so vehemently at the sight of
the crucifix "þat hir teerys copiously doune rennynge on þe kirke-
paumente shewed where she ȝeed" ("Lyf of s. Marye," p. 137). She tried
in vain to control her emotions, but as her biographer points out, "wher
as she enforced hir to restreyne hir wepynge, þere encresed meruelously
teerys moor and moor" ("Lyf of s. Marye," p. 137). Mary then tried to
hide her tears from others, but that effort proved tedious and time-
consuming: "And while beoþ daye and nyghte contynuelly water wente
awaye by hir eyen, and not only hir terys in hir chekys but also leste they
shulde be perceyued in þe paumente, she kepte hem in kerchefs wiþ þe
whiche she couerd hir heed; and siche lynnen cloþes she vsed fulmany, þe
whiche sche nedid often to chaunge, þat, as on wette, anoþere myghte
drye" ("Lyf of s. Marye," p. 138). Her compassion with Christ's suffering became so intense that the mere mention of his torments on behalf of
all mankind rendered her prostrate: "She myghte not byholde an ymage
of the crosse, ne speke ne heere oþere folke spekynge of the passyone, but
if sche felle in to a swounynge for hyȝ desyre of herte" ("Lyf of s. Marye,"
p. 137). Christ finally took pity and relieved her suffering somewhat by
sparing her visions of his crucifixion: "And in þe passyone vmwhile oure
lorde apperyd in þe crosse, but selden, for vnneþes myght she suffir þat"
("Lyf of s. Marye," p. 173).

Like St. Mary, Margery wept copious tears of compassion whenever
she was reminded of Christ's sacrifice. This habit started during her
pilgrimage to the Holy Land, where a vision of Christ's passion touched
off violent paroxysms of "cryings" and "roarings." In Norwich, for
example, she once saw a *pièta*, "and thorw þe beholdyng of þat pete hir
mende was al holy occupyed in þe Passyon of owr Lord Jhesu Crist & in

þe compassyon of owr Lady, Seynt Mary, þe whech sche was compellyd to cryyn ful lowde & wepyn ful sor, as þei sche xulde a deyd" (p. 148). Margery claims she too would have liked to conceal her grief, but, like Mary, "þe mor þat sche wolde wythstonde it er put it a-wey, þe mor strongly it wrowt in hir sowle wyth so holy thowtys þat sche xulde not sesyn. Sche xulde sobbyn & cryen ful lowde al a-geyn hir wyl þat many man & woman also wondryd on hir þerfore" (p 98). Unlike Mary, however, Margery ultimately eagerly accepted God's gift of tears as her personal means of preventing others from falling victim to sin and perdition. In a rare demonstration of humility she acknowledges her debt to God for bestowing this singular gift of grace upon her, which alone gives meaning and purpose to her existence: "I schal not sesyn, whan I may wepyn, for to wepyn for hem plentyuowsly, spede ȝyf I may. And ȝyf þu wylt, Lord, þat I sese wepyng, I prey þe take me owt of þis world. What xulde I don þerin but ȝyf I myth profityn? For, thow it were possibyl þat al þis world myth be sauyd thorw þe teerys of myn eyne, I wer no thank worthy. Þerfor alle preysyng, al honowr, al worshep mot ben to þe Lord" (p. 142).

Both Mary and Margery eventually came under fire for their disruptive weeping during mass. Priests especially seem to have resented their boisterous demonstrations of compassion, which invariably reached their climax during the week before Easter. Once on Maundy Thursday a priest admonished Mary and "badde þat she shulde praye softely and latte be hir wepynge, [and] she, sooþly, as she euer was shamfaste & in alle thinges sympil as a doufe, didde hir bisynesse to obey" ("Lyf of s. Marye," p. 138). But since she could not stay her tears, Christ himself came to her assistance to silence the priest's criticism once and for all:

Þenne she, knowynge hir vnmyghte, went priuely oute of þe chirche and hidde hir in a priue place fer fro alle folk: and gate graunte of oure lorde with terys þat he wolde shewe to þe same preste þat hit is not in mannes powere to wiþholde þe stronge streme of teerys. . . . Wherfore þat preste, þe while he sange masse þat same daye, was so ouercomen wiþ abundauns of terys, þat his spirite was wel nyghe strangelyd; and þe more þat hee biseyd hym to reffreyne his terys, þe moor not oonly hee but also þe buke and þe autor-clothes were wette wiþ water of wepynge: soo þat hee vnavisyman, he þat blamer of Crystes mayden, leeryd with schame by experiens what hee schulde do þat hee wolde not firste knowe by meeknesse and compassyone. For ofer many sobbynges, pronounsynge many wordes vnordynatly now and now, atte laste vnneþes hee skaped from perille. ("Lyf of s. Marye," p. 138)

This little miracle vindicated Mary fully and apparently silenced similar criticism among her contemporaries. From that day on, Jaques de Vitry reports, this priest "þat bouþ sawe and knewe," defended Mary's tears as genuine gifts of divine grace. Mary, though "sympil as a doufe," on this occasion could not refrain from gloating just a little over her victory: "Sooþly, þen longe tyme after the messe was endid, Cristes mayden, turnynge ageyne & wondirly as if she hadde be presente vmbreidynge tolde what felle vnto þe preste. "Now, 'quod sche, 3ee haue leeryd by experyens þat hit is not in a man to wiþholde þe fersenes of þe wynde whanne þe sowth bloweþ' " ("Lyf of s. Marye, " p. 138).

Margery reports a similar event having taken place in her home town of Lynn when a famous preaching friar refused to preach as long as Margery was in the congregation. After having suffered her "boisterous weeping" on several occasions, he apparently lost patience, and not even the persuasion of a local doctor of divinity and her confessor could sway him: "So þei went, boþe preystys to-gedyr, & preyid þe good frer as enterly as þei cowde þat he wolde suffyr þe sayd creatur quyetly to comyn to hys sermown & suffyr hir paciently 3yf sche happyd to sobbyn er cryen as oþer good men had suffyrd hir be-fore. He seyd schortly a-3en, 3yf sche come in any cherch wher he xulde prechyn & sche made any noyse as sche was wone to do, he xulde speke scharply a-geyn hir, he wolde not suffryn hir to crye in no wyse" (p. 150).

Even their efforts to incline him favorably toward Margery through gifts of good wine were ultimately unsuccessful, so convinced was the friar that Margery's tears were a sham. Again the two clerics "wentyn to þe sayd frer as þe good preystys dedyn beforn & sentyn for wyne to cheryn hym wyth, preyng hym of hys charite to fauyr þe werkys of owr Lord in þe sayd creatur & grawntyn hir hys beneuolens in supportyng of hir 3yf if happyd hir to cryen er sobbyn whyl he wer in hys sermown. & þes worthy clerkys telde hym þat it was a 3yft of God & þat sche cowde not haue it but whan God wolde 3eue it, ne sche myth not wythstande it whan God wolde send it, & God xulde wythdrawe it whan he wilde, for þat had sche be reuelacyon, & þat was vnknowen to þe frer" (pp. 150–51). He, however, "neythur 3euyng credens to þe doctowrys word-ys ne þe bachelerys, . . . seyd he wolde not fauowr hir in hir crying for nowt þat any man myth sey er do, for he wolde not leuyn þat it was a 3yft of God" (P. 151). Instead, he suggested that it might be "a cardiakyl er sum oþer sekenesse," and if she would signify that indeed she suffered from some terrible disease, "he wold haue compassyon of hir & steryn þe pepil to prey for hir, and vndyr þis condicion he wolde han paciens in hir

& suffyr hir to cryen a-now" (p. 151). Needless to say, Margery was outraged at such a suggestion, for "hir-self knew wel be reuelacyon & be experiens of werkyng it was no sekenes, & þerfor sche wolde not for al þis world sey oþerwyse þan sche felt" (p. 151). The controversy ended in an apparent victory for the friar. For the rest of his stay in Lynn, Margery was banished from his sermons for "þei myth not acordyn" (p. 151).

Ultimately, though, this affair turned out to be an important victory for Margery. The friar, who kept condemning Margery's behavior in his sermons, supposedly turned many people against her, among them the priest who later was to revise and expand her life's history: "And þan many of hem þat pretendyd hir frenschep turnyd a-bakke for a lytyl veyn drede þat þei haddyn of hys wordys & durst not wel spekyn wyth hir, of þe whech þe same preyste was on þat aftirward wrot þis boke & was in purpose neuyr to a leuyd hir felyngys aftyr" (p. 152). But at this point the Lord himself intervened on Margery's behalf. He sent to the priest a bachelor of divinity, who made him read Jaques de Vitry's *Vita b. Mariae Oigniacensis* to convince him that Margery's tears were indeed a divine gift of grace.[11] This ploy was so successful that after having read the account of St. Mary's weeping and God's conversion of the doubtful priest, "owr Lord drow hym a-ȝen in schort tyme, blissed mote he ben, þat he louyed hir mor & trustyd mor to hir wepyng & hir crying þan euyr he dede be-forn" (p. 152). The preaching friar evidently never changed his opinion about the source of Margery's tears. But in respect to him, she too, like St. Mary, considered herself ultimately fully vindicated, if not in man's eyes, so in God's eyes. For, as God himself assured her, "ther is no clerk can spekyn a-ȝens þe lyfe whech I teche þe, &, ȝyf he do, he is not Goddys clerk; he is þe Deuelys clerk" (p. 158).

Beside the Life of St. Mary of Oigny, MS Douce 114 also contains the translations of the Latin *vitae* of two other thirteenth-century Belgian Beguines, *Þe lyfe of s. Elizabeth of Spalbeck in þe shyre of Losse bisyde an abbey of nunnys þat is called Herkenrode*, and *Þe lyfe of s. Cristyne þe meruelous of þe town of S. Trudous in Hasban*.[12] Whether Margery was familiar with these translations cannot be ascertained, but since both of these Lives exhibit some of the most prominent religious practices and beliefs that were later to characterize the Lives of so many German Dominican nuns, lay mystics, and Margery herself, it may be useful to mention just a few items that are sufficiently similar to Margery's experiences as she relates them in her book. Elizabeth of Spalbeck (d. 1266), who eventually lived as a recluse in a Cistercian house, according to this Life, was especially fond of approximating both the sufferings of Christ and the ingenious tortures of his tormentors on her own body as preparation for the celebration of the seven canonical hours. But what is of interest here is her response to the elevation of the Eucharist during the mass. Even when she was too ill to participate, she observed the proceedings from a cot in her cell which was so positioned that she could see the altar: "Anone as she seeþ þe eleuacyon of the sacramente, in þe selfe momente of þe sighte þere-of, sche berith ouer wiþ a merueilous monynge alle hir body ouerthwarte þe bedde, strecchynge forþe hir armes on booþ sydes hir, & makith a crosse of hir-selfe, and so sche abidith allestarke as a stok in a swogh and rauishynge."[13]

This behavior closely resembles Margery's "roarings," with which she was to confound and dismay her fellow citizens for many years. The first instance of her threshing about on the ground with outstretched arms occurred while she was on pilgrimage in the Holy Land: "& whan þei cam vp on-to þe Mownt of Caluarye, sche fel down that sche myght not stondyn ne knelyn but walwyd & wrestyd wyth hir body, spredyng hir armys a-brode, & cryed wyth a lowde voys & þow hir hert xulde a brostyn a-sundyr, for in þe cite of hir sowle sche saw veryly & freschly how owyr Lord was crucifyed. . . . & sche had so gret compassyon & so gret peyn to se owyr Lordys peyn þat sche myt not kepe hir-self fro krying & roryng, þow sche xuld a be ded þerfor" (p. 68). Elizabeth of Spalbeck's biographer may have applauded such a dramatic exhibition of grief, but Margery's English traveling companions were mortified by such exotic behavior, and as Margery herself reports, "þerfor sufferyd sche mych despite & mech reprefe" (p. 68). Some of them said "it was a wikkyd spiryt vexid hir; sum seyd it was a sekenes; sum seyd sche had dronkyn to mech wyn; sum bannyd hir; sum wisshed sche had ben in þe hauyn; sum wolde sche had ben in þe se in a bottumlas boyt" (p. 69).

But more than Elizabeth of Spalbeck's Life, that of Christina mirabilis(d. 1224) would have attracted Margery, if she had any knowledge of its existence. And indeed, this exact translation of Thomas of Cantimpré's vita exhibits some interesting parallels to Margery's book. As Margery was to do later, Christina often bewailed the indifference of the world toward Christ's sufferings on behalf of all mankind: " 'Þou wrecchende worlde, arte turnyd aweywarde; þou hast closed þyne eiȝen & wilte not vndirstonde.' And she, seiynge þese wordes, cryed as a womman trauelynge, and wryþed to-gadir hir membrys & walowed in þe erþe, wiþ ful grete weymentacyone."[14] Like Margery, Christina was illiterate, but nevertheless, "she vndirstood sooþly alle latyn and knewe plenirly alle the menynge in scripture, þof sche neuer knewe lettir syþen she was borne" ("Lyf of s. Cristyne," p. 129). Her concern for the clergy parallels Margery's, who, like Christina, often felt herself mistreated by them, but nevertheless respected them and admonished them, as she insisted, not in a spirit of vindictiveness, but "lest by her excesses þey schulde scorn þe good name of Cryste amonge þe pepil" ("Lyf of s. Cristyne," p. 129).

Like Margery later, Christina drew attention to herself wherever she went. Her method of repairing her wardrobe, for example, must have impressed many witnesses as peculiar, to say the least. Although the convent of St. Catherine to which she was attached was a Benedictine house, she, like Mary before her, wore the white coat and scapulary Margery was to covet for herself. But whenever "she wantid a sleue in hir cote or an hode in hir scapulary: if she mette any body of whome she knewe by spyrite þat she shulde take hit of, she preyed hym; and if he wolde gif hit, sche þanked hym; and if he denyed, she toke hit agayne his wille and sewyd it to hir owne cloþes" ("Lyf of s. Cristyne," p. 126). Lacking thread, she would sew these items to her clothes with strips of tree bark, which could not have improved the appearance of the garments. Since she paid no attention to matching the sleeves or hoods to her own gowns, the resulting outfit apparently resembled the getup of a court fool. Christina, however, according to her biographer, remained undaunted: "She shamed not þogh þe sleues in o coot were party and of dyuerse colours" ("Lyf of s. Cristyne," p. 126).

Moreover, Christina at times exhibited such strange behavior that even those who knew her and loved her considered her mad. Occasionally she vexed the nuns of St. Catherine's when suddenly, in the midst of a disputation about Christ, she had mysterious and frightening fits: "Sodeynly and vnsupposid alle hir body was taken of spirite & turnyd in to a whirlynge about as a scoprelle or a toppe þat childer pleye with, soo þat for houge swiftnesse of whirlynge, þere myghte be perceyud no forme ne schape of membrys in hir body" ("Lyf of s. Cristyne," p. 128). But it was her penchant for living in trees to escape the stink of human corruption that finally convinced her two older sisters, fellow Beguines, that Christina needed to be confined for her own good: "For suchemaner doynge hir sistres & frendes were greetly ashamyd þat men trowyd hir ful of fendes . . . [and] atte laste with grete laboure toke hir and bonde hir with chaynes of yren." God, however, released her from her imprisonment. One night he miraculously undid her fetters. She escaped, fled to the woods, and there once more she lived for the next nine weeks "as bryddes doon, in trees" ("Lyf of s. Cristyne," p. 121).

Obviously, not even Margery's eccentricities could match such outlandish behavior, but she too relates how during the postpartum depres-

sion that precipitated her religious career she was locked up and fettered
to protect her from herself:

> Þis creatur went owt of hir mende & was wondyrlye vexid &
> labowryd wyth spyritys half ȝer viij wekys & odde days. And in þis
> tyme sche sey, as hir thowt, deuelys opyn her mowthys al inflaumyd
> wyth brennyng lowys of fyr as þei schuld a swalwyd hyr in, sum-tyme
> rampyng at hyr, sum-tyme thretyng her, sum-tym pullyng hyr &
> halyng hir boþe nygth & day. . . . Sche slawndred hir husbond, hir
> frendys, and her owyn self. . . . Sche wold a fordon hir-self many a
> tym at her steryngys & a ben damnyd with hem in Helle, & in-to
> witnesse þerof sche bot hir owen hand so vyolently þat it was seen al
> hir lyfe aftyr. And also, sche roof hir skyn on hir body a-ȝen hir hert
> wyth hir nayles spetowsly, for sche had noon oþer instrumentys, &
> wers sche wold a don saf sche was bowndyn & kept wyth strength
> boþe day & nygth þat sche mygth not haue hir wylle. (pp. 7–8)

Margery too eventually escaped her confinement through Christ's direct
intervention. He appeared to her in person when "sche lay a-loone and
hir kepars wer fro hir" (p. 8) and healed her from her affliction.

Perhaps the most notable characteristic Margery shares with both St.
Mary of Oigny and Christina *mirabilis* is her anxiety to avoid the pains of
purgatory and a corresponding desire to help those already there. Mary
once had a vision of a multitude of hands praying. Unable to determine
the meaning of this sight, she begged God for illumination, "and she was
answeryd of god þat soulles þe whiche be peyned in purgatory asked
helpe of hir prayers or of an oþere, wiþ þe which her sorowes were
softenyd as with a precyous oynemente" ("Lyf of s. Marye," p.142). Not
only did Mary pray for these wretched souls, she also engaged the prayer
of others in easing their pain and reducing their punishment. Once, for
example, as she witnessed the burial of a dead woman, she "sawe þe soule
of hir, þat was neuer in þis worlde playnly purged, be putte to purgatorye, to fulfille þat wanted of hir peyne. For hir husbonde was a
merchaunte and hadde goten summe goodes be gyle, as is merchauntȝ
maner; also she hadde receyued in hir ostry summe men of þe dukys
meynye of Louayne þat hadde mykel spendid in hir hous of wrangegoten
goodes" ("Lyf of s. Marye," p. 156). When Mary told all this to the
"deuoute virgyne Margarete of Villambroc and hir sistirs," the prayers of
these women provided such powerful restitution on behalf of the dead
woman that soon thereafter she appeared to Mary in a vision with a soul
"clenner þan glass, whitter þan snowe, briȝhter þanne þe sunne . . .
holdynge þe boke of lyfe in hir handes, [and] radde þerre-vpon" ("Lyf of
s. Marye," p. 156). Mary herself, so God assured her in a vision, eventually would also read from the book of life without hindrance or delay, for

he granted her "aboue alle oþere thinges, at she shulde passe to paradys wiþouten purgatory peyne" ("Lyf of s. Marye," p. 148).

In addition to weeping and praying for hours on end for the sake of the souls in purgatory, Margery, in her zeal even provided information to relatives concerned for their welfare. Before going on pilgrimage to Jerusalem, for example, she was approached by a widow who "preyd þis creatur to preyn for hir husbond & wete yf he had ony nede of help" (p. 46). As Margery prayed for him, she found out from God "þat hys sowle xuld be xxx зer in Purgatory les þan he had bettyr frendys in erthe" (p. 46). She informed the widow of her findings, suggesting a remedy to ease the dead man's plight: "зyf ye wyl don almes for hym iij pownd er iiij in messys & almes-зeuyng to powyr folke, зe schal hyly plesyn God & don þe sowle gret esse" (pp. 46–47). Margery's efforts to ease the punishment of this departed soul were less successful than similar efforts by Mary. Apparently the widow thought the price for her husband's relief too steep, for "þe wedow toke lytyl hede at hir wordys & let it pasyn forth" (p. 47). Like St. Mary, however, Margery was also granted her desire not to suffer "non oþer Purgatory . . . but in þis werld only" (p. 157). Upon passing out of this world, she was to enjoy the "blysse of Heuyn . . . wyth-in þe twynkelyng of an eye" (pp. 16–17).

But it is again the Life of Christina *mirabilis* which presents the most unusual treatment of this concern with the pains of purgatory. Because God chose her to rescue many souls from purgatory and lead them to paradise, she even rose from the dead. While the priest celebrated her funeral mass, she, like the persona of the poet Dante, traveled through hell and purgatory and was finally "broзhte to þe trone of goddes mageste." There God himself revealed her mission to her:

"For certeyne, my swetynge," quod he, "þou haste be wiþ me heer, but now I putte to þe choys of two þinges: þat is to seye, wheþer þou has leuer dwelle stille with me now, or turne ageyne to þy body, þere to suffre peynes of an vndeedly soule by a deedly body wiþ-outen harme of hitselfe, and to delyuere wiþ þy peynes alle þes soulles of þe whiche þou haddest pite in þe place of purgatorye, and also with ensaumple of þy peyne and lyfe stir men to repentauns & penauns and to forsake her synnes & be trewly turnyd to me; and after alle this is doon, þen þou schalte come ageyne to me wiþ many medys." ("Lyf of s. Cristyne," pp. 120–21)

Needless to say, Christina made the correct choice, returned to earth, and the first of the "many medys" God had promised her was that "sche hadde graunte of god þat sche liuynge in body, shulde suffre purgatorye in þis worlde" ("Lyf of s. Cristyne," p. 119).

In his extensive study of the origins and development of the Beguine

movement in Flanders, Ernest W. McDonnell points to the close spiritual ties that existed between these *mulieres religiosae* and the various
monastic orders entrusted with their spiritual care.[15] The Church, from
the inception of this popular religious movement, was searching for ways
of controlling its members who, because of their lack of formal incor-
poration and freedom of adherence to a specific monastic rule, defied
strict ecclesiastical supervision. Placing the Beguines under the spiritual
tutelage of an established monastic order was one means of providing
proper spiritual guidance and at the same time preserving orthodoxy
within the movement. In the early history of the Beguine movement, this
spiritual supervision had been entrusted mainly to the Cistercian order,
and as McDonnell's study indicates, many of the mystical concepts of the
most influential mystic of the twelfth century, Saint Bernard of Clairvaux, were apparently transmitted to the Beguines through their direct
contact with Cistercian spirituality.

   With the rise of the mendicant orders, the responsibility of supervising
the spiritual development and orthodoxy of the Beguines was transferred
to the Franciscans and, much more frequently, to the Dominicans. This
transfer was of utmost importance to the development of continental
feminine mysticism because through it Beguine spirituality infiltrated
the newly established Dominican convents which in the course of the
thirteenth century sprang up in great abundance in Germany and nowhere more prominently than in the Rhineland.[16] As they took on
pastoral care of these lay women, the Dominicans, like other orders
charged with that task before them, tried to gain as much direct control
over them as possible. Most frequently they did this by attaching Beguines to Dominican convents or by actually converting Beguine establishments into Dominican houses and simultaneously incorporating
their inhabitants into the Dominican order.[17]

   The second decisive event in the development of feminine mysticism in
the Dominican convents occurred when in addition to being the spiritual
mentors of the Beguines, the Dominican friars became the teachers and
confessors of the Dominican nuns as well. In 1267 Pope Clement V
entrusted the *fratres docti,* the teachers and lectors of the Dominican
order, with the *cura monialium,* the pastoral care of the women who
flocked to the Dominican nunneries in ever-increasing numbers. These
fratres docti, by being teachers and confessors to both the Beguines and
the Dominican nuns, may have served as yet another channel for the
transmission of Beguine spirituality and religious practices to the inhabitants of the Dominican convents.[18] Most importantly, though, these
friars through their sermons and private instruction introduced these

nuns, most of them well-educated members of the nobility,[19] to the secrets of scholasticism. Moreover, many of the *fratres docti* had themselves strong mystical leanings; Meister Eckhart, the creator of German speculative mysticism, and his two famous disciples Johannes Tauler and Heinrich Seuse (Suso) were the most prominent of the *fratres docti*. And the women, through their desire to retreat from the world and through the strict ascetic exercises customarily observed in these houses, were very receptive to mystical ideas. The result of this confluence of spiritual currents was a flourishing of visions and religious experiences in these Dominican convents which found no equal in European religious history.

The mysticism of such women as Hildegard von Bingen and the instruction of such eminent teachers as Meister Eckhart, Tauler, and Suso promised the development of a speculative feminine mysticism in the Dominican houses comparable to that of Julian of Norwich in England. But this potential was never realized. What Josef Quint observes with respect to the Beguine Mechthild von Magdeburg,[20] the most important German mystic of the thirteenth century, and her equally influential Dutch contemporary Hadewijch, becomes increasingly characteristic of the Dominican women mystics who follow them: "One looks in vain for something like a speculative system in these two mystics. The center of their mysticism, its driving concern, is not Eckehart's unlimited desire for understanding, but the love of Bernard for the heavenly bridegroom."[21] The religious experiences and practices of the Dominican brides of Christ do reflect some of the teachings of the eminent theologians and mystics of their time. However, far more prominently they exhibit the major characteristics of Beguine spirituality, which itself owes much to St. Bernard, including some of the embarrassingly pathological manifestations of faith which at times attended the religious careers of the *mulieres religiosae*. And in turn, this kind of mysticism, attended by an even more severe distortion of mystical concepts, is the most notable feature in *The Book of Margery Kempe*.

The Beguines, the Dominican nuns, and Margery Kempe all practiced a systematic *imitatio* of the Virgin Mary, whom all Christian mystics acknowledge as "the archetype of all mystical experience, and at the same time as the benevolent and powerful helper and mediator of all mystical grace."[22] The virtues the early Church Fathers had associated with Mary—her humility, the total surrender of her own will to God's will, her inner peace, her union with God, and her strength in suffering—became the virtues all mystics emulated. And although various mystics in their imitation of the Virgin stressed different aspects of her characteristics, they all considered the emulation of Mary's qualities as the key to the *visio beatifica* and the union of the soul with God.

The particular kind of veneration the women under discussion here accorded the Virgin Mary points to the influence of Eckhart, Tauler, and Suso, whose own *imitatio* of Mary focused on her as the mother of God incarnate. According to Eckhart, Mary gave spiritual birth to Christ in her soul before giving birth to him physically, and he stresses that without having done so, she would not have been chosen to become the mother of God.[23] No one else, of course, can give physical birth to Christ as Mary had done; however, every faithful Christian can emulate Mary by giving spiritual birth to Christ in his own soul. As a matter of fact, it is ultimately of greater value to God that Christ be born spiritually by every virgin and pure soul than that he was born physically by the Virgin Mary, "because through such a process his birth can never be reduced to a mere historical event, but is transformed into an everlasting present event."[24] In his speculations concerning the proper *imitatio* of Mary, Eckhart insists on her being seen as a symbol of Christian perfection in whom man can discern the conditions which make the spiritual birth of Christ possible in his own soul. As Tauler summarizes this concept, Mary was much more blessed by having borne God spiritually in her soul than by having brought him into the world physically, and he who wants to experience this spiritual birth of God in himself must observe Mary's qualities. He must be as Mary was, physically and spiritually a mother, isolated from the affairs of the world. Suso, finally, in contrast to both Meister Eckhart and Tauler, rejects the concept of Mary as a symbol of Christian perfection in favor of emphasizing her human aspect as a real mother of a real child, experiencing all the joys and all the pains of actual motherhood.

Understandably, the *imitatio* of the Virgin Mary as the real mother of a real child was especially attractive both to the many widows who entered convents and Beguinages after having reared children, and to the unmarried women who upon entering a convent could not hope to have children of their own. Especially at Christmas time these women often experienced visions depicting the motherhood of Mary. St. Mary of Oigny, for example, witnessed Jesus "as in Criste-masse lyke a childe soukynge þe pappes of þe moder-mayden and weymentynge in cradel-cloþes—& þanne she hadde hir to hym as to a childe, hauynge diuerse affeccyouns and desyre after dyuerse shewynges; and so solempnites were renewed euery ȝeere" ("Lyf of s. Marye," p. 173). However, in contrast to devout men for whom the imitation of the Virgin Mary always remained the spiritual exercise it was meant to be, the women mystics, perhaps because of their sex, frequently lost sight of the spiritual nature of their *imitatio,* translating spiritual concepts into purely physical sensations and experiences. Their visions of Christ's infancy are generally accompanied by their own efforts to provide motherly care to the Christ child. At times they court blasphemy in their apparent usurpation of the Virgin's position as the child's mother. Again St. Mary's description of being Christ's nursemaid provides a good illustration of this problem: "Sumtyme thre dayes to-gedir or more, as hir semyde, she clypped oure lorde as a litil babbe dwellynge bitwix hir pappys & hidde hymselfe, þat oþere shulde not se hym; sumtyme she kyssunge played wyþ hym as with a childe" ("Lyf of s. Marye," p. 172).

In the Dominican nunneries the visions of the motherhood of Mary and the childhood of Christ sometimes also exhibit rather disturbing characteristics. The *Schwesternbücher,* the collections of nuns' Lives composed in the various Dominican convents during the thirteenth and fourteenth centuries,[25] testify to an embarrassing insistence of these nuns to know even the minute details concerning Mary's impregnation by the Holy Spirit. One sister from Oetenbach, for example, reports that "she was illuminated to such a degree that she was able to discern fully the purity of Our Lady's body. In the same light she was also able to witness fully how the Holy Spirit came to her and covered her, and how her blood and her flesh were joined with God and God with her." Such visions, however, ultimately did not satisfy these nuns' cravings to emulate all aspects of Mary's life. Especially the later Lives describe with increasing frequency the sisters' experiencing, particularly at Christmas time, all the joys, pains, and physical sensations associated with an actual pregnancy. Similar distortions of mystical concepts also mar the accounts of the Dominican nuns' adoration of the infancy of Christ. One nun of the house of Töss, for example, describes herself as sucking, like Christ, on Mary's breast, while another nun from the same convent, in her efforts to provide physical comfort for the infant, offers her own skin as a diaper.[26]

Like the Dominican nuns, Margery attached extreme importance to the emulation of the motherhood of Mary and the adoration of the infant Christ, because she, even more than they, considered such worship as a means of achieving the *unio mystica.* Like the nuns, Margery frequently describes herself as Christ's nursemaid, whose services are unfailingly rewarded with the *visio beatifica:* "Sodeynly sche sey, . . . owr Lady in þe fayrest syght þat euyr sche say, holdyng a fayr white kerche in hir hand & seying to hir, 'Dowtyr wilt þu se my Sone?' & a-non forthwyth sche say owr Lady han hyr blyssyd Sone in hir hand & swathyd hym ful lytely in þe white kerche þat sche myth wel be-holdyn how sche dede. Þe creatur had þan a newe gostly joye & a newe gostly comfort, wheche was so meruelyows þat sche cowde neuyr tellyn it as sche felt it" (p. 209). At Christ's birth, Margery "swathyd hym wyth byttyr teerys of compassyon, hauyng mend of þe scharp deth þat he schuld suffyr for þe lofe of synful men, seyng to hym, 'Lord, I schal fare fayr with ȝow; I schal not byndyn ȝow soor. I pray ȝow beth not dysplesyd wyth me' " (p. 19). Far from being displeased, Christ himself is most appreciative, time and again thanking her profusely for a job well done: "Þan owr Lord mad a maner of thankyng to hir, for-as-meche as sche in contemplacyon & in medita-cyon had ben hys Modyrs maydyn & holpyn to kepyn hym in hys childhod & so forth in-to þe tyme of hys deth" (p. 203).

Margery, unlike the nuns in the Dominican convents, never carried her *imitatio* of the Virgin so far as to claim to have experienced Mary's pregnancy in her own body. Nevertheless, her emulation of Mary ex-hibits equally questionable manifestations of divine grace. The sisters' distortion of Eckhart's metaphor and their at times pathological devo-tions to the infant Christ may very well be considered as pathetic man-ifestations of repressions of maternal feelings and experiences their status as nuns prohibited them from enjoying in real life. Margery, on the other hand, a mother of fourteen children, apparently channeled all her mater-nal affections into the adoration of the Christ child at the expense of her own children. Her constant wanderings from one church to another and from one shrine to another could not have left her with much time to lavish on her own children, and her book mentions only her son Thomas in passing.

Moreover, her need to occupy the center of the stage, coupled with her complete misunderstanding of the concept of mystical participation in biblical events, caused her, to an even higher degree than the nuns and the Beguines, to court blasphemy in the descriptions of her visions. Instead of being a mere spectator, she becomes the main actor, as is readily apparent in her descriptions of events surrounding the nativity of the Virgin and of Christ. Not content with being St. Anne's handmaiden and servant, "sche besyde hir to take the chyld [Mary] to hir & keepe it tyl it wer twelve ȝer of age wyth good mete & drynke, wyth fayr whyte clothys & whyte kerchys" (p. 18). She steals the angel Gabriel's thunder by telling the twelve-year-old Mary, "Lady, ȝe schal be þe Modyr of God" (p. 18). As Mary's servant, she completely displaces St. Joseph: "And þan went þe creatur forth wyth owyr Lady, to Bedlem & purchasyd hir herborwe euery nyght wyth gret reuerens, & owyr Lady was receyud wyth glad cher. Also sche beggyd owyr Lady fayr whyte clothys &

kerchys for to swathyn in hir Sone whan he wer born, and whan Ihesu was born, sche ordeyned beddyng for owyr Lady to lyg in wyth hir blyssed Sone. And sythen sche beggyd mete for owyr Lady & hyr blyssyd chyld" (p. 19). Likewise, during the Holy Family's stay in Egypt, it is Margery who "day be day [was] purueyng hir herborw wyth gret reuerens" (p. 19).

The most serious aberrations in the visions of all these women, however, occur in their embarrassingly fleshly versions of the supposedly spiritual *unio mystica*. Mechthild von Magdeburg, Germany's most famous thirteenth-century Beguine, clothed her descriptions of her soul's relationship to the heavenly bridegroom in the formal language and conventions of courtly love literature, thus avoiding excesses of erotic expression. Most often, though, the Beguines of the thirteenth century follow the tradition established by St. Bernard and describe their visions of Christ the bridegroom seeking his bride in the erotically charged language of the Song of Songs and eventually lapse into unrestrained eroticism.[27] St. Mary of Oigny's experiences as they are described by Jaques de Vitry, are typical examples of this corruption of the central event of all Christian mysticism:

> Also vpon a tyme whanne she hadde liggen three dayes in hir bedde and restyd esely wiþ hir spouse, for swetnesse of houge myrþe so mykel dayes wente priuely aweye, þat her semed atte she hadde liggen vnneþes a momente. For oþere-while she hungyrde god wiþ wondir chaungynge of affeccyouns, and vmwhile she toke hym. And for it is written: "Þey þat ete me shalle ʒit hunger, and þey þat drynke me shalle ʒitte thriste," euer þe more she felte oure lorde, þe more hir desyre encresed: she was greuyd & cryed, and besoȝhte þat hee wolde abyde; and leste he shulde go, she helde hym as halsynge by-twix hir armes and preyed with wepynge atte he wolde shewe hym mor to hir. ("Lyf of s. Marye," p. 172)

Similar distortions of the Bernardine concept of the spirtual union of the mystic's soul with the Godhead can be observed in great numbers in the Lives of the Dominican nuns. Adelheid von Trochau, for example, a nun at Engeltal, so eagerly desired to be united with Christ that while in a visionary trance, she went into the cloister garden and embraced all the trees, pressing them to her breast in the delusion of holding Jesus, her soul's bridegroom, in her arms. Elsbeth Bechlin, a nun at Töss, is beside herself with desire to adore the infant Christ until he finally appears to her in a vision. While the child is sitting on her lap and she plays with him, he suddenly changes into a man. While she did not dare kiss the child, she immediately asks for permission to kiss the man: "Thus spoke she out of heartfelt love: O beloved of my heart, do I dare kiss you? Then he said: Yes, according to your heart's desire, as much as you would like."[28]

One prominent feature of the *Schwesternbücher* is the Dominican nuns' insistence on spotless virginity as the most important prerequisite for achieving the *unio mystica*. The Lives of those nuns who entered the convents as virgins endlessly and exuberantly praise their subjects for their cleanness. The Lives of those women, however, who had entered the convents only after they became widows or had dissolved their marriages are testimonies of excruciating spiritual torment.[29] Although some of the greatest saints of the Catholic Church had not been virgins and had achieved sainthood even after having lived sinful and unchaste lives, these women obviously perceived their status as former wives of fleshly husbands as an insurmountable impediment in their efforts to become perfect brides of Christ. The Church, which had always regarded the state of matrimony as the less perfect state and less conducive to spiritual perfection in effective service to God, did nothing to relieve their anxieties.

These women's feelings of inadequacy produced visions that clearly indicate an unhealthy and pathetic state of mind. Adelheid von Breisach of the convent of Adelhausen provides an excellent example:

> She suffered great sorrow about her virginity, because she was a widow and cried day and night over her lost maidenhood. After many years of this an angel appeared to her and said: God will grant you your request [union with the heavenly bridegroom] as far as it is possible for him to do so. Speaking thus, he took her with him into the air where there were angels with a winepress. In this winepress they pressed her so severely that she believed that not a drop of blood would remain in her body. But the angels said to her: All the blood in your body that has ever sinned we have pressed out of you. In exchange for it virgins shall pour their blood into you, and you yourself shall be like a virgin as much as it is possible for you to do so. But never could you become truly a virgin again.[30]

Mechthild von Hundersingen from the convent of Weiler found Christ much more willing to forgive and forget her having yielded her virginity to an earthly lover. In a sermon she hears that the blood of our Lord does not unite itself as intimately and as lovingly with a rueful heart as with the soul of a virgin. Because of that she falls into deep grief, since she had been in the world. Thereupon God comforts her and says: "I will purify you with my rose red blood and make you as spotless as if you were taken from the baptismal font, and I will adorn you and crown you with my own virginity."[31]

The Christian mystics who were inspired by the mysticism of St. Bernard are fond of describing their soul's intimacy with the Godhead through the metaphors of marriage and conjugal felicity. All the women under discussion here do so, but again the spiritual content of these metaphors is either blurred or altogether missing, and no one shows this more clearly than Margery Kempe, whose descriptions of her marriage to Christ are far more detailed and extensive than any one found in the Lives of the Beguines or the German Dominican nuns. Soon after her husband's public renunciation of his rights over her person, Margery celebrated her marriage to her heavenly bridegroom. Before embarking on her pilgrimage to the Holy Land in the fall of 1413, "the forseyd creatur had a ryng þe whech owyr Lord had comawndyd hir to do makyn whil she was at hom in Inglond & dede hir gravyn þerup-on, 'Ihesu est amor meus,' " which Margery refers to as "my bone maryd ryng to Ihesu Crist" (p. 78). She claims she did this in answer to God's command: "Dowtyr, I wil han þe weddyd to my Godhede, for I schal schewyn þe my preuyteys & my cownselys, for þu xalt wonyn wyth me wyth-owtyn ende" (p. 86). The ceremony itself, however, was not performed until the feast day of St. John the Lateran, November 9, 1414. After this suitably long period of engagement, God the bridegroom in the Church of the Apostles in Rome, before all the saints of heaven, the apostles, and a great multitude of angels, recited the age-old wedding vow which Margery's earthly husband had probably recited years earlier in pledging his troth to her: "I take þe, Margery, for my weddyd wyfe, for fayrar, for fowelar, for richar, for powerar, so þat þu be buxom & bonyr to do what I byd þe do. For, dowtyr, þer was neuyr childe so buxom to þe modyr as I xal be to þe boþe in wel & in woo,—to help þe and comfort þe. And þerto I make þe suyrte" (p. 87).

To an even higher degree than the Lives of those Dominican nuns who had entered the convent in a lesser state that perfect maidenhood, *The Book of Margery Kempe* reveals the anxieties married women apparently suffered upon embarking on a spiritual life devoted to God without benefit of spotless virginity. To reassure Margery of her worthiness as his bride even though she did not come to him as a pure maiden, Christ frequently declares his ardent love for her. He brushes aside her insistence that she is not a maid and therefore not worthy of him by asserting his freedom to choose as his brides whomever he wishes, regardless of their station in life: "3a, dowtyr, trow þow rygth wel þat I lofe wyfes also, and specyal þo wyfys whech wolden levyn chast, 3yf þei mygtyn haue her wyl, & don her besynes to plesyn me as þow dost, for þow þe state of maydenhode be mor parfyte & mor holy þan þe state of wedewhode, & þe state of wedewhode mor parfyte þan þe state of wedlake, 3et dowtyr, I lofe þe as wel as any mayden in þe world" (p. 49).

Far from being reassured, Margery remains doubtful, so Christ more explicitly points out his affection for her: "I haue telde þe be-for-tyme þat þu art a synguler louer, & þerfor þu xalt haue a synguler loue in Heuyn, a synguler reward, & a synguler worshep. &, for-as-mech as þu art a mayden in þi sowle, I xal take þe be þe hand in Heuyn & my Modyr be þe oþer hand, & so xalt þu dawnsyn in Hevyn wyth oþer holy maydens & virgynes, for I may clepen þe dere a-bowte & myn owyn derworthy derling" (p. 52). To convince her once and for all of her fitness to be his bride, Christ finally exhorts her to compare her status to that of the many wives who can never escape the state of matrimony to serve him properly, but who nevertheless will be richly rewarded for their modest accomplishments: "Dowtyr, ȝyf þu knew how many wifys þer arn in þis worlde þat wolde louyn me & seruyn me ryth wel & dewly, ȝyf þei myght be as frely fro her husbondys as þu art fro thyn, þu woldist seyn þat þu wer ryght meche beheldyn on-to me. & ȝet ar þei putt fro her wyl & suffyr ful gret peyne, & þerfor xal haue ryght gret reward in Heuyn, for I receyue euery good wyl as for dede" (p. 212).

Despite Christ's reassurances, Margery never quite overcame her feelings of inadequacy. When Christ had first exhorted her to become his bride during one of her many pregnancies, she had refused regretfully by saying: "Lord Ihesu, þis maner of leuyng longyth to thy holy maydens," reminding him of her continued sexual relationship with her husband manifested in the pregnancy (pp. 48–49). Later, after she had decided to heed Christ's call, she forever bewailed the loss of her maidenhood to a worldly husband: "A, Lord, maydenys dawnsyn now meryly in Heuyn. Xal I not don so? For be-cawse I am no mayden, lak of maydenhed is to me now gret sorwe; me thynkyth I wolde I had ben slayn whan I was takyn fro þe funtston þat I xuld neuyr a desplesyd þe, & þan xuldyst þu, blyssed Lorde, an had my meydenhed wyth-owtyn ende" (p. 50). The abundance of such statements and God's comforts throughout *The Book of Margery Kempe* are eloquent testimony to Margery's lifelong feelings of inferiority, which even her heavenly bridegroom could never fully dispel.

Ironically, the attainment of her highest goal, becoming the bride of Christ, turned out to be less satisfactory than Margery had anticipated. A woman endowed with strong sexual appetites, Margery struggled with her fleshly desires for the rest of her life, and her self-imposed abstinence resulted in serious aberrations. One of these, as T.W. Coleman observes, was her lifelong inordinate fear of rape.[32] In 1413, the year in which she and her husband agreed to live chastely, Margery went on pilgrimage to the Holy Land. In Constance, abandoned by her companions, she charged Christ, her new fiancé, with the responsibility of preserving her virtue. Identifying herself with the woman taken in adultery, she begs Christ: "Lord, as þow dreve a-wey hir enmys, so dryfe a-wey myn enmys,

& kepe wel my chastite þat I vowyd to þe, & late me neuyr be defowlyd, for ȝyf I be, Lord, I make myn a-vow I wyl neuyr come in Inglonde whil I leue" (p. 65).

Advancing age did nothing to relieve Margery's dread of defilement; quite the contrary, her fears increased with age. During her last pilgrimage in Germany in 1433, when Margery was about sixty years old, she was still terrified of becoming a victim of rape: "And on nyghtys had sche most dreed oftyn-tymys, & perauentur it was of hir gostly enmy, for sche was euyr a-ferd to a be rauishyd or defilyd. Sche durst trustyn on no man; whedir sche had cawse er non, sche was euyr a-ferd. Sche durst ful euyl slepyn any nyth, for sche wend men wolde a defylyd hir. Þerfor sche went to bedde gladliche no nyth les þan sche had a woman er tweyn wyth hir. For þat grace God sent hir, wher-so sche cam for þe most party maidenys wolde wyth good cher lyn be hir, & þat was to hir gret comfort" (p. 241). But not even the company of young women reassured her for long. On her way to Aachen "sche had mech drede for hir chastite & was in gret heuynes. Þan went sche to þe good wife of þe hows, preying hir to han sum of hir maydenys þat myth lyn wyth hir þat nyght. Þe good wife assygnyd tweyn maydenys, þi whech weryn wyth hir al þat nyght, ȝet durst sche not slepyn for dred of defilyng. Sche woke & preyid ny al þat nyght þat sche myth be preseruyd fro al vnclennes & metyn wyth sum good felashep þat myth helpyn hir forth to Akun" (pp. 236–37). Thus Margery's abnormal fears resulted in the ludicrous situation of an old crone's virtue being guarded by young women instead of their honor being protected by an old woman past her prime and sexual allure.

Margery's suppressed sexual appetites manifest themselves most blatantly in her sexual fantasies, many of which involved clerics. On one occasion, when she was traduced into thinking that her visions of damned souls in hell came from the devil and not from God, God punished her disbelief by removing all his spiritual blessings from her and by making her have visions of things she claims she least wanted to see. She "sey as hir thowt veryly men of religyon, preystys, & many oþer, bothyn hethyn & Cristen comyn befor hir syght þat sche myth not enchewyn hem ne puttyn hem owt of hir syght, schewyng her bar membrys vn-to hir & þerwyth þe Deuyl bad hir in hir mende chesyn whom sche wolde han fyrst of hem alle & sche must be commown to hem alle. & he seyd sche lykyd bettyr summe of hem þan alle þe oþer. Hir thowt þat he seyd trewth; sche cowde not sey nay; & sche nedys don hys byddyng, & ȝet wolde sche not a don it for alle þis worlde" (p. 145). This "torment" lasted for twelve whole days.

Like the Beguines and the Dominican nuns, Margery channeled her suppressed sexual needs into her adoration of the heavenly bridegroom, and as was the case with these women who preceded her, it is in this aspect of her religious utterances and experiences where the most serious perversions of mystical concepts occur. Her consistent inability to differentiate between metaphor and actual experience appears with most embarrassing clarity in her descriptions of her soul's marriage to the Godhead. Margery perceived the *unio mystica* as the human sex act; accordingly, Jesus behaves like a fleshly husband eager to enjoy his conjugal rights. Like a magnanimous husband lecturing his worldly-wise bride on their future relationship before consummating the marriage, Christ tells Margery: "It is conuenyent for þe wyf to be homly wyth hir husbond. Be he neuyr so gret a lorde & sche so powr a woman whan he weddyth hir, ȝet þei must ly to-gedir & rest to-gedir in joy & pes. Ryght so mot it be twyx þe & me, for I take non hed what þu hast be but what þu woldist be. And oftyntymes haue I telde þe þat I haue clene forȝoue þe alle thy synnes. Þerfore most I nedys be homly wyth þe & lyn in þi bed wyth þe" (p. 90). Margery's efforts to describe a spiritual concept which her experience of married life compelled her to perceive strictly in physical terms produce not only a falsification of the mystical concept of the soul's being Christ's couch on which he rests within the body of the believer, they also result in an abundance of such ludicrously mixed metaphors as the following: "Dowtyr, thow desyrest gretly to se me, & þu mayst boldly, whan þu art in þi bed, take me to þe as for þi weddyd husbond, as thy derworthy derlyng, & as for thy swete sone, for I wyl be louyd as a sone schuld be louyd wyth þe modyr & wil þat þu loue me, dowtyr, as a good wife owyth to loue hir husbonde" (p. 90). On one occasion Christ even thanks his bride "for alle þe tymys þat þu hast herberwyd me & my blissyd Modyr in þi bed" (p. 214).

With few exceptions, the scholars who have studied continental feminine mysticism comment on the increasing superficiality and falsification of mystical ideas in the course of its development. Of special interest in respect to this problem is the contradictory role of the *fratres docti*. On the one hand they encouraged and furthered the development of feminine mysticism by introducing women under their care to mystical concepts, imagery, and terminology; on the other hand, many of them were scandalized by the "exaggeration, humanization, and concretization" of the most profound and ineffable mystical experiences observable in the "revelations" of their charges. One of the most outspoken critics of such abuses was the thirteenth-century Franciscan David von Augsburg, whose concern suggests that decay was evident even before the development of continental feminine mysticism reached its climax early in the fourteenth century.[33] David's mystical tracts had been translated and issued to convents and monasteries in the form of "Mirrors" to "introduce novices to the concepts of spiritual religiosity and to inspire them to develop similar depths of emotional sensitivity in response to the Godhead."[34]

But the author of "The Mirror of Monks," "The Mirror of Novices," and "The Mirror of Spiritual Men" preached in vain against the abuses his own tracts had helped to create. For a time the decay of feminine mysticism could be contained in the Dominican convents because of the relative seclusion of these houses. It defied such containment, however, "once mysticism became a popular movement and spread from these convents to the layfolk, without the supervision and guidance of the masters."[35] Once that happened, mystical concepts became totally misunderstood and misapplied to describe delusions and self-deceptions which had nothing to do with mystical experiences.

This spread of mysticism from the convents to the layfolk occurred in the second half of the fourteenth century. One reason for this widening interest in and acceptance of mysticism was an increased contact between the populace and the mystical sermons preached in the monastic houses, as more and more laymen became members of the audience. The Dominican nuns, through their letters, *vitae*, legends, and poems also disseminated mystical concepts among lay audiences.[36] In the wake of such disasters as the Black Death, lay interest in mysticism manifested itself in two ways. The threat of sudden death without benefit of absolution drove many people to join such extremist groups as the flagellants, who, with their public confessions, penances, and self-castigations, at least suggested a possibility of gaining salvation in the absence of clergy and sacrament.[37] Others, mainly women, became lay mystics.

Nothing testifies to the ultimate decay of continental feminine mysticism more blatantly than *The Book of Margery Kempe*. More than even the Lives of the Dominican nuns, the *Book* presents divine miracles as "the mere decoration of the personality of the beneficiary, serving as nothing more than the legitimization of her devout life. The glorification of God in the miracle can be seen only as it is fractured in the prism of the personality of its recipient."[38] In Margery's case, God is frequently reduced to a crude miracle worker who amazes simple-minded audiences with displays of thunder and lightning. Whenever Margery needed a visible sign of divine approbation, she asked God for a "tokne of leuyn, thundyr, & reyn so þat it hyndir ne noy no-thyng þat I vnworthy may þe raþar fulfillyn thy wil" (p. 103), and God, dutiful as always, fulfilled her desire: "Dowtyr, dowte it not, þu xalt haue þat tokyn be þe thryd day"

(p. 103). As promised, "erly in þe morwenyng, as sche lay in hir bed, sche sey gret leuyn, sche herd gret thundyr & gret reyn folwyng, & as swyþe it passyd a-wey & was fayr wedir a-geyn" (p. 104).

Her enemies and detractors soon realized it was not wise to meddle with her because the Lord did not at all hesitate to frighten them with thunder and lightning if they did. The people of Leicester, for instance, fell victim to God's wrath when their "wicked" mayor imprisoned two innocent fellow pilgrims while detaining Margery on suspicion of Lollardy. After assuring her "þat þe pepil xal be ryth fayn to letyn hem gon & not longe kepyn hem . . . owr Lord sent sweche wederyng of leuenys, thunderys, & reynes contynuyng þat al þe pepil in þe town wer so afrayd þei wist not what to do. Þei dreddyn hem it was for þei had put þe pylgrimys in preson" (p. 114). Sure enough, as soon as they were released, "a-non þe tempest sesyd, & it was fayr wedir, worschepyd be owre Lord God" (p. 114). While Margery was forced to remain in Leicester until the Bishop of Lincoln's letter arrived which was to absolve the mayor of all judicial responsibility for Margery's arrest and trial, "þer fellyn gret thunderys & leuenys & many reynes þat the pepil demyd it was for veniawns of þe sayd creatur, gretly desyryng þat she had ben owt of þat cuntre" (p. 119).

This simplistic concept of God's visible signs of grace is most dramatically presented in the account of the great fire of Lynn, which provided Margery with the golden opportunity to function as the patroness of her own home town by saving it singlehandedly from certain destruction. After the Guild Hall of the Trinity had burned to the ground, everyone realized that St. Margaret's Church and the entire town would fall victim to the conflagration "ne had grace ne myracle ne ben" (p. 162). For a while there was hope that carrying the Holy Sacrament to the fire would contain the flames; Margery herself had advised the parish priest to do so. The Host, however, proved no match for this disaster, and Margery, following the priest about, beheld "how þe sparkys comyn in-to þe qwer thorw þe lantern of þe Cherch" (p. 163). This emergency called for immediate divine intervention, and Margery was ready to initiate it. She cried: "Good Lord, make it wel & sende down sum reyn er sum wedyr þat may thorw þi mercy qwenchyn þis fyer & esyn myn hert" (p. 163). God immediately did both, for while Margery still cried and wept, there came to her "iij worschepful men wyth whyte snow on her clothys, seying vn-to hir, 'Lo, Margery, God hath wrowt gret grace for vs & sent us a fayr snowe to qwenchyn wyth þe fy. Beth now of good cher & thankyth God þer-for' " (p. 163). Margery had every reason to do just that; both her home town and her reputation were safe. "With a gret cry sche ȝaf preysyng & thankyng to God for hys gret mercy & hys goodnes, & specyaly for he had seyd to hir be-forn þat it xulde be ryth wel whan it was ful vn-lykely to ben wel saf only thorw myrakyl & specyal grace" (p. 163).

Such proofs of divine approbation, simple-minded as they may be, are ultimately quite harmless. But Margery's exploitation of divine grace to further her own ends from time to time takes on a decidedly vicious turn, as for example in her account of her good offices on behalf of her husband John when he was old and in his dotage. When John at the age of sixty or more fell and hurt himself so seriously as to require constant care, she begged God to save his life, not out of love and charity for him, but out of concern for her own safety: "Whan he had fallyn & greuowsly was hurt . . . þe pepil seyd, ȝyf he deyid, it was worthy þat sche xulde answeryn for his deth" (p. 180). To avoid any danger of prosecution for having neglected John, "sche preyid to owr Lord þat hir husband myth leuyn a ȝer & sche to be deliueryd owt of slandyr" (p. 180).

The Lord, as usual, granted her wish, but Margery almost immediately regretted having asked for this boon. First of all, God insisted that she take John to her own home and nurse him. Margery, vexed, refused outright: "Nay, good Lord, for I xal þan not tendyn to þe as I do now" (p. 180). Thereupon God lectured her on the virtue of charity and the debts she owed her husband: "Þu hast seyd many tymys þat þu woldist fawyn kepyn me. I prey þe now kepe hym for þe lofe of me, for he hath sumtyme fulfillyd þi wil & my wil boþe, and he hath mad þi body fre to me þat þu xuldist seruyn me & leuyn chast & clene, and þerfor I wil þat þu be fre to helpyn hym at hys nede in my name" (p. 180). Only after God assured her "þu xalt haue as meche mede for to kepyn hym & helpyn hym in hys nede at hom as ȝyf þu wer in cherche to makyn þi preyerys" (p. 180), did she reluctantly agree to care for him in her own home. But Margery never really enjoyed playing the role of the good Samaritan, especially since God did not comply with her wish of letting John live only long enough to silence malicious gossip. John, after reverting to the state of an infant unable to control his bodily functions, lived for a number of years, and Margery resented the unpleasant task and the expense and considered his care a punishment designed to keep her from her accustomed dalliance with her heavenly bridegroom: "And þerfor was hir labowr þe mor in waschyng & wryngyng & hir costage in fyryng & lettyd hir ful meche fro hir contemplacyon þat many tymys sche xuld an yrkyd hir labowr saf sche bethowt hir how sche in hir ȝong age had ful many delectabyl thowtys, fleschly lustys, & inordinat louys to hys persone. & þerfor sche was glad to be ponischyd wyth þe same persone &

toke it mech þe mor esily & seruyd hym & helpyd hym, as hir thowt as sche wolde a don Crist hym-self" (p. 181).

Margery's singular lack of modesty in her claims of spiritual acomplishments provides equally persuasive evidence for the decline of medieval feminine mysticism. As a "peler of Holy Cherch," Margery claims to have been granted the power to save people by the hundreds of thousands by divine fiat. Furthermore, God himself put all the angels of heaven at her disposal to help her achieve this awesome task: "Þer is no seynt in Heuyn but ȝyf þu wilt speke wyth hym he is redy to þe to comfortyn þe & spekyn to þe in my name. Myn awngelys arn redy to offyrn thyn holy thowtys & þi preyerys to me & þe terys of thy eyne also, for þi terys arn awngelys drynk, & it arn very pyment to hem" (pp. 160–61).

Even toward the heavenly bridegroom himself, Margery exhibits none of the humility appropriate to the soul searching for God's grace and illumination. Margery frequently ignored his commands, so that he often had reason to complain of her negligence: "And I haue oftyn-tymys bodyn þe so myself, & ȝet þu wilt no don þeraftyr but wyth meche grutchyngs" (p. 218). But instead of punishing her, he always hastened to assure her of his approval of anything she did: "& ȝet am I not displesyd wyth þe, for, dowtyr, I haue oftyn seyd on-to þe þat wheþyr þu preyist wyth þi mowth er thynkyst wyth thyn hert, wheþyr þu redist or herist redyng, I wil be plesyd wyth þe" (p. 218). In fact, God at times resembles a henpecked husband, meekly pointing out what gifts Margery "awt" to thank him for, and he spends a conspicuous amount of time thanking her for all her good deeds on his behalf. One long list of thanks for all conceivable favors begins like this: "Þan owr Lord mad a maner of thankyng to hir, for-as-meche as sche in contemplacyon & in meditacyon had ben hys Modyr's maydyn & holpyn to kepyn hym in hys childhod & so forth in-to þe tyme of hys deth" (p. 203).

As these and all the rest of her illustrations of divine grace indicate, Margery never progressed beyond the most primitive stage of spiritual illumination. Part of the responsibility for this failure lies with her spiritual advisers, none of whom, as David Knowles observes, made the least effort to guide and develop what spiritual gifts she may have had along the guidelines set forth by Walter Hilton in *The Scale of Perfection*. But Margery too, like the Dominican nuns before her who had ignored the advice and corrections of their spiritual counselors, frequently dismissed the commands of her mentors. Unrestrained by any disciplined spiritual guidance, Margery's mysticism became what Sheila Delany describes as "a spiritual economics as schematic as anything produced by the Puritans. The money consciousness that pervaded her world and social class pervades her mysticism as well. Every prayer and every good deed are the commodities which produce a hundred pecent profit in heaven, as Christ, the executor of Margery's spiritual estate, reminds her at every opportunity."[39]

At the end of this study, two items remain to be clarified. How typical was Margery's religious behavior of English popular piety in the four-teenth and fifteenth centuries, and how did she become exposed to the most common elements of continental feminine mysticism which form such a prominent part of her own religious life? The first question is not difficult to answer. Even a casual reading of her book reveals that Margery's expressions of piety were not the norm in her native England. Her descriptions of the derision and hostility with which her fellow citizens of all classes greeted her "boisterous" demonstrations of faith are far too numerous and far too realistic to be dismissed as the obligatory persecution of God's saint commonly featured in the hagiographies.

Furthermore, throughout her religious career Margery betrays a cur-ious affinity for Germans, whom she clearly considered more tolerant and helpful than her own countrymen. Her book mentions a consider-able number of them as her hosts, confessors, and helpers in need, tolerant of her habits and eager to assist her. During her stay in Canter-bury, for example, she stayed "at a Dewchmannys hows" (p. 29). In the Holy Land, when none of her fellow Englishmen would help her, two German pilgrims led her safely to the the city of Jerusalem: "Þan, for joy þat sche had [upon seeing the Holy City of the first time] & þe swetnes þat sche felt in þe dalyvance of owyr Lord, sche was in poynt to a fallyn of hir asse, for sche myth not beryn þe swetnesse & þe grace þat God wrowt in hir sowle. Þan tweyn pylgrymes of Duchemen went to hir & kept hir fro fallyng, of þe whech þe on was a preste. And he put spycys in hir mowth to comfort hir, wenyng sche had ben seke, & so þei holpyn hir forth to Jerusalem" (p. 67). In Rome she attended a number of sermons preached by "Duchemen," although she could not understand what was being said and suffered from the resulting lack of spiritual nourishment. As her confessor during her stay in Rome she chose a German priest named Wenslawe, even though at first they could communicate only through the help of an interpreter.

Like all the other German acquaintances Margery mentions in her book, Wenslawe supported her against her detractors, and in time he became a true friend to her. To ease their communication problem, God provided Wenslawe with the ability to understand Margery's English, although, as the book asserts, he remained incapable of understanding the speech of any other Englishman. In order to minister to Margery's needs, he gave up other duties: "He forsoke hys office be-cawse þat he wolde supportyn hir in hir sobbyng & in hir crying whan alle hir cuntremen had forsakyn hir" (p. 83). His tolerance of her exotic be-havior apparently incited the ill will of Margery's countrymen, who had already forced the brethren of the Hospital of St. Thomas of Canterbury in Rome to expel her, for "þei wer euyr ageyn hir & a-geyn þe good man whech supportyd hir" (pp. 83–84). When Margery at last departed from Rome in the spring of 1415, their parting was tearful. She "toke hir leue of hir frendys in Rome, & most specyaly of hir gostly fadyr, whech, for owr Lordys lofe, had supportyd hir & socowrd hir ful tenderly a-geyn þe wykked wyndys of hir invyows enmyis, whos departyng was ful lament-abyl as wytnessyd wel þe pur watyrdropys rennyng down her chekys" (p. 100).

How Margery became familiar with continental feminine mysticism is mainly a matter of conjecture. But since she obviously felt comfortable and appreciated in the company of Germans, it is reasonable to assume that she also was drawn to the feminine mysticism which had flourished in the Rhineland in the preceding centuries. Translations of saints' lives as those recorded in the MS Douce 114 may have been available to her to acquaint her with the religious practices of some of the famous Beguines of the Low Countries, as her direct references to St. Mary of Oigny imply. But what knowledge Margery had of the mysticism that had flourished in the Dominican convents is more difficult to assess. Her "lak of vndir-stondyng" of German may have prevented any significant direct impact of German Dominican mystical traditions on Margery, even though on her pilgrimage to Jerusalem she passed directly through the Rhineland.

The Book of Margery Kempe gives no indication of how familiar Margery may have been with the importance of such cities as Cologne, Strasburg, and Constance to the development of German feminine mys-ticism. She does mention staying in Constance on her way to the Holy Land, but how long she was there is impossible to determine; her stay could not have been extensive. According to Meech, Margery traveled from Lynn to Venice in two months' time, and later from Rome back to Norwich in less than a month.[40] Traveling such distances in such a short time could not have given her much time to absorb local mystical traditions, especially without any knowledge of the language. Further-more, as the book points out, Margery's stay in Constance was filled with problems which might have kept her too distracted to explore the rich local legacy of feminine mysticism. Because her English traveling companions were extremely hostile to her and abandoned her in Constance, Margery may have spent most of her time there making new arrangements for the safe continuation of her pilgrimage.

None of these difficulties, however, would have prevented her becoming acquainted with the life and mysticism of Dorothea von Montau (or von Preussen, as she is also called), the patroness of the Teutonic Knights, and through her with German feminine traditions. After having lived most of her life as a lay mystic in the town of Danzig, Dorothea became Prussia's first anchoress at the Dominican cathedral chapter of Marienwerder near Danzig. After her death, her confessor and biographer Johannes von Marienwerder wrote a series of Latin accounts of Dorothea's life, visions, and revelations for the papal legates in charge of the canonization inquiry which, had it been brought to a successful conclusion, would have established this widely venerated woman as Prussia's first native saint. For the local populace and the Teutonic Knights, Johannes Marienwerder composed a vernacular biography, *Des Leben der zeligen frawen Dorothee clewsenerynne in der thumkyrchen czu Marienwerdir des landes czu Prewszen,* which, because of its tremendous popularity, furnished the text for the firt book to be printed in Prussia.

Margery nowhere mentions Dorothea in her own book. However, her life and spiritual career bear such a striking resemblance to the life of Dorothea as it is recorded in Johannes Marienwerder's vernacular biography as to support the conclusion that Margery probably knew about Dorothea and consciously or unconsciously patterned her own mysticism on Dorothea's example. A close textual analysis of both works supports such a conclusion. The close mercantile ties which Lynn and Danzig enjoyed under the auspices of the Hanseatic League, Margery's lifelong association with Germans and her abiding interest in German affairs, her visit to Danzig in her later years, and her family ties to Prussia indicate the channels through which Dorothea's influence could have reached Margery over a long period of time.[41] Since Dorothea's own mysticism is solidly based on Rhenish mystical traditions and since she had undertaken two lengthy pilgrimages to the Rhineland and had lived in the famous hermitic community of Einsiedeln for almost two years, her mysticism in many ways also constitutes the most likely link of transmission between Margery's spirituality and that of the Belgian Beguines and the German Dominican nuns.

Unlike many of the saintly women she imitated, Margery, at least officially, never became "a peler of Holy Cherch." But, as Miss Collis asserts, like the biographers of these venerated women, she may have succeeded in writing a book of inspiration. The wives and daughters of the members of the new middle classes, the merchants, the aldermen, the mayors, the master craftsmen, the artisans—these, like herself, "had almost insatiable appetites for improving literature." Furthermore, like the biographers of famous Beguines or nuns, "the pious laity were not the only audience Margery could hope to address. Her orthodoxy had been fully attested under the Archbishop of Canterbury's seal. Nuns and other religious persons could safely read her book." Nothing is known about the circulation of Margery's book. But if it was read widely by middle-class women and religious personages, it was probably a great success with these audiences, for "here was not a remote God speaking only in the words of the mass, or of the scriptures. He was like an elder brother, or an ideal husband: simple, direct, and dependable."[42]

NOTES

1. *The Book of Margery Kempe,* ed. Sanford Brown Meech and Hope Emily Allen, EETS, o.s. 212 (London: Oxford Univ. Press, 1940), p. 4.

2. Eric Colledge, "Margery Kempe," *Month* 28 (1962): 28.

3. Julian of Norwich, *Revelations,* quoted by R.M. Wilson, "Three Middle English Mystics," *Essays and Studies by Members of the English Association* 9 (1956): 104.

4. David Knowles, *The English Mystical Tradition* (New York: Harper, 1961), p. 142.

5. Wilson, "Three Mystics," p. 111, quoting from dissertation entitled "Julian of Norwich, Sixteen Revelations of Divine Love, Edited from MS Sloane 2499," by Sister Anna Maria of St. Joseph's College, Bradford.

6. Louise Collis, *The Apprentice Saint* (London: Michael Joseph, 1964).

7. Carl Horstmann, ed., "Þe lyf of s. Marye of Oegines," *Anglia* 8 (1885): 106; hereafter cited as "Lyf of s. Marye."

8. Meech, *Book of Margery Kempe,* p. 274. In the fifteenth century a number of widows apparently took such a vow before their bishop and then assumed white garments and wore a wedding ring.

9. Allen, *Book of Margery Kempe,* p. 273.

10. Margery's stay in Rome extended from August 1414 until Easter 1415. She assumed the white robes against the wishes of her German confessor, Wenslawe, who frequently counseled her to continue wearing a black habit.

11. On page 153, Margery's book gives a very accurate summary of this event in St. Mary's life. Margery's priest must have read the Latin *vita* because the book states that this event is described in ch. 19; the Middle English translation in the MS Douce 114 relates it in ch. 5.

12. According to Horstmann's introduction to the Life of Elizabeth of Spalbeck, little is known about this Beguine. The original Latin *vita* is lost, and Horstmann's edition of the Middle English translation marks the first time for the only surviving document concerning her life to appear in print. The author of the lost Latin original identifies himself as Dan Philip de Clarevall, apparently a Cistercian monk, who during his visitations of chapter houses had heard about Elizabeth's holy life, but "gaf no credens to hem þat tolde me, til-tyme þat I come my-selfe and sawe and proued þat I hadde not herde þe halfe."

13. Carl Horstmann, ed., "Þe lyfe of s. Elizabeth of Spalbeck in þe shyre of Losse bisyde an abbey of nunnys þat is called Herkenrode," *Anglia* 8 (1885): 115.

14. Idem, "Þe lyfe of s. Cristyne þe meruelous of þe town of S. Trudous in Hasban," *Anglia* 8 (1885): 129; hereafter cited as "Lyfe of s. Cristyne."

15. Ernest W. McDonnell, *The Beguines and Beghards in Medieval Culture* (New Brunswick, N.J.: Rutgers Univ. Press, 1954).

16. Herbert Grundmann, "Die geschichtlichen Grundlagen der deutschen Mystik," in *Altdeutsche und altniederländische Mystik*, ed. Kurt Ruh, (Darmstadt: Wissenschaftliche Buchgesellschaft, 1964), p. 83. According to Grundmann, the Dominicans were active in eighteen so-called provinces of western and southern Europe. In the province of Germany, eighty Dominican convents for women were established in the thirteenth century, more than in the remaining seventeen provinces combined. A concentration of these convents occurred in and around the major towns of the Rhine area, namely Cologne, Strasburg, Freiburg, and Constance. Strasburg alone boasted seven of these houses within the city proper. The population within the convents ranged from forty to sixty women.

17. The seven Dominican convents under discussion in this essay are all located in the Rhineland, and most of them belong to the diocese of Constance. They are Unterlinden near Colmar, Adelhausen near Freiburg, Katharinenthal near Diessenhofen, Kirchberg near Sulz, Weiler in Esslingen, Oetenbach near Zurich, and Töss near Winterthur. Of these seven, four had been Beguine establishments before being converted to Dominican nunneries. Individual Beguines entered Dominican convents in such great numbers that in 1260 Humbert de Romans, minister general of the Order of the Preachers, had to issue an order which forbade the convents to admit any *mulieres religiosae* beyond the number of inhabitants set for each given convent. Apparently their influx strained the resources of many of these houses to a point where the sisters found it difficult to maintain themselves (McDonnell, *Beguines and Beghards*, p. 92).

18. An analysis of Meister Eckhart's and Johannes Tauler's sermons, according to Grundmann in "Grundlagen der deutschen Mystik," pp. 76–77, suggests that they were directed mainly toward nuns and Beguines under the spiritual supervision of the Dominicans and the Franciscans: "Und soweit sich aus den Predigten Eckharts und Taulers überhaupt Schlüsse ziehen lassen auf die Hörerschaft, vor der sie gehalten sind, deuten sie gleichfalls ausschliesslich auf solche Frauenklöster hin oder auf Beginenhäuser, d.h. jene religiösen Frauengemeinschaften, die der Seelsorge der Dominikaner oder Franziskaner unterstellt waren,

ohne eigentlich diesem Orden inkorporiert zu sein. . . . Alles das und vieles
andere weist eindeutig darauf hin, dass man zunächst in besonders engen geistlichen Beziehungen zwischen den Dominkanern in Deutschland und bestimm-
ten religiösen Frauengemeinschaften, Dominikanerinnen-Klöstern und Be-
ginenhäusern, den geschichtlichen Boden für die deutsche Mystik in ihren
verschiedenen Ausdrucksformen zu suchen hat."

19. Carl Boeckl, "Die Bedingtheiten der deutschen Mystik des Mittelalters,"
in *Aus der Geisteswelt des Mittelalters,* ed. Albert Lang et al. (Münster: Aschendorff, 1935, p. 1015. In discussing the high social status of the female inhabitants
of German Dominican convents, Boeckl reiterates Wilhelm Preger.

Herbert Grundmann, "Die Frauen und die Literatur im Mittelalter," *Archiv
für Kulturgeschichte* 26 (1936): 93, gives a good survey of the level of education
among the women of nobility and their influence on the development of German
vernacular literature during the Middle Ages. He compares the development of
mysticism in Germany to that in other countries, stating: "Nur hat diese Be-
wegung in Deutschland vornehmlich Frauen erfasst und zwar vor allem die
Frauen des Adels, der ritterlichen Geschlechter und des städtischen Patriziats."

20. Mechthild von Magdeburg (ca. 1210–1285) came from a noble family.
Late in life she entered the famous Cistercian nunnery of Helfta near Eisleben in
Saxony. Under the guidance of her Dominican confessor Heinrich von Halle, she
composed the first great mystical work in the German language, *Das fließende
Licht der Gottheit.* This Low German tract, a mixture of poetry and prose, was
translated into Latin ca. 1290, and ca. 1344 Heinrich von Nördlingen, the
Dominican confessor of the famous Dominican mystic Christine Ebner (1291–
1351), translated the work into High German. The Low German original is lost,
and the only extant copy of the High German translation is MS 277 at the
Benedictine library of Einsiedeln, Switzerland, a famous hermitic community
throughout the Middle Ages. Einsiedeln was also the site of four communal
houses, presumably Beguinages, which owned a copy of Mechthild's work,
rotating it among their establishments for the edification of their inhabitants.
Thus Mechthild's work not only exerted a powerful influence on religious
women in Saxony and Swabia, but in Switzerland as well.

21. Josef Quint, "Mystik," *Reallexikon der deutschen Literaturgeschichte,* ed.
Werner Kohlschmidt and Wolfgang Mohr, 2d ed. Berlin: de Gruyter, 1962),
2:549. "Nicht aber kann man bei Hadewijch, ebenso wie bei Mechthild von
spekulativer Mystik reden. So etwas wie ein spekulatives System sucht man bei
beiden Mystikerinnen vergebens. Das Zentrum ihrer Mystik, ihr treibender
Faktor, ist nicht der unendliche Erkenntnisdrang Eckeharts, sondern die Minne
Bernhards zum himmlischen Bräutigam." All translations from the German are
my own.

22. Anton Pummerer, "Maria in der Mystik," *Geist und Leben* 20 (1947): 54.
"So steht sie vor uns als Urbild und Vorbild aller mystischen Begnadigung und
zugleich ist sie die gütige und mächtige Helferin und Mittlerin jeder mystischen
Gnade."

23. Peter Meinhold, "Die Marienverehrung in der deutschen Mystik," *Saeculum* 27 (1976): 186–87.

24. Ibid., p. 187. "Er [Meister Eckhart] entnimmt diesem Vorgang den Vorrang der geistlichen Geburt vor der leiblichen und kann sich sogar zu der Außerung steigern, daß: es für Gott wertvoller sei, daß: Christus von einer jeden Jungfrau und guten Seele geistlich geboren werde, als daß: er in Maria leiblich geboren wurde"; p. 189: "So gehört die Christgeburt nicht der Vergangenheit an, sondern sie ist immerwährende Gegenwart."

25. The oldest of these collections of nuns' *vitae* comes from Unterlinden. It was composed in Latin by the prioress Katharina von Gebweiler and consists of 43 *vitae*. All others are written in German, and none of them was composed later than 1350. The *Schwesternbuch* of Adelhausen, the oldest of the Dominican convents, was written by Anna von Munzingen and contains 34 Lives. The collection of Katharinenthal contains 54 Lives; that of Kirchberg (two editions) comprises 64 and 23 Lives respectively; the *Schwesternbuch* of Oetenbach comprises only three extensive Lives, but contains numerous short episodes. The two most famous collections are those of the house of Weiler and the house of Töss near Winterthur. The Töss collection was written by Elsbeth Stagel, who recorded and in so doing preserved the German writings of Heinrich Suso. This collection of 40 Lives differs considerably from the others and is generally considered to be the first collection of biographies in the German language.

26. Walter Blank, *Die Nonnenviten des 14. Jahrhunderts* (Freiburg: K. Müller, 1962), p. 204: ". . .ward si also erleuchtet, das si erkennen ward die reinikeit unser frauen leibes und in demselben ward ir auch erkennen, wie der heilig geist über si kam und si beschattet, und wi ir plut und ir fleisch geeinbart ward mit got und got mit ir." See also p. 263.

27. St. Bernard's mysticism, in contrast to that of Meister Eckhart and his disciples, focuses on emulating the Virgin Mary in her aspect as the perfect bride of Christ so that the mystic, like Mary, may marry his soul to the Holy Spirit and thus achieve the *unio mystica*. It is based on the Song of Songs, which St. Bernard and his spiritual descendants interpreted as the wedding of Mary, the perfect bride, to the Holy Ghost, the heavenly bridegroom. St. Bernard's mystical concepts were disseminated all over Europe, and in the literature of German medieval mysticism they are most cogently expounded in the twelfth-century vernacular poem the St. *Trudperter Hohelied,* which was composed specifically for nuns.

28. Blank, *Nonnenviten,* p. 263. See p. 171: "Also sprach sy von hertzlicher min: Ach herz trut, getar ich dich gekussen? Do sprach er: Ja, nach dines hertzen gird, wie fil du wilt."

29. Blank, ibid., on p. 263, gives a lengthy catalog of women who entered Dominican convents after legally having dissolved their marriages. On pp. 178–79 he lists a number of women who entered these convents as widows. The Lives of all these women are included in the *Schwesternbücher* of the Dominican houses under discussion in this article.

30. Ibid., p. 26. "Sie hatte groß Leid um ihr Magdtum, denn sie war eine Witwe und weinte Tag und Nacht um ihre (verlorene) Jungfräulichkeit. Nach vielen Jahren erschien ein Engel und sagte, Gott wird dich erhören, soweit es möglich ist. Damit nahm er sie mit sich in die Luft, wo Engel mit einer Weinpresse waren. Darin preßten sie sie so sehr, daß sie glaubte, kein Tropfen Blutes bleibe in ihrem Leibe. Die Engel aber sagten zu ihr: Alles Blut, was in dir gestündigt hatte, haben wir aus dir gepresst. Dafür sollen dir Jungfrauen ihr Blut eingießen, und du sollst Jungfrauen gleich werden soweit du kannst, aber Jungfrau kannst du nicht mehr werden."

31. Ibid., pp. 26–27. ". . . daz daz plut unseres herren sich nicht als mynniklich und alz andechtiklich vereinet mit einem rewigen hertzen alz mit einer megde sel. Da von kom si in grossen jammer, wan sie in der werlt waz gewesen. Da tröst sie unser herr und sprach zu ir: 'Ich will dich mit meinem rosenvarben plut und alz lawter machen, alz du auz der tauff kömde, und will dich zieren und krönen mit mein selbes magtum.' "

32. T.W. Coleman, *English Mystics of the Fourteenth Century* (Westport, Conn.: Greenwood Press, 1971), p. 158.

33. Blank, *Nonnenviten*, p. 141. "Dieses mehr oder weniger äuß Sehen findet im Visionswesen seit dem 13. Jahrhundert weite Verbreitung. Wenn sich auch die späteren Mystiker meist ablehnend dagegen verhalten, hat doch keiner so scharfe Kritik daran geübt wie David von Augsburg, ein Zeichen dafür, daß schon vor der eigentlichen Blütezeit der Mystik das Visionswesen im Schwange war." Blank goes on to say that of the three most famous *fratres docti* of the fourteenth century, Meister Eckhart was the most outspoken critic of the feminine mystics' distortions, whereas Suso, predictably, seems to have encouraged them in their practices.

34. Wolfgang Stammler, "Studien zur Geschichte der Mystik in Nord-deutschland," in *Altdeutsche und altniederländische Mystik*, p. 428. "Manche der niederdeutschen Traktate waren in erster Linie bestimmt, die männlichen und weiblichen Novizen in die neue Gefühlsreligiosität einzuführen und sie zu ähnlicher Erlebnisfähigkeit anzuspornen. Da sind vor allem die Novizenanweisungen Davids von Augsburg zu nennen, die er lateinisch verfasste und die unter verschiedenen Titeln und Verfassernamen umliefen. Mitunter wird daraus eine Zusammenstellung unter dem Titel 'Spiegel der Mönche,' 'Spiegel der Novizen' oder 'Spiegel geistlicher Leute.' Auch je nach Orden wurden Davids Schriften, der selbst Franziskaner war, umgearbeitet."

35. Friedrich Wilhelm Wentzlaff-Eggebert, *Deutsche Mystik zwischen Mittelalter und Neuzeit*, 3rd ed. (Berlin: de Gruyter, 1960), p. 130. "Wenn die Anzeichen des beginnenden Verfalls auch zunächst noch eingeschränkt wurden durch die Abgeschlossenheit der Klöster, so muß sich die Wirkung vervielfältigen, sobald die Mystik zur Volksbewegung wurde und sich über die Klöster hinaus unter den Laien, ohne Kontrolle und Zucht der Meister ausbreitete."

36. K. Bihlmeyer, "Die Selbstbiographie in der deutschen Mystik des Mittelalters," *Theologische Quartalschrift* 114 (1953): 520. "Auch Laienkreise, Verwandte der Nonnen, Beichtkinder der Dominikanermystiker und Zuhörer ihrer

Predigten in den Klosterkirchen wurden in das gleiche Interesse hineingezogen und gaben sich dem Streben nach einem höheren geistlichen Leben hin. So wurde die Mystik, die bisher gewissermaßen mehr aristokratisch geartet und auf enge Kreise beschränkt gewesen war, popularisiert.

"Jene Dominikanernonnen schrieben nicht nur die Predigten ihrer Ordensbrüder nach und überlieferten sie so der Nachwelt, sie wurden selbst zur Schriftstellerei angeregt, zeichneten ihre religiösen Erfahrungen schlicht und unkritisch auf und verarbeiteten sie weiter in geistlichen Memoiren, Briefen, Traktaten, Legenden und Gedichten. Dadurch übten sie wiederum unter Gleichgesinnten in Kloster und Welt eine wirksame Propaganda für die mystischen Ideen aus" (pp. 520–21).

37. Wentzlaff-Eggebert, *Deutsche Mystik*, p. 75. "Bevor es zur Beteiligung der unvorbereiteten Menge an den Geiess-zetlerzügen kam, blieb es auch bei der Wirkung des mystischen Gedankengutes in den Konventikeln, Orden und Klöstern, das durch die Predigt nach außen drang. Äußere Wirren und Wunden der Zeit aber, wie der schwarze Tod zwingen auch das Volk in die Frömmigkeitsbewegung hinein,—die die so lange abseits geblieben waren, und die nun die Fanatiker der Geißlerbewegung von 1349 werden."

38. Blank, *Nonnenviten*, p. 248. "Das Wunder wird zur Dekoration der Persönlichkeit und dient zum Ausweis ihrer heiligen Lebensführung, und nur dazu. Die Verherrlichung Gottes im Wunder zeigt sich nur noch im Prisma des Subjekts gebrochen."

39. Sheila Delany, "Sexual Economics, Chaucer's Wife of Bath, and *the Book of Margery Kempe*," *Minnesota Review* 5 (1975): 110, 111.

40. Meech, *Book of Margery Kempe*, pp. 284, 306.

41. My dissertation, "The Influence of Dorothea von Montau on the Mysticism of Margery Kempe" provides a detailed study of the possible relationship between the two women.

42. Collis, *Apprentice Saint*, pp. 249–50.

Contributors

THOMAS J. HEFFERNAN is Associate Professor of English at the University of Tennessee. He has written widely on Middle English Literature and is currently completing a book on "Sacred Biography: Saints and their Biographers in the Middle Ages, Continuity and Change." He is the editor of *Studies in the Age of Chaucer*.

D.W. ROBERTSON, Jr., Professor of English Literature Emeritus of Princeton University, is the author of *A Preface to Chaucer, Chaucer's London, Abelard and Heloise,* and *Essays in Medieval Culture*. He is currently a Visiting Professor at Duke University.

LEONARD E. BOYLE, O.P. is the Prefect of the Vatican Library. He is the author of many articles in diplomatics and medieval philosophy.

JUDITH SHAW, Associate Professor of English at the University of Georgia, is the author of various essays on the subject of law and medieval literature. She is currently at work on a monograph on John Gower's Ovidian borrowings.

BRUCE A. ROSENBERG is Professor of English and Chairman of the American Civilization Program at Brown University. His books include *The Art of the American Folk Preacher* (winner of the 1970 James Russell Lowell Prize) and *Custer and the Epic of Defeat*. He is currently completing a book on "Folklore Methodology and Literary Criticism."

STANLEY J. KAHRL is a Professor of English at Ohio State University. Among his numerous publications in the area of medieval English is *Traditions of Medieval English Drama*.

EDMUND REISS has published extensively on medieval literature. His books include *Sir Thomas Malory, Elements of Literary Analysis, The*

Art of the Middle English Lyric, William Dunbar, Boethius, and, most recently, *Arthurian Legend and Literature: An Annotated Bibliography.*

DEREK BREWER is Master of Emmanuel College, Cambridge, and Professor of English in the University. He has written a number of books and articles mainly on English medieval literature.

JOHN V. FLEMING, the Fairchild Professor of English and Comparative Literature at Princeton, is the author of several books concerning medieval art and literature including *The Roman de la Rose: A Study in Allegory and Iconography, An Introduction to the Franciscan Literature of the Middle Ages, From Bonaventure to Bellini,* and *Reason and the Lover.*

GEORGE R. KEISER, Professor of English at Kansas State University, is the editor of *The Middle English Boke of Stones: The Southern Version* and is the author of numerous essays on Middle English literature.

ROBERT ADAMS is Associate Professor of English at Sam Houston State University. He has published articles on Chaucer and Langland and currently is editing a treatise from the thirteenth-century mendicancy controversy, the *Liber de Antichristo et eius ministris.*

JOHN H. FISHER is the Hodges Professor of English at the University of Tennessee, Knoxville. He is the author of numerous articles and books; his most recent book is *An Anthology of Chancery English.*

WILLIAM F. POLLARD, is Associate Professor of English at Belmont College, Nashville. He has written on *Sir Gawain and the Green Knight* and is completing a book-length study of "Theology and Apocalypse in Sir Gawain and the Green Knight" for *Salzburg Studies in English.* He is also editing from manuscript an anthology of late medieval English verse and prose prayers.

UTE STARGARDT is Assistant Professor at Alma College. Her scholarly interests focus on medieval female mystics, and several of her articles on that subject have been accepted for publication. She also reviews German language publications on medieval mysticism for *The Mystics Quarterly.*

Index

Aarne, A. *Types of the Folktale* 67, 68, 70, 71, 83n, 131–47 passim
Abelard, Peter 33, 34, 36
Abraham 227
Abraham and Isaac (Brome) 93, 94
Acts of Andrew 116
Acts of John 264
Acts of Paul and Thecla 116
Acts of Thomas 116
Adams, Robert 231n, 232n
Adelheid von Breisach 296
Adelheid von Trochau 295
Aers, David *Chaucer, Langland, and the Creative Imagination* 233n
Alberic of Monte Cassino 238
Alberigo, J. 37n
Albertanus of Brescia 11
Albertus Magnus 41n, 224; *Postilla super Isaiam* 236n
Alexander 110, 129n
King Alexander 109, 112
Alexander of Bremen 199
Alexiou, Margaret *Ritual Lament in Greek Tradition* 169, 172, 191n, 192n
Alfonso, Pedro *Disciplina Clericalis* 136
Alford, John 235n
Allen, Hope Emily 105n, 193n, 282, 308n; ed., *English Writings of Richard Rolle* 261–76 passim
Alliterative Morte Arthure 109, 113, 172
Alphabet of Tales 135
Amadace 112, 128n
Ambrose, St. 56
Amis and Amiloun 77, 109, 113, 115, 119, 120, 124, 126
Anciaux, P. *La Théologie du sacrement de pénitence au XIIe siècle* 37n
Ancrene Wisse 58n, 85

Andersson, T.M. 146n
Anna Maria, Sr. 308n
Anna von Munzingen *Schwesternbuch* 311n
Anne, St. 89, 179, 294
"Appeal to all Mothers" 188n
Apuleius *Golden Ass* 116, 125
Aquinas, St. Thomas 213, 234n; *De articulis fidei et ecclesiae sacramentis* 40n; *Summa theologiae* 36, 37n
Arabian Nights 134
Armstrong, C.A.J. 167, 168, 190n, 192n
Arnold of Villanova 199
Arnold, Thomas 60n
Arnould, E.J. 47, 273n; *Le Manuel des péchés* 43n, 59n
"Arte lacrimandi" 188n
Arthour and Merlin 112, 114, 119, 242
Arthur 86, 110, 112, 120–21, 134, 172
Artonne, A. 39n
Arundel, Thomas 13, 282
Aspin, Isabel, ed., *Anglo-Norman Political Songs* 23n
"Assumption of Our Lady" 188n
Assumption of Our Lady 171
Astesanus of Asti *Summa de casibus Astesana* 40n
Aston, Margaret *Thomas Arundel* 26n
Athelston 75, 77
Aubrey, John 157
Augustine, St. 159, 195, 197, 202, 203, 216, 223, 229n, 231n, 255, 257; *City of God* 197, 202, 229n; *De musica* 254, 272n; *Enarrationes in Psalmos* 206, 215, 272n; *Letters* 229n; *On Christian Doctrine* 326n; *Sermon 32* 271n
Augustine (Pseudo) *De vera et falsa poenitentia* 33, 36

Ault, W.O., ed., *Court Rolls of the Abbey of Ramsey and of the Honor of Clare* 24n, 25n
Awntyrs of Arthur 113, 120–21
Axton, Richard *European Drama of the Early Middle Ages* 27n, 86, 104n
Azo of Bologna 60

Bacon, Robert *Opus Tertium* 230n
Baildon, W.P. 25n, 29n
Baker, Donald C. 107n
Bakhtin, M. *Rabelais and His World* 143, 147n
Balbi, John *Catholicon* 40n
Baldwin, J.W. *Masters, Princes, and Merchants* 37n
Baldwin, Ralph *Unity of the "Canterbury Tales"* 151, 152
"Ballad of Hind Horn" 64
Barber, C.L. 88
Barbour, John *Bruce* 109
Barrow, Sarah P. *Medieval Society Romances* 128n
Basevorn, Robert 41n
Basil, St. 257
Bataillon, L.J. 39n
Bateson, Mary *Borough Customs* 26n; ed., *Records of the Borough of Leicester* 27n, 29n
Baugh, A.C. 129n, 240–41, 242–43, 250n
Beadle, Richard 107n
Bechlin, Elsbeth 295
Bede 211, 220, 221, 236n
Bedier, Joseph *Les Fabliaux* 137, 146n
Beichner, Fr. P. 68, 82n
Bellow, Saul 61
Bennett, J.A.W. 201; ed (with G.V. Smithers) *Early Middle English Verse and Prose* 146n; *Poetry of the Passion* 168, 183, 184, 191n, 193n; *Piers Plowman* 232n
Benson, L.D. ed. (with T.M. Andersson) *Literary Context of Chaucer's Fabliaux* 146n; ed. (with S. Wenzel) *Wisdom of Poetry* 193n
Beowulf 68
Bercovitch, Sacvan 130n
Bernard of Clairvaux, St. 168, 271n, 290, 291, 295, 296, 311n; *In cantica canticorum* 206
Bernard of Pavia 60n
Béroul *Tristan* 125
Bestul, T.H. 175, 192n
"Betrayed Maiden's Lament" 15

Bettenson, Henry 229n
Bettridge, William 68, 82n
Bevington, David *From Mankind to Marlowe* 87, 105n; ed., *Medieval Drama* 276n
Bevis of Hamptoun 73, 76, 77, 110, 111, 112, 115, 118, 119, 242
Bible 20, 21, 27n, 44, 116, 140, 162, 163, 170, 181, 182, 194–326 passim
Bignami-Odier, Jeanne *Etudes sur Jean de Roquetaillade* 229n
Bihlmeyes, K. 312n
Bird, Joanna, (et al.) ed., *Collectanea Londiniensia* 165n
Blanch, Robert, ed., *Style and Symbolism in "Piers Plowman"* 236n
Blank, Walter *Die Nonnenviten des 14. Jahrhunderts* 311n, 312n, 313n
"Blessed Virgin's Appeal to the Jews" 188n
"Blessed Virgin to her Son on the Cross" 188n
Block, K.S. 105, 107n, 190n
Bloomfield, Morton 186, 193n, 198, 199, 229n; *Essays and Explorations* 127n; ed., *Incipits* 39n, 40n, 41n, 43n; *"Piers Plowman" as a 14th Century Apocalypse* 194, 222, 229n, 230n, 234n, 235n, 236n
Blunt, John Henry 60n
Boccaccio 111, 137, 152, 240; *Decameron* 63, 81, 82n, 133, 136, 138, 139, 145
Boeckt, Carl 310n
Boehmer, H., ed., *Libelli de lite Imperatorum et Pontificum saec. XI et XII* 235n
Boitani, Piero 239; *English Medieval Narrative in the 13th and 14th Centuries* 250n
Bonaventure 199, 252–76, 280; *Itinerarium mentis in Deum* 253; *Meditations vitae Christi* 103; *De perfectione vitae ad sorores* 271n; *De triplici via* 252, 259; *Vitis mystica* 258, 259, 266, 270, 272n, 273n, 276n
Bonaventure (pseudo) *Meditationes* 175
Book of Vices and Virtues 43n, 57, 60n
Booth, John 24n
Bordman, Gerald *Motif-Index of English Metrical Romances* 126n
Bosch 102
Bousset, Wilhelm *Der Antichrist* 230n
Bowers, A. Joan 230n

Boyle, L.E. 40n, 59n; *Pastoral Care, Clerical Education and Canon Law* 39n, 59n; *Setting of the "Summa theologiae" of St. Thomas* 37n
Bracton, H. 60n
Bramley, H.R., ed., *Psalter or Psalms of David with Trans. by Rolle* 257–76 passim
Brandeis, Arthur 59n
Brent, Cecil 165n
Breughel 102
Brewer, Derek 129n, 130n, 146n, 147n; ed., *Chaucer and Chaucerians* 190n; *Chaucer and His World* 146n; ed., *Chaucer: The Critical Heritage* 146n; *Chaucer: The Poet as Storyteller* 147n; *Symbolic Stories* 141, 147n
Bridget, St. *Revelations* 175
Brinton, Bishop 15
Brody, Alan *English Mummers and Their Plays* 87, 105n
Bromyard, John *Opus trivium* 40n
Bronson, Bertram *In Search of Chaucer* 240, 250n
Broomfield, F. 58n
Brown, Beatrice D. 275n
Brown, Carleton 128n; ed., *English Lyrics of the 13th Century* 24n, 27n; (with R.H. Robbins) *Index of Middle English Verse* 188n–90n; ed., *Religious Lyrics of the 14th Century* 25n, 27n; ed., *Religious Lyrics of the 15th Century* 187n, 190n
Brown, Peter 229n
Brown, R.E. *Birth of the Messiah* 193n
Brunner, Karl 146n; ed., *Der mittelenglische Versroman uber Richard Löwenherz* 128n, 129n
Bruno of Segni 229n
Bühler, Curt F. 275n
Buonaiuti, E. 235n
Burgess, Glyn S., ed., *Court and Poet* 146n
Burial of Christ (Bodley) 106n
Burial of Christ (Digby) 171, 178, 190n
Burnham, John 277
Burnley, J.D. *Chaucer's Language and the Philosophers' Tradition* 177, 191n, 192n
Burrow, J.A. 236n
Butterworth, G.W. 272n
Buttimer, Charles 272n

Calendar of Inquisitions Post Mortem 28n
Capgrave, John xii
Caplan, Harry 191n

Carruthers, Mary 251n
Cartula 11
Carus-Wilson, E.M., ed., *Essays in Economic History* 23n
Cassidorus 261, 274n
Castle of Perseverance 87, 90, 91, 105n
"Cato" 11
Cavalca, Domenico *Disciplina degli spirituali:* 35
Cawelti, John G. 81n
Cawley, A.C. 107n; ed., *Everyman* 105n; ed., *Wakefield Pageants in the Townley Cycle* 92, 105n–106n
Caxton, William 113
Cervantes *Don Quixote* 113, 144
Chambers, E.K. 102; *Medieval stage* 105n
Chambers, Mr. 100
Chambers, Robert, ed., *Book of Days* 27n
Chapman, Hugh 165n
Charland, T.M., ed., *Artes praedicandi* 41n
Charlemagne 110, 112, 115, 129n
Chaucer, Geoffrey xi, xii, 8, 11, 15, 16, 21, 23, 26n, 37, 50, 58, 59n, 61, 64, 66, 79, 88, 94, 109, 110, 111, 112, 113, 128n, 137–40, 144, 148–66, 167, 168, 169, 175, 176, 184, 234n, 237–51; *Astrolabe* 244, 247, 249; *Boece* 244, 247, 249; *Book of Duchess* 242, 243; *Canon's Yeoman's Prologue* 245; *Canon's Yeoman's Tale* 79; *Canterbury Tales* 11, 16, 37, 57, 116, 125, 128n, 133, 139, 145, 146n, 148–66 passim, 190n, 191n, 193n, 243–47; *Clerk's Tale* 68, 167, 184, 185, 246; *Complaint of Venus* 139; "Envoy to Bukton" 247; *Equatorie* 249; *Franklin's Tale* 80–81; *Friar's Tale* 139; *General Prologue* 16, 153, 161, 163, 244–45, 247; *House of Fame* 242, 243, 244; *Knight's Tale* 111, 125, 158, 161, 191n; *Legend of Good Women* 111, 243, 244; *Legend of Good Women Prologue* 243; *Man of Law's Tale* 71, 73, 75, 111, 167, 184, 185, 186, 190n, 192n, 193n, 245–46; *Melibee's Tale* 243, 244, 247, 249; *Merchant's Tale* 139, 144; *Miller's Headlink* 243; *Miller's Tale* 68, 74, 82n, 125, 139, 161; *Nun's Priest's Tale* 139, 157; *Pardoner's Prologue* 55, 161; *Pardoner's Tale* 234n, 245; *Parliament of Fowls* 242, 243; *Parson's Tale* 26n, 37, 50, 54, 55–56, 59n, 158, 159, 243, 244,

Chaucer *(cont.)*
247; *Physician's Tale* 167, 184, 185;
Prioress's Tale 167, 179, 185–87, 191n,
192n, 193n; *Reeve's Headlink* 245;
Reeve's Tale 139, 161; *Retraction* 243;
Second Nun's Prologue 243; *Shipman's
Tale* 139; *Squire's Tale* 111, 244;
Summoner's Tale 139; *Sir Thopas*
111–12, 114, 122, 128n, 242; *Troilus
and Criseyde* 26n, 125, 128n, 151,
239, 240–41, 244, 247, 250n, 251n;
Wife of Bath's Prologue 16, 144, 145,
246, 247; *Wife of Bath's Tale* 111, 244
Cheney, C.R. 37n, 38n, 39n, 40n, 59n;
English Synodalia of the 13th Century
38n, 59n, 60n
Chester Cycle 104n, 106n, 190n
Chestre, Thomas *Sir Launfal* 69
Chevalere Assigne 77
Child, Francis J. 64; ed., *English and
Scottish Popular Ballads* 82n
Chobham, Thomas *Summa confessorum*
58n
Chrétien de Troyes 108, 109; *Erec et
Enide* 117; *Lancelot* 117, 125; *Yvain*
69, 75, 117, 242
Christ 44, 51, 52, 54, 102, 103, 114,
116, 141, 167–93 passim, 195–236
passim, 252–76 passim, 279–313
passim
Christine de Pisan *Epistre d'Othea* 268,
275n
Chrysostom, John 254; *Expositio in
Psalmum XLI* 272n
Cicely of York 167, 190n, 192n
Cicero (pseudo) *Rhetorica ad Herennium*
170, 238
City Governments in Winchester 26n
Clanchy, M.T. 3, 10, 21; *From Memory to
Written Record in England* 23n, 25n,
28n
Clareno, Angelo 199
Clark, Elaine 24n
Clark, John 165n
Cleanness (Purity) 116
Sir Cleges 109, 132, 146n
Clement V 290
Clement of Alexandria 254; *Exhortation
to the Greeks* 271n; *Recognitions* 116
Cloud of Unknowing xii, 280
Cobsam, Adam *The Wright's Chaste Wife*
134
Cohen, Jeremy *Friars and the Jews* 192n
Cokwold's Dance 134
Coldewey, John 107n

Coleman, T.W. *English Mystics of the 14th
Century* 298, 312n
Colet, John 149, 164
Colledge, Eric 278, 308n
Collette, C.P. 191n
Collis, Louise *Apprentice Saint* 280,
307–308, 308n, 313n
"Complaint of Our Lady" 190n
Conciliorum oecumenicorum decreta 37
Constance, St. 298, 306–307
Constantine 234n, 235n
Copland, William 113, 134
Corbett, J.A. 42n
Cords, R. 188n
Corpus iuris canonici 58n, 60n
Cotton, Sir Robert Bruce 92
Courson, Robert 33, 37n
Court Rolls of the Borough of Colchester 18
Court Rolls of the Manor of Carshalton 25n
Courtney, Francis 58n
Coventry Plays 99
Cowper, J.M. 189n
Cox, A.C. 272n
Cox, Edward G. 83n
Coy, J., ed. (with J. de Hoz) *Estudios
sobre Los Generos Literarios* 146n
Craig, Hardin 102; *English Religious
Drama of the Middle Ages* 106n; ed.,
Two Coventry Corpus Christi Plays 99
Crane, R.S. *Vogue of Medieval Chivalric
Romance* 128n
Crawford, William *Bibliography of
Chaucer 1954–63* 238, 250n
"Crescentia" 82n
Cristina, St. 285, 286, 287, 288, 289
Crow, Elizabeth 98
Crow, M.M., ed. (with C.C. Olson)
Chaucer Life Records 249n
Crow, Robert 97–99, 101, 106n
Cunningham, I.C. 146n
Cursor Mundi xii, 112, 128n, 137, 179,
188n, 189n
Cutler, J.L. 187n–90n

Dale, M.K. *Court Rolls of Chalgrave
Manor* 28n
Dame Sirith 131, 146n
Daniel, E.R. *Franciscan Concept of Mission*
231n
Dante 163, 239, 240, 249, 289; *Paradiso*
259
da Todi, Jacopone *Laude* 268, 275n
David 117, 210, 211, 212, 216, 218,
219, 224, 228, 234n, 235n, 236n,
254, 255, 256, 257, 258, 261, 266,

David (cont.)
268, 270
David von Augsburg Mirrors 300, 301,
312n
Davidson, Clifford 176, 192n
Davis, J.F. 153, 165n
Davis, Norman 93, 97, 104n, 106n,
129n, 274n
Deanesley, Margaret 252, 271n
de Beauchamp, Guy 21
de Besançon, Etienne Alphabetum
narrationum 135
de Bilby, John 19
de Bolon, Godefridi 21
de Breton, Richard 155
de Burgh, Elizabeth 27n
de Burgh, John Pupilla oculi 39n
de Cantilupe, Walter 48
de Cessolis, Jacobus De ludis saccorum
42n
de Clarevall, Dan Philip 309n
de Cobeley, Richard 19
Sir Degaré 69–72, 73, 74, 76, 83n, 113,
119
Sir Degrevant 77
de Hoz, J. 146n
de Insulis, Alanus Liber parabolum 11
de la Halle, Adam Le Jeu de la Feuillé
27n
Delany, Sheila 251n, 304, 313n
Delargy, J.H. 147n
de Loring, Sir Nigel 20, 28n
de Lubac, Henri 231n Exégèse médievale
230n, 235n
de Mampton, Roger 19
de Meun, Jean 15, 152, 240, 249, 269,
276n
de Monte Rocherii, Guido Manipulus
curatorum 39n
Dentone, William 18
Denyas, Sir Robert 100
de Spordon, John 19
Destruction of Troy 109, 112, 114, 129n
de Thoresby, John 42n, 43n, 49; Lay
Folks' Catechism 52, 55, 59n, 60n
D'Evelyn C. 193n, 275n
de Vinck, José 273n
de Vitry, Jaques Vita b. Mariae
Oigniacensis 280, 284, 285, 295
de Vocht, Henry, ed., Earliest English
Translations of Erasmus' Colloquia 165n,
166n
de Worde, Wynkyn 113, 133, 134, 181,
278
"Dialogue between Our Lady and Jesus

on the Cross" 188n
"Dialogue of the Virgin and Child" 188n
Dickens, Charles 241
Dietterle, J. 40n
Digby Plays 106n
Dighton, Mr. 100–101
Disney, Walt 67, 82n
"Disputation between Mary and the
Cross" (Vernon) 173, 177, 178, 188n
Dives et Pauper 43n
Donaldson, D. 129n
Donaldson, E.T. 210, 229n, 233n, 236n
Donckel, E. 231n
Dondaine, A. 37n
Doomsday 98
Dorothea von Montau (von Preussen)
307, 313n
Dorson, Richard 79, 80, 82n
Douglas, Mary 143, 147n
Doyle, A.I. 188n, 193n, 247, 251n
Dream of the Rood 264
Drennan, J.F. 190n
Du Boulay, F.R.H. Age of Ambition 24n
Dugdale, William 21; Monasticon
Anglicanum 29n
Dunbar, William Twa Maritt Wemen and
the Wedo 27n
Dunn, Charles W. 64
Dunn, E.C. 129n
Duranti, William (the Elder); Aureum
confessorium et memoriale sacerdotum
40n; Rationale divinorum officiorum
42n; Speculum iudiciale 40n

Earl of Toulouse 113
Ebner, Christine 310n
Eccles, Mark 104n, 105n
Eckhart, Meister 291, 292, 294, 309n,
311n, 312n
Edward III 5, 12, 14, 22, 24n, 234n
Edward, the Black Prince 20
Eger and Grime 242
Sir Eglamour 73, 75, 76, 77, 112, 113,
115, 119, 122, 123–24, 130n
Elder, E.R., ed., Spirituality of Western
Christendom 192n
Elizabeth I 89
Elizabeth of Spalbeck 285, 286
Elkerlijc 104–105n
Emaré 72, 73, 75
Emmerson, Richard Antichrist in the
Middle Ages 205, 232n, 233n
England, George 106n, 190n, 274
Erasmus 15, 148–66; Colloquia 149,
165n, 166n; Peregrinatio religionis ergo

Erasmus *(cont.)*
  149, 163–64
Erbe, T. 193n
Die Erlösung 268, 275n
Esch, A., ed., *Chaucer and seine Zeit*
  250n
"Eustace-Constance Group" 116, 122
Everett, Dorothy *Essays on Middle English
  Literature* 127n, 128n
Everyman 87, 104–105n
Exeter Book 65

Facetis 11
"False Fox" 15
Fanna, F. 271n
Ferri, Giovanni 275n
Ferumbras 129n
Fielding, Henry 239, 241
"Filius regis mortuus est" 171, 189n
Finberg, H.P.R. 11; *Tavistock Abbey* 25n;
  Gloucestershire Studies 26n
Finlayson, John 127n, 128n, 129n
Finnegan, Ruth *Oral Poetry* 82n
Fisher, Jane 239, 250n
Fisher, John H. 250n; *John Gower;* ed.
  (with Jane Fisher and Malcolm
  Richardson) *Anthology of Chancery
  English* 239, 250n; ed., *Complete Poetry
  and Prose of Geoffrey Chaucer* 80, 82n,
  250n
Fitzralph, Richard 199–200
Fleming, John V. 165n; *Introduction to
  the Franciscan Literature of the Middle
  Ages* 24n; *"The Roman de la Rose"*
  276n
Fletcher, Reginald J. *Pension Book of
  Gray's Inn* 249n
Floris and Blancheflur 113, 119, 126
Fluck, R. 42n
Folklore, Types: "Bear's Son" 68;
  "Cinderella" 67, 141; "Flood" 68, 74;
  "Forgotten Fiancée" 75; "Girl as
  Helper in the Hero's Plight" 69;
  "Griselda" 68, 82n; "King Discovers
  His Unknown Son" 71, 74; "Maiden
  without Hands" 71, 74; "Man On A
  Quest For His Lost Wife" 75;
  "Matron of Ephesus" 142; "Misplaced
  Kiss" 74; "Oedipus" 70, 74; "Patience
  of a Sultaness" 68; "Prince Finds
  Heroine in Woods" 70; "Rip van
  Winkle" 80; "Snow White" 67;
  "Sohrab and Rustum" 73; "Stupid
  Ogre" 141; "Three Hunchbacks" 142
"Follies of Fashion" 16

Forebille, Raymonde *Le Jubilé de Saint
  Thomas Becket* 165n
Fowler, Kenneth, ed., *Hundred Years
  War* 27n
Fox and the Wolf 131, 146n
Francis, St. 231n, 259
Francis, W. Nelson 43n, 60n
Frank, H.L. 192n
Frank, Robert W. 193n; *Chaucer and the
  Legend of Good Women* 193n; *"Piers
  Plowman" and the Scheme of Salvation*
  229n
Fredoli, Berengarius *Le Liber de
  excommunicatione* 40–41n
French, W.H., ed. (with C. B. Hale)
  Middle English Metrical Romances 129n
Frere, W.H. 165n
Frere and the Boye 133, 134
Fretté, S.E. 234m
Freud, Sigmund *Jokes and Their Relation
  to the Unconscious* 143, 147n
Friedberg, Aemilius 58n
Froissart, Jean *Chronicles* xii, 21
Frye Northrop *Anatomy of Criticism*
  127n, 129n, 130n, 174–75, 176,
  192n, 239; *Secular Scripture* 114, 116,
  128n, 129n
Furber, E.C., ed., *Essex Sessions of Peace*
  28n
Furley, J.S. 12; *City Government in
  Winchester* 27n
Furnivall, F.J. 43n, 58n, 189n, 190n,
  275n; ed., *Political, Religious, and Love
  Poems* 188n

Galloway, David, ed. (with John
  Wasson) *Collections XI* 104n, 105n
Gamelyn 75, 77, 110, 113, 119, 125,
  128n, 129
Gardner, John 239
Garrett, R.M. 188n
Gawain and the Carl of Carlisle 76, 77,
  114
Sir Gawain and the Green Knight 76, 77,
  78, 86, 104, 113, 114, 116, 117,
  122–24, 125, 128n, 129n, 130n, 247,
  274n
Gawain-poet ("*Pearl*-poet") 109, 110,
  116, 123, 249
Gaylord, A.T. 165
Generides 112, 113, 114, 119, 120, 121,
  122
Geoffrey of Vinsauf 170; *Poetria Nova*
  191n
Georgianna, Linda *Solitary Self* 58n

Gerard of Borgo San Donnino 199
Gerhoch of Reichersberg *De quarta vigilia noctis* 235n
Gesta Pilati 179
Gesta Romanorum 132, 146n
Gibbs, Marion 47; (with Jane Lang) *Bishops and Reform* 58n, 59n
Gibson, Gail McMurray 28n, 105n, 107n
Gilbert of Tournai *De modo addiscendi* 42n; *Rudimentum doctrinae* 42n
Gill, Chris 65, 82n
Glossa ordinaria 212, 220
Godfrey of Bouillon 110
Golden Fleece 98, 101
Gollancz, I. 188n
Gordon, E.V. 104n, 129n, 274n
Gospel of Nicodemus 190n
Gottfried von Strassburg 109
Gower, John 94; *Confessio Amantis* 57, 247
Gradon, Pamela *Form and Style in Early English Literature* 127n
Graelent 68
Gray, Douglas *Themes and Images in the Medieval English Religious Lyric* 168, 191n, 274n, 275n
Great Revolt of 1381 5
Green, D.H. *Irony in Medieval Romance* 128n, 130n
Greene, R.L., ed., *Early English Carols* 188n, 189n, 190n
Gregory I ("the Great") *Moralia in Job* 206
Gregory IX 46
Grosseteste, Robert 59, 267; *Templum domini* 39n; *De modo confitendi* 40n; *De decem mandatis* 41n; *Stans puer ad mensam* 11
Grundmann, Herbert 309n, 310n
Guido de Terrena 220
Guillaume d'Angleterre 73
Guy of Warwick 76, 110, 111, 112, 113, 114, 115, 118, 119, 120, 128n, 129n
Guyot, B.G. 39n, 40n, 41n, 43n

Hadas, Moses 129n
Hadewijch 291, 310n
De haeretico comburendo 153
Hale, C.B. 129n
Hall, Hubert *Antiquities and Curiosities of the Exchequer* 25n
Hall, Joseph 129n
Halmota Prioratus Dunelmensis 24n, 25n
Hanna, Ralph 130n

Harriss, G.L. *King, Parliament, and Public Finance in Medieval England* 23n
Hart, G.W. 165n
Hartzheim, J., ed., *Concilia Germaniae* 40n
Harvey, Barbara F. *Westminster Abbey and Its Estates in the Middle Ages* 24n
Harvey, P.D.A. 10
Harvey, Ralph 271n
Havelok the Dane 17, 76, 77, 110, 112, 119
Hay, Charles E. 232n
"Haymo of Halberstadt" 234n
Hazlitt, W.C. *Early Popular Poetry* 133, 146n
Hefele, C.J. (with H. Leclercq) *Histoire des conciles* 58n
Hegge, Richard 92
Heinrich von Halle 310n
Heinrich von Nordlingen 310n
Heliodorus *Ethiopica* 116
Hemneon, M. de W. 26n; *Burgage Tenure in Medieval England* 26n
Hennecke, Edgar 193n
Henry II 14
Henry III 14
Henry V 239, 248
Henry VII 89
Henry VIII 89, 101, 149, 150, 153
Henry of Langenstein 220–21
Herbert, George 276n; "Easter" 270
Hervé of Bourgdieu 217–18, 224–25; *Commentaria in Isaiam* 236n
Hesychias 229n
Heynes, Nicholas 98
Hibbard, G.R. 106n
Hildegard von Bingen 291
Hill, D.M. 127n
Hill, Thomas 228, 236n
Hilton, R.H., ed., *Stoneleigh Leger Book* 24n, 29n
Hilton, Walter 184, 265, 266, 280; *Scale of Perfection* 267, 275n, 304
Hirsh, John C. 186, 191n, 193n
Hirsh-Reich, Beatrice 230n, 232n, 234n
Hoccleve, Thomas 247; "Compleynte of the Virgin" 173, 188n; *Regement of Princes* 188n
Hodgson, P. 43n
Hodkinson, Terence *English Medieval Alabasters* 107n
Hofmann, Gustav 165n
Holbiche, Thomas 91
Holcot, Robert *Wisdom Commentary* 22
Holmstedt, Gustaf 43n, 60n

Holzapfel, Otto, (et al.) ed., *European Medieval Ballad* 83n
Homer 241
Hoops, Reinald 127n
Hopkins, A. *Select Rolls of Chester City Courts* 28n
Hopkins, Gerard Manley 260, 273n
Ho Presbys Hippotes (The Old Knight) 112
Horn et Rimenild 64
Hornstein, Lillian 108, 126n
Horstmann, Carl 179, 190n, 192n, 252, 308n, 309n; ed., *Yorkshire Writers* 189n, 270n
"How a Merchande dyd hys Wyfe Betray" 132, 146n
How the Plouman lerned his Paternoster 134
Howard, D.R. 39n
Hudson, William 27n
Hugh of Bologna *Rationes dictandi prosice* 238
Hugh of St. Cher 216, 235n, 236n; *Opera omnia in universum Vetus et Novum Testamentum* 229n; *Speculum ecclesiae* 41n
Hugh of St. Victor 222; *Disdiscalicon* 272n; *Exegetica de scripturis* 268, 275n
Hugh of Strasbourg *Compendium theologicae veritatis* 41n
Huizinga, Johan 167
Humbert de Romans 309n
Hume, Kathryn 126n, 127n, 129n
Hundred Mery Tales 135
Huon de Meri 227
Huon of Burdeux 77
Huppé, B.F. 233n
Hurst, J.G. 24n
Hussey, S.S. 275n; ed., *"Piers Plowman": Critical Approaches* 232n
Hutton, Thomas 19

Ingram, R.W. 98, 106n–107n; ed., *Coventry* 105n, 106n–107n
Innocent III 30, 31, 35, 44, 54, 58
Interludium de clerico et puella 86, 131, 146n

Ipomedon 112, 113, 114, 120, 122
Isabella (concubine of Thomas of Pipe) 22
Isidore of Seville 234n, 257; *Etymologiarum sive originum* 272n, 275n
Sir Isumbras 73, 76, 110, 112, 113, 115, 117, 118, 119, 120, 122, 124, 129n

Iswolsky, Helene 147n
Ives, Burl 27n

Jackson, K.H. 138 *International Popular Tale and Early Welsh Tradition* 146n, 147n
Jackson, Kenneth 145
Jacob, E.F. 229n
Jacobs, Nicolas 128n, 129n
Jacob's Well 50, 57, 59n, 60n
Jambeck, T.J. 176, 177, 191n, 192n
James, Margery K. 27n
James, M.R. 274n
Jeayes, I.H., ed., *Court Rolls of the Borough of Colchester* 28n
Jeffrey, D.L. *Early English Lyric and Franciscan Spirituality* 24n, 27n
Jelier, I. 27n
Jerome, St. 116, 213, 220, 221, 230n
Joachim of Fiore 195, 198, 199, 200, 201, 202, 203, 204, 205, 218, 220, 221, 230n, 231n, 233n; *Concordia Novi ac Veteris Testamenti* 230n, 234n, 235n; *Expositio in Apocalypsim* 229n, 232n; *De prophetia ignota* 231n; *Tractatus super quatuor Evangelia* 219, 235n Joachim (Pseudo)- *Super Isaiam Prophetam* 234n
Johannes von Marienwerder *Des Leben der zeligen frawen Dorothee* 307
John (natural son of Thomas of Pipe) 22
John of Bridlington 218, 219
John of Freiburg *Summa confessorum* 40n, 41n
John of Garland, 238, 250n; *Parisiana Poetria* 191n
John of Gaunt 13
John of Rupescissa 198, 199, 222; *Liber secretorum eventum* 229n
John, St. 53
Johnston, Alexandra F. 24n
John the Lateran, St. 297
Joliffe, P.S. *Check-list of Middle English Prose Writing of Spiritual Guidance* 25n, 43n
"Jolly Jankyn" 15
Jones, Douglas *Church in Chester 1300–1540* 28n
Jordan, Robert M. 239, 240n, 250n; *Chaucer and the Shape of Creation* 232n
Joseph, St. 294
Joyce, James 163; *Ulysses* 113
"Judas" 64

Julian of Norwich xii, 265, 280, 291;
    Revelations 265, 275n, 279, 308n

Kabealo, T.B. 39n
Kaeppeli, T. ed., *Scriptores ordinis
    praedicatorum medii aevi* 40n
Kahrl, S.J. 106n, 146n; ed., *Collections
    VIII* 105n, 107n; *Traditions of
    Medieval English Drama* 104n
Kalevala 66
Kamlah, Wilhelm *Apokalypse und
    Geshichtstheologie* 229n
Kane, George 229n, 233n; *Middle
    English Literature* 127n, 129n
Kaske, Robert E. 166n, 229n, 234n
Kastan, D.S. 165
Katharina von Gebweiler 311n
"Katherine Group" xii
Kean, P.M. 232n, 236n; *Chaucer and the
    Making of English Poetry* 185, 193n
Kellogg, Robert 239
Kempe, John 277, 280, 281, 303
Kempe, Margery xii, 90, 184, 265,
    277–313; *Book of Margery Kempe*
    105n, 187, 193n, 251n, 277–313
Kempe, Thomas 278, 294
Kennedy, Arthur C. 244
Kennedy, V.L. 37n
Ker, N.R. 251n; *Medieval Mss. in British
    Libraries* 193n
Kerrison, Sir Edward 93
Kimball, Elizabeth G. ed., *Rolls of the
    Gloucestershire Sessions of Peace* 28n;
    Some Sessions of Peace in Lincolnshire
    25n
King and the Barker 134
King Horn 64, 76, 77, 110, 111, 112,
    113, 114, 115, 118, 119, 129n, 188n
King of Tars 113, 115, 120
King Robert of Sicily 109, 113, 115, 117,
    120, 124
Kingsford, C.L. 28n
Kirkby, Margaret *Form of Living* 261
Kittredge, George L. 73, 82n, 151; ed.
    (with Helen Sargent) *English and
    Scottish Popular Ballads* 82n, 83n
"Klage der Mutter Jesu" 188n
Knapp, Daniel 165n
Knowles, David *English Mystical
    Tradition* 279–80, 304, 308n
Kohlschmidt, Werner, ed. (with
    Wolfgang Mohr) *Reallexikon der
    deutschen Literaturgeschichte* 310n
Kölbing, E. 146n
Kolve, V.A. 103

Köster, Kurt 165n
Kristensson, G., ed., *John Mirk's
    Instructions for Parish Priests*
Krohn, Kaarle *Folkloristische
    Arbeitsmethode* 82n, 83n
Kuttner, S. 40n

Laing, David *Early Popular Poetry of
    Scotland and the Northern Border* 133
"Lamentacio dolorosa" 188n
"Lamentacioun of Oure Lady" 179–84,
    190, 193n
Lang, Albert, (et al.) ed., *Aus der
    Geistewelt des Mittelalters* 310n
Lang, Jane 47, 58n, 59n
Langland, William 94, 101 *Piers
    Plowman* xii, 22, 37, 137–38,
    194–236, 247, 249
Langton, Stephen 41n
Lateran Council (First) 31
Lateran Council (Third) 33
Lateran Council (Fourth) 30–43, 44, 45,
    46, 47
Laud Troy-Book 112, 122, 128n
Sir Launfal 68, 69, 76, 78, 114, 119,
    120
Laurent of Orléans *Somme le roi* 35
Lavagnini, Bruno *Le origini de romanzo
    greco* 130n
Lawlor, Traugott 191n
Lawrence, D.H. 79
Lawrence of Arabia (film)
Lay Folks' Mass Book 51, 60n, 103
Leach, A.F., ed., *Beverley Town
    Documents* 26n
Leclercq, H. 58n
Lecoy, Félix 276n
Legge, M. Dominica *Anglo-Norman
    Literature* 128n
Lerner, Robert 220, 230n, 235n
Levett, Ada E. 10
Libeaus Desconus 111, 113, 115, 119,
    120, 129n
Liber figurarum 202, 230n, 231n, 234n,
    235n
Lillywhite, Bryant *London Signs* 156,
    157, 165n
Lindsay, W.M. 272n, 275n
Lionel, Duke of Clarence 27n
Little, A.G. *Franciscan Papers, Lists, and
    Documents* 276n; *Liber exemplorum* 42n
Lobel, M.D. *Borough of Bury St. Edmunds*
    28n
Lombard, Peter *Sentences* 253
Longstaffe, W.H.D., ed. (with John

Longstaffe *(cont.)*
  Booth) *Halmota Prioratus Dunelmensis*
  24n
Longus *Daphnis and Chloe* 125
Lönnrot, Elias 66
Loomis, L.H. 72, 128n, 129n
Loomis, Roger S. 65, 83n
Love, Nicholas 103
Lowes, John L. 151
Lucan 241
Ludolf of Saxony 184
Ludus Coventriae 105n, 107n, 190n;
  Trial of Mary 16
Luers, Grete *Die Sprache der deutschen*
  Mystik des Mittelalters 274n
Lumby, J.R. 129n
Lumiansky, R.M. 104n, 190n *Of Sondry*
  Folk 250–51n
Lydgate, John 28n; *Guy of Warwick* 116;
  "Quis dabit meo" 189n; *Siege of Thebes*
  116; *Troy-Book* 116
Lyfe of S. Cristyne 285, 289n, 309n
Lyfe of S. Elizabeth of Spalbeck 285, 309n
"Lyfe of S. Marye" 281, 282, 283, 284,
  288, 289, 292, 293, 295, 308n

MacCracken, H.N. 189n
McDonnell, Ernest W. *Beguines and*
  Beghards in Medieval Culture 290,
  309n
McGinn, Bernard *Visions of the End* 233n
McKinnon, Sarah M. 24n
McKnight, G.H. 129n, 188n; ed., *Middle*
  English Humorous Tales in Verse 132,
  143, 145n, 146n, 147n
McNeill, J.T. *History of the Cure of Souls*
  58n
Macro Plays 87, 104n, 105n
Madicott, J.R. *English Peasantry and the*
  Demands of the Crown 23n
Madigan, M.F. Sr., 183; *Passion Domini*
  Theme in Works of Rolle 192n, 193n
Maitland, F.W. 60n; ed. (with W.P.
  Baildon) *Court Baron* 25n, 29n
Mâle, Emile *Gothic Image* 193n
Malory, Thomas 108, 116, 128n
Manegold of Lautenbach 236n
"Man in the Moon" 10
Mankind 87, 90, 104, 105n
Manly, John M. 151
Mannyng, Robert 9; *Handlyng Synne* 35,
  43n, 45, 53, 55, 56, 57, 58n, 59n,
  137, 267, 275n
Manorial Records of Cuxham 25n
Maré, P. 234n

Margaret of Anjou 89
Margaret, St. 90
Margarete of Villambroc 288
Mari, Giovanni 250n
Marie de France 16; *Lais* 68, 109, 116,
  125
Markus, R.A., ed., *Augustine* 229n
Marlowe, Christopher 87, 105n
Mary 13, 52, 93, 101, 102, 103, 149,
  150, 155, 160, 167–93, 202, 266,
  279, 291, 292, 293, 294, 295, 304,
  311n
Mary Magdalen 93, 182, 202
"St. Mary's Lamentation to St. Bernard"
  189n
Mary of Oigny, St. 280, 282, 285, 288,
  289, 292, 295, 306
Mary of Walsingham, St. 165n
Mary Tudor 89
Mason, John *Letters* 28n
Massingberd, W.O. trans., *Court Rolls of*
  the Manor of Ingoldmells 25n
Matami, A. 42n
Maurer, Friedrich 275n
Mauricius Hibernicus 39n
Maurus, Rabanus 162, 211, 212
Mechthild of Hackeborn *Liber speciales*
  gratiae 264
Mechthild von Hundersingen 296
Mechthild von Magdeburg 266, 275n,
  291, 295, 310n; *Das fließende Licht der*
  Gottheit 310n
MED 54, 85, 233n
Meditations on the Life and Passion of
  Christ 109, 266, 267, 270, 275n
Meditations on the Supper of Our Lord
  171, 189n
Meech, Sanford Brown 105n, 193n, 278,
  306, 308n, 313n
Meersseman, G.G. *Ordo fraternitatis* 42n
Megarry, R.E. *Inns, Ancient and Modern*
  249n
Mehl, Dieter 239, 240, 241, 244, 246,
  250n, 251n; *The Middle English*
  Romances of the 13th and 14th Centuries
  127n, 128n, 129n
Mehl, J.M. 42n
Meinhold, Peter 311n
Melton, Sir Robert 94
Melton, William 276n
Melville, Herman *Moby Dick* 113
Meredith, Peter 106n
Merrifield, Ralph 165n
Merry Ieste of a Shrewde and curst Wyfe
  lapped in Morrelles skin 134

Michael of Northgate *Ayenbite of Inwit* 35, 43n
Michand-Quantin, P. *Sommes de casuistique et manuels de confession au moyen âge* 37n, 40n
"Midsummer Day's Dance" 17, 19
Mill, A.J. 193n
Miller, J. Hillis *Disappearance of God* 273n
Mills, David 104n, 190n
Mills, Maldwyn 127n, 129n
Milton, John *Paradise Lost* 228
Minnis, A.J. 192n
Mirk, John *Instructions for Parish Priests* 39n, 49, 50, 52, 54, 57, 59n, 60n
Mirk's Festival 179, 193n
Miroir du monde 35
Mirror of Lewed Man 109
Misyn, Richard 259, 260, 271n
Mitchell, J. 288n
Mohr, Wolfgang 310n
Morel, P. Gall 275n
Morris, R. 43n, 128n, 188n, 189n
Mortimer, R.C. *Origins of Private Penance* 58n
Moses 162, 163, 212, 224, 226, 227
Murphy, James J. *Rhetoric in the Middle Ages* 238, 250n
Murray, A. *Reason and Society in the Middle Ages* 146n
Muscatine, Charles 137, 146n, 190n, 239 *Chaucer and the French Tradition* 130n, 184n, 193n
"Mylner that stale the nuttes of the tayler that stale a sheep"
Myroure of Oure Ladye 52, 60n

N-Town Cycle 28n, 90, 91, 106n, 107n; *Trial of Joseph and Mary* 102; *Passion* 102
Nabokov, Vladimir 5, 83n
Nelson, A.H. 105n; *Medieval English Stage* 26n
New Riddle Book or a Whetstone for Dull Wits 136
Newstead, Helene 128n, 129n, 130n
Newton, K.C. *Manor of Writtle* 24n; *Thaxted in the 14th Century* 26n
Nicholas, Master 18
Nicholas of Lyra 210, 213; *Postilla super totam Bibliam* 233n, 234n
Nichols, John G. *Pilgrimages* 165n
Nims, M.F. 191n
Nolloth, R.E. 42n
Northern Passion 103

Nykrog, P. *Les Fabliaux* 130n, 137, 146n, 239, 250n

Oakden, J.P. *Alliterative Poetry* 127n
Obermann, Heiko 168, 191
O'Connor, M.C. *Art of Dying Well* 42n
Octavian 73, 112, 113, 114, 115, 119, 125
OED 85, 157
Offord, N.Y. 128n
"Of Our Lady and Her Son" 189n
"Of the Passion" 189n
Olivi, Peter John 195, 199
Olson, C.C. 249n
Omnis utriusque sexus 31, 32, 34, 35, 36, 37, 45
Ong, Walter 238–39, 240, 241, 244
Sir Orfeo 73, 77, 83n, 113, 119, 120, 122
Orme, Nicholas *English Schools in the Middle Ages* 25n, 99, 101, 107n
Ormulum ix–xi
"O Thou, with Heart of Stone" 189n
Otinel 129n
"Our Lady's Imprecation" 189n
"Our Sir John" 15
Ovid 241
Owen, Charles *Pilgrimage and Story-Telling* 244, 250n
Owen, D.M. *Church and Society in Medieval Lincolnshire* 27n

Page, Barbara 251n
Page, Frances M. *Estates of Crowland Abbey* 25n
Palmer, George Herbert 276n
Pantin, W.A. 28n
Panton, G.A. 129n
Panzer, F.W. *Studien zur germanische Sagengeschichte* 68, 83n
Parkes, Malcolm B. 247; ed. (with A.G. Wilson) *Essays Presented to N.R. Ker* 251n
Parliament of the Three Ages 112, 128n
Parsons, Wilifred Sr., 229n
Partonope 76, 112, 113, 114, 119, 120, 121
Paschini, P. 231n
Passavanti, Jacopo *Specchio della penitenza* 35
Pater, Walter 143
Patience 116
Paul, St. 160
Payen, J.C. 37n, 47; *Motif du repentir* 59n

Payne, Robert O. 185; *Key of Remembrance* 192n, 193n
Peacock, Edward 59n
Pearl 116
Pearsall, Derek 26n, 108, 126n, 127n, 146n, 232n
Peckham, John 38n, 42n, 48, 49, 51, 56, 59n
Peckam, W.D. 24n, 28n
"Peniworth of Witte" 132, 146n
Pepwell, Henry 278
Perry, Ben E. *Ancient Romances* 129n, 130n
Peter of Peckham *Lumière as lais* 35
Peter, St. 141–42, 156
Peter the Chanter 33, 37n
Petrarch 240, 249
Petronius *Satyricon* 125
Peyraut, Guillaume ("Peraldus") 37n; *Summa de vitiis et virtutibus* 35, 36, 41n
Pfander, H.G. 43n, 59n
Phillip III (of France) 35
Platt, Colin *Medieval Southampton* 27n
Play Called Corpus Christi 107n
Play of Antichrist 233n
Play of the Sacrament 104
Pollard, Alfred W. 106n
Pontal, O. *Les Statuts synodaux* 38n
Poore, Richard 35, 39n, 47, 49, 50, 51, 59n
Pore Caitiff 43
Poschmann, Bernard *Penance and the Anointing of the Sick* 58n
Powicke, F.M., ed. (with C.R. Cheney) *Councils and Synods* 37n, 38n, 39n, 40n, 59n
Powicke, M.R. 28n
Pratt, Robert A. 251n
Preger, William 310n
Preston, Raymond *Chaucer* 238, 250n
Prick of Conscience x, 3
Propp, Vladimir *Morphology of the Folktale* 75, 76, 83n
Pummerer, Anton 310n
Putnam, B.H., ed., *Proceedings before the Justices of Peace in the 14th and 15th Centuries* 28n
Pynson, Richard 113

Queste del Saint Graal 119
Quilligan, Maureen 236n
Quint, Josef 291, 310n
Quivil, Peter 59n *Summula* 39n, 48

Raftis, J.A., ed., *Pathways to Medieval Peasants* 24n; *Warboys* 25n
Ranke, Kurt ed. *Folktales of Germany* 72, 83n
Ransom, John Crow 245
Raymond, Bishop of Nîmes 39n
Raymond of Pennafort 34, 46; *Summa de casuum* 47; *Summula de poenitentia* 40n, 41n, 59n
Records of the Borough of Nottingham 19
Redmond, James *Themes in Drama* 107n
Reeves, Marjorie 231n, 232n (with Beatrice Hirsh-Resch) *Figurae of Joachim* 230n, 232n, 234n; *Influence of Prophesy* 230n, 232n, 235n
Reiss, Edmund 128n
Remigius of Auxerre 217
Renaud, J.G.N. 165n
Repyngdon, Philip 88, 281, 282
Resurrection (Bodley) 106n
Reynolds, Anna Maria Sr., 275n
Reynolds, Susan *Introduction to the History of English Medieval Towns* 26n
Richard I 110
Richard II 23n, 24n, 26n, 111
Richard III 89
Richard Coer de Lyon 112, 113, 115, 120, 122, 128n
Richard of St. Victor *Sermo in die paschae* 258, 262, 266, 270, 273n, 274n
Richards, Angela 147n
Richardson, Cynthia C. 251n
Richardson, F.E. 130n
Richardson, Malcolm 239, 250n
Richmond, Velma B. *Laments for the Dead in Medieval Narrative* 192n; *Popularity of Middle English Romance* 126n, 128n, 129n
Richmond, W. Edson 65, 82n, 83n
Rickard, P. (et al.) ed., *Medieval Comic Tales* 146n, 147n
Riehle, Wolfgang 264, 274n
Riga, Peter *Aurora* 234n
Ritchie, Nora 23n
Riz, Juan *Libro de Buen Amor* 136
Robbins, R.H. 187n–90n, 239, 250n *Secular Lyrics of the 14th and 15th Centuries* 27n, 28n
Roberts, P.B. 41n *Stephanus de Lingua-Tonante* 42n
Robertson, D.W. 23n, 43n, 59n, 151, 236n; *Chaucer's London* 27n; (with B.F. Huppé) *"Piers Plowman" and Scriptural Tradition* 233n; *Preface to Chaucer* 151

Robertson, W.A. Scott 165n
Robin Hoods ballads 134
Robin Hood Play 87
Robinson, F.N., ed., *Works of Geoffrey
    Chaucer* 26n, 59n, 128n, 191n
Robinson, J.W. 105n, 107n
Rock, Daniel *Church of Our Fathers* 154,
    165n
Rolle, Richard xii, 176, 183, 184, 192n,
    252–76- *English Psalter* 252, 257;
    Form of Living 264; *Incendium amoris*
    252, 254, 255, 259, 260, 264, 271,·
    280; *Jubilatio* 257, 259; *Meditations on
    the Passion* 261; *Melos amoris* 260, 266,
    267, 272n, 273n; *Song to the Love of
    Jesus* 262, 274n
Roman de la Rose 109, 162, 264, 269,
    276n
Romanus, Aegidius *De regimine
    principum* 22
Rose, Donald M., ed., *New Perspectives in
    Chaucer Criticism* 165n
Rosenberg, Bruce A. 70, 79, 82n, 83n,
    127n
Rossiter, A.P. 102; *English Drama from
    Early Times to the Elizabethans* 107n
Roswall and Lillian 77
Rotuli Parliamentorum 23n, 24n
Rouse, M.A. 39n, 40n
Rouse, R.H. (with M.A. Rouse)
    Preachers, Florilegia and Sermons 40n
Rowland, Beryl, ed., *Chaucer and
    Medieval Studies* 146n, 250n;
    Companion to Studies 240, 250n
Ruggiers, Paul G. 247
Ruh, Kurt, ed., *Altdeutsche und altnieder
    ländische Mystik* 309n
Ruodlieb 116
Rupert of Deutz 212, 229n; *De Trinitate
    et operibus eius* 236n
Russell, G.H. 43n
Russell, John 229n

Sabellius 201
Sacchetti, Franco 136
Sachs, Hans 136
Sackur, Ernst *Sibyllinische Texte und
    Forschungen* 233n
Sampson, Peter 39n
Sandquist, T.A., ed. (with M.R.
    Powicke) *Essays in Medieval History* 28n
Sands, Donald B., ed., *Middle English
    Verse Romances* 63, 83n, 127n
Sargent, Helen C. 83n
Sawicki, J.T. *Bibiliographia synodorum*

Sawicki *(cont.)*
    particularium 38n
Saxl, F. 42n
Sayers, Peig 145
Sayles, G.O., ed., *Select Cases in the Court
    of King's Bench* 29n
Scales, Lord 89, 90
Schelp, Hanspeter *Exemplarishe
    Romanzen* 127n
Schiller, Friedrich 114
Schiller, Gertrud *Iconography of Christian
    Art* 192n
Schirmer, Walter 250n
Schmidt, A.V.C., ed. (with Nicolas
    Jacobs) *Medieval English Romances*
    128n, 129n
Schmitz, H.J. *Die Bussbücher und die
    Bussdiciplin der Kirche* 41n
Schneemelcher, Wilhelm 193n
Schneyer, J.B. *Repertorium der lateinischen
    Sermones des Mittelalters* 42n; *Wegweiser
    zu lateinischen Predigtreihen* 42n
Schoeck, Richard, ed. (with Jerome
    Taylor) *Chaucer Criticism* 82n
Schwänke 136
Schwesternbücher 293, 296
Scoles, Robert E. (with Robert Kellogg)
    Nature of Narrative 239
Scrope, Stephen 275n
Second Shepherd's Play 86
Seeberg, Reinhold *Text-Book of History of
    Doctrines* 232n
Seligman, J. 192n
Seven Sages of Rome 132, 133, 146n
Severs, J. Burke, ed., *Manual* 64, 70, 73,
    83n, 126n, 128n, 129n, 130n; ed.,
    *Recent Middle English Scholarship and
    Criticism* 126n
Shakespeare, John 19
Shakespeare, William 88, 140; *Henry IV*
    (part 1) 143; *Henry IV* (part 2) 143;
    King Lear 207; *Midsummer Night's
    Dream* 27n, 90; *Taming of the Shrew*
    134
Sharp, Thomas 88
Sharpe, R.R., ed., *Calendar of Letter
    Books* 27n–28n
Shaw, Judith 60n
Shelton, James 273n
Shrewsbury Fragments 106n; *Pastores*
    96–97
Sidney, Sir Philip *Apology for Poetry* 142
Siege of Jerusalem 109, 112, 114, 128n
Siepmann, Ferdinand 236n
Simmons, T.F. 60n; (with R.E. Nolloth)

Simmons *(cont.)*
  The Lay Folks' Catechism 42n
Skeat, W.W. 151
Smalley, Beryl 229n
Smith, Lucy Toulmin 106n, 190n
Smith, Philip A. *History of Education for
  the English Bar* 249n
Smithers, G.V. 146n
Smyth, John *Lives of the Berkeleys* 28n
Solch, G. 41n
Song of Igor's Campaign 65, 83n
Sophocles 70
"Sorrowing Mary" 190n
"Sorrows of Mary" 189n
South English Legendary 103, 179, 193n
Southern, R.W. *Making of the Middle
  Ages* 129n
Spector, Stephen 176, 192n
Speculum Christiani 43n, 54, 60n
Speirs, John *Medieval English Poetry* 130n
Spencer, Brian 165n
Spenser, Edmund *Faerie Queene* 205
Squyr of Lowe Degre 76
Stagel, Elsbeth *Schwesternbuch* 311n
Stammler, Wolfgang 312n
Standring, Bernard 274n
Stanley, D.A.P. *Historical Memorials of
  Canterbury* 166n
Stanstede, John 18
Stargardt, Ute, 313n
Statius 241
Statutes of the Realm 23n, 24n
Stavensby, Alexander 48, 56, 59n;
  Tractatus de septem criminalibus peccatis
  40n
Steadman, John M. 250n
Steenstrup, Johannes *Medieval Popular
  Ballad* 83n
Steger, Hugo *David Rex et Propheta* 256
Steinbeck, John 79
Sterne, Laurence 241; *Tristram Shandy*
  113
Stevens, John *Medieval Romance* 128n,
  129n, 130n
Stevenson, W.H., ed., *Records of the
  Borough of Nottingham* 28n
Stewart, Ann H. 65, 83n
Sticca, Sandro, ed., *Medieval Drama*
  191n
Strom, Melvin 166n
Stow, John *Survey of London* 28n, 157
Strachey, James 147n
Der Stricker 136
Strohm, Paul 127n, 128n
Stugrin, Michael 191n

Suso, Heinrich 291, 292, 311n, 312n
Sylvester 235n

Taill of Rauf Coilyear 77, 110
Tancred of Bologna *Summa de sponsalibus
  et matrimonio* 41n
Tatlock, John S.P. 151, 244
Tauler, Johannes 291, 292, 309n
Taylor, G.C. 82n, 170, 187n–90n
Taylor, Jerome, ed. (with Alan H.
  Nelson) *Medieval English Drama* 105n
Teetaert, A. 41n
Telesforus of Cosenza 199, 221, 231n
Thomas, S.H. *Writings of Robert
  Grosseteste* 39n, 40n, 41n
Thomas, Earl of Oxford 90
Thomas IV, Lord Berkeley 21
Thomas Hibernicus *Manipulus florum*
  39n
Thomas Martyr, St. 86, 148
Thomas of Canterbury, St. 148–66
  passim, 306
Thomas of Cantimpré 286
Thomas of Pipe 21, 22
Thompson, Stith 68, 69, 70, 71, 131–47
  passim *Motif-Index of Folk-Literature*
  67, 84n 146n; *Folktale* 82n, 83n
Thornton, Gladys H. *History of Clare,
  Suffolk* 27n
Thrupp, S.L. *Merchant Class of Medieval
  London* 146n
Titus and Vespasian 112
Tobit 116
Tole, William 19
Tolkien, J.R.R. 104n, 129n, 274n
Topfer, Bernhard *Das Kommende Reich
  des Friedens* 230n
Li tornoiemenz Antecrit 236n
Torrent 73, 77
Towneley Cycle (*See Wakefield/Towneley
  Cycle*)
Transitus Mariae 179
Sir Triamour 113, 115, 119
Tristan (Prose) 112
Sir Tristrem 77, 119
Trevisa, John 249
Trivet, Nicholas 74, *Chronicle* 71, 75
Trounce, A.M. 127n
St. Trudperter Hohelied 311n
Tupper, F. *Riddles of the Exeter Book* 65,
  84n
Tournament of Totenham 17, 135
Twycross, Meg 88, 103, 107n

Ubertino de Casale 199

Usk, Thomas 249
Utley, F.L. 68, 73, 82n, 84n

Valentine and Orson 73
Van Meteren 16
Vaughan Williams, Ralph *Five Mystical Songs* 270
Veale, E.W.W., ed., *Great Red Book of Bristol* 26n; ed., *Studies in the Medieval Wine Trade* 27n
Verdict (film) 103
Vernay, E. 41n
Vinaver, Eugène *Rise of Romance* 128n
Vincent of Beauvais 235n
Virgil 241

Wace 116
Wagner, Louis A. 83n
"Wakefield Master" 92, 97, 103, 104
Wakefield/Towneley Cycle 86, 92, 94, 106n, 190n, 274n; *Christ and the Doctors* 94; *Coliphizacio* 103; *Crucifixion* 176, 191n, 263; *Death of Abel* 103; *First Shepherd's Play* 104; *Harrowing of Hell* 94; *Last Judgment* 12, 94; *Pharaoh* 94, 95–96; *Resurrection* 94; *Second Shepherd's Play* 85, 92, 93, 135
Waleys, Thomas 41n
Wasson, John 104n, 105n
Watkins, O.D. *History of Penance* 58n
Watson, A.G. 251n
Wedding of Gawain and Dame Ragnell 76, 109, 114
Wehmer, Carl 165n
Weissman, H.P. 191n
Wells, John *Manual* 126n
Welsch, Roger L. 82n
Welter, J.T., *L'Exemplum dans la littérature religieuse didactique du moyen âge* 42n
Welty, Eudora 241
Wenslawe 305–306, 308n
Wentzlaff-Eggebert, F.W. *Deutsche Mystik zwischen Mittelalter und Neuzeit* 312n, 313n
Wenzel, Siegfried 40n, 193n; *Sin of Sloth* 56, 59n, 60n; *Verses in Sermons* 60n
Weseham, Roger *Instituta* 51, 55
West-Country Historical Studies 26n
"Who Cannot Weep, Come Learn at Me" 190n
Wilkins, David *Concilia Magnae Britanniae et Hiberniae* 59n
Wilkinson, Bertie 28n

William of Pagula; *Oculus sacerdotis* 39n, 41n, 49, 59n; *Speculum praelatorum* 42n
William of Palerne 73, 76, 77
William of Paris *Summa de administratione sacramentorum* 41n
William of St. Amour 27n, 199
William of Tournai *De instructione puerorum* 42n
William of Waddington *Manuel des péchés* 35, 267
Wilmart, A. 39n
Wilson, R.M. 308n
Wilson, R. McL. 193n
Wimmer, Georg 236n
Winwar, Francis 82n
Wisdom Who is Christ 87
Wittig Susan, *Stylistic and Narrative Structures* 127n
Wolfram von Eschenbach 109; *Parzival* 119
Wolfson, Harry A. *Philosophy of the Church Fathers* 232n
Woodruff, D., ed., *For Hillaire Belloc* 191n
Wooing of Etain 73
Woolf, Rosemary *English Mystery Plays* 27n, 106n; *English Religious Lyric in the Middle Ages* 168, 191n, 193n, 274n
Wright, C.E. *English Vernacular Hands* 106n
Wright, John 233n
Wright, Thomas, ed., *Political Poems and Songs* 235n
Wülfing, J.E. 128n
Wunderlich, A. 41n
Wycliffe, John 152, 249 *Ten Comaundementis* 57, 60n
Wyfe in Morrelles Skin 134

Xenophon *Ephesian Tale* 116, 125

Yevele, Henry 16
York Cycle 92, 94, 106n, 176, 190n; *Crucifixion* 261, 264; *Last Judgment* 101; *Passion* 192n; *Pastores* 96–97; *Pharaoh* 95–96
"York Realist" 92, 97, 105n, 107n, 192n
Young, Karl 102
Ywain and Gawain 74, 242

Zupitza, Julius 129n